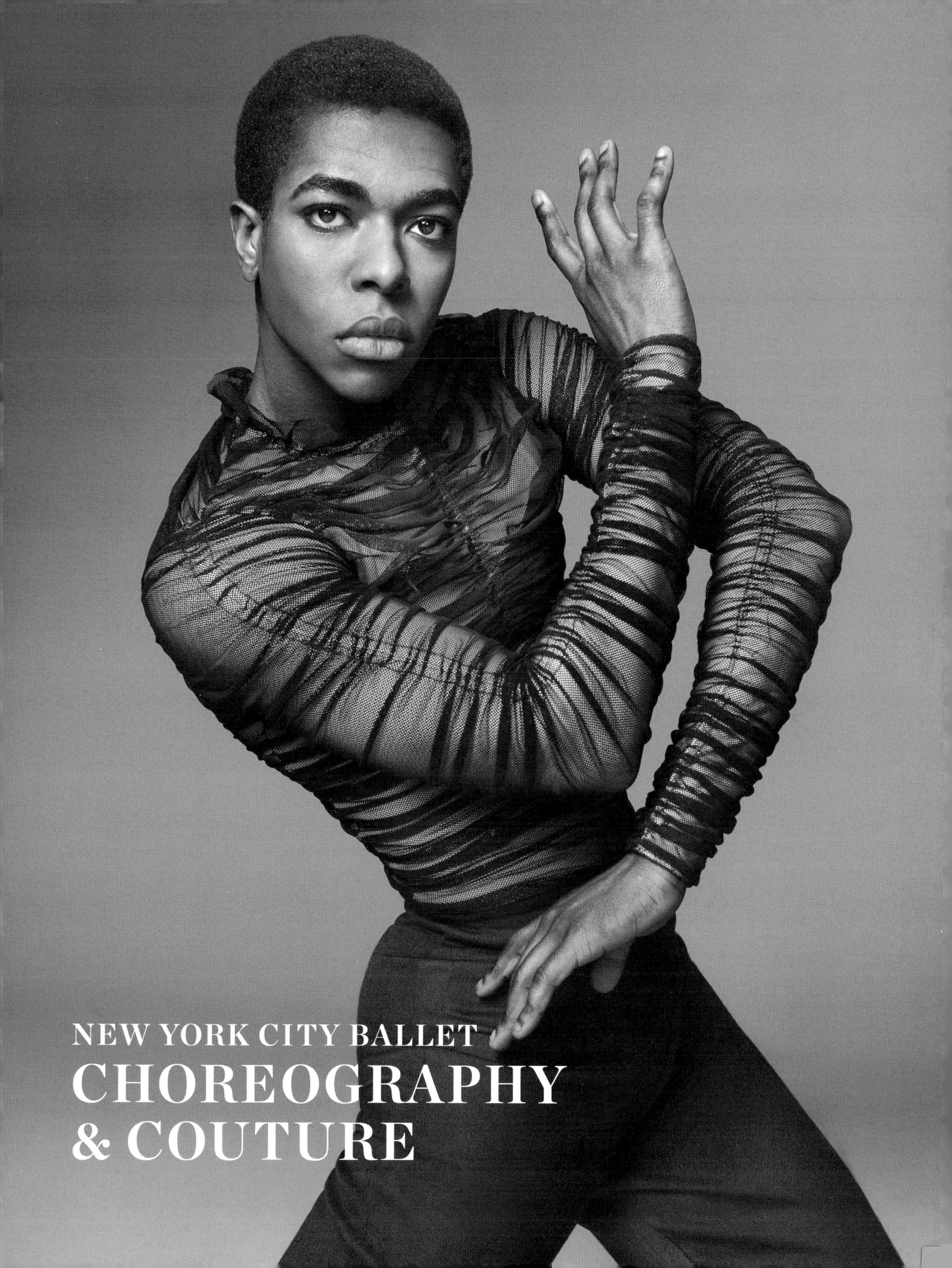

NEW YORK CITY BALLET

CHOREOGRAPHY & COUTURE

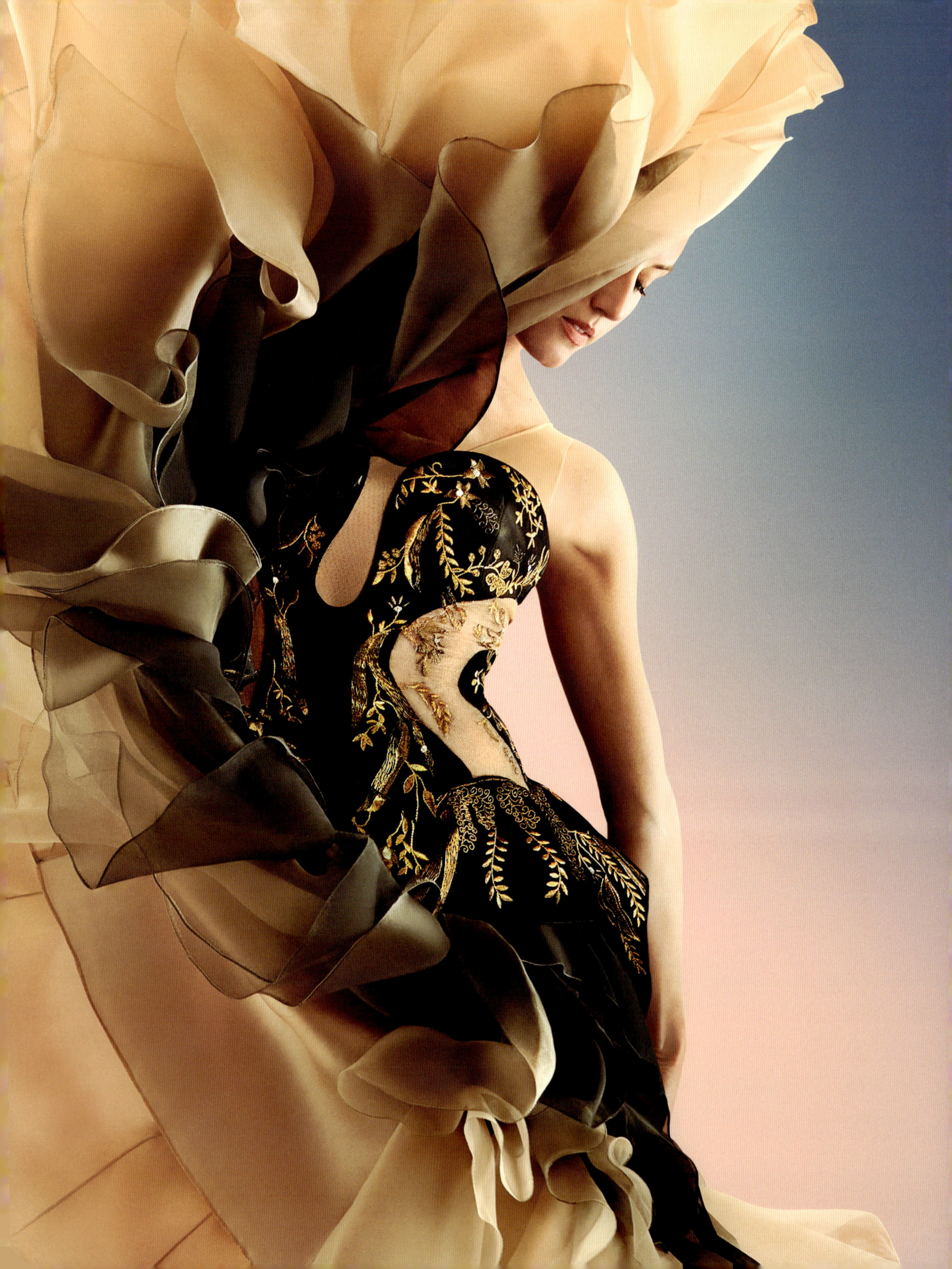

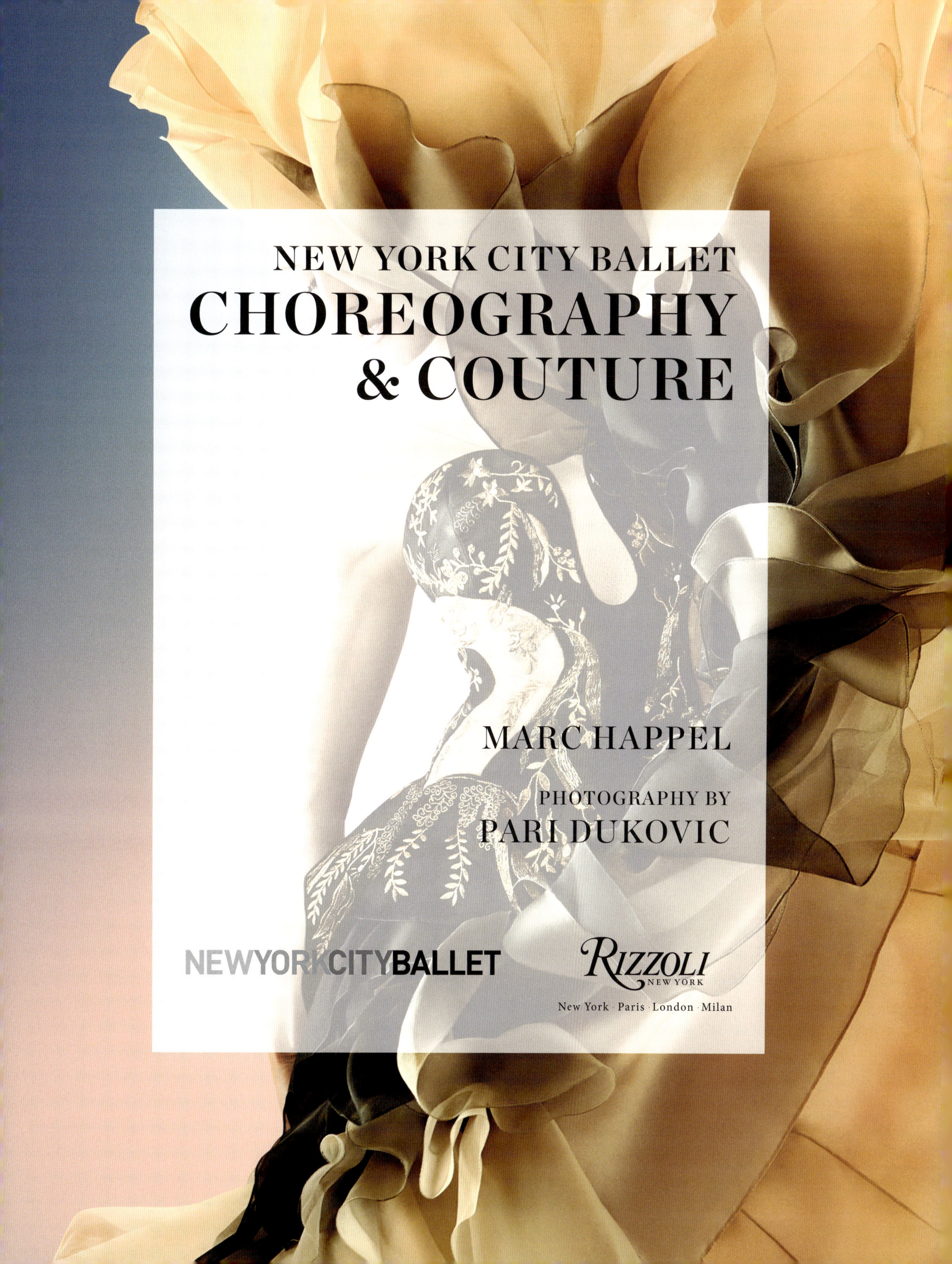

NEW YORK CITY BALLET

CHOREOGRAPHY & COUTURE

MARC HAPPEL

PHOTOGRAPHY BY
PARI DUKOVIC

NEWYORKCITYBALLET

RIZZOLI
NEW YORK

New York · Paris · London · Milan

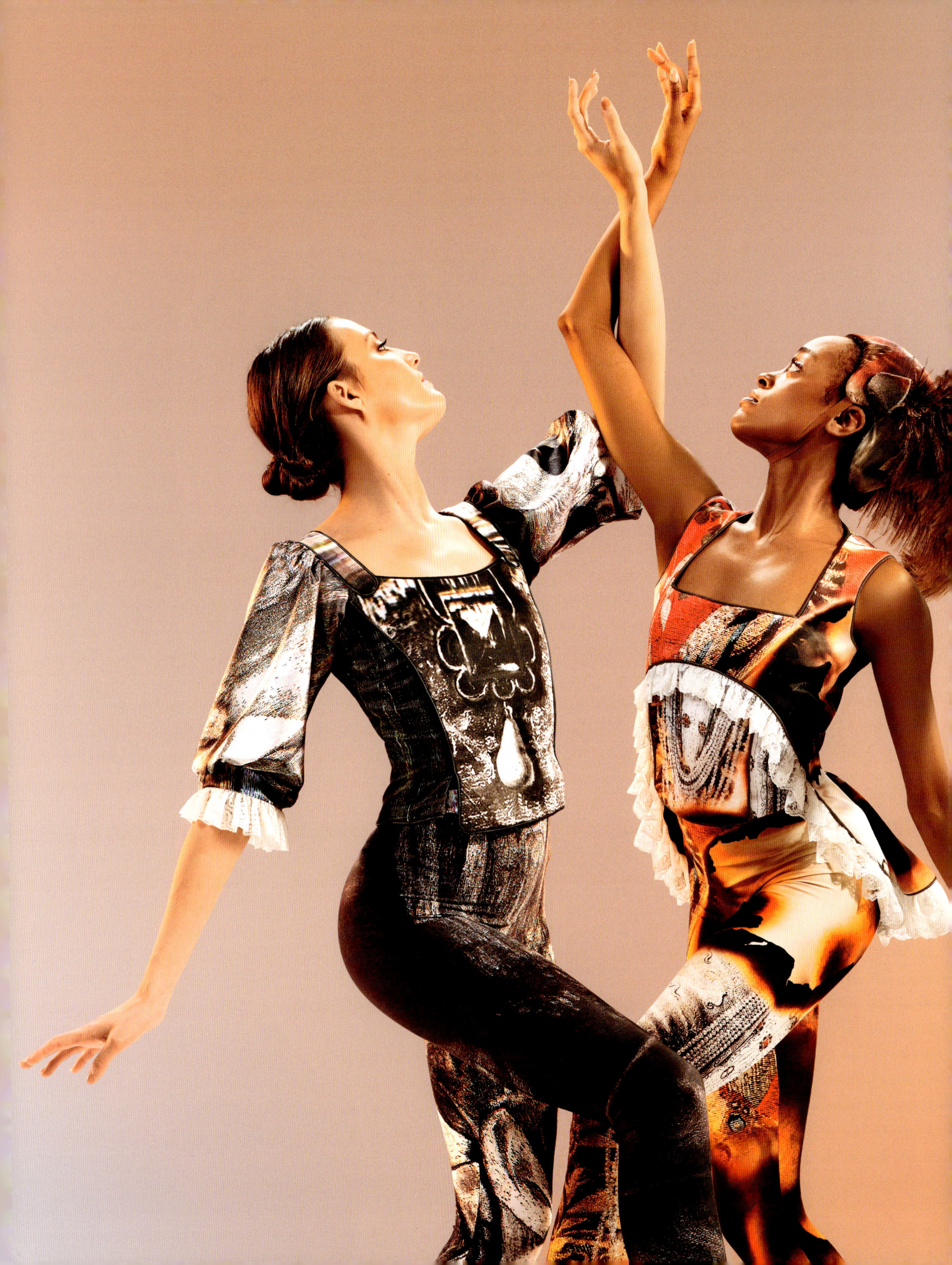

CONTENTS

7 **FOREWORD**
SARAH JESSICA PARKER

9 **INTRODUCTION**
MARC HAPPEL

2012
10 **VALENTINO**

2013
20 **PRABAL GURUNG**
26 **OLIVIER THEYSKENS**
32 **IRIS VAN HERPEN**

38 **ESSAY**
PATRICIA MEARS

2014
40 **THOM BROWNE**
46 **SARAH BURTON FOR ALEXANDER MCQUEEN**
52 **CAROLINA HERRERA**
58 **MARY KATRANTZOU**

2015
62 **PETER COPPING OF OSCAR DE LA RENTA**
70 **HUMBERTO LEON OF OPENING CEREMONY & KENZO**
78 **HANAKO MAEDA OF ADEAM**
84 **MARTA MARQUES & PAULO ALMEIDA OF MARQUES'ALMEIDA**
90 **ZUHAIR MURAD**

94 **ESSAY**
TONNE GOODMAN

2016
96 **JASON WU**
102 **ROSIE ASSOULIN**
108 **NARCISO RODRIGUEZ**
116 **DRIES VAN NOTEN**

2017
120 **JONATHAN SAUNDERS**
126 **VIRGIL ABLOH OF OFF-WHITE™**
132 **FERNANDO GARCIA & LAURA KIM OF MONSE & OSCAR DE LA RENTA**
136 **TSUMORI CHISATO**

2018
144 **GILES DEACON**
150 **GARETH PUGH**
156 **ALBERTA FERRETTI**

2019
160 **ANNA SUI**
164 **ZAC POSEN**

2021
172 **CHRISTOPHER JOHN ROGERS**
178 **ESTEBAN CORTÁZAR**

2022
184 **GILES DEACON**
190 **RAF SIMONS**
194 **ALEJANDRO GÓMEZ PALOMO FOR PALOMO SPAIN**

202 **DESIGN & CHOREOGRAPHY CREDITS**
205 **ACKNOWLEDGMENTS**
207 **AUTHOR BIOS**
208 **PHOTO CREDITS**

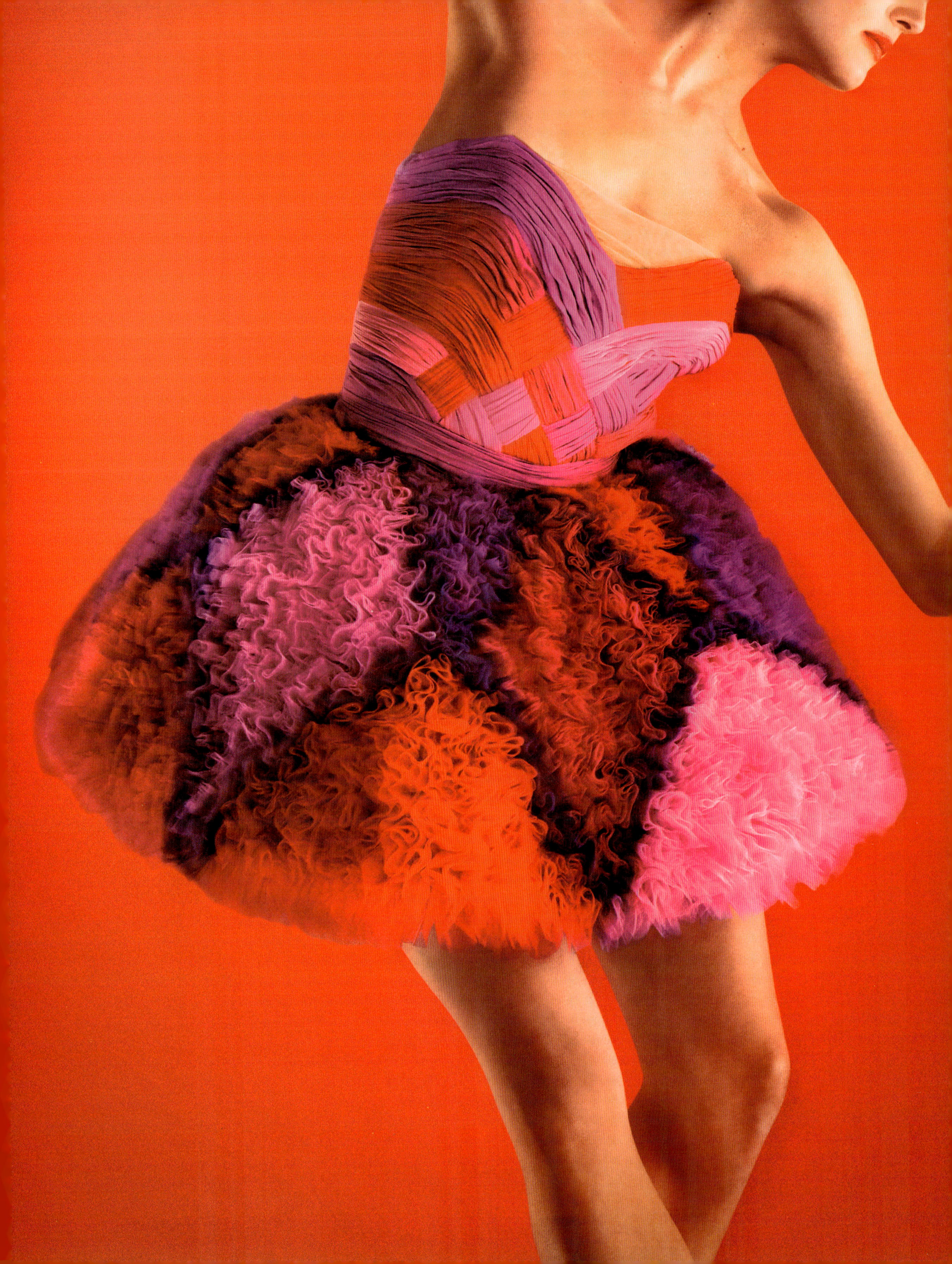

FOREWORD

GEORGE BALANCHINE, THE LEGENDARY co-founder of New York City Ballet, once said "there is only now." Today New York City Ballet continues to take those words to heart. The Company doesn't just honor Balanchine by preserving his works, they honor him by keeping ballet in the now—by taking risks, by pushing the art form forward, and by creating opportunities for the next generation. The annual Fall Fashion Gala has become part of that enduring legacy.

First launched in 2012, the seeds for the event were planted two years before when Lincoln Center, home to New York City Ballet since 1964, began hosting New York Fashion Week. With so much creativity and experimentation right on our doorstep, we decided to harness it, and the idea of regularly inviting designers of high fashion into City Ballet was born.

Over the years, the designers, drawing inspiration from NYCB's unparalleled history of artistic excellence, have wowed us with beauty and elegance. They've captured our imagination through their ability to tell stories with their costumes. And, once in a while, they break the mold wide open, completely redefining what a ballet costume can be.

But the innovation isn't limited to the costumes. Since its inception the Fall Fashion Gala has presented 28 world premiere ballets by some of the dance world's most renowned choreographers, as well as exciting newcomers looking to make their mark.

Each year the great reward is being in the audience on the night of the Fall Fashion Gala to see these singular creations come to life, to feel the meaning and hear the echo of Balanchine's edict that "there is only now."

Sarah Jessica Parker
A Vice Chair of the New York City Ballet Board of Directors,
Sarah Jessica Parker conceived the Company's Fall Fashion Gala in 2012.

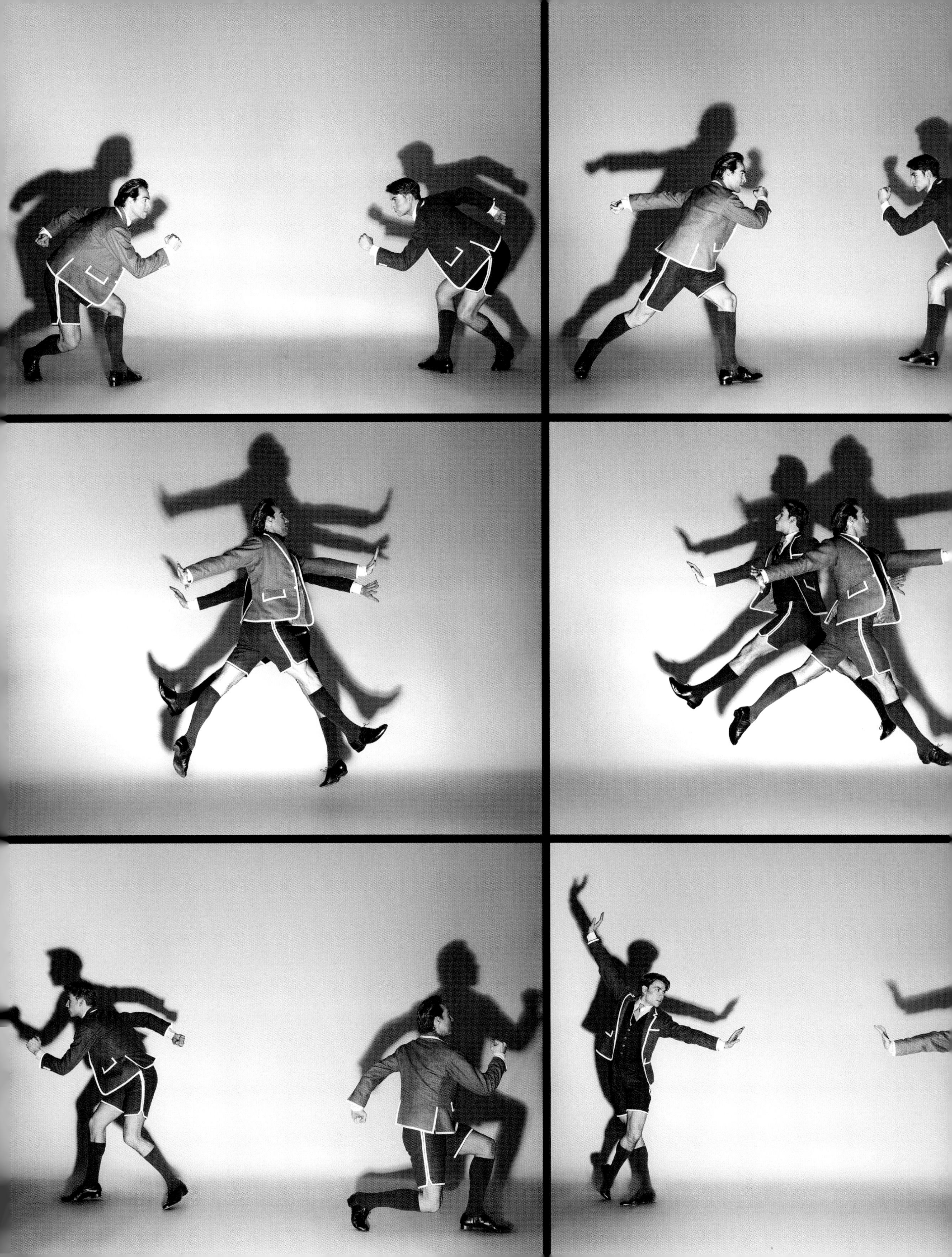

INTRODUCTION

WHEN I WAS FIRST APPROACHED about the idea of a fashion gala, an event that would bring fashion designers together with choreographers, it seemed a natural marriage. There was a personal excitement for me in the possibility of working with world-class fashion designers, remembering my early years as a young gay costumer poring over the endless fashion monographs and always wondering if this was a direction I should have pursued.

For the first gala in 2012, it was suggested that we seek out young and newly developed designers from the fast-moving world of New York fashion. But when our Company's director at the time, Peter Martins, tapped his dear friend Valentino to design a ballet for the evening it led to the entire evening—four ballets in all—being designed solely by Valentino. This was a thrilling period for me, meeting one of the icons of fashion and after a while feeling like we had developed a trust and friendship with each other. His excitement in being a part of this new project and completely immersing himself in the many designs for the evening was truly inspiring.

As the seasons have progressed we have had the good fortune of working with designers from not only New York, but also Antwerp, Paris, Beirut, and Tokyo, just to name a few; a total, as of the 10th anniversary, of nearly 30 designers. Each has brought their own distinctive design concept to the world of ballet, some for the very first time, and others with past experience. Each time there have been new challenges in helping to make their designs "danceable," working with them to bring their creations from the world of fashion runways and red carpets to the David H. Koch Theater with its uncompromising stage lights, detail-erasing distance, and the dancers' sweat-soaked athleticism. This was always my mission: to absolutely keep the integrity of the fashion designers' concepts while making them work for dance. After all, why would you ask Thom Browne to design a ballet that, in the end, does not look like Thom Browne?

But, of course, it is the amazing dancers who bring these ballets and the often elaborate costumes to life. So many times, they have come into our fitting rooms and been presented with a costume that is nothing like what they are accustomed to wearing. Their enthusiasm and patience as these world-renowned fashion designers drape, cut, and sometimes tape costume mockups on them has been a highlight for me. I've enjoyed their enthusiasm for the process as well as their collaborative feedback.

Throughout the years, the designers and I have been incredibly lucky to be surrounded and supported by the immensely talented artisans of the New York City Ballet Costume Shop. They are true heroes. Drapers, stitchers, dyers, fabric shoppers who have been asked to work long hours to create costumes using techniques that are many times unfamiliar to them (who can forget the plastic shards of Iris van Herpen's futuristic costumes?!). I have been awed and remain eternally grateful for their dedication. Their work demonstrates that, as a team, there is no limit to what we can accomplish.

MARC HAPPEL
Director of Costumes, New York City Ballet

2012

VALENTINO
BAL DE COUTURE, NOT MY GIRL, SOPHISTICATED LADY

I first met Peter Martins when he was a dancer. He came to Paris to be photographed for GQ *by Bruce Weber wearing my menswear collection. We developed a friendship and I would often attend the openings of the ballet seasons. I started to learn more about the production and all of the "behind-the-scenes" of these incredible performances. Over the years, we often discussed how we might work together for a special ballet where I would design the costumes.*

Then my dear friend Sarah Jessica Parker had the wonderful idea to bring the ballet and fashion worlds together to create magic on the stage. She and Peter invited me to design costumes for the very first Fall Fashion Gala, and I was honored. —VALENTINO

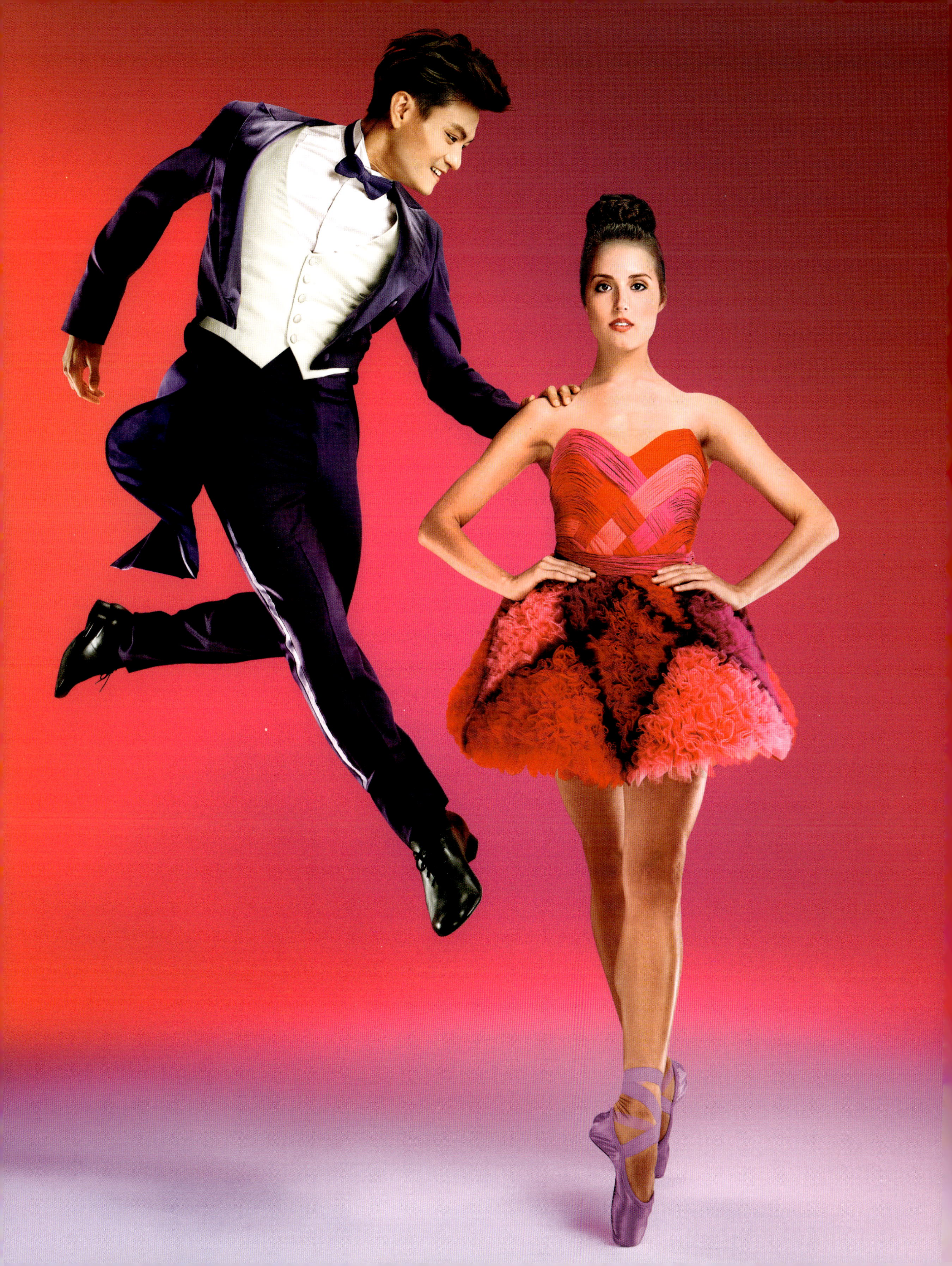

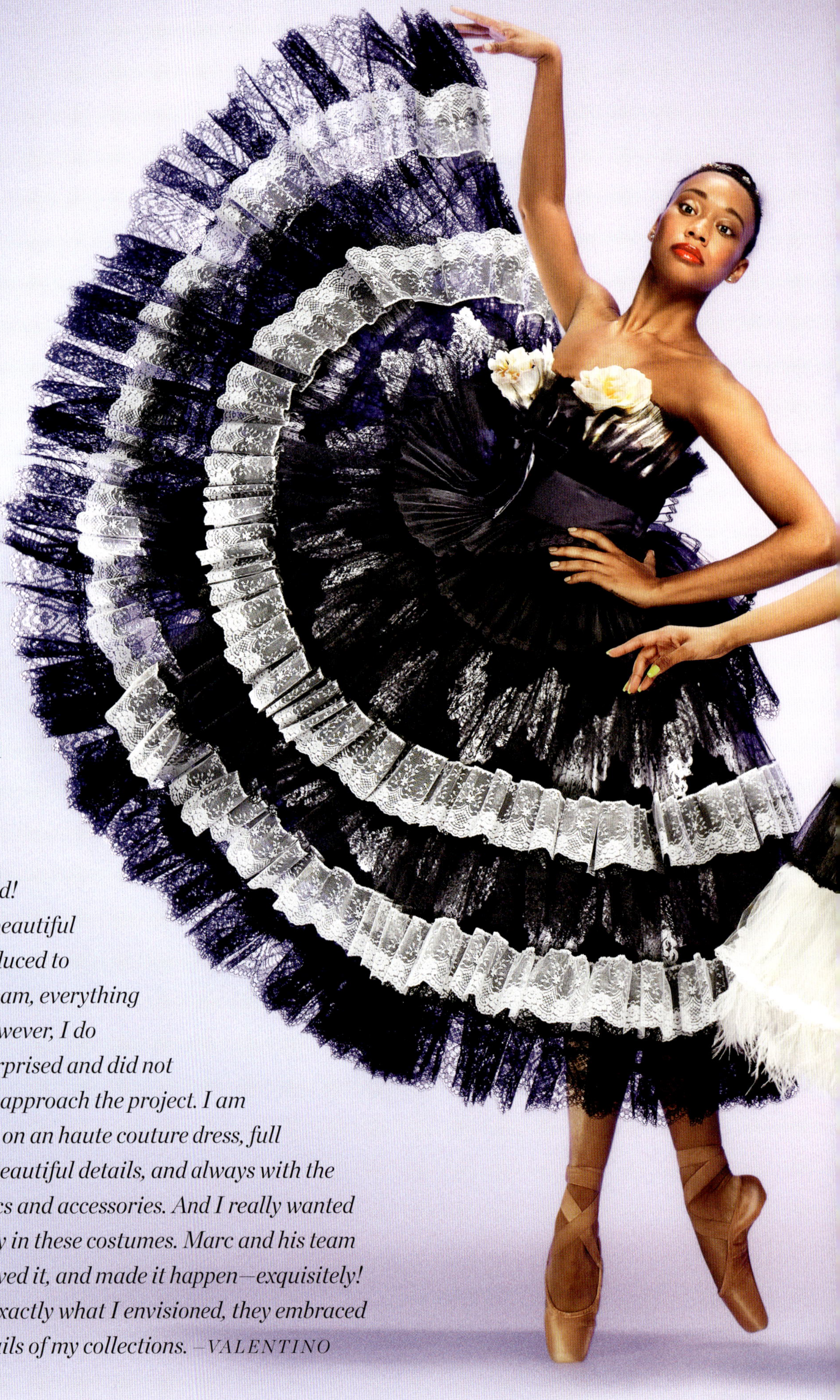

I wanted very much to design for the entire evening of this first celebration myself, and they agreed. This included three ballets for Peter: Bal de Couture, Sophisticated Lady, *and* Not My Girl, *as well as* This Bitter Earth *for Christopher Wheeldon. I was thrilled! This was the start of a beautiful experience. I was introduced to Marc Happel and his team, everything was going perfectly. However, I do think they were a bit surprised and did not anticipate how I would approach the project. I am used to always working on an haute couture dress, full of fine techniques and beautiful details, and always with the highest quality of fabrics and accessories. And I really wanted to have the same quality in these costumes. Marc and his team accepted the process, loved it, and made it happen—exquisitely! They not only created exactly what I envisioned, they embraced the techniques and details of my collections.* —VALENTINO

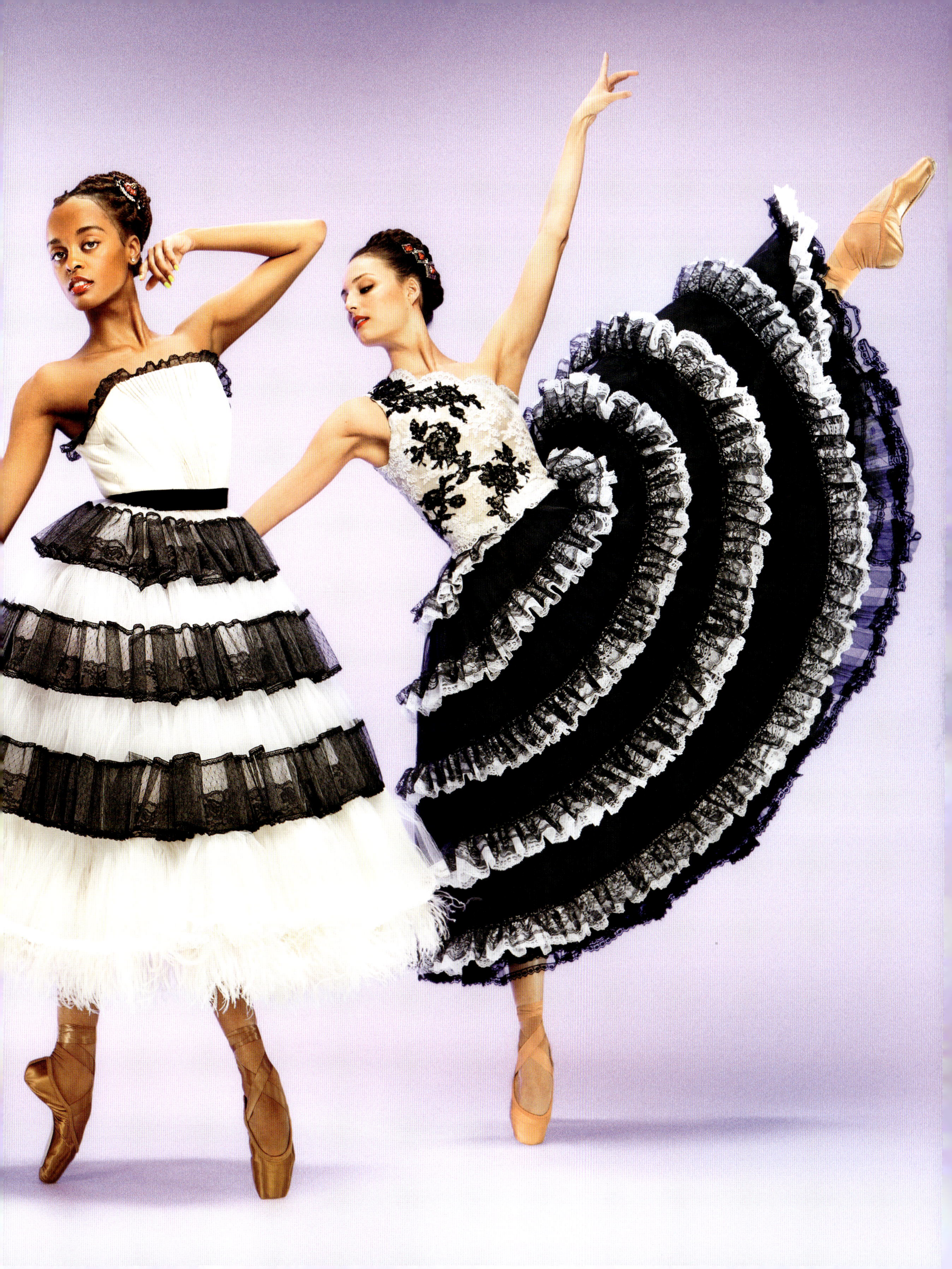

I remember that, at one point, I had an idea for another dress and wanted to add it to the ballet, because it was a particularly special one. Peter decided to change the choreography in order to accommodate my wish!

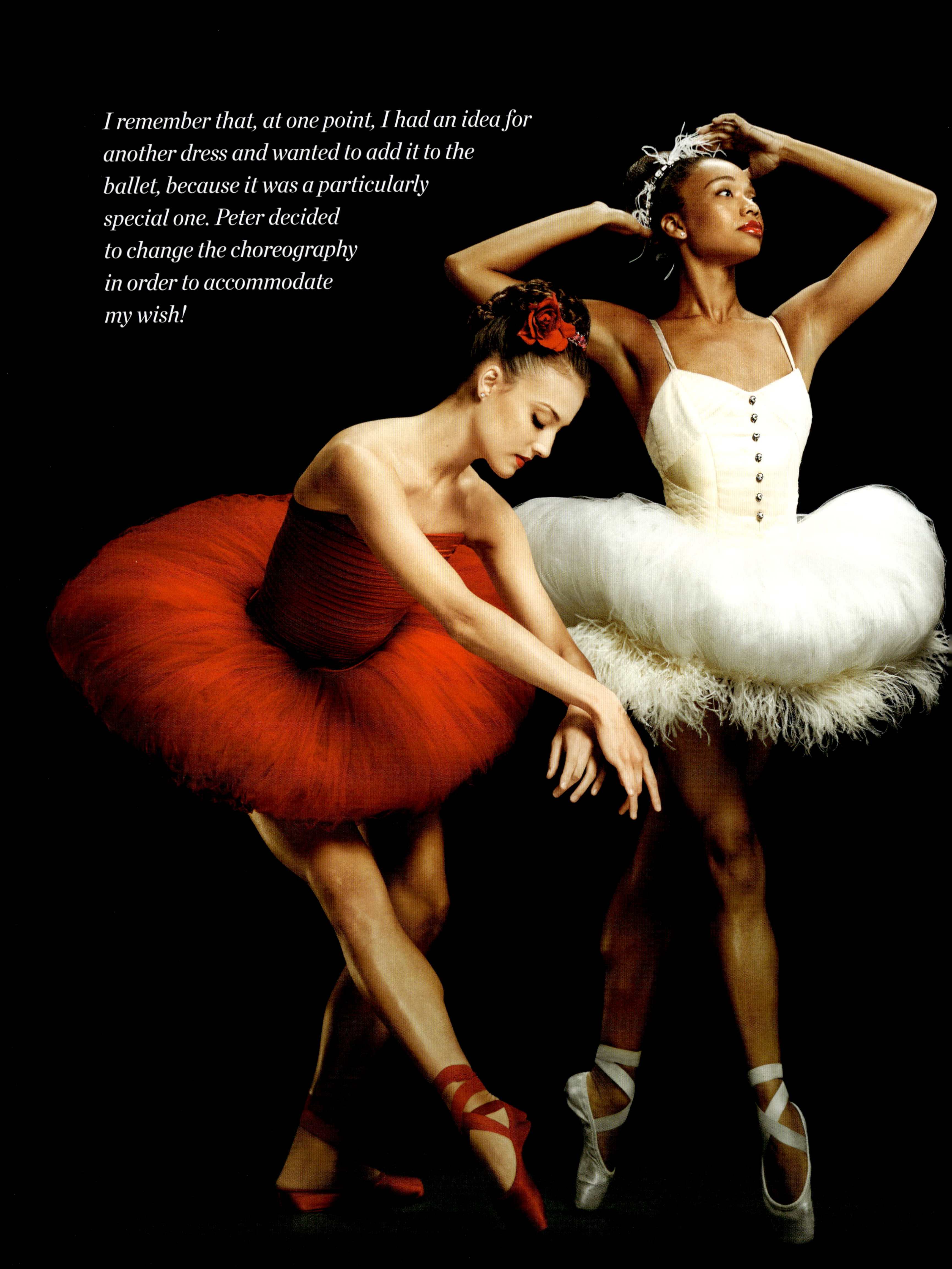

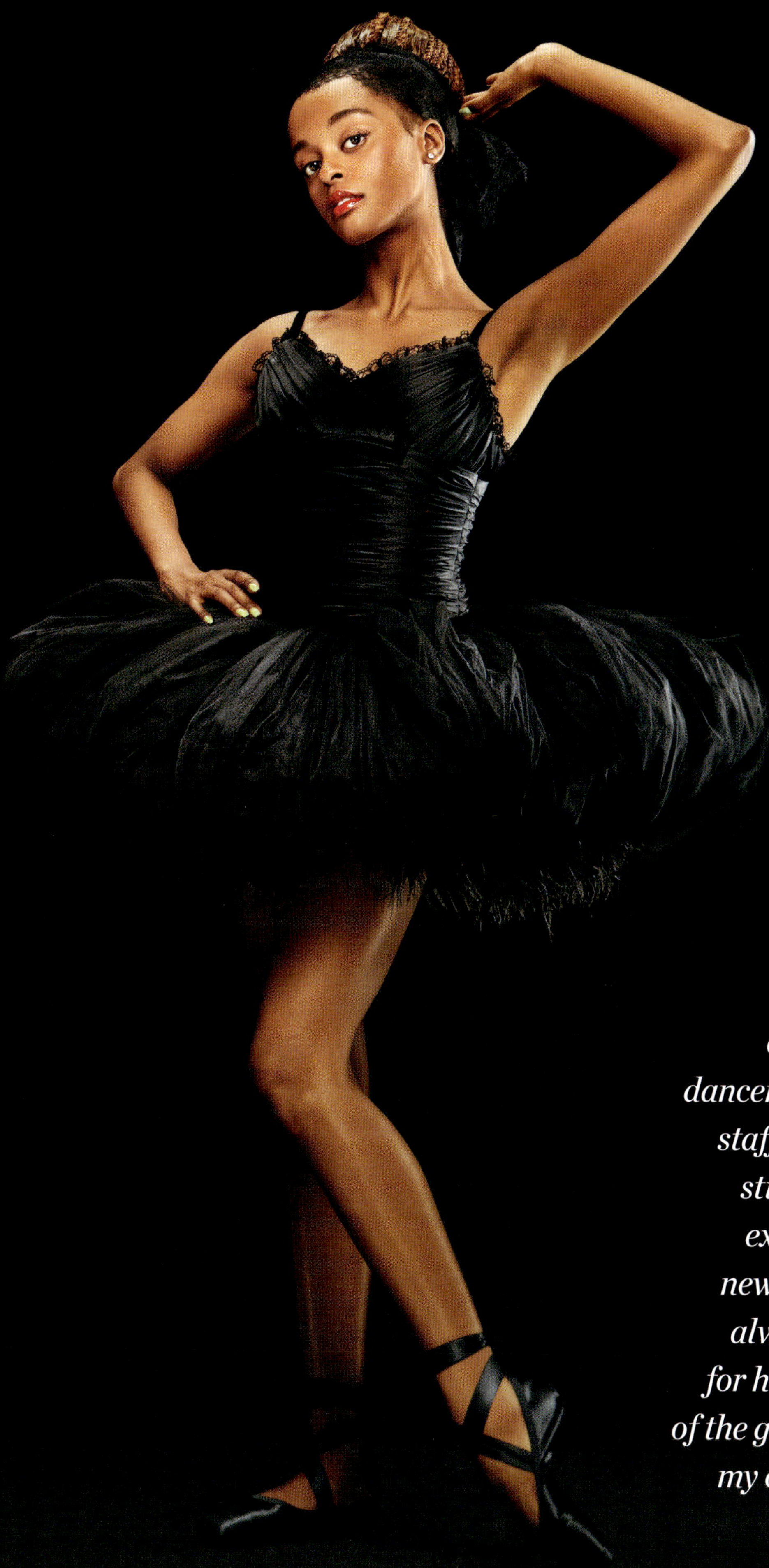

I have never in my life enjoyed such an enthusiastic group of people—from the dancers to the production staff to the drapers and stitchers—so ready to experiment and have new experiences! I will always thank them all for having given me one of the greatest moments of my career. —VALENTINO

The fashion gala is always a magical collaboration and the extra focus on what we're wearing stretches the imagination of every creative involved.

—*MEGAN FAIRCHILD, Dancer*

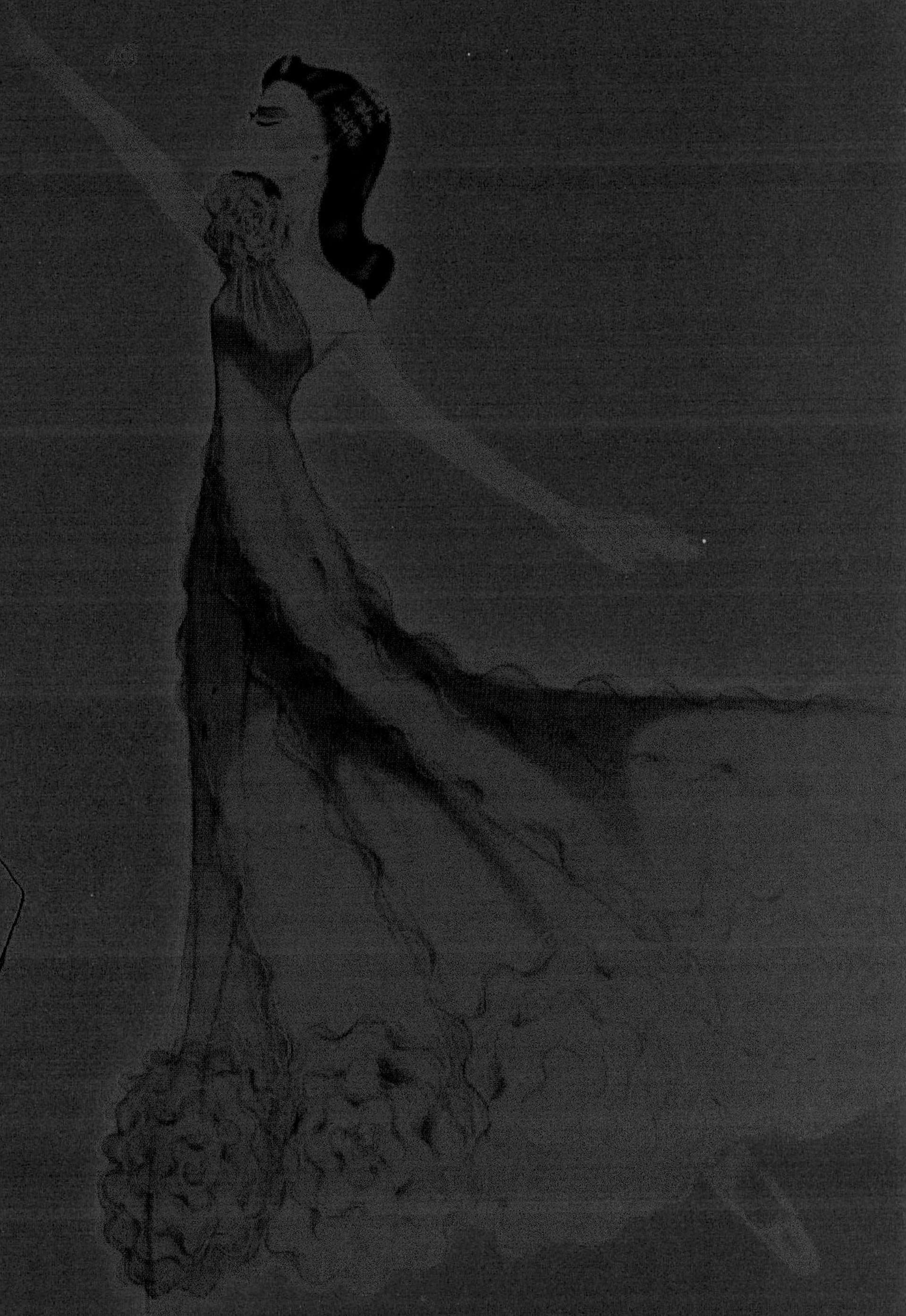

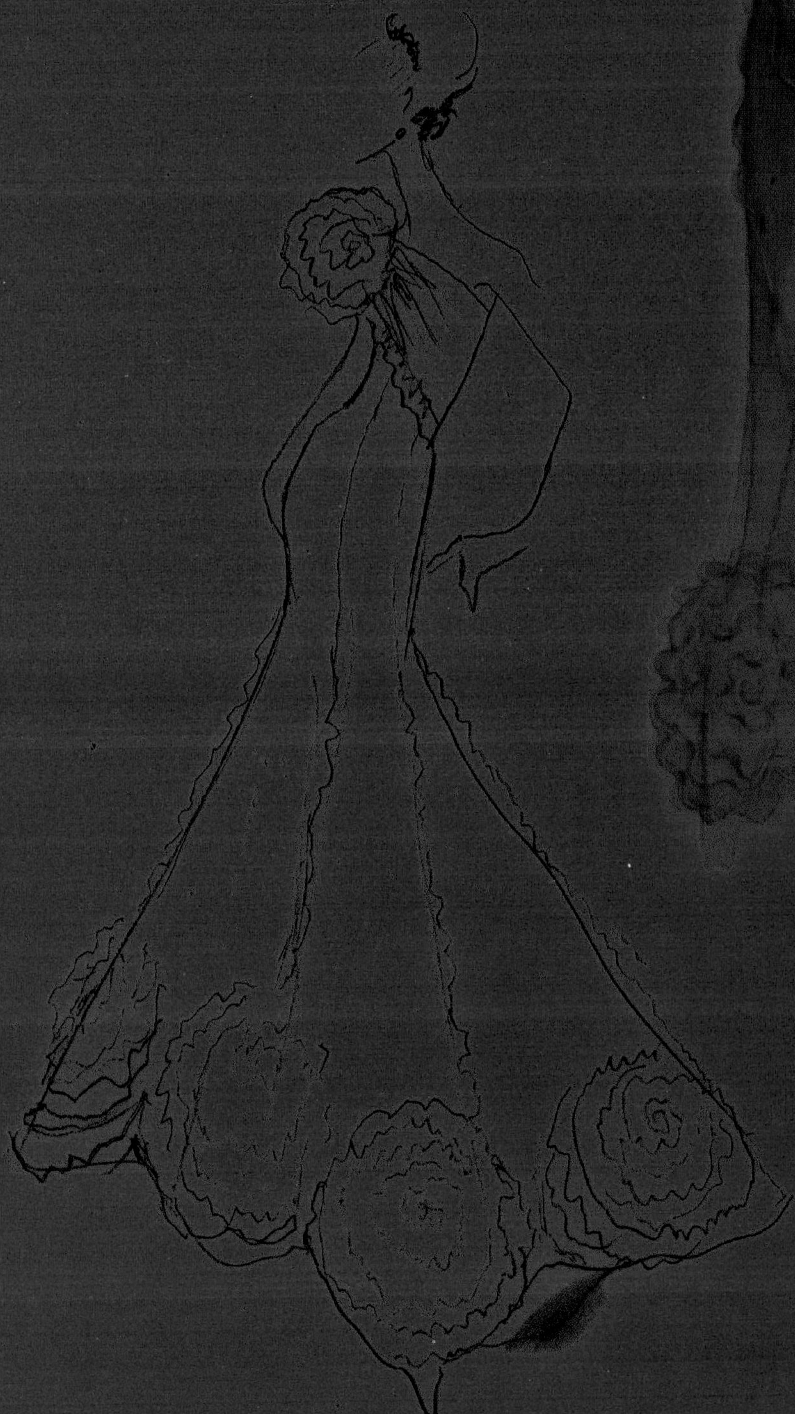

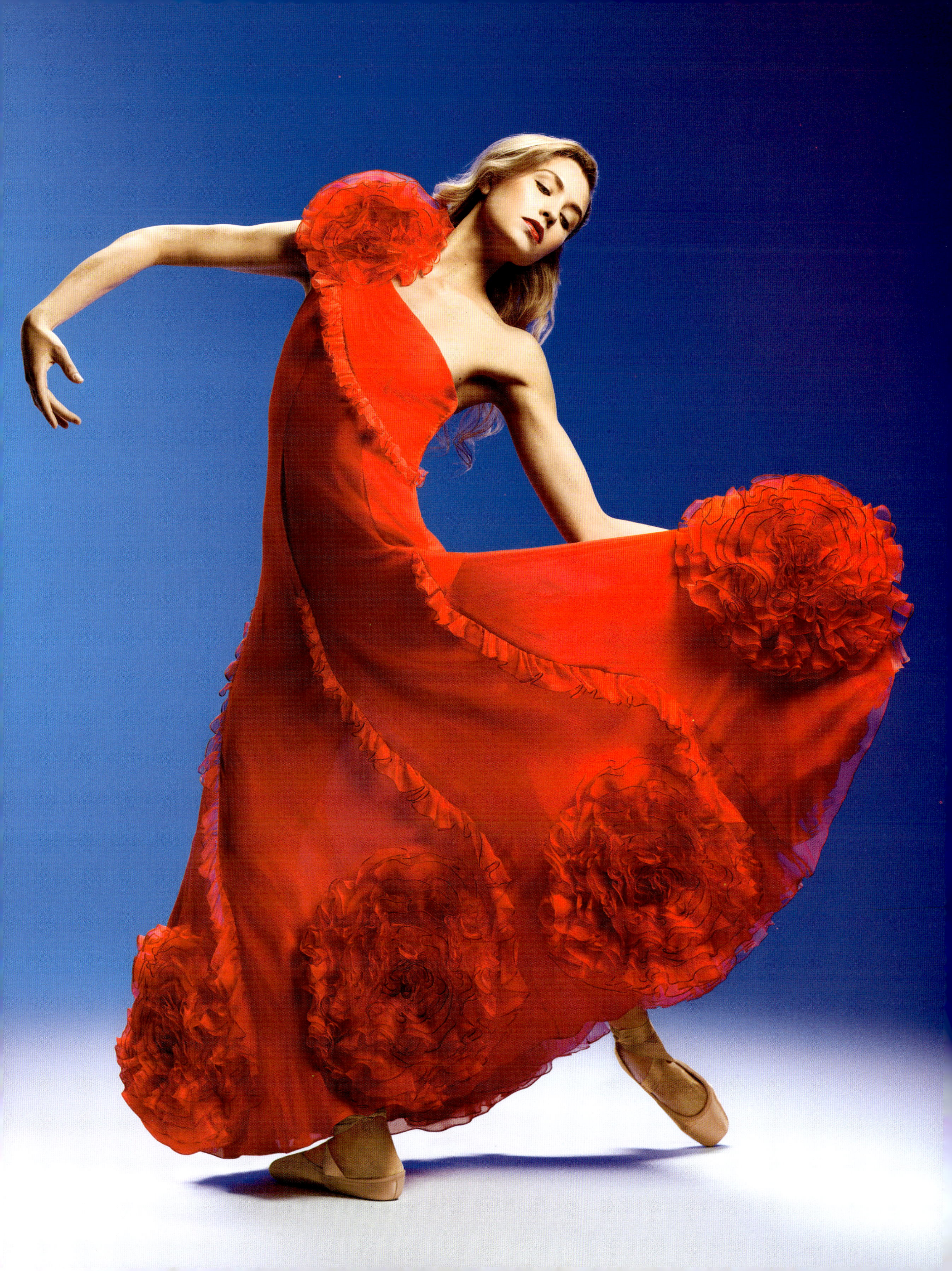

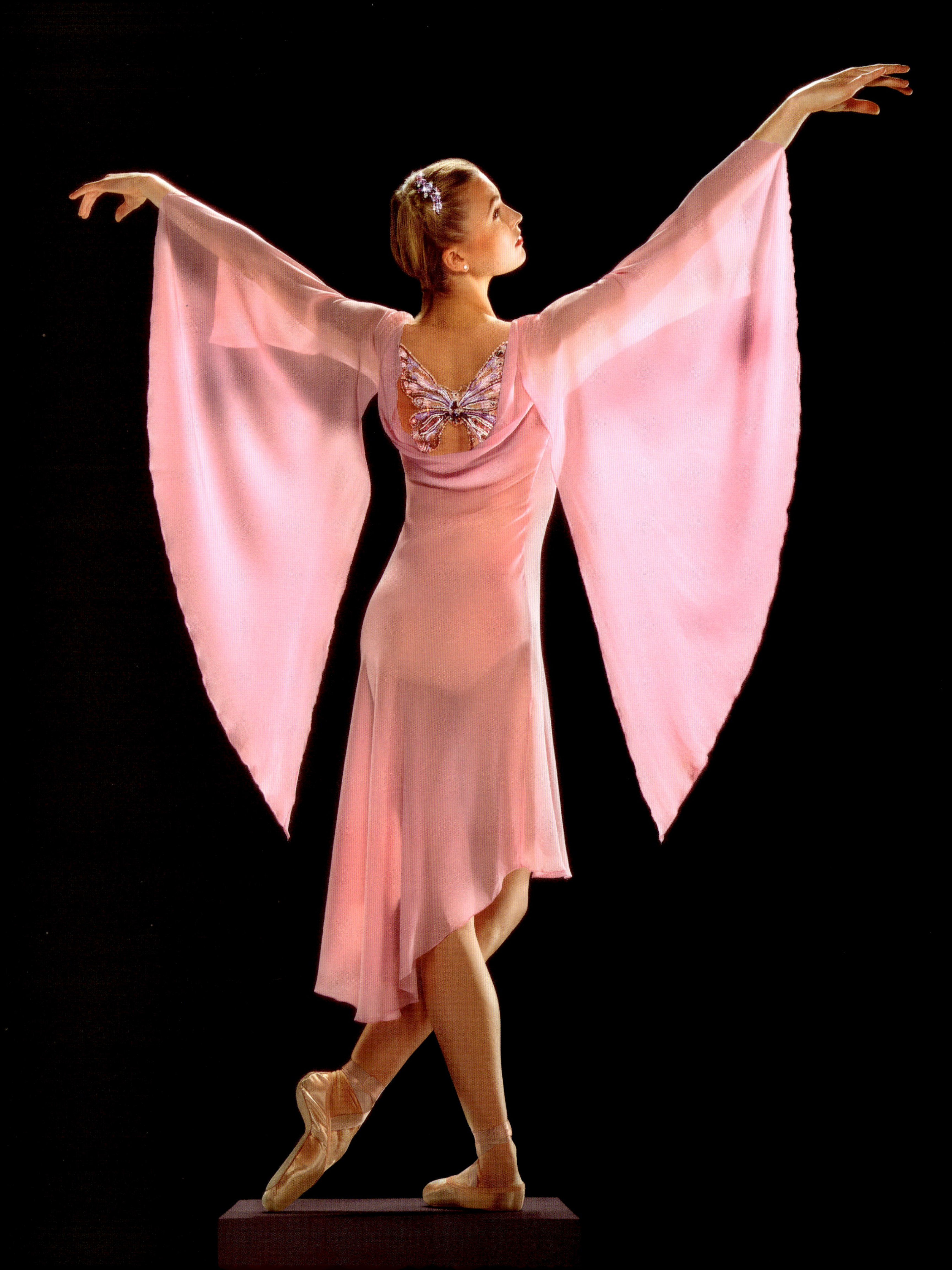

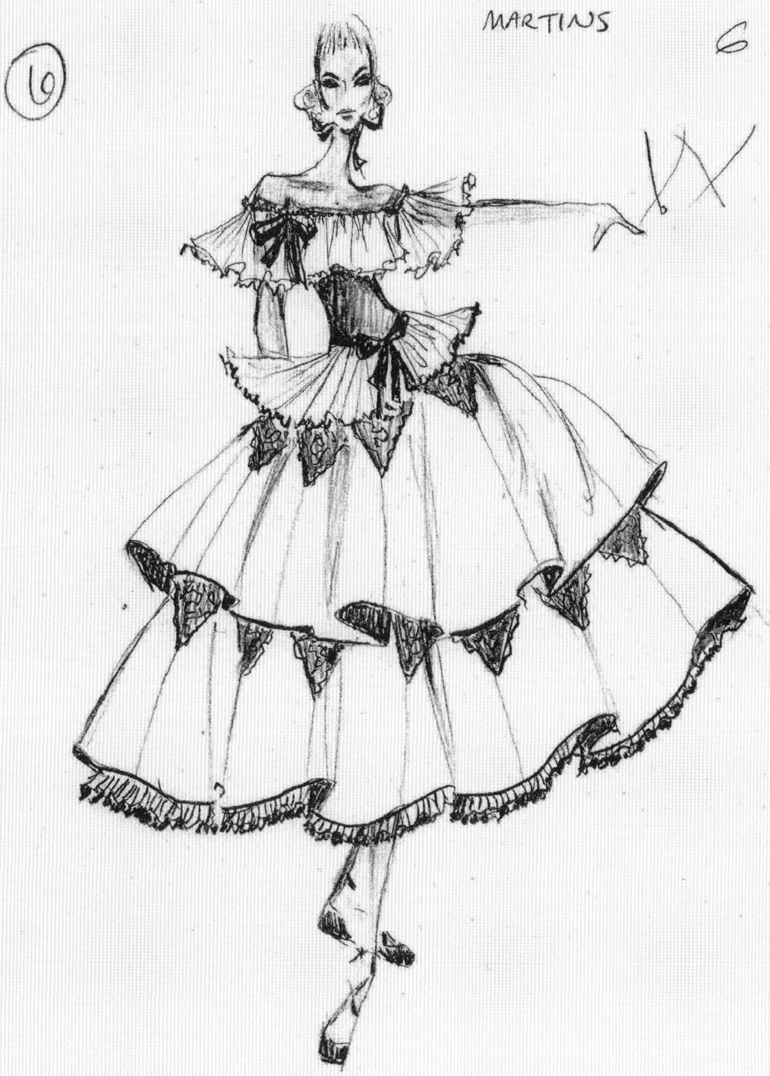
MARTINS
6

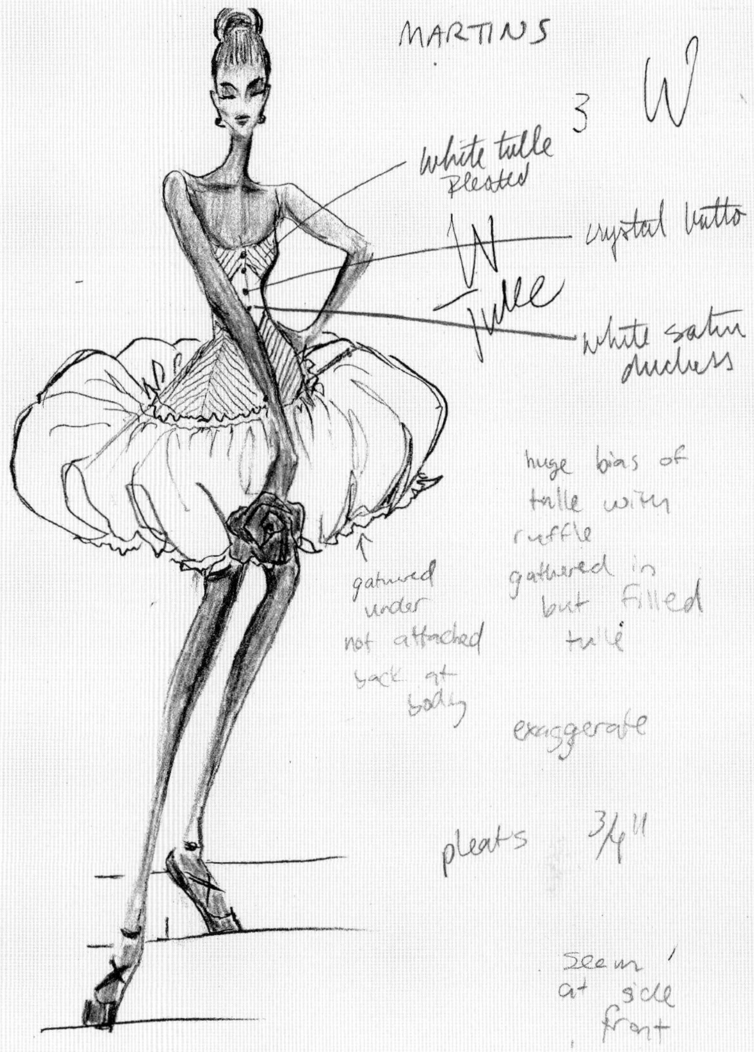
MARTINS
3 W
white tulle Pleated
crystal butto
W Tulle
white satin duchess
huge bias of tulle with ruffle gathered in but filled tulle
gathered under not attached back at body
exaggerate
pleats 3/4"
seam at side front

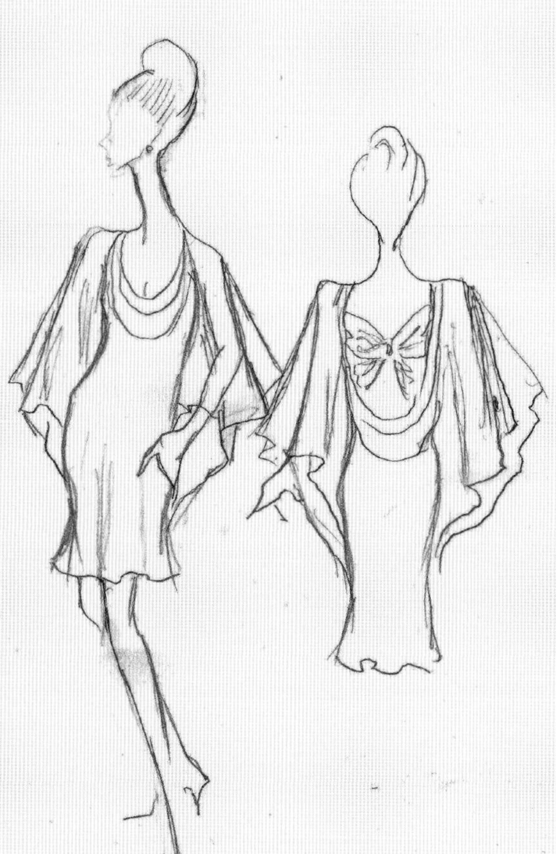

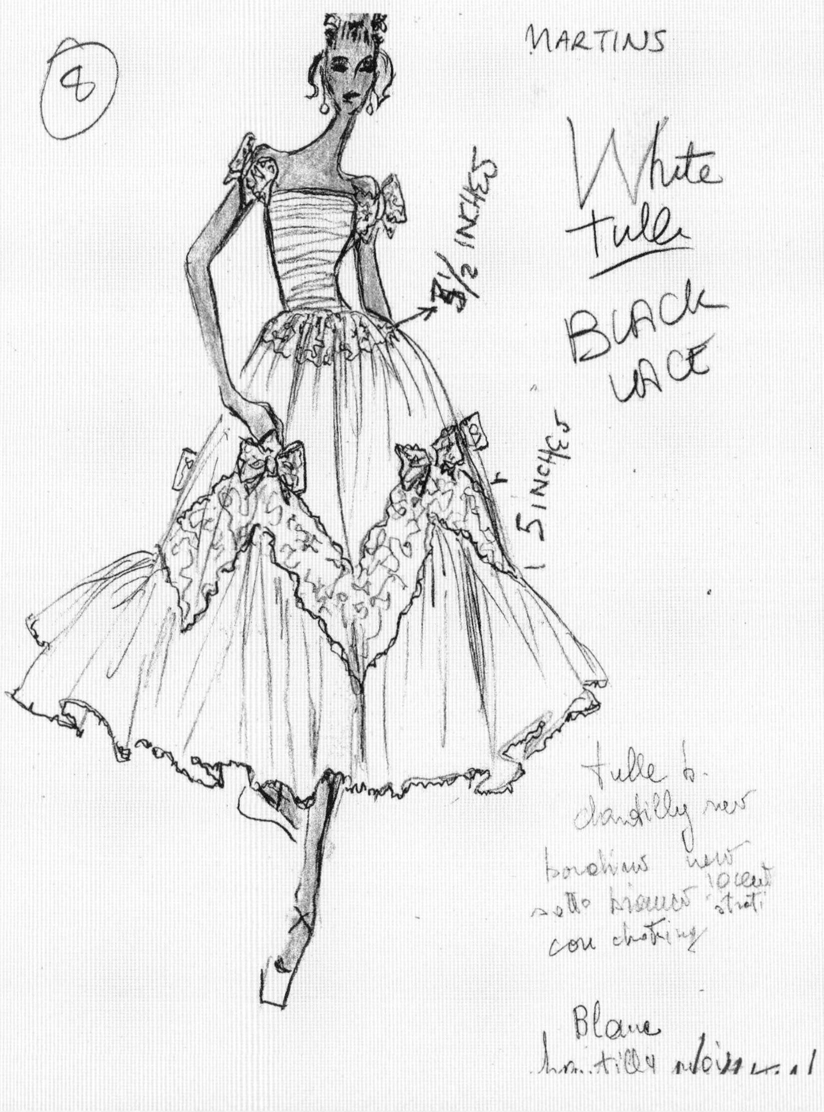
MARTINS
8
3 1/2 INCHES
White tulle
BLACK LACE
5 INCHES
Blanc

2013

PRABAL GURUNG *CAPRICIOUS MANEUVERS*

As a lover of all forms of art, seeing fashion and dance come together was a marvelous experience.

—PRABAL GURUNG

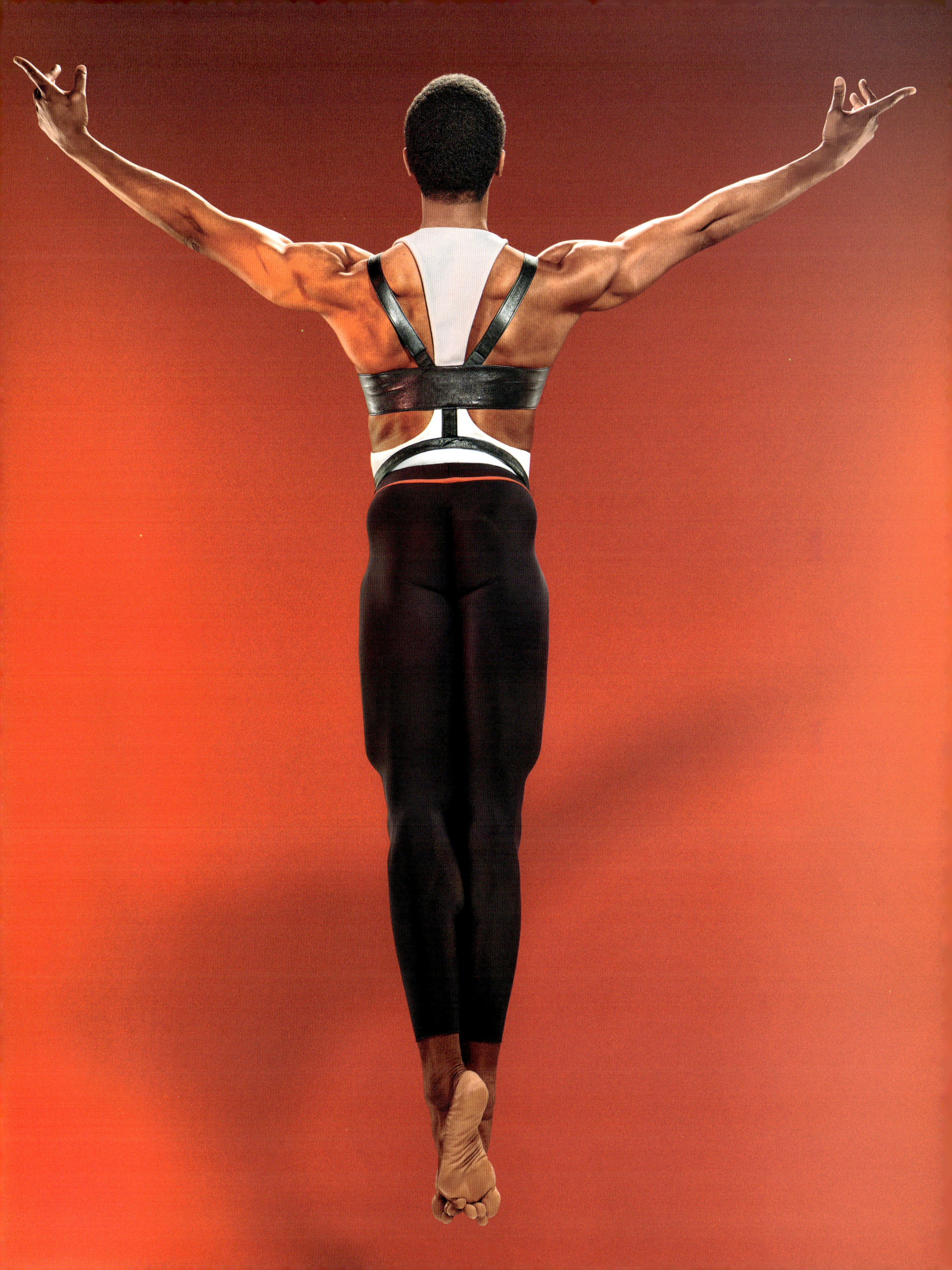

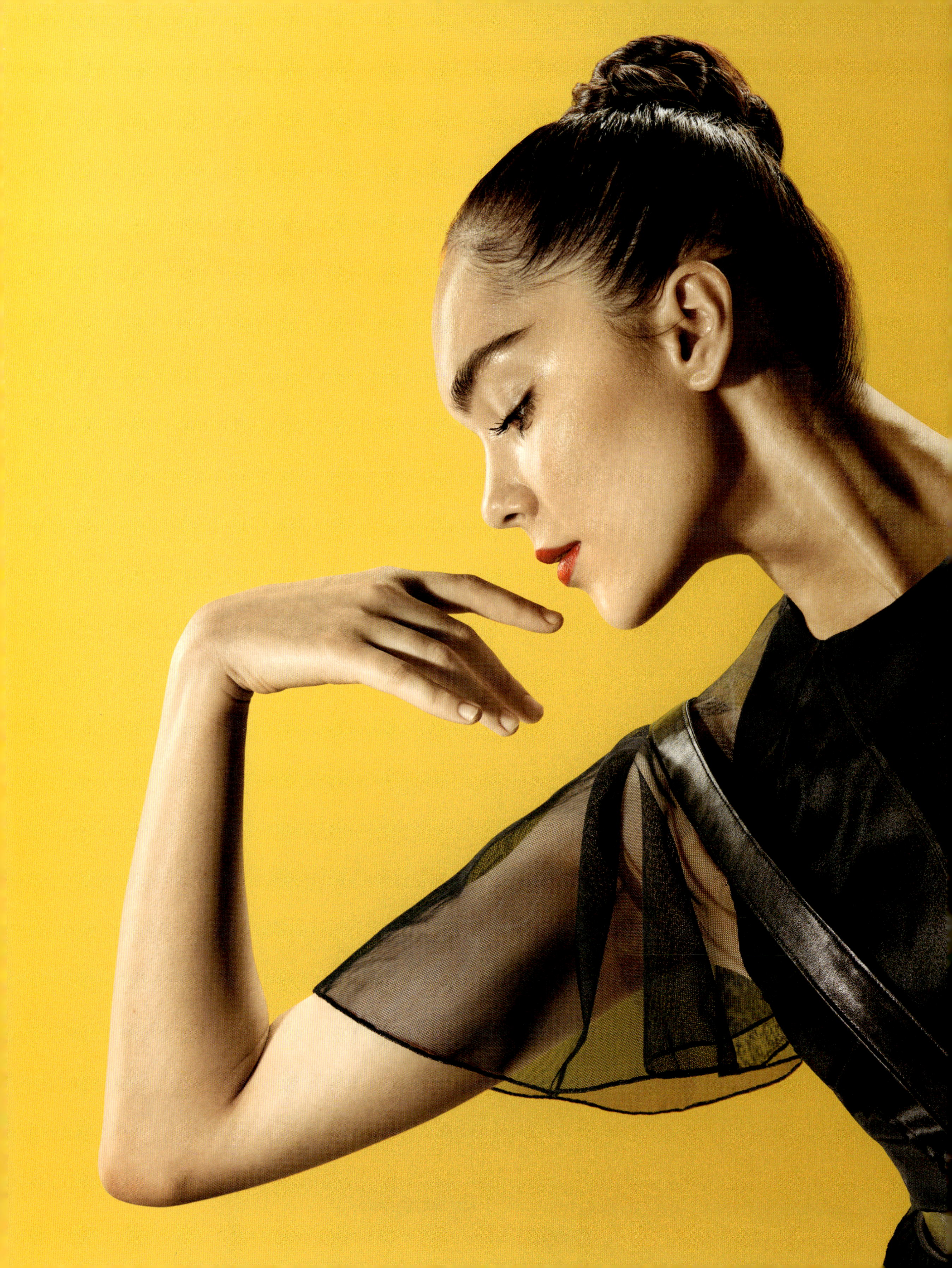

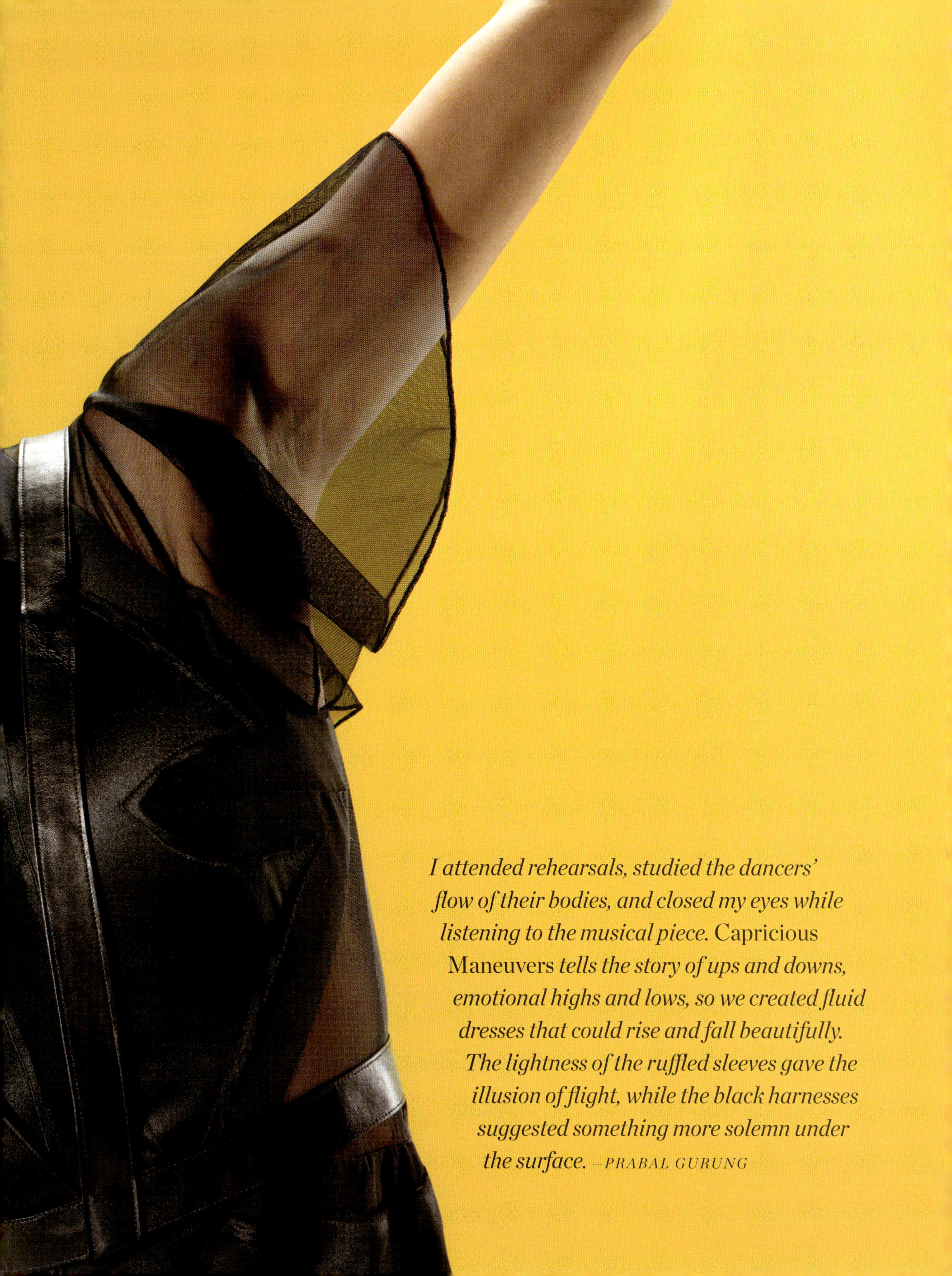

I attended rehearsals, studied the dancers' flow of their bodies, and closed my eyes while listening to the musical piece. Capricious Maneuvers *tells the story of ups and downs, emotional highs and lows, so we created fluid dresses that could rise and fall beautifully. The lightness of the ruffled sleeves gave the illusion of flight, while the black harnesses suggested something more solemn under the surface.* –PRABAL GURUNG

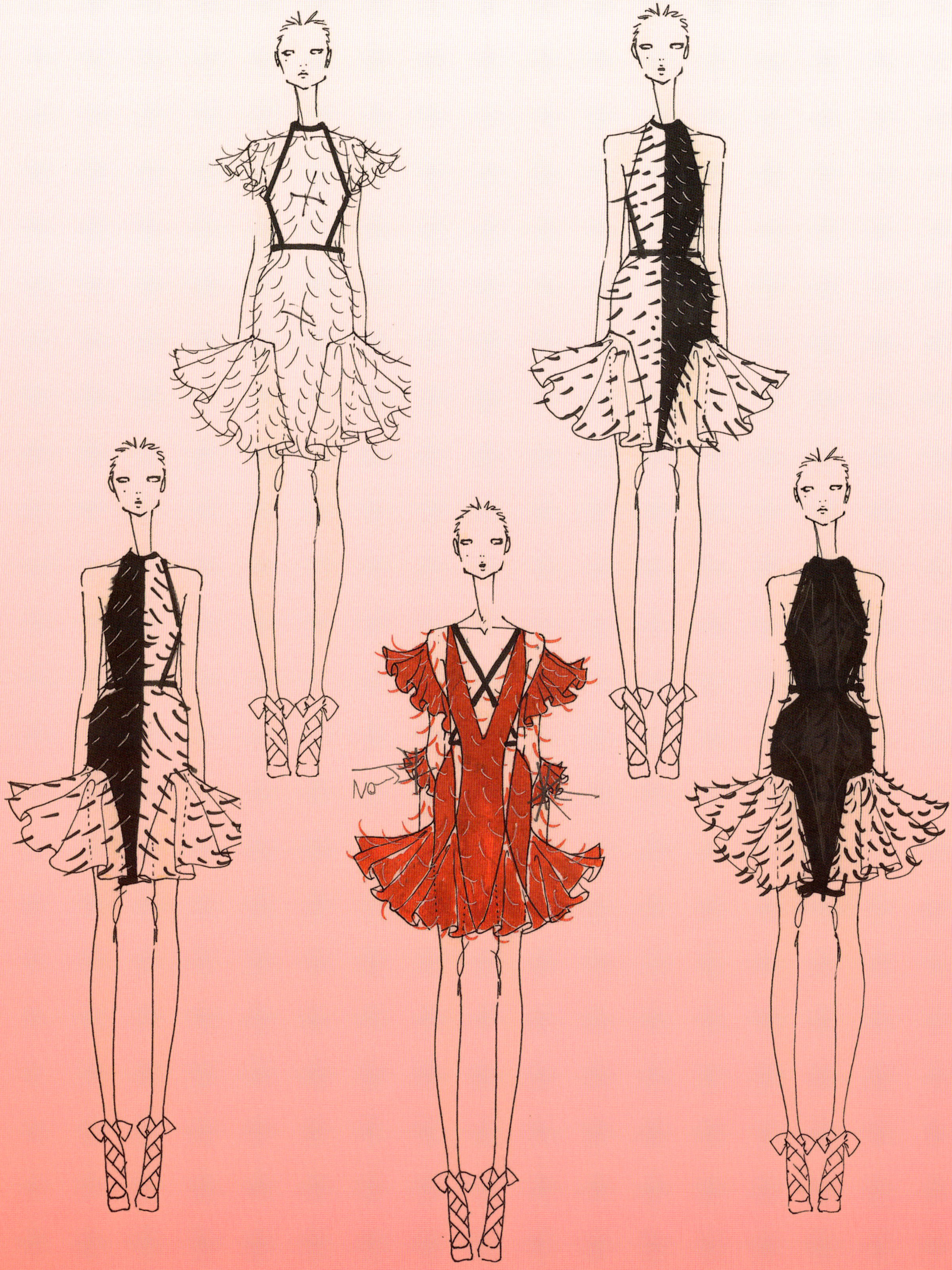
No

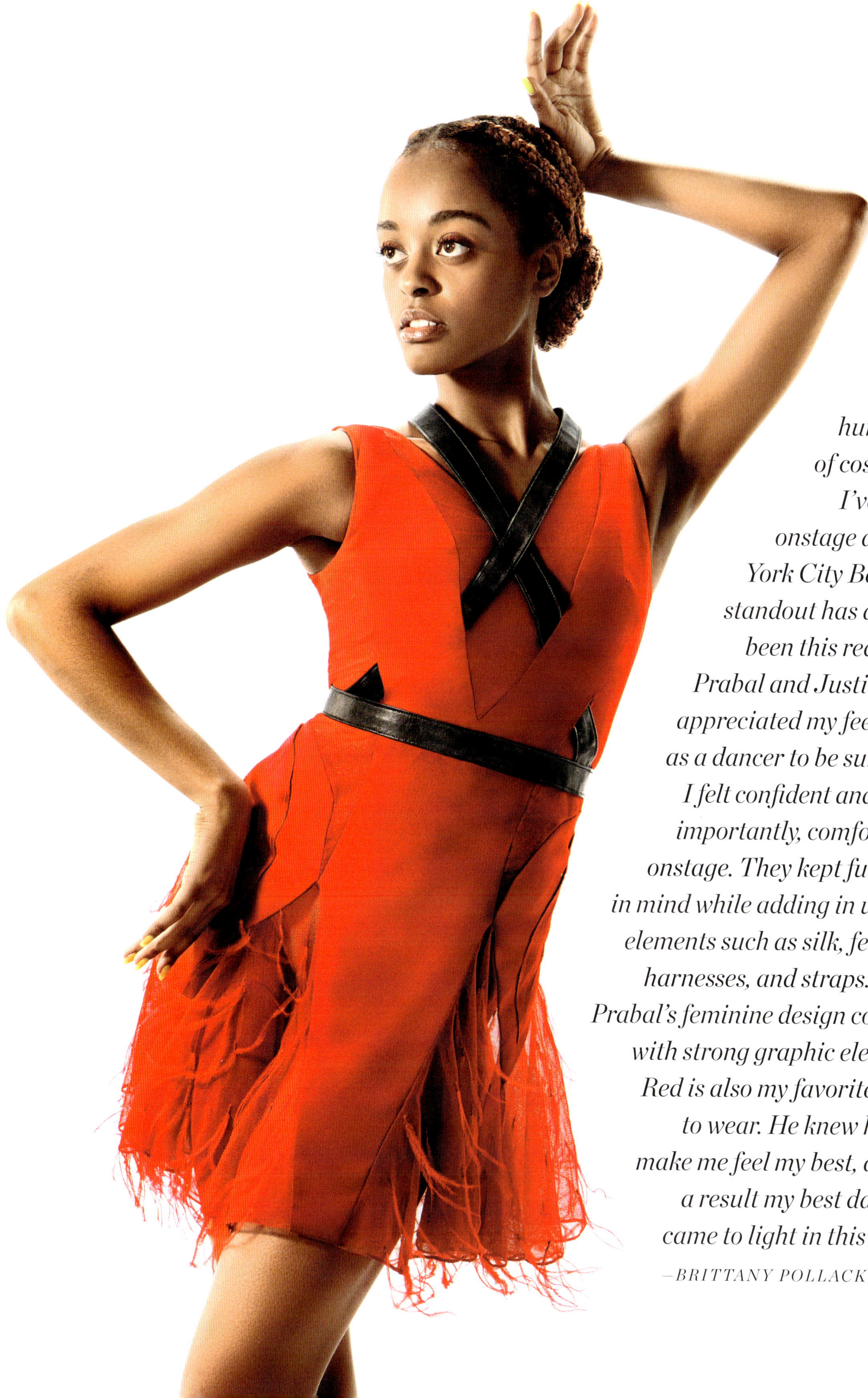

Of the hundreds of costumes I've worn onstage at New York City Ballet, a standout has always been this red dress. Prabal and Justin Peck appreciated my feedback as a dancer to be sure that I felt confident and, most importantly, comfortable onstage. They kept function in mind while adding in unique elements such as silk, feathers, harnesses, and straps. I love Prabal's feminine design coupled with strong graphic elements. Red is also my favorite color to wear. He knew how to make me feel my best, and as a result my best dancing came to light in this ballet.

—BRITTANY POLLACK, *Dancer*

2013

OLIVIER THEYSKENS *SPECTRAL EVIDENCE*

I have always been interested in creating for the dance field, but when Angelin Preljocaj came with the theme of The Crucible *for the piece I was struck by the story which resonated totally with my creative world.*

Angelin gave me total freedom to create the costumes. I'll be always thankful to him for welcoming me into his world through the most fascinating tale of the witches of Salem.

—OLIVIER THEYSKENS

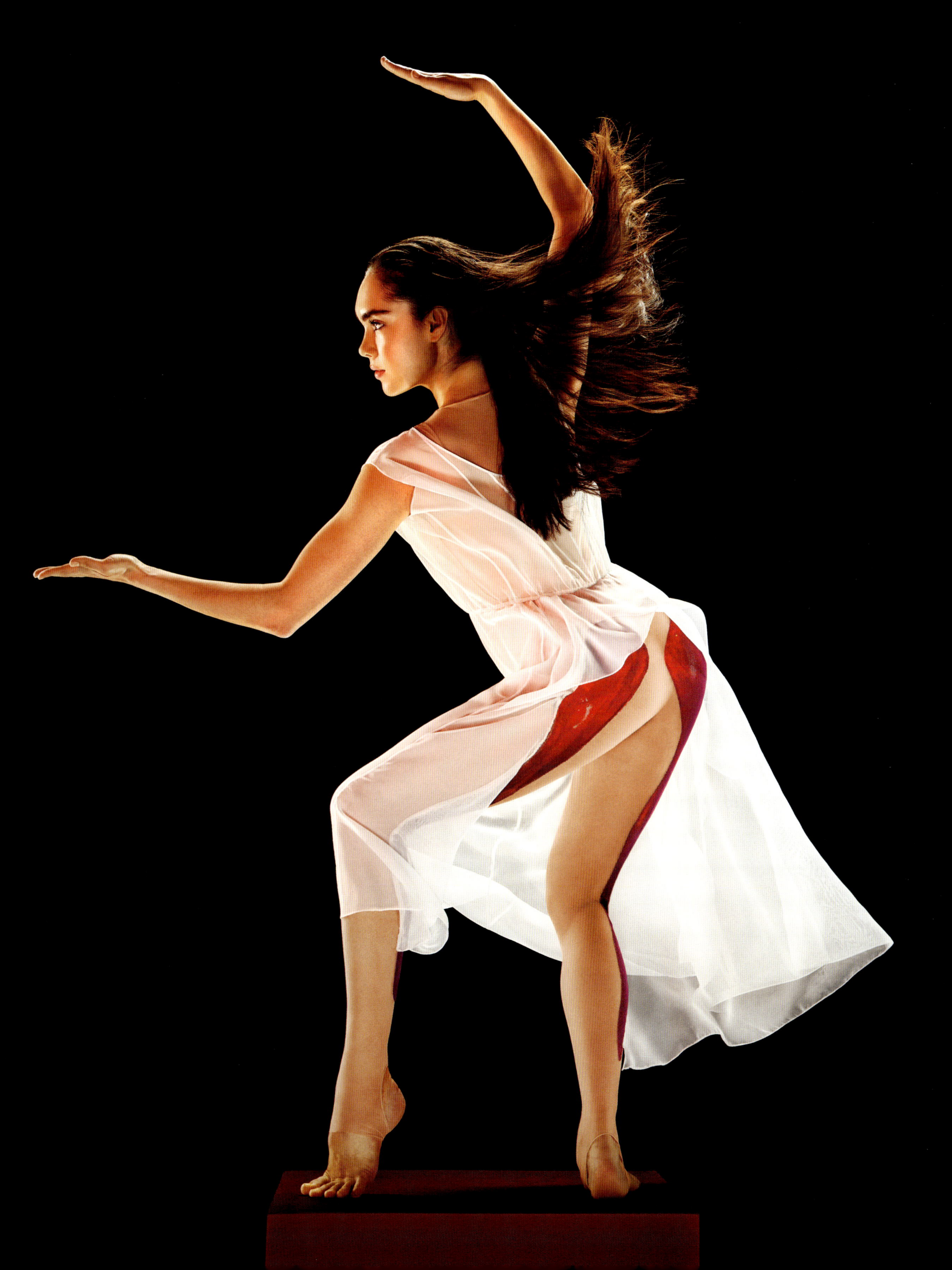

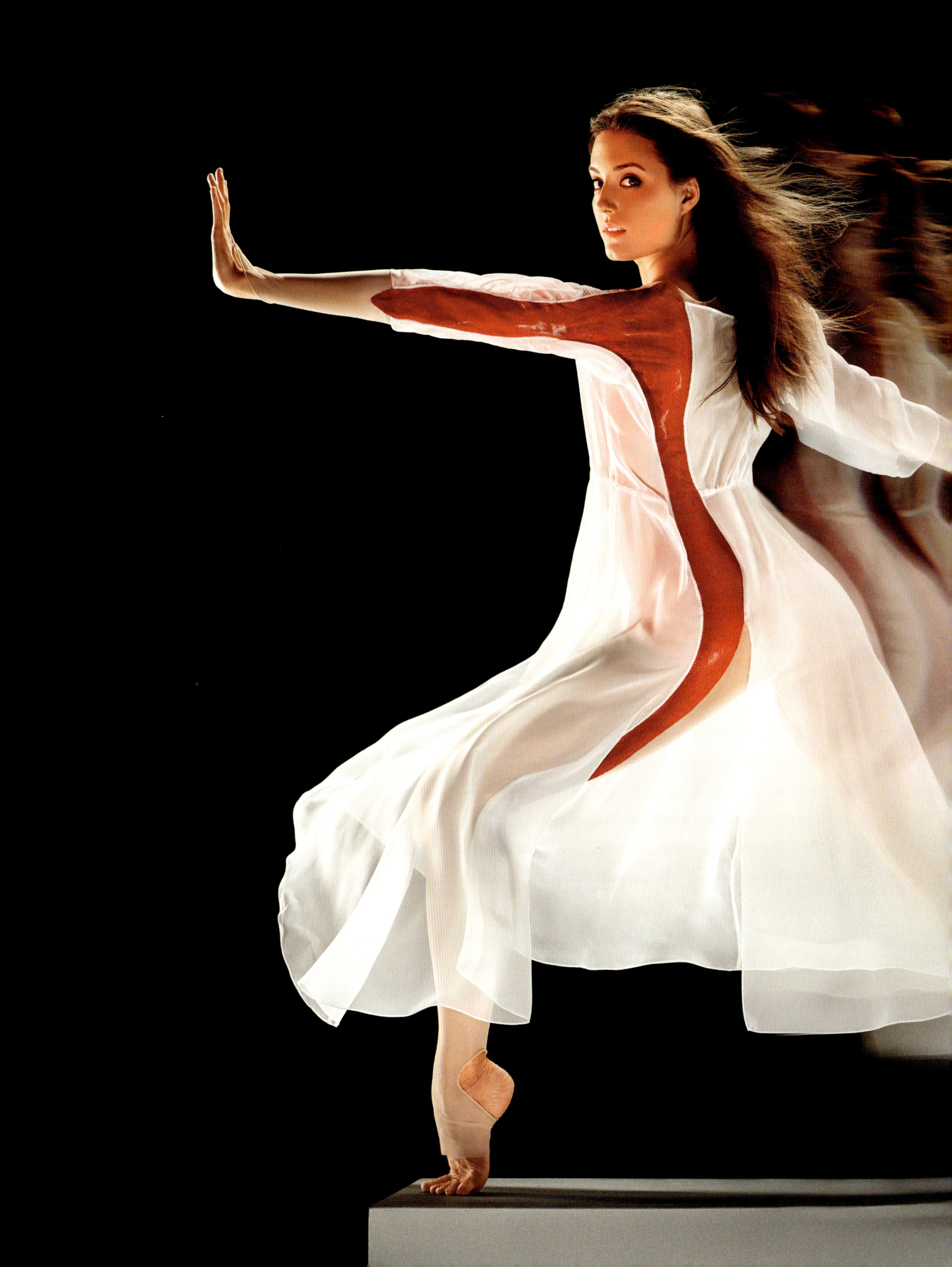

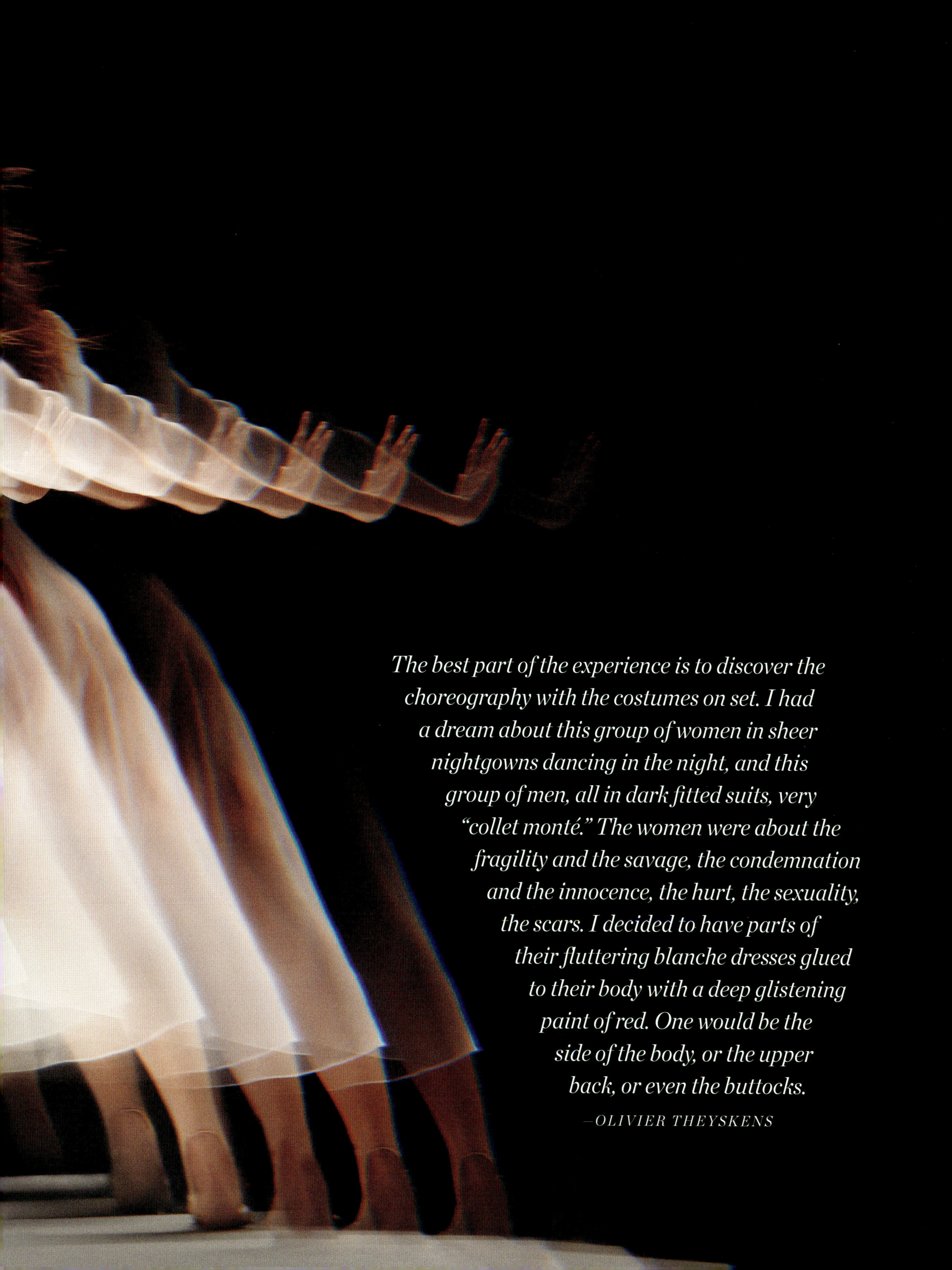

The best part of the experience is to discover the choreography with the costumes on set. I had a dream about this group of women in sheer nightgowns dancing in the night, and this group of men, all in dark fitted suits, very "collet monté." The women were about the fragility and the savage, the condemnation and the innocence, the hurt, the sexuality, the scars. I decided to have parts of their fluttering blanche dresses glued to their body with a deep glistening paint of red. One would be the side of the body, or the upper back, or even the buttocks.

—OLIVIER THEYSKENS

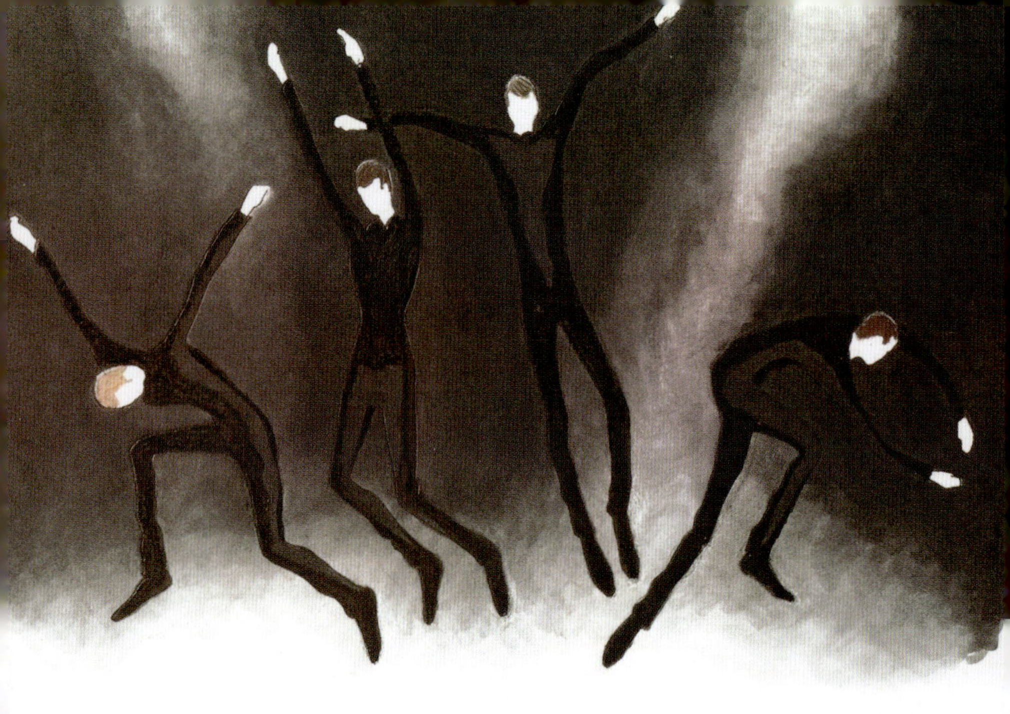

It's like a contamination—Olivier contaminates my creativity, and I hope I will contaminate his creativity.

—ANGELIN PRELJOCAJ, *Choreographer*

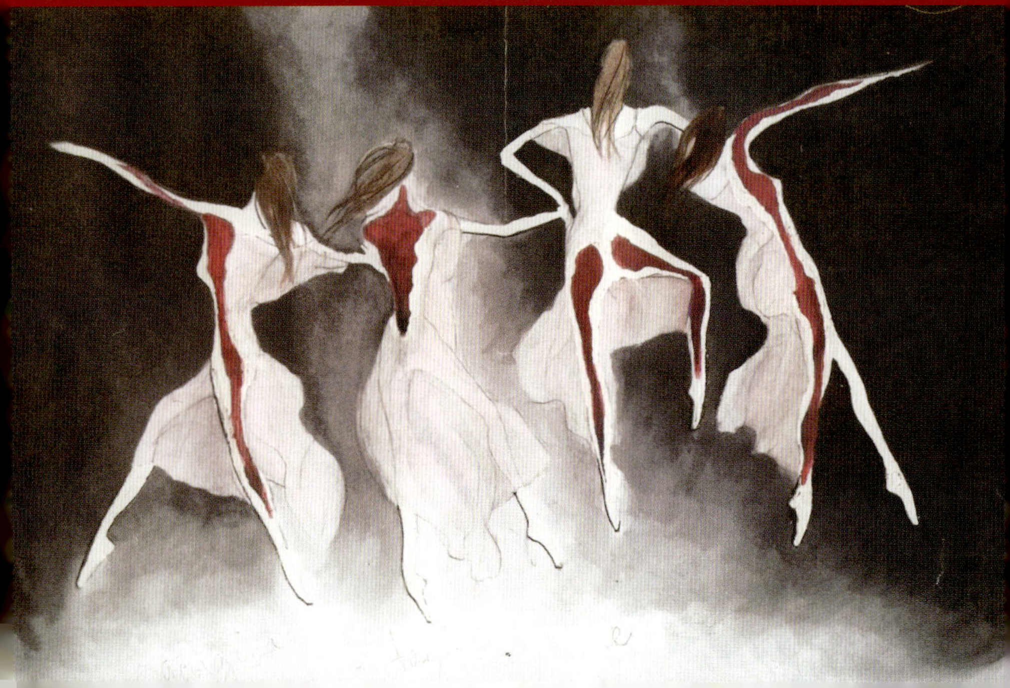

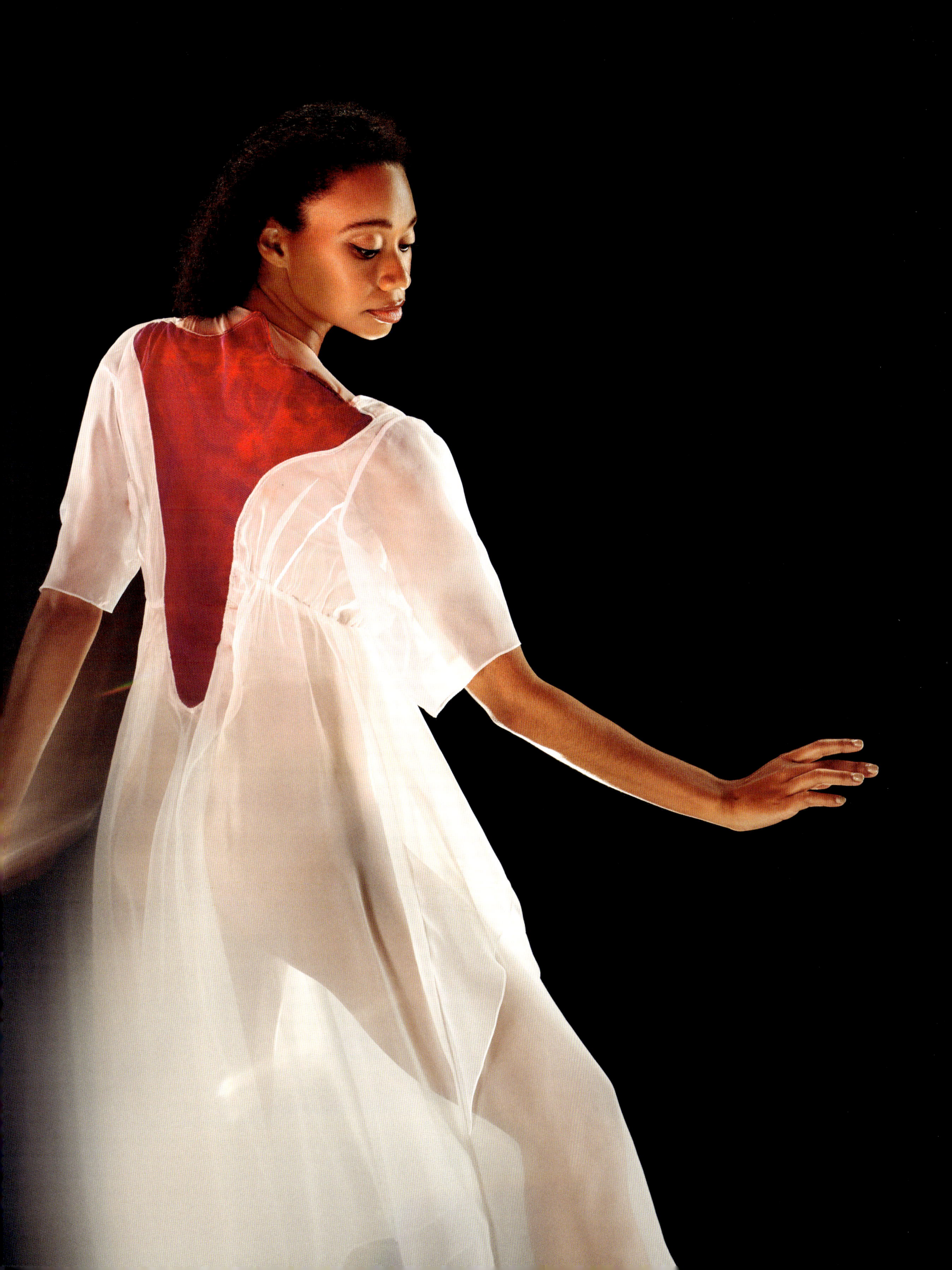

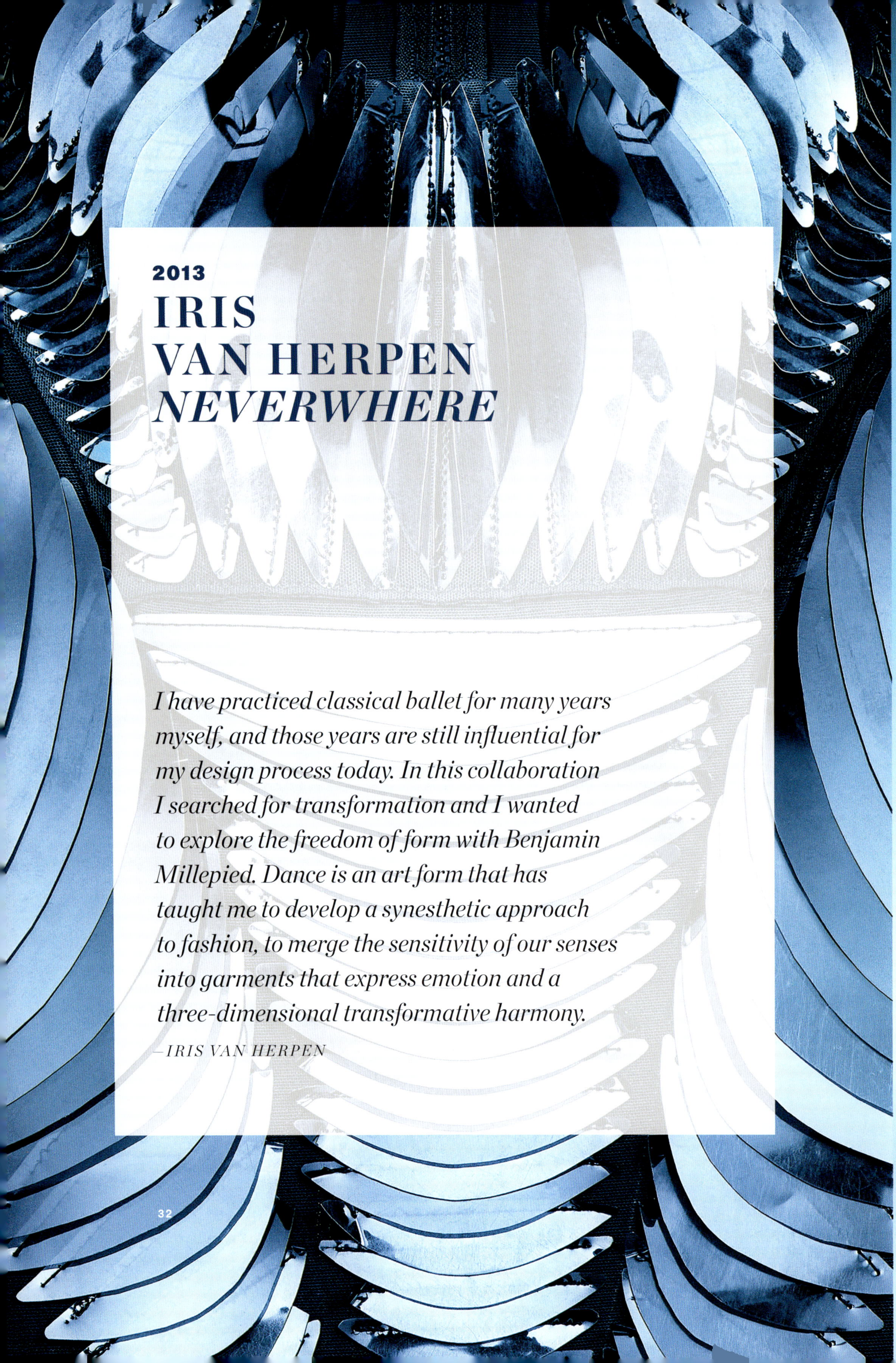

2013

IRIS VAN HERPEN *NEVERWHERE*

I have practiced classical ballet for many years myself, and those years are still influential for my design process today. In this collaboration I searched for transformation and I wanted to explore the freedom of form with Benjamin Millepied. Dance is an art form that has taught me to develop a synesthetic approach to fashion, to merge the sensitivity of our senses into garments that express emotion and a three-dimensional transformative harmony.

—IRIS VAN HERPEN

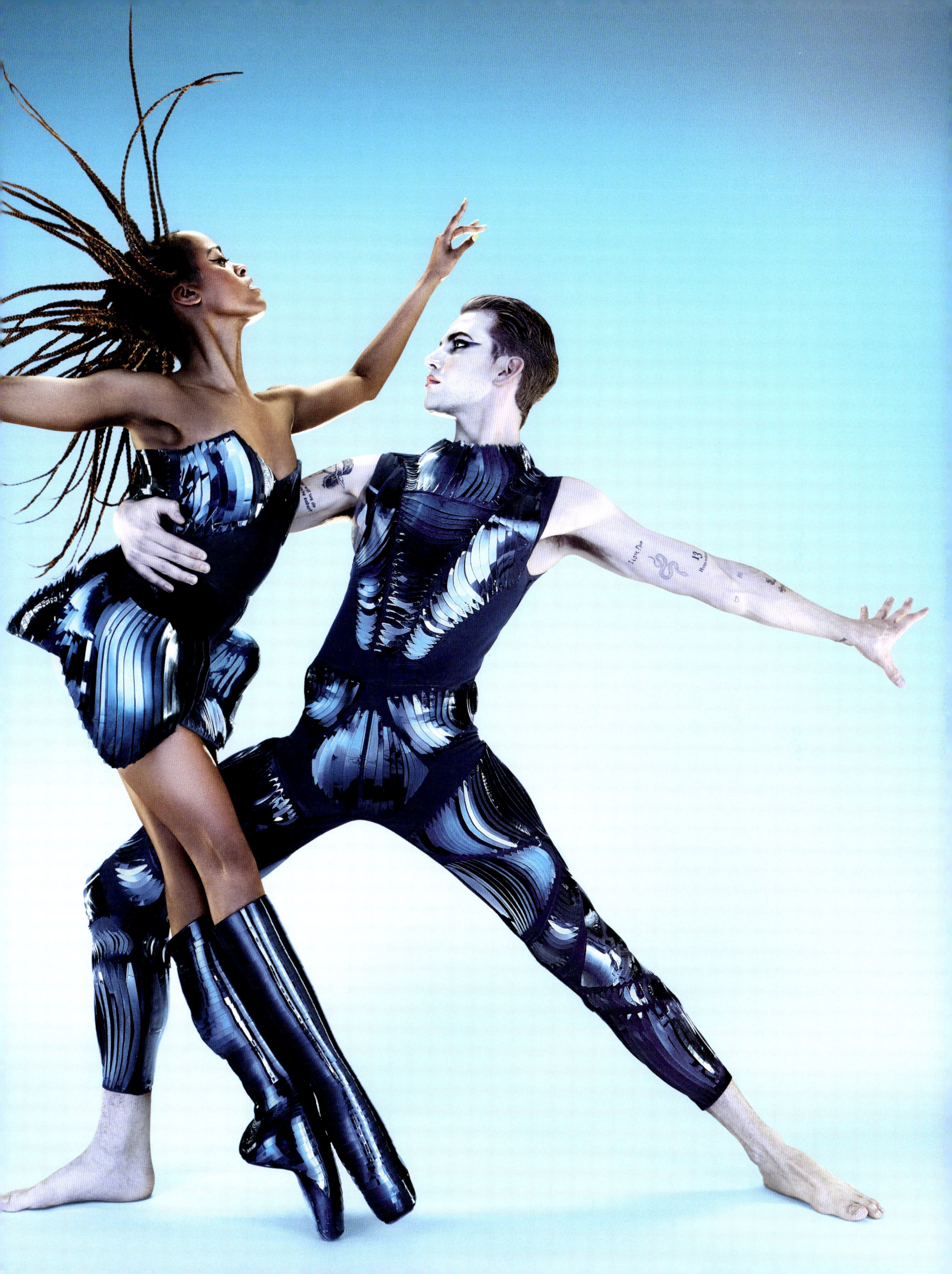

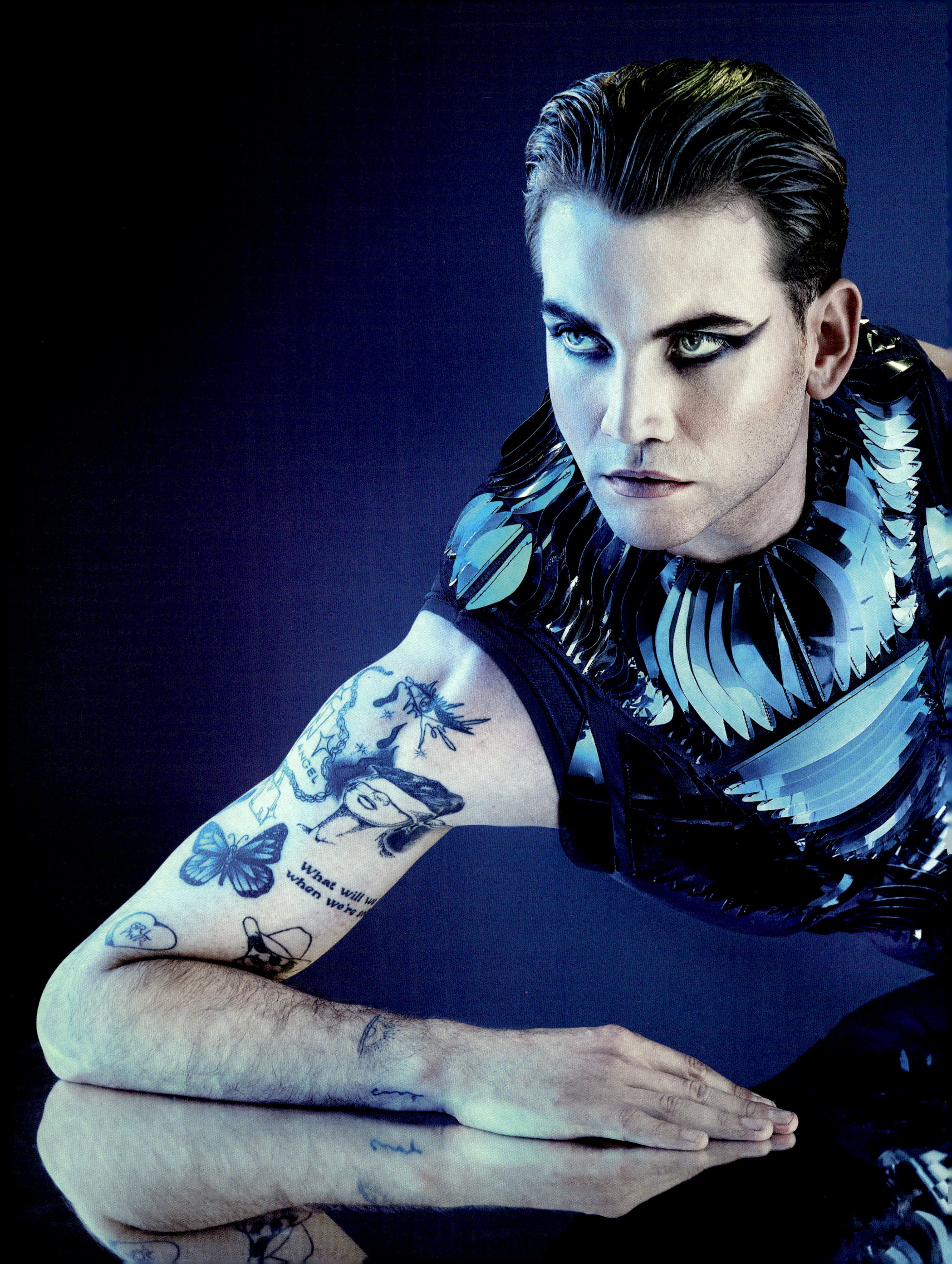

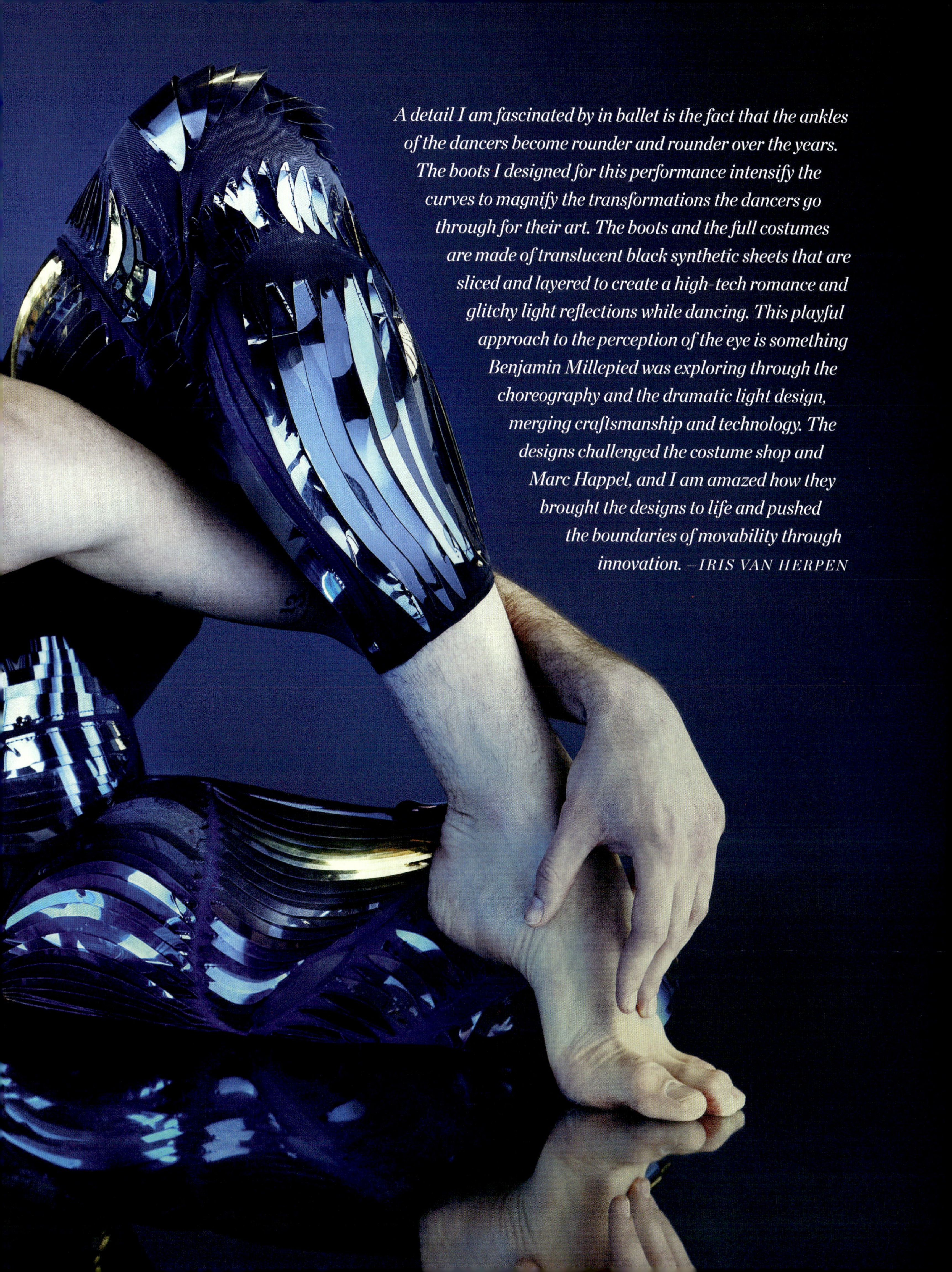

A detail I am fascinated by in ballet is the fact that the ankles of the dancers become rounder and rounder over the years. The boots I designed for this performance intensify the curves to magnify the transformations the dancers go through for their art. The boots and the full costumes are made of translucent black synthetic sheets that are sliced and layered to create a high-tech romance and glitchy light reflections while dancing. This playful approach to the perception of the eye is something Benjamin Millepied was exploring through the choreography and the dramatic light design, merging craftsmanship and technology. The designs challenged the costume shop and Marc Happel, and I am amazed how they brought the designs to life and pushed the boundaries of movability through innovation. —IRIS VAN HERPEN

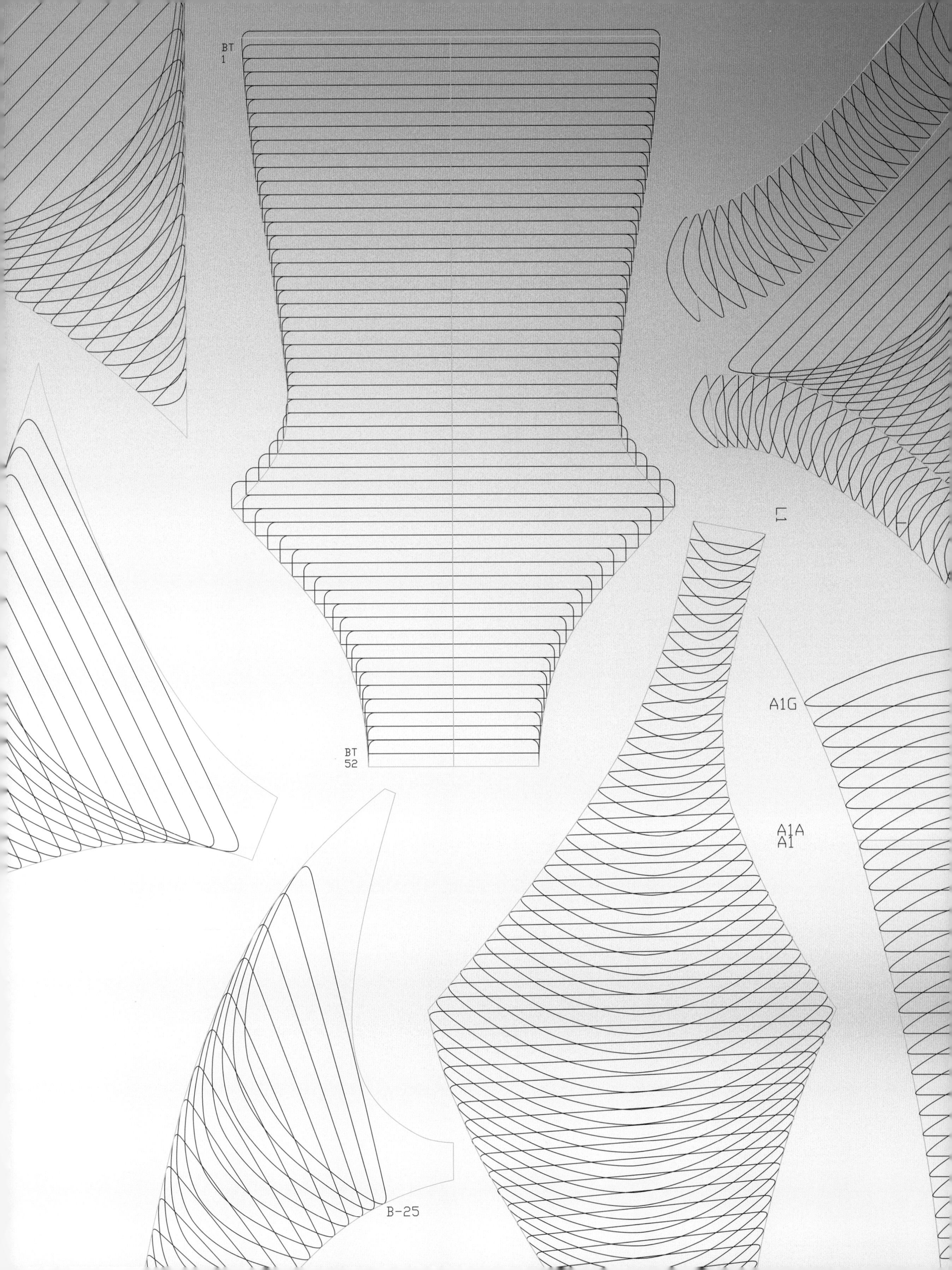
BT
1
BT
52
L1
A1G
A1A
A1
B-25

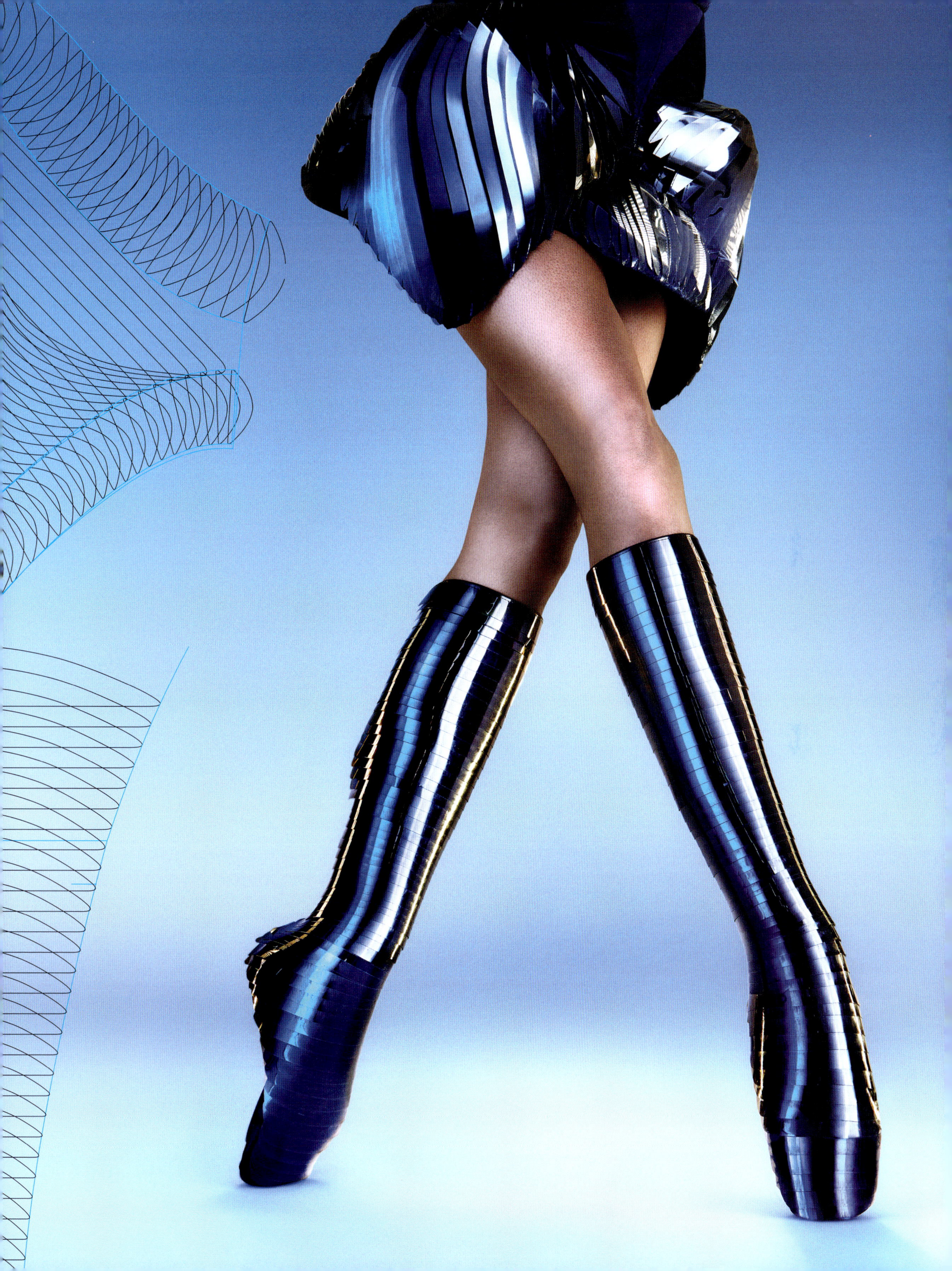

PATRICIA MEARS

BALLET AND FASHION HAVE LONG, intertwined histories. This companionable relationship has been a natural fit as both art forms rely on the human physique as a point of departure for their creative expressions. Today, we take for granted that classical dancers, especially ballerinas, have had a major impact on modern fashion. Even those who have never seen a ballet or have little knowledge of it can readily recognize the key elements of the ballerina's professional raiment, whether for practice—knitted leotards, legwarmers, and flat slippers—or performance—fitted satin bodices and frothy tutu skirts, tights, and satin pointe shoes.

From its creation and codification in France during the reign of Louis XIV, to its elevation as a supreme art form in late czarist Russia, to its mid-twentieth century modernization in America, ballet consistently reflected the latest fashion trends. Fashion, however, rarely adapted elements from classical dance until the interwar years of the twentieth century. The Parisian debut of Sergei Diaghilev's (1872–1929) Ballets Russes in 1909, ignited a firestorm of enthusiasm with its revolutionary marriage of music, sets and costumes, and choreography. The Company helped hasten the inversion of western Europe's traditional social order; soon, the intelligentsia, socialites, artists, writers, and the working classes alike began flocking to ballet performances. This craze for ballet, or "balletomania" as it was called by some, was both widespread and profound.

Ballet inspired an array of other fields including art, film, photography, and fashion. The legendary editor Diana Vreeland stated that the Ballets Russes was the "only avant-garde I've ever known." Dance coverage abounded in leading fashion magazines such as *Vogue* and *Harper's Bazaar*, a phenomenon that continued for the next several decades. Even advertisers took note as goods from stockings to nightgowns were advertised using ballerinas or packaged with balletic elements, clearly drawing a connection between these products and the elegant qualities of classical ballet.

Fashion too mirrored the rise of classical ballet, especially romantic, full-length works such as *Giselle* and *Swan Lake*. From the 1920s through the 1950s, French and British couturiers regularly designed ballet-inspired gowns with boned bodices and voluminous tulle skirts. Among them were Jeanne Lanvin (whose eighteenth-century-style dresses were called *La Camargo* after the rococo-era star ballet dancer), Charles James, Norman Hartnell, Christian Dior, Pierre Balmain, and even avowed moderns such as Coco Chanel and Madeleine Vionnet. Perhaps it is not surprising that ballerinas strove to wear couture-like creations whenever possible. Most dancers did not have the means to do so, but a lucky few, such as Margot Fonteyn and Maria Tallchief, were fortunate enough to acquire notable couture garments by Dior that helped burnish their images and further elevated the status of ballerinas.

Ballet also inspired fashion in America from the 1940s through the 1970s. However, rather than make versions of the tutu, ready-to-wear female designers, such as Claire McCardell, Mildred Orrick, and Vera Maxwell, and later Bonnie August of Danskin, to name a few, created an array of knitted separates and wrap dresses that were daytime versions of leotards and other ballet practice clothing worn in class or in rehearsal. In 1942, McCardell became the first designer to pair actual ballet slippers with her innovative garments. She later collaborated with Capezio, and together they created the first street-worthy ballet flats.

Knitted sportwear separates paralleled a new style of ballet advanced by the great choreographer and New York City Ballet co-founder George Balanchine. Although his breadth of creativity was vast, he became perhaps best known for works that were sleek, fast, and often plotless. Indeed, a number of Balanchine's most celebrated masterpieces were performed in knitted leotards and tights. Such fashion innovations presaged today's athleisure phenomenon by several decades.

The connections between ballet and fashion also encompassed art and popular culture. Cecil Beaton, Christian Bérard, Marcel Vertes, and Salvador Dalí designed ballet costumes (Beaton and Bérard collaborated with Ukrainian-born Barbara Karinska, the couturier who later became NYCB's legendary costumier), and they regularly incorporated ballet elements into their fashion illustrations. Photographers from George Platt Lynes to Richard Avedon not only captured images of ballet-inspired fashions, they also chose ballerinas as models in their fashion editorials. Dancers were frequent subjects for painters including Paul Cadmus and Laura Grant, while a few, such as Leslie Caron and Cyd Charisse, became world famous movie stars.

Even though ballet's influence on fashion had waned by the 1980s, it had not evaporated. The tutu was worn by Madonna during the early years of her career, albeit in a decidedly punk way, and Sarah Jessica Parker in the opening credits of the hit television series *Sex and the City*. Likewise, the leotard, or bodysuit, remained a mainstay of designers such as Donna Karan and Azzedine Alaïa. Fashion could also be found on the ballet stage. In 1988, American Ballet Theatre's revival of Léonide Massine's 1938 *Gaîté Parisienne* was enhanced and enriched thanks to the costumes by couturier Christian Lacroix.

The creation of ballet costumes by leading fashion designers reached its apex in 2012 with the debut of New York City Ballet's Fall Fashion Gala. Spearheaded by NYCB Board Vice Chair Sarah Jessica Parker, it has become the preeminent ballet and fashion event. But the annual pairings of choreographer and fashion creator could only come to fruition thanks to the Company's Director of Costumes Marc Happel and his team. It is they who have translated brilliant but often unorthodox and impractical fashions into danceable, stage-worthy wearables.

This cross-disciplinary collaboration between artists and artisans is the contemporary manifestation of the centuries-old relationship between classical ballet and high fashion. We are the privileged recipients of these dynamic, unexpected, and expertly crafted costumes that signify the continued richness and vitality that connect these two beloved art forms.

PATRICIA MEARS
Deputy Director, The Museum at FIT

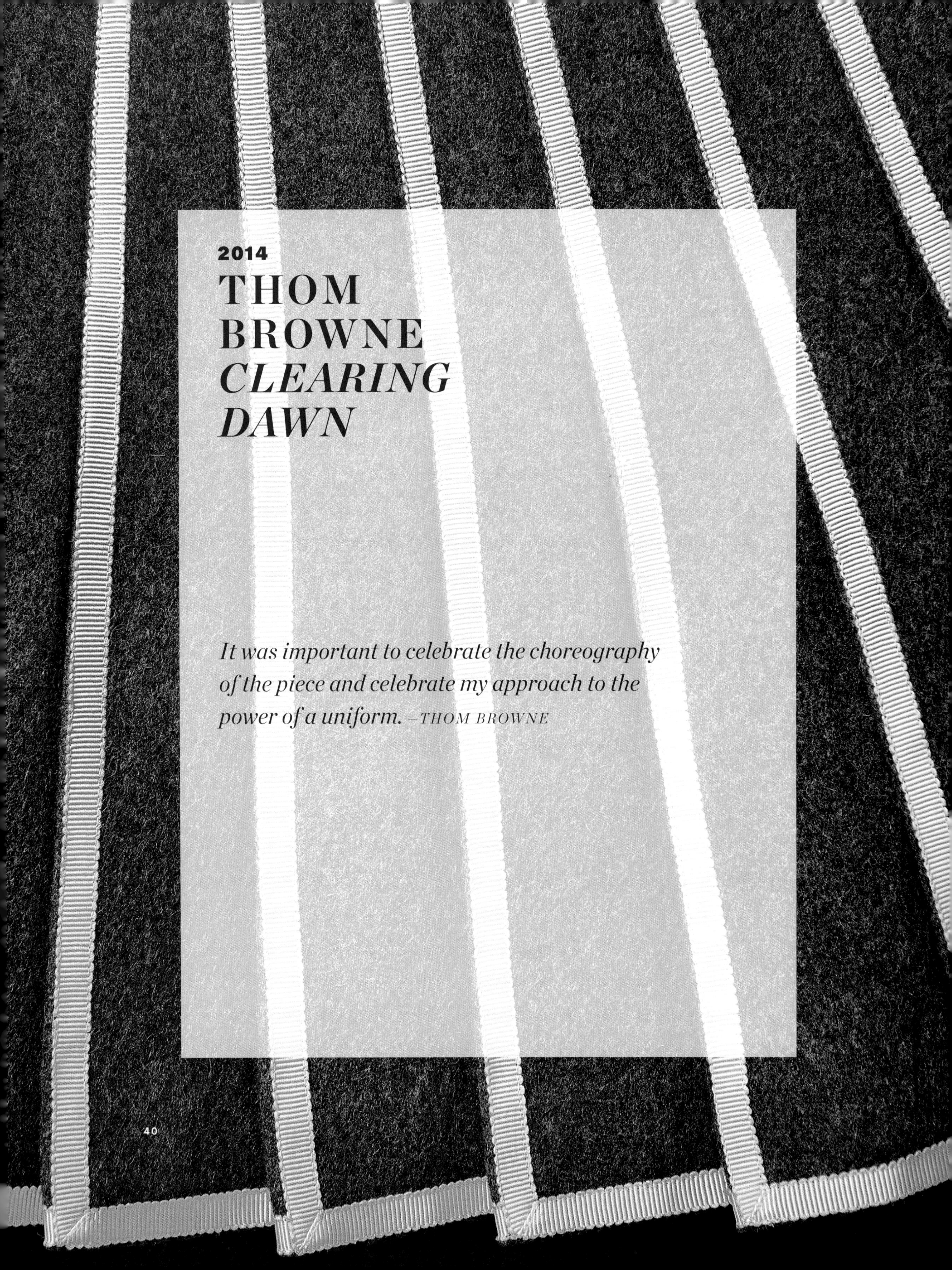

2014

THOM BROWNE *CLEARING DAWN*

It was important to celebrate the choreography of the piece and celebrate my approach to the power of a uniform. —THOM BROWNE

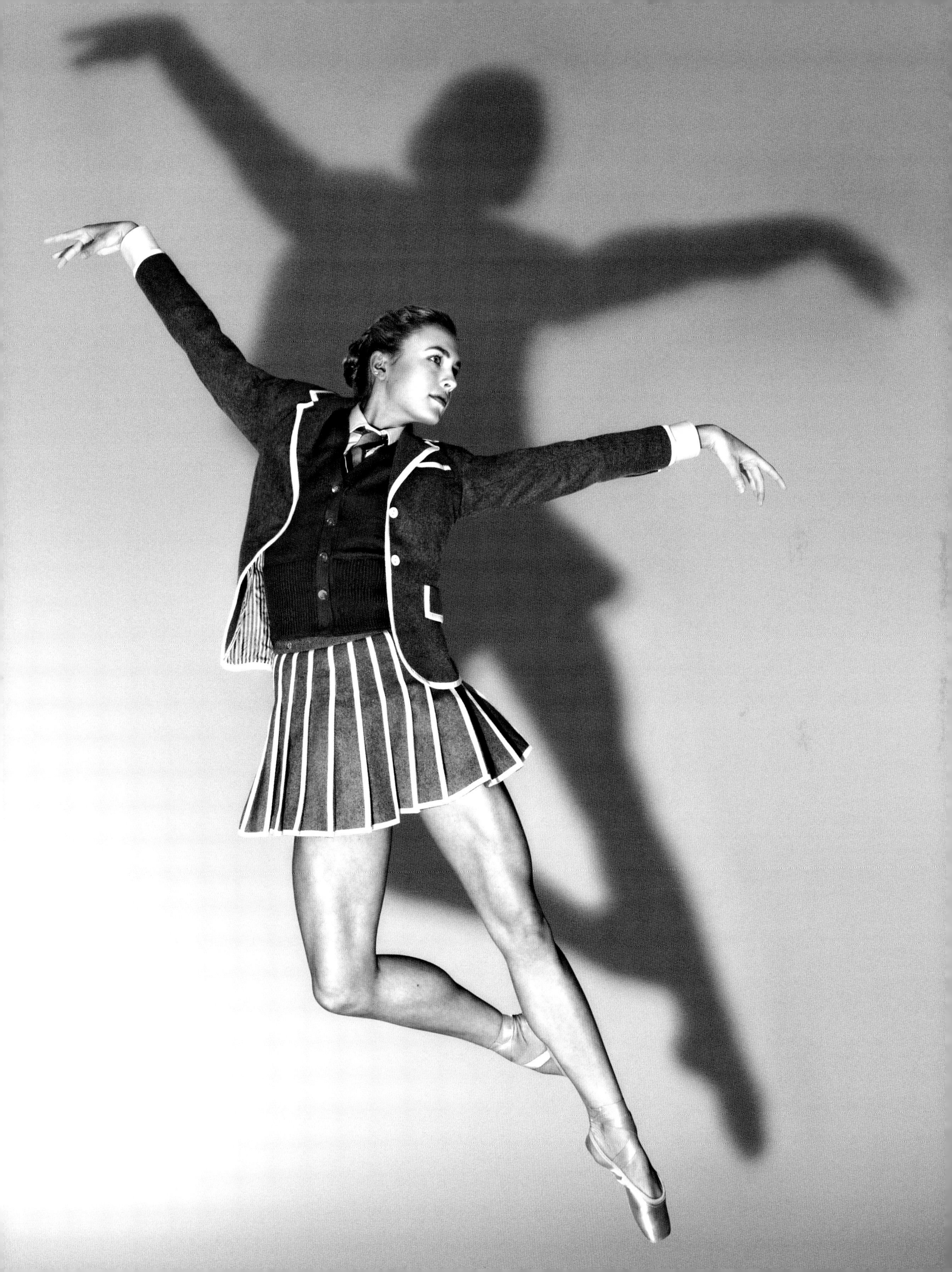

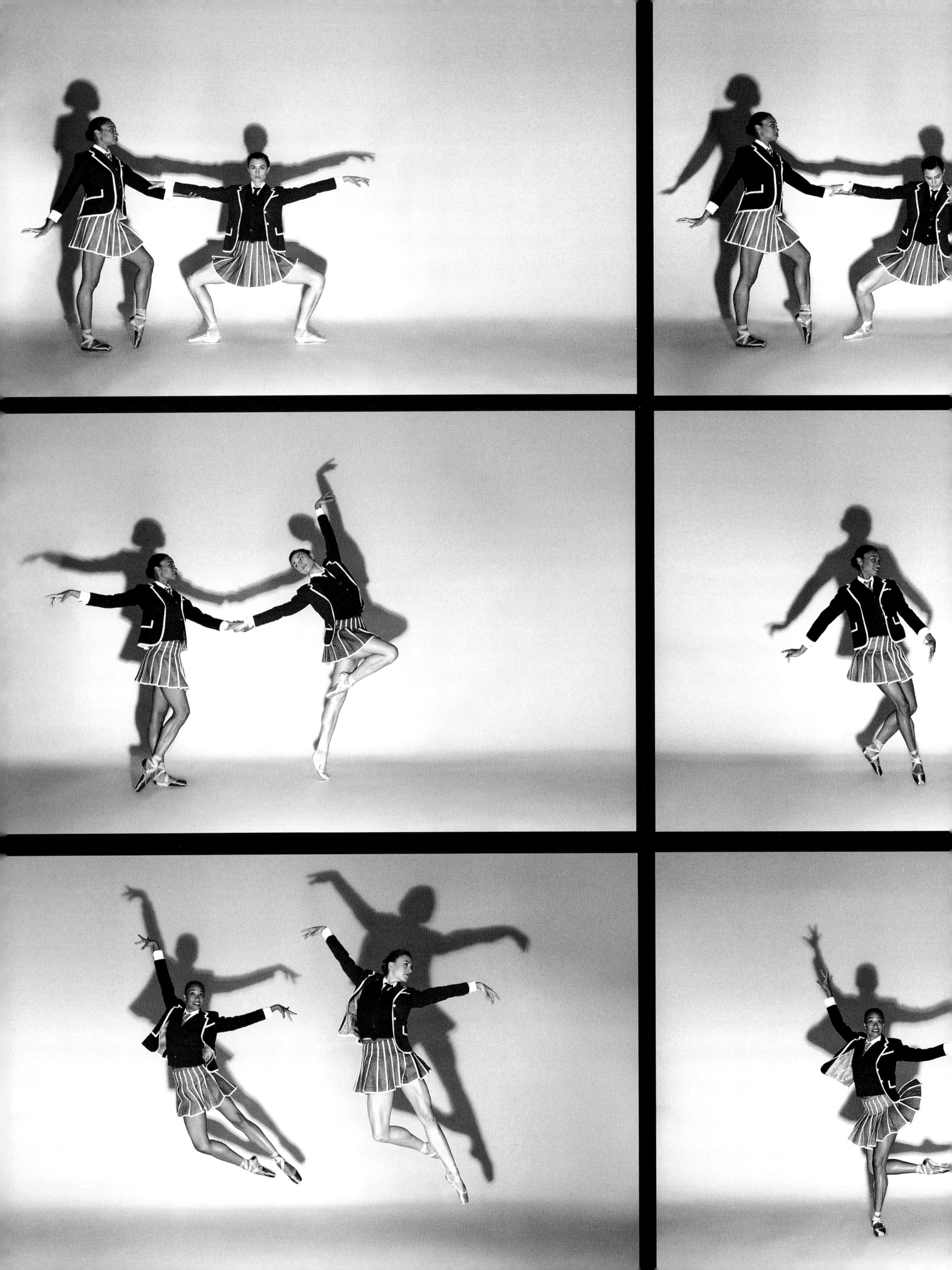

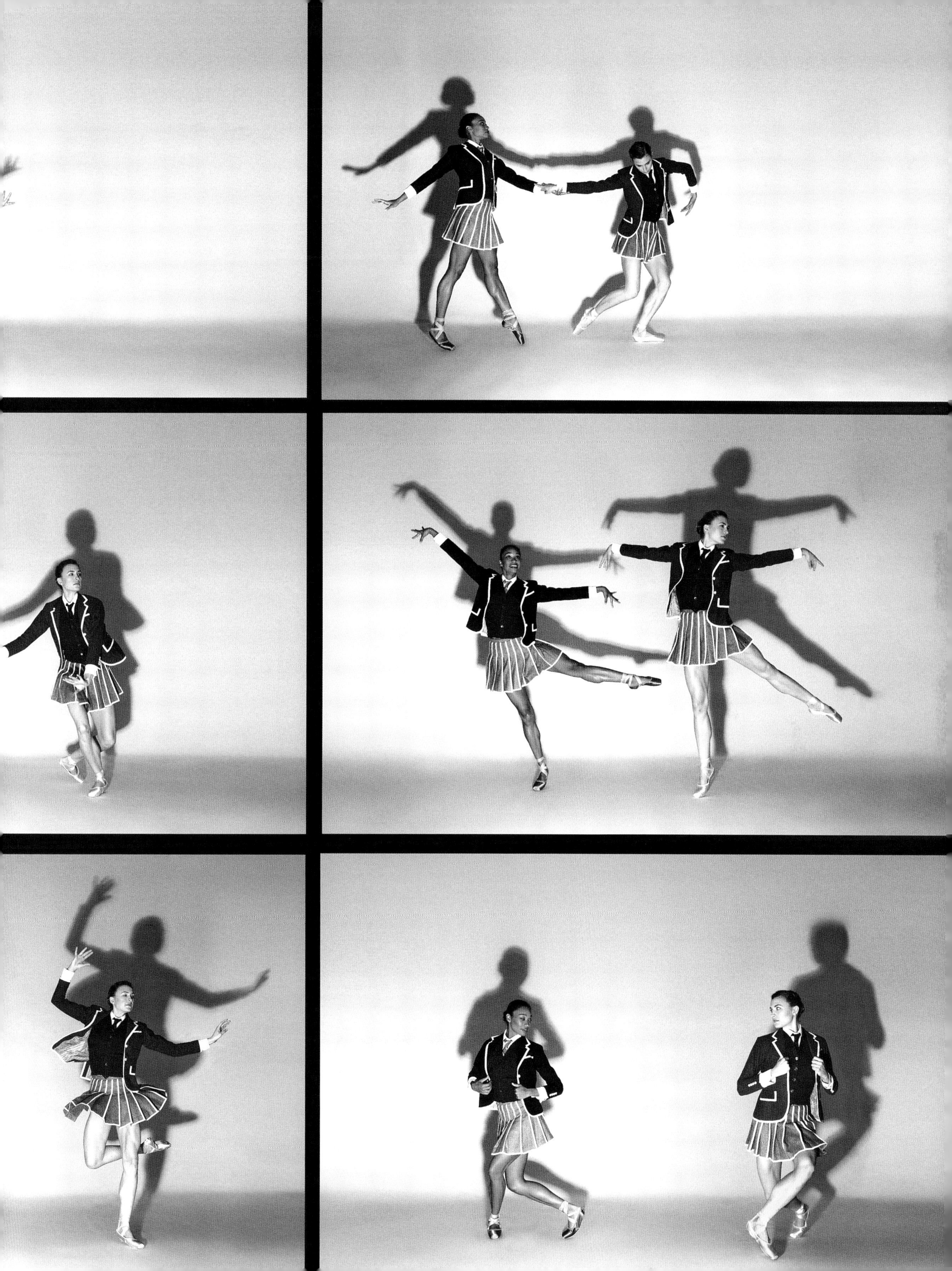

When Thom and I were discussing our ballet, Clearing Dawn, *he was experimenting with boxy, geometric shapes. We thought our ballet could be an opportunity to blend those oversized shapes with his re-inventive, distinct tailoring. During the collaborative process, he showed me sketches for some very fun, oversized overcoats with shoulders that referenced football shoulder pads. I immediately had the idea of using the coats as both costumes and set pieces that would, early on in the ballet, suddenly fly off the dancers, as if a metaphorical weight had been lifted, allowing them to be free, and share a magical moment.* —*TROY SCHUMACHER, Choreographer*

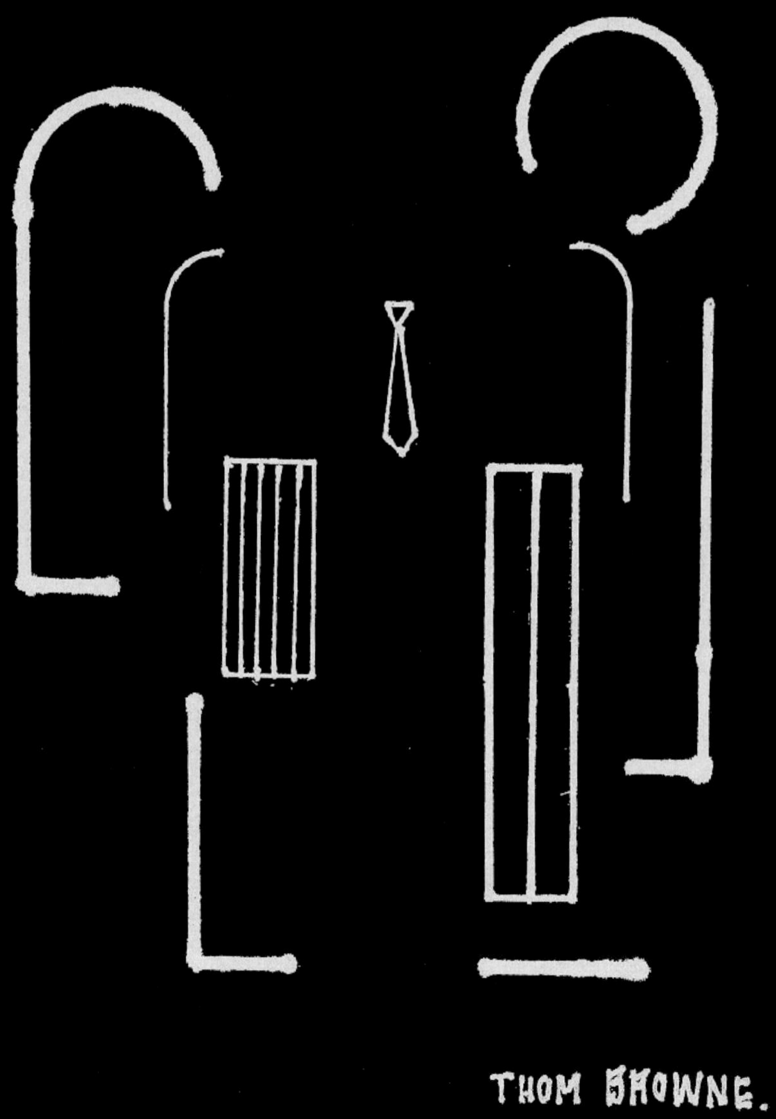

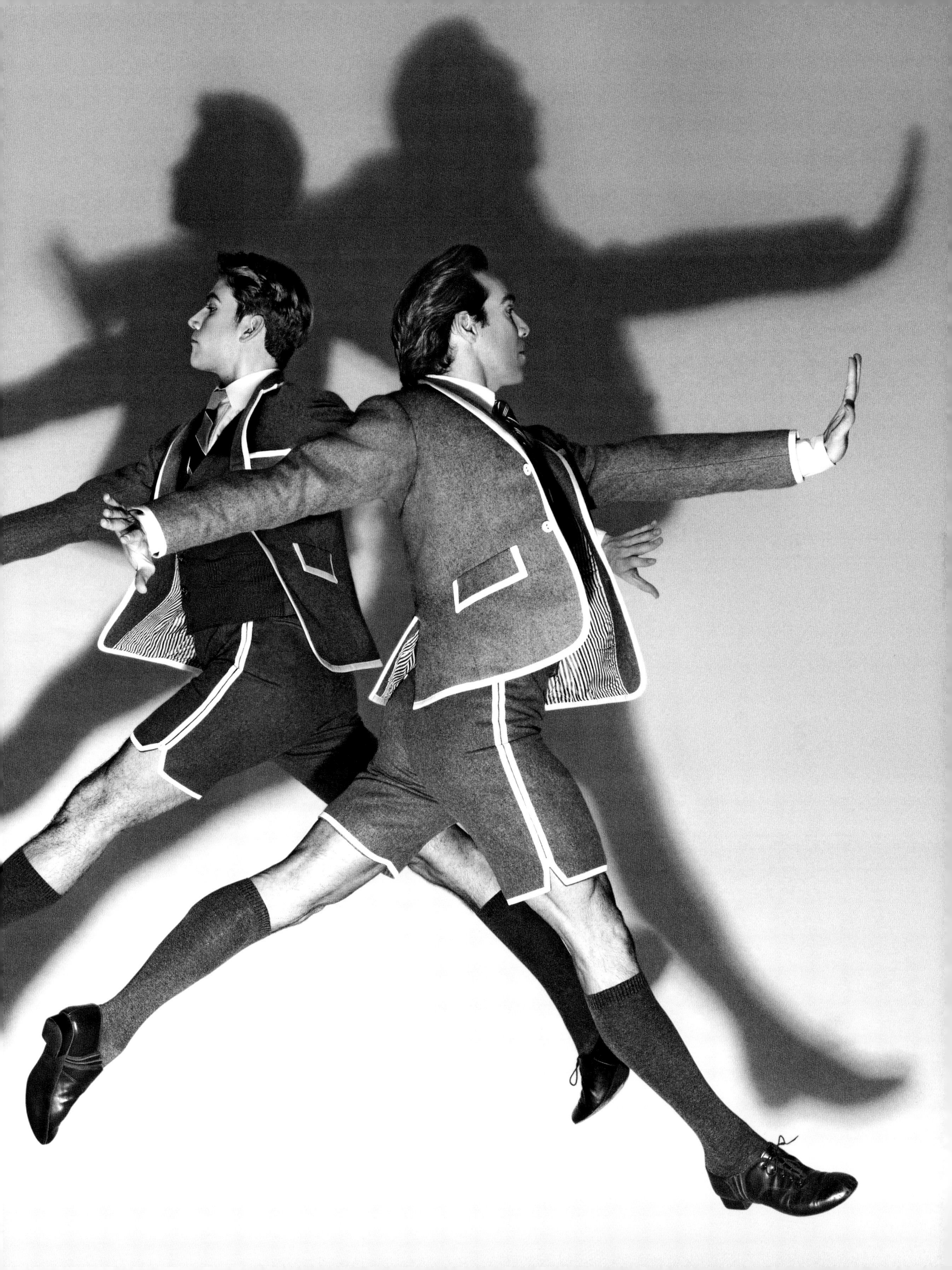

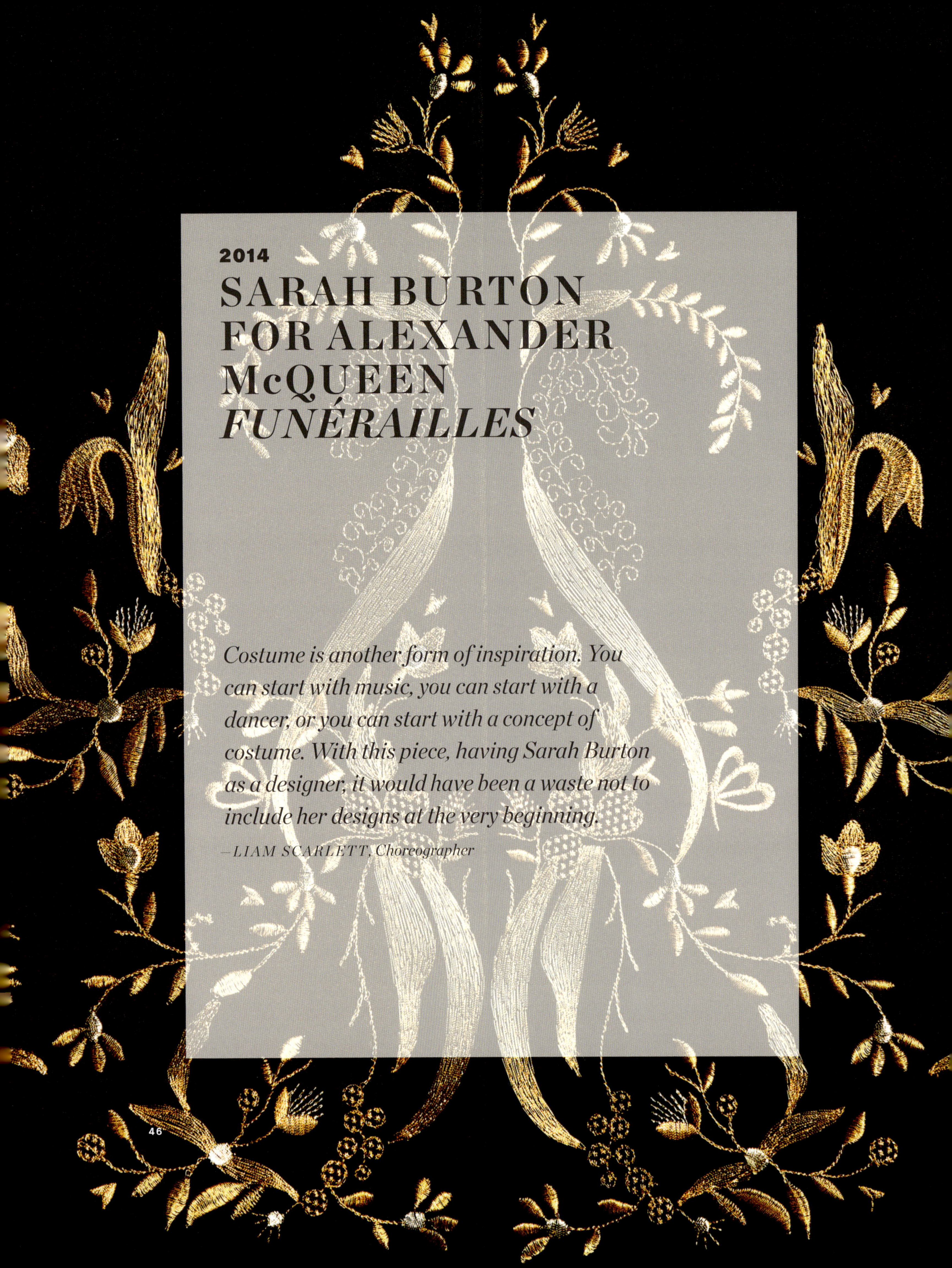

2014

SARAH BURTON FOR ALEXANDER McQUEEN *FUNÉRAILLES*

Costume is another form of inspiration. You can start with music, you can start with a dancer, or you can start with a concept of costume. With this piece, having Sarah Burton as a designer, it would have been a waste not to include her designs at the very beginning.

—LIAM SCARLETT, Choreographer

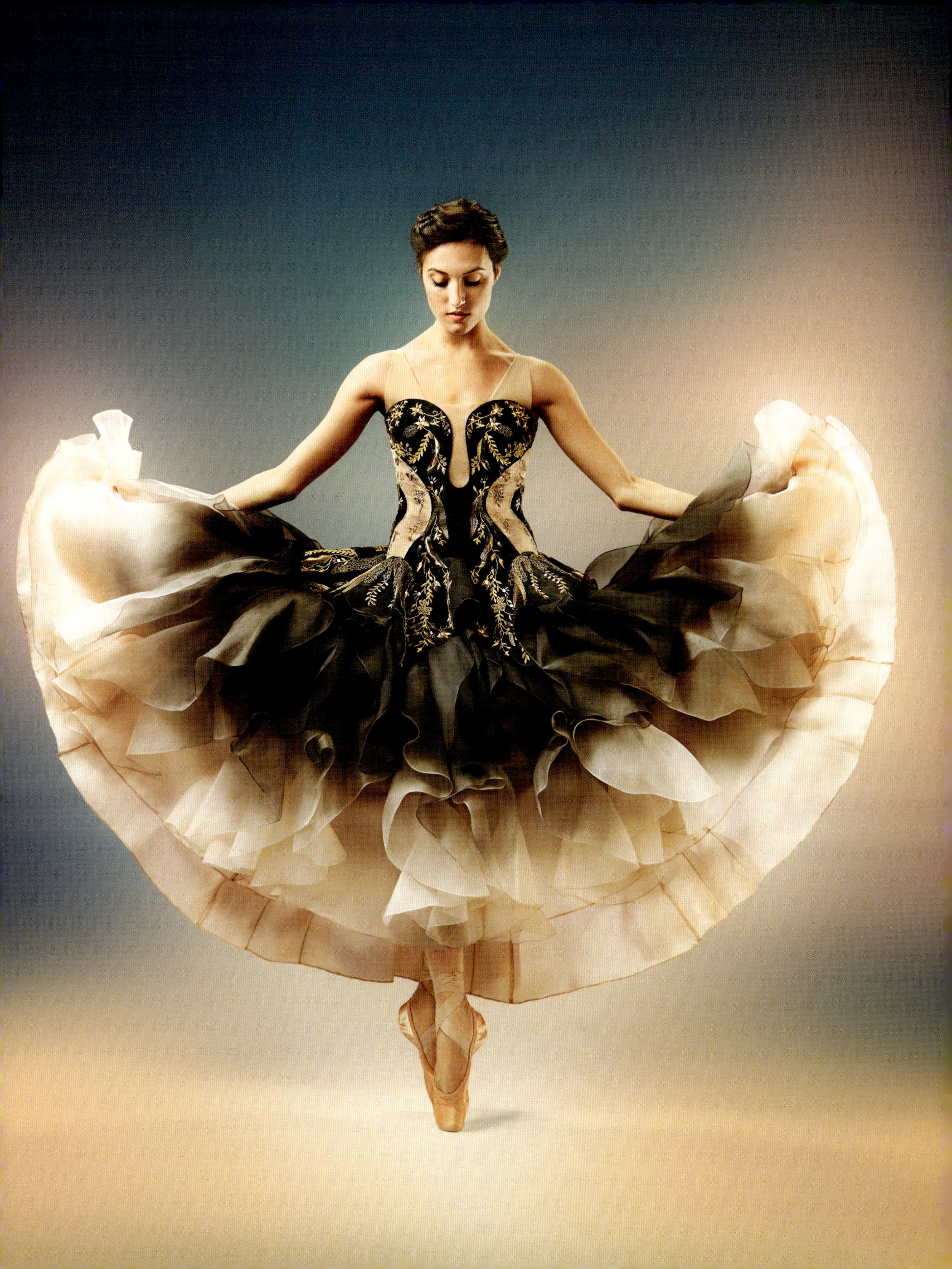

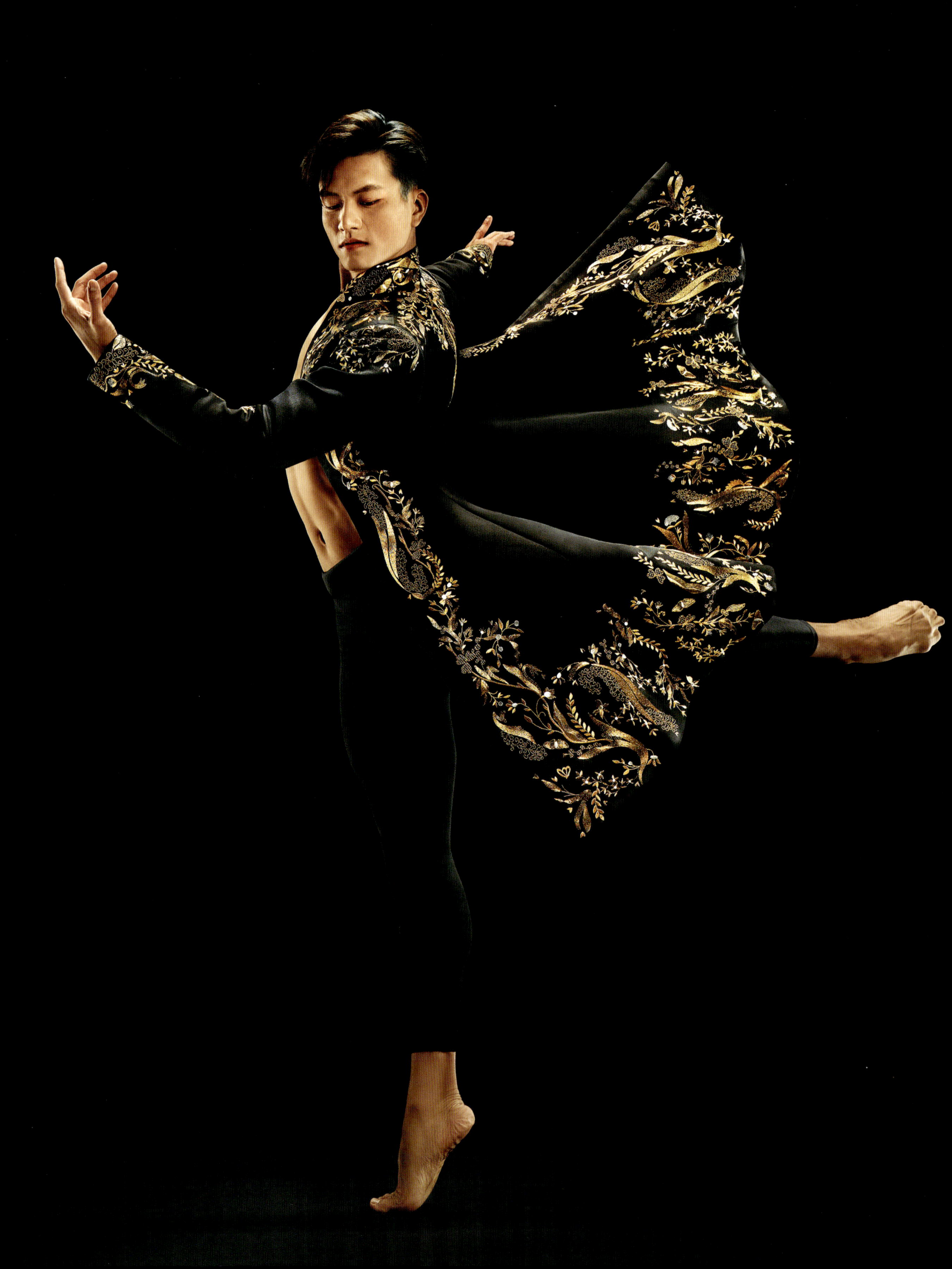

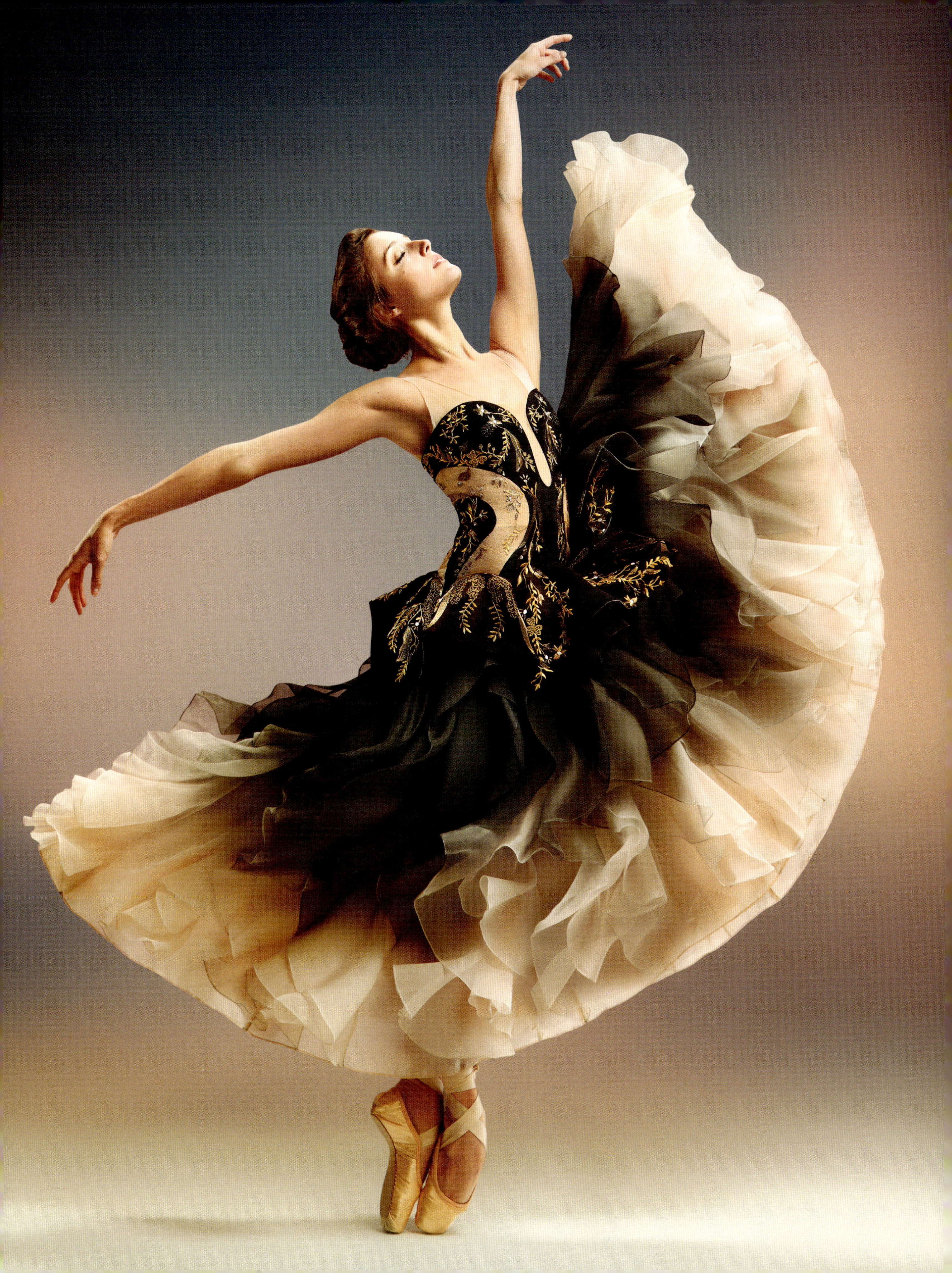

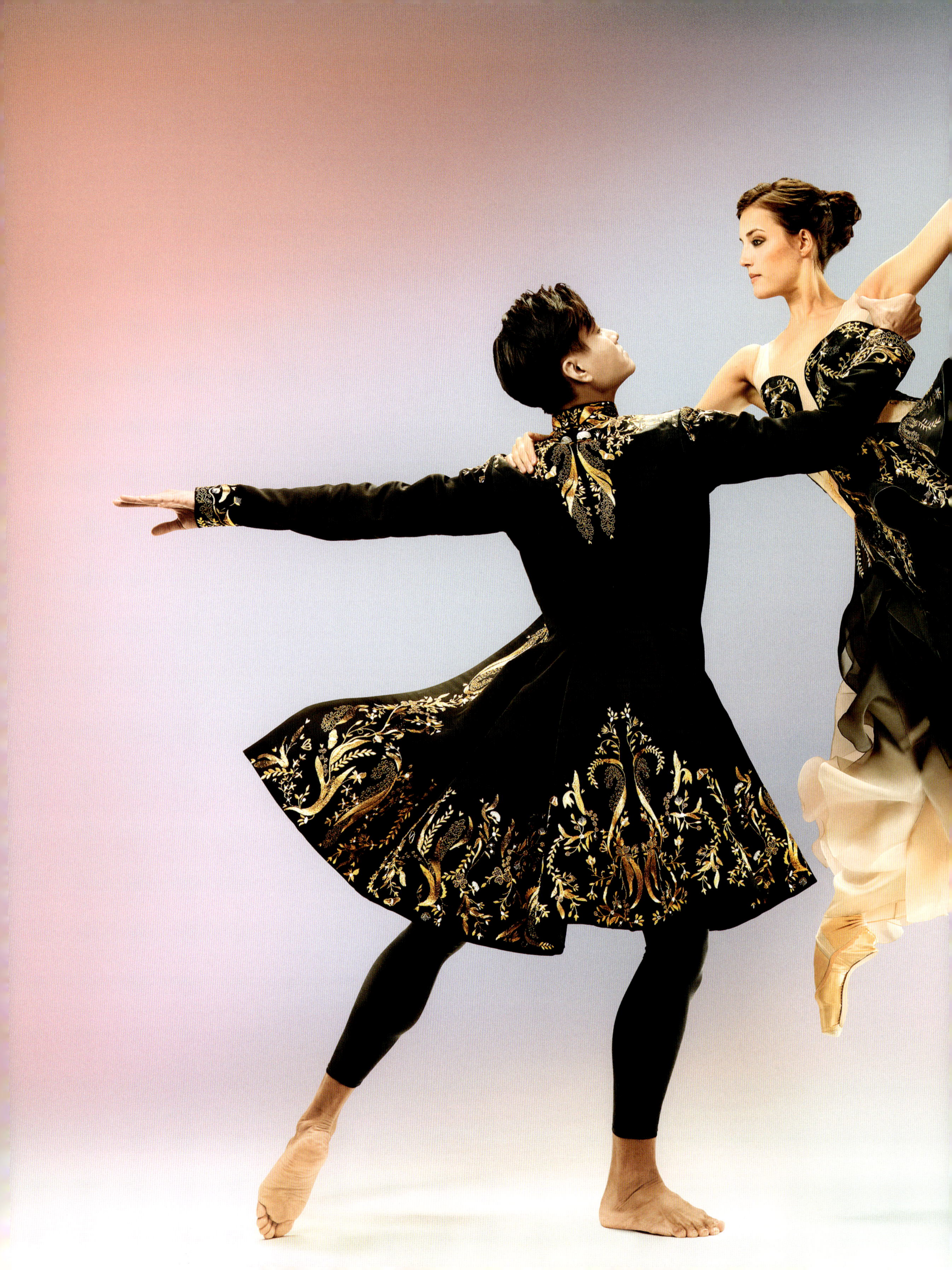

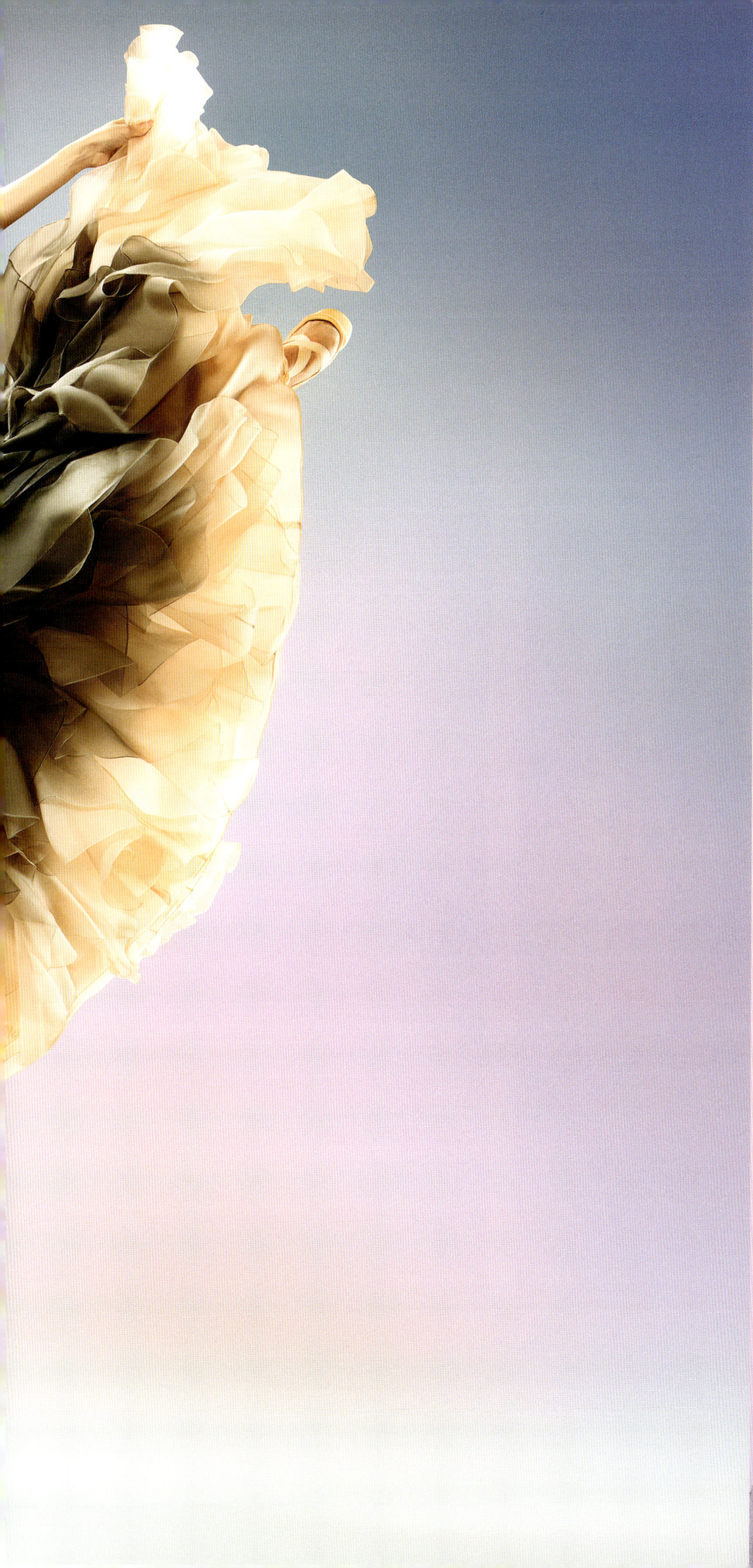
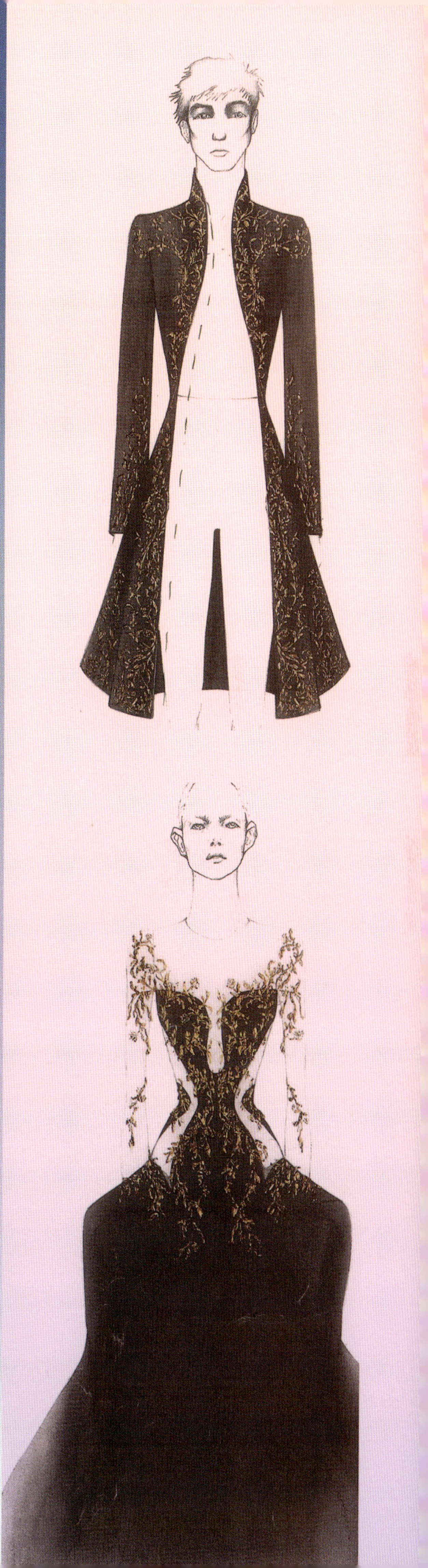

2014

CAROLINA HERRERA *MORGEN*

I've loved ballet since I was a child. So when Peter Martins asked me if I could design the costumes for Morgen, *with his beautiful choreography and music by Richard Strauss, I said yes immediately. Working with Marc Happel and the talented dancers inspired me to create pieces that were elegant and easy to move in. There are a lot of things to think about when designing costumes for ballet dancers. For me it was an unforgettable experience.* –CAROLINA HERRERA

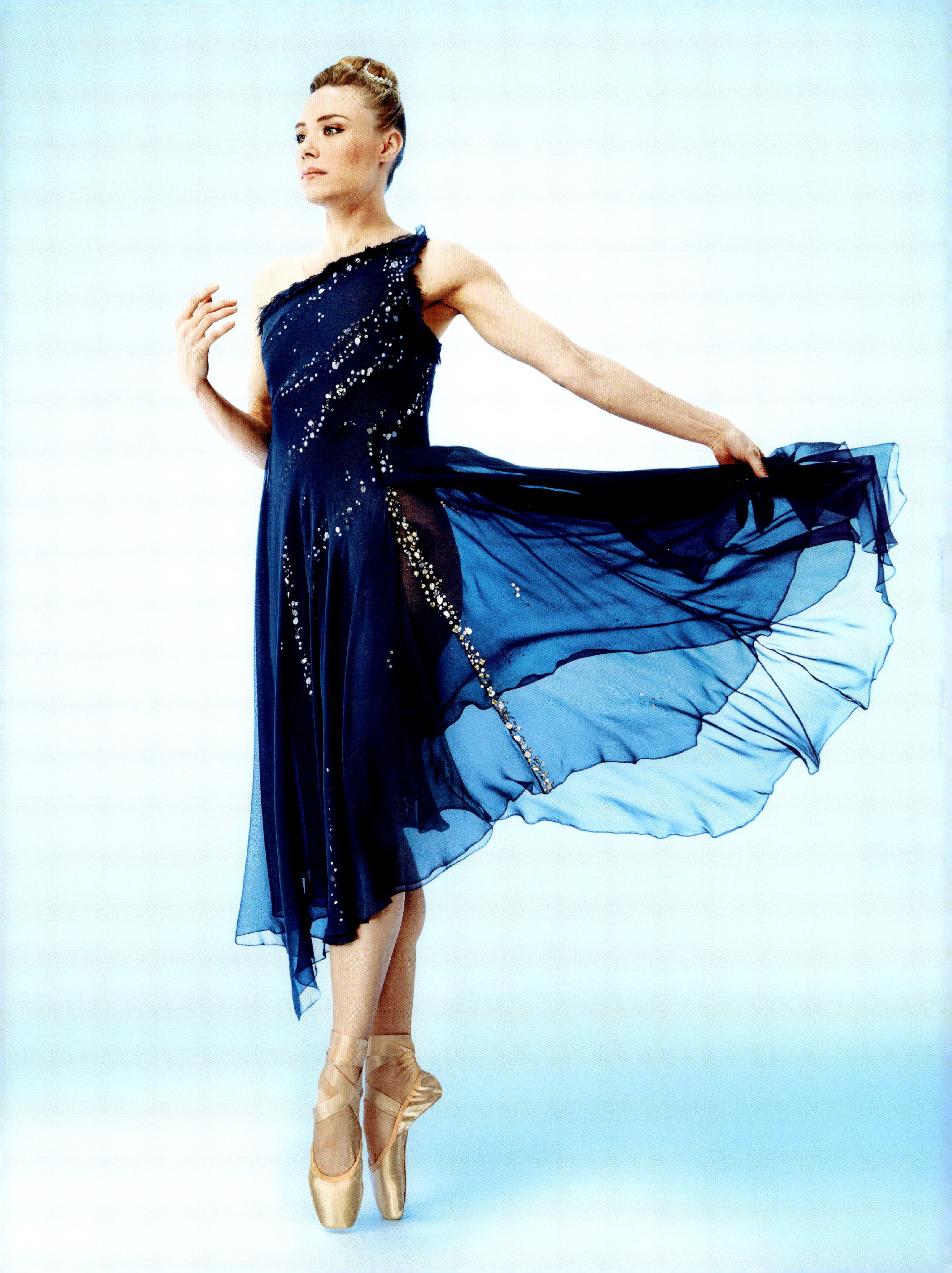

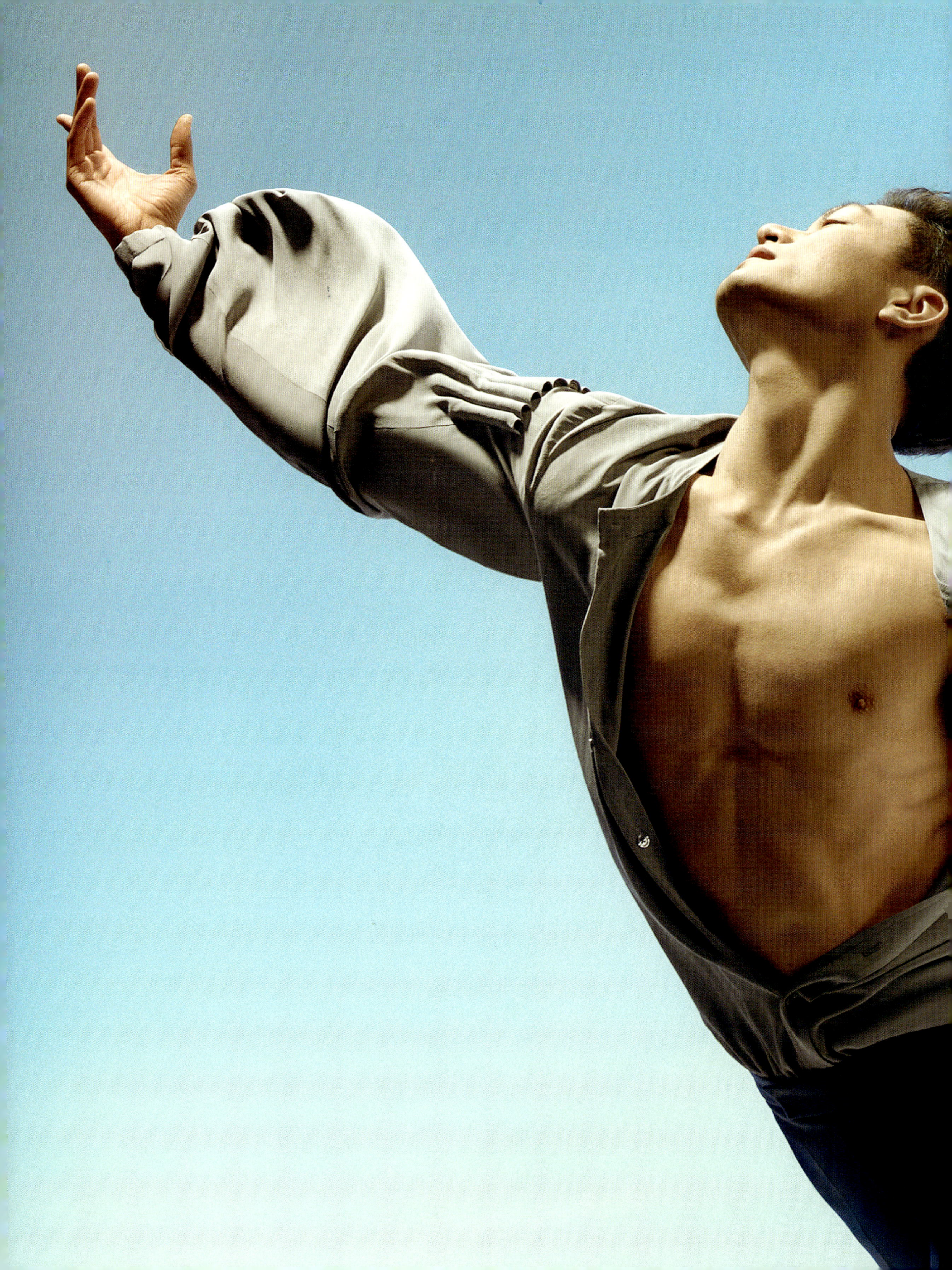

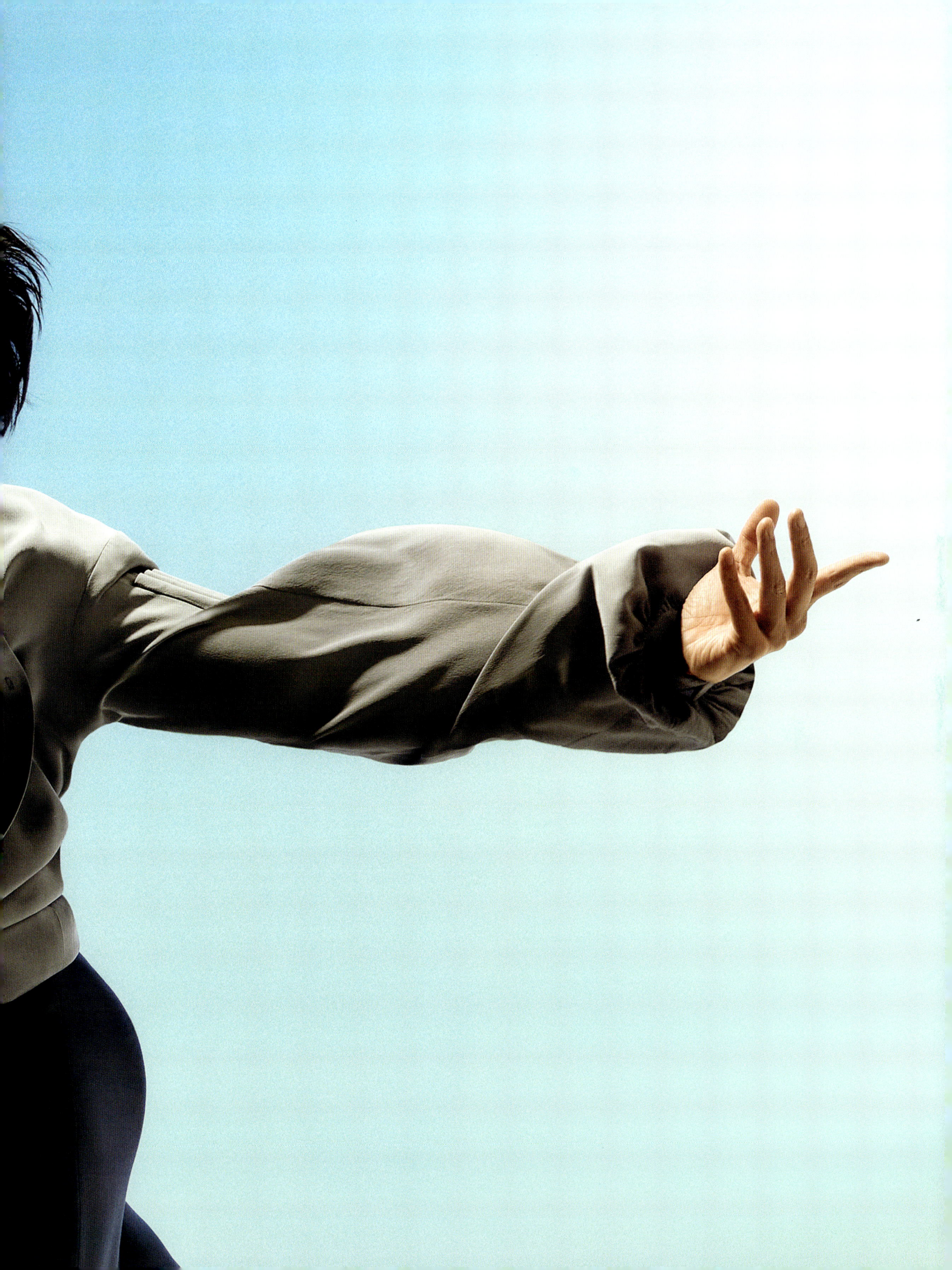

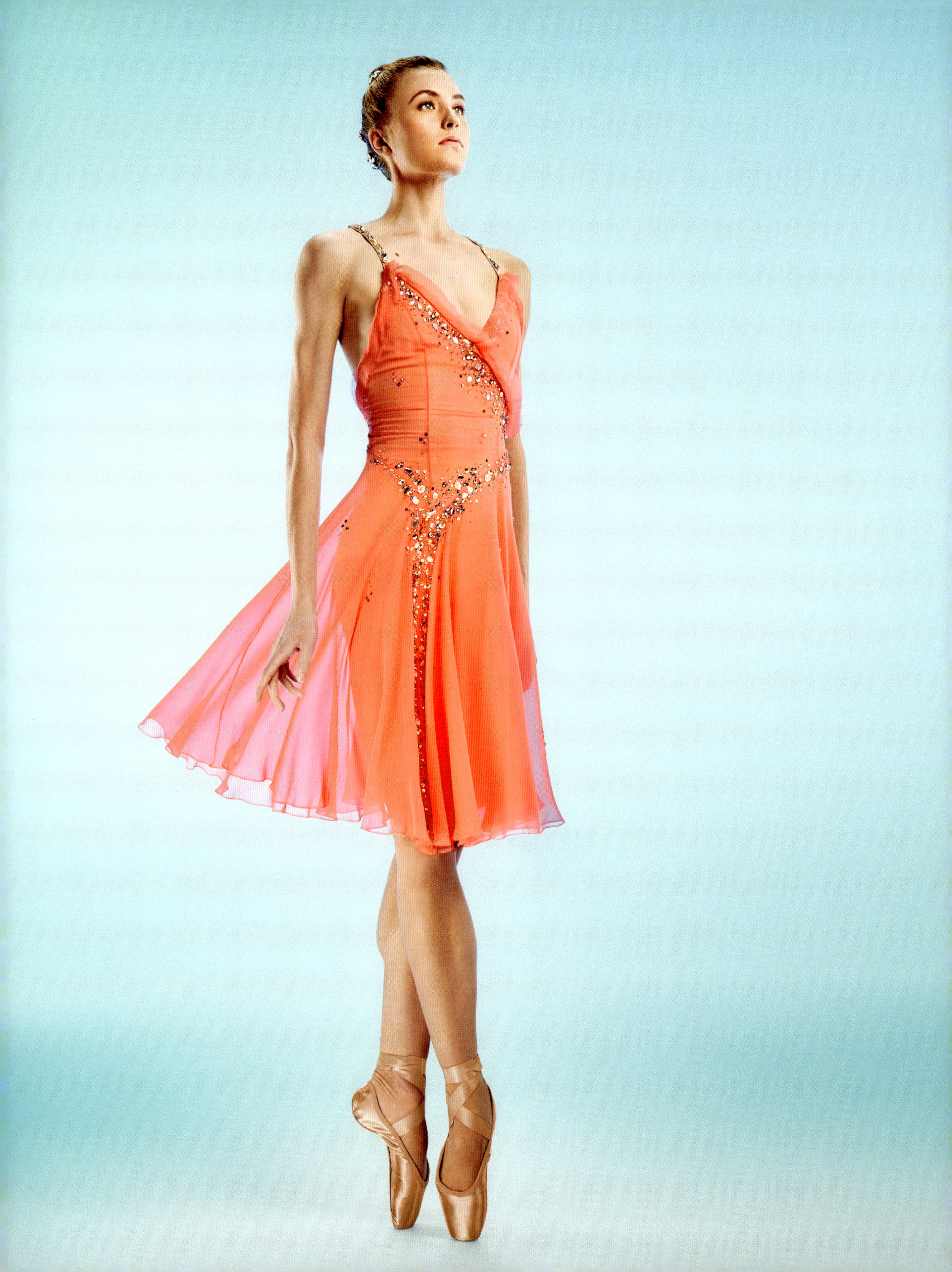

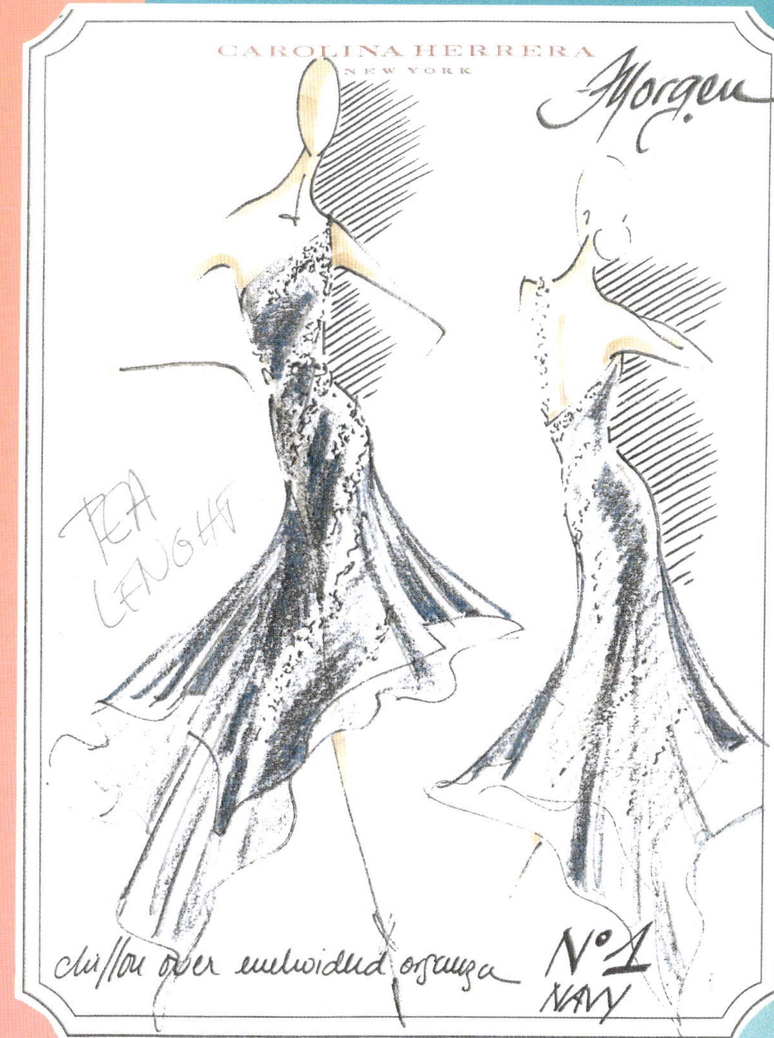

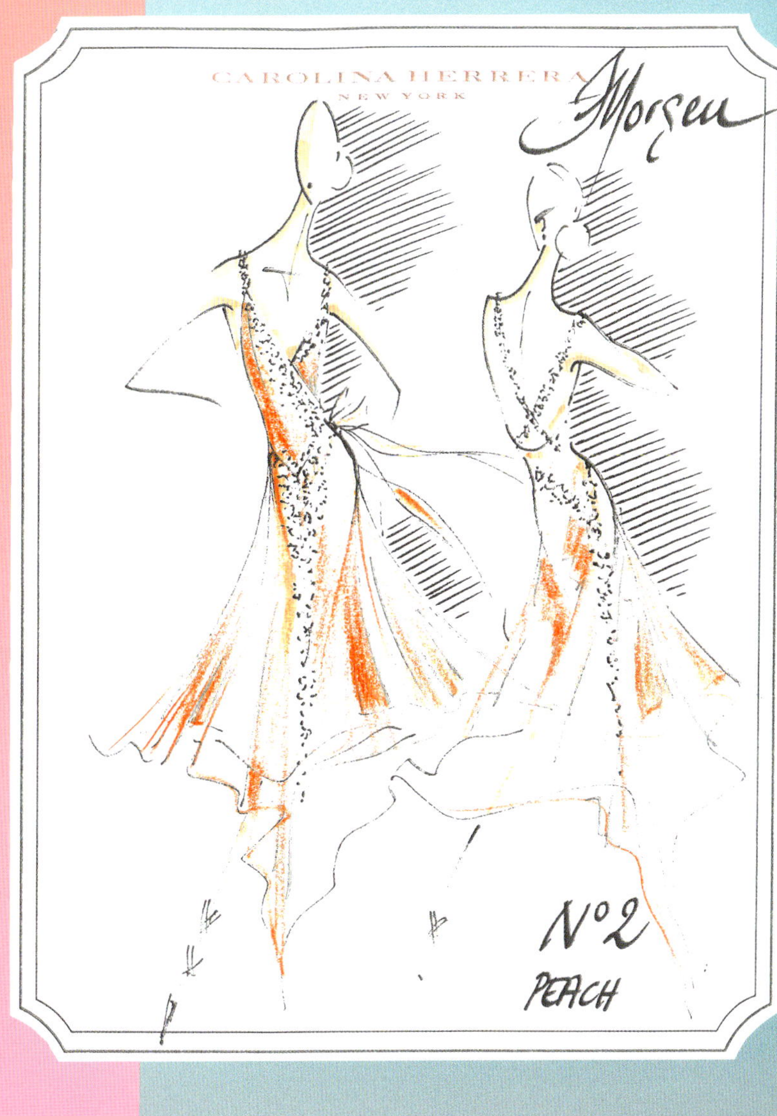

Carolina is so tuned into the world of ballet. The body is paramount, and the dress, of course, is also paramount but it has to be a perfect marriage.

—PETER MARTINS, *Choreographer*

2014

MARY KATRANTZOU

BELLES-LETTRES

I thought, "Why don't we do something that's a second skin instead of something with lots of volume or construction?" I wanted to do something subtle. Justin Peck's work is very clean. It evokes a certain emotion, and I wanted the costumes to mimic that. —MARY KATRANTZOU

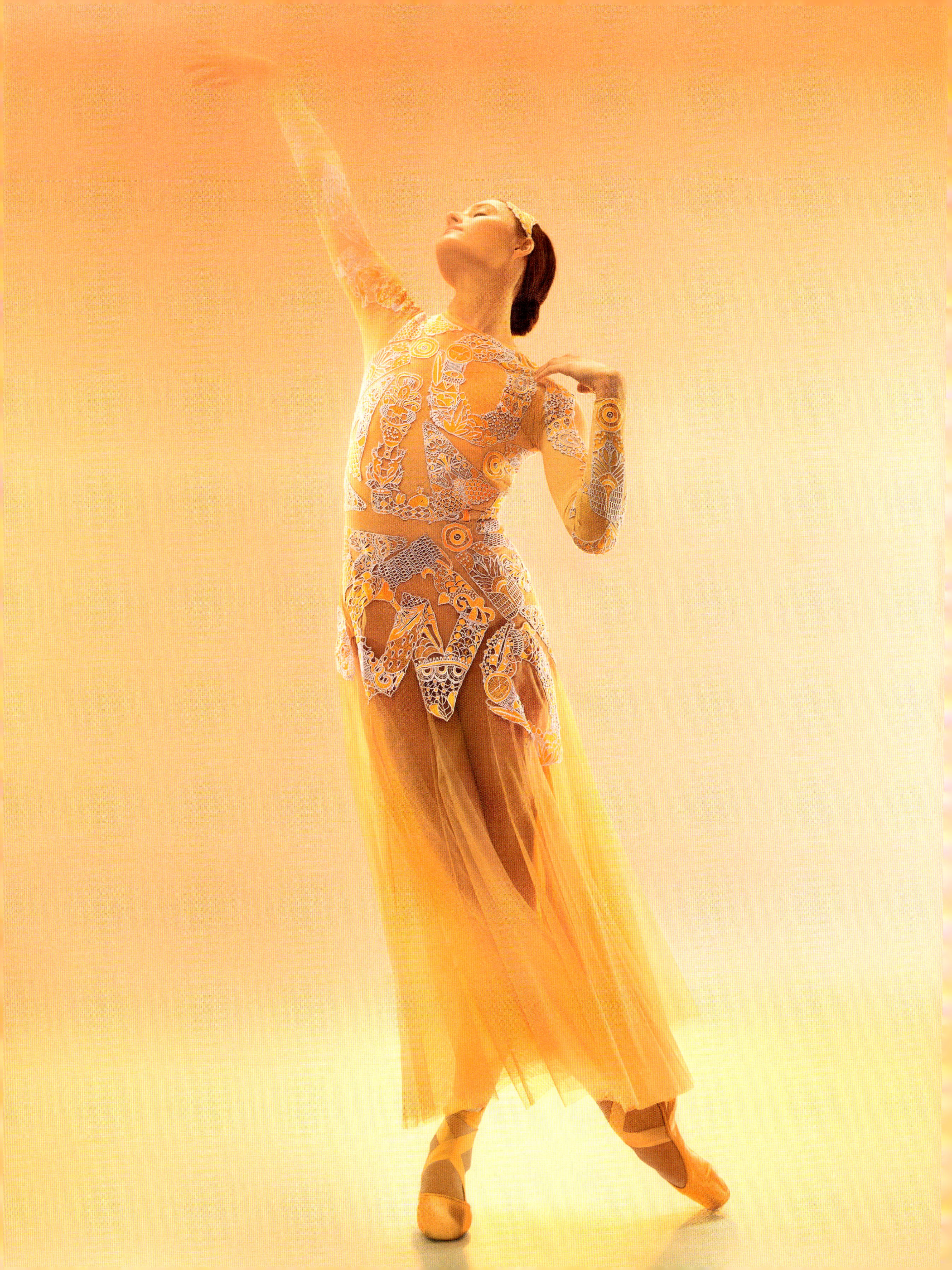

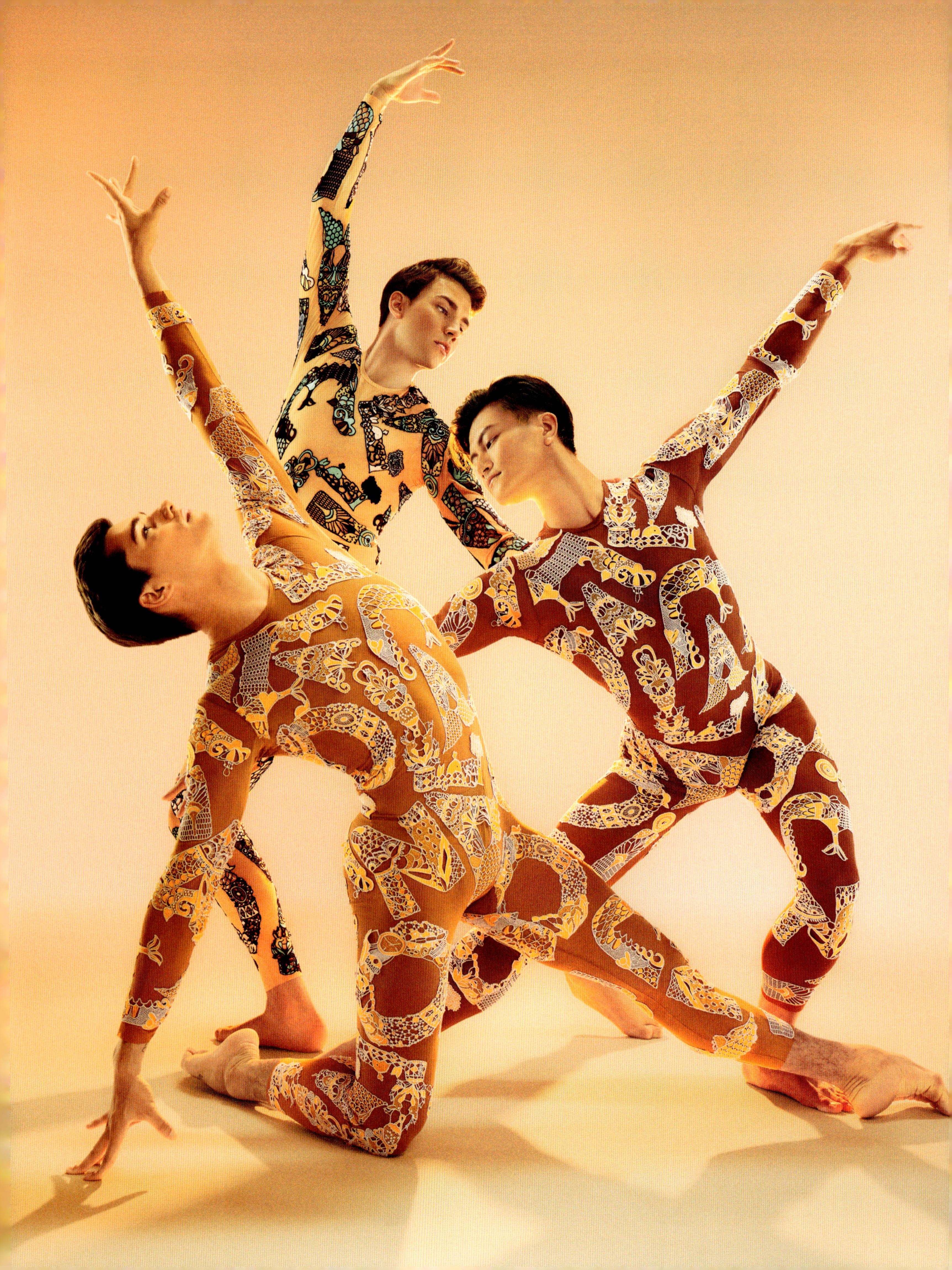

The world of fashion and art are in constant dialogue, and I love the idea of cross-pollinating disciplines. While designing the costumes, my focus was on elevating the movement of the dancers while combining creativity, functionality, and performance. It all came down to the physicality of the dancers and making sure it really was like a second skin for them.

—MARY KATRANTZOU

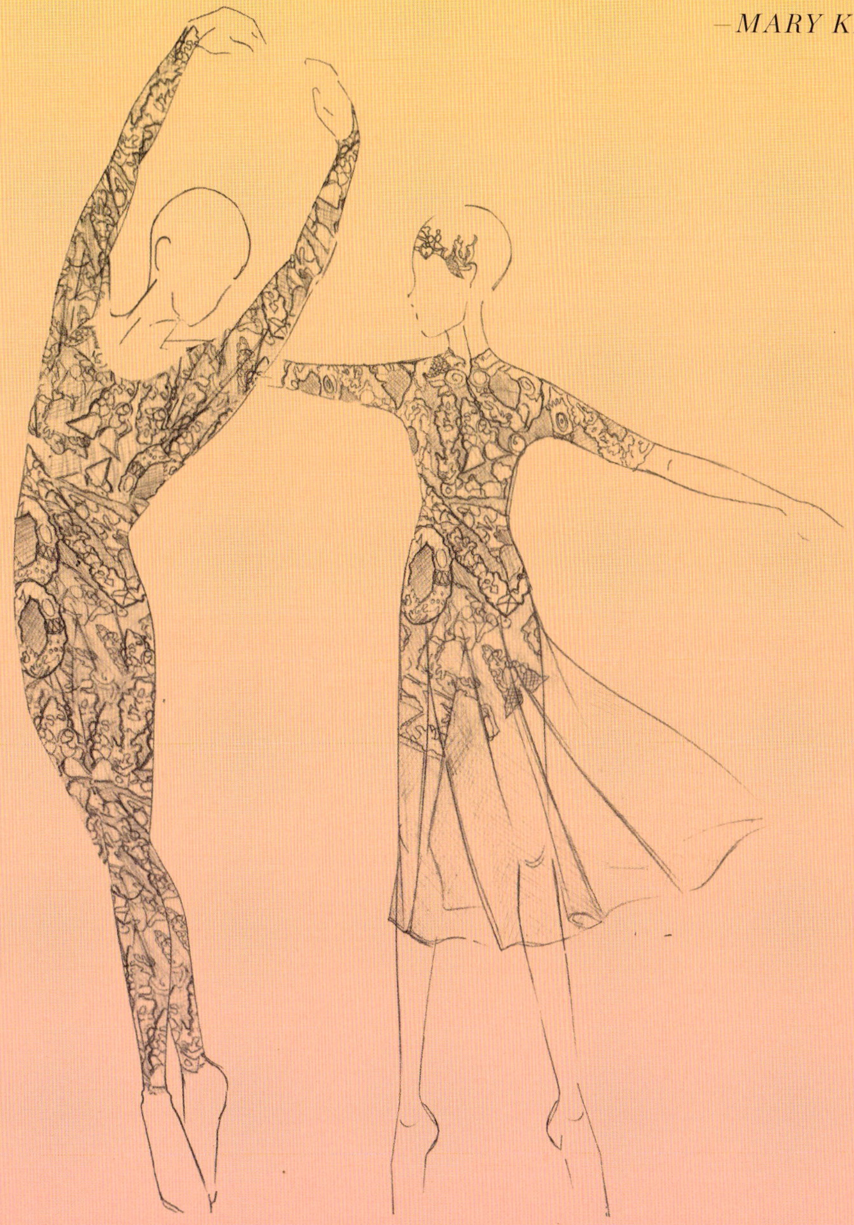

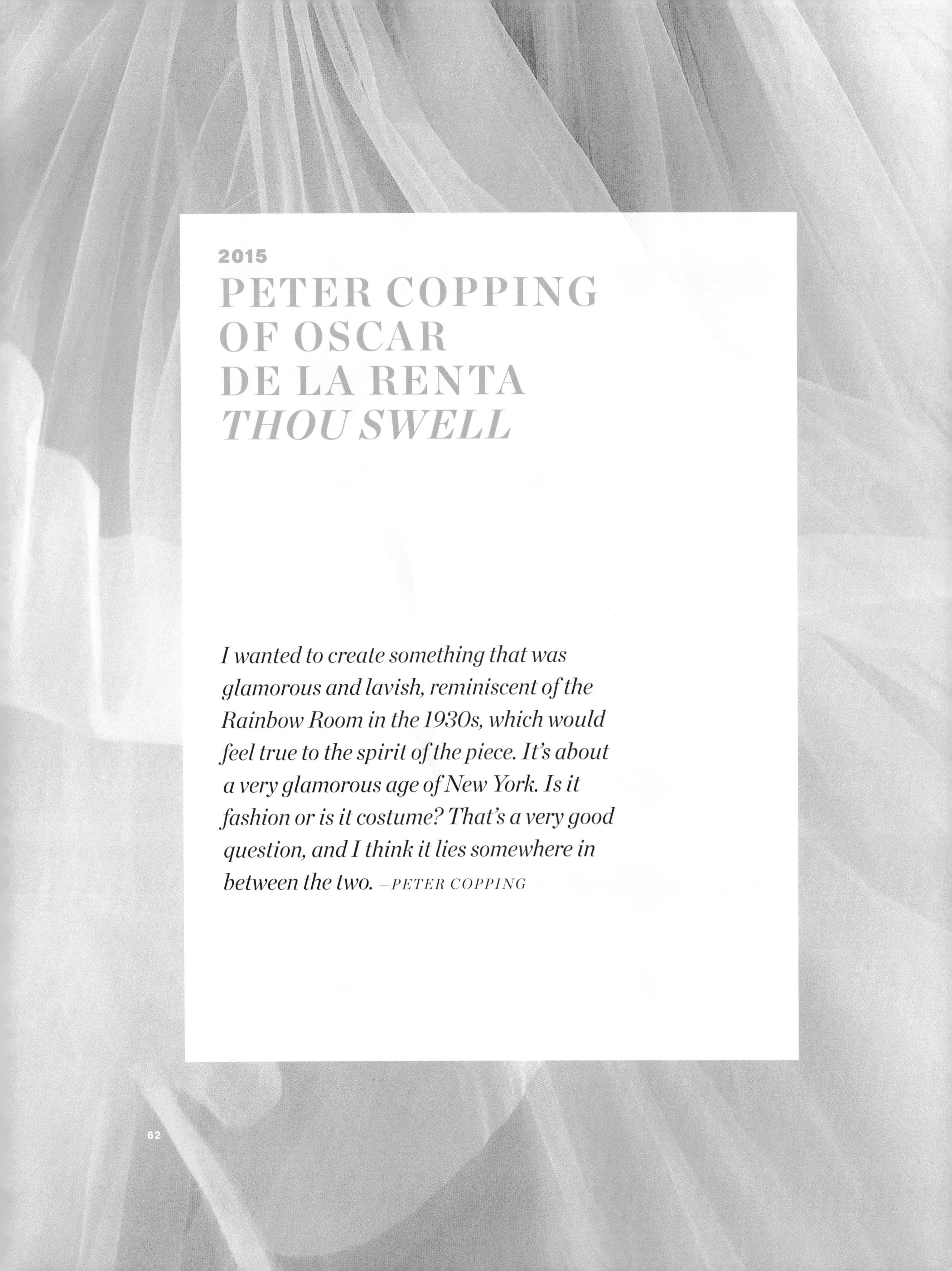

2015

PETER COPPING OF OSCAR DE LA RENTA *THOU SWELL*

I wanted to create something that was glamorous and lavish, reminiscent of the Rainbow Room in the 1930s, which would feel true to the spirit of the piece. It's about a very glamorous age of New York. Is it fashion or is it costume? That's a very good question, and I think it lies somewhere in between the two. —PETER COPPING

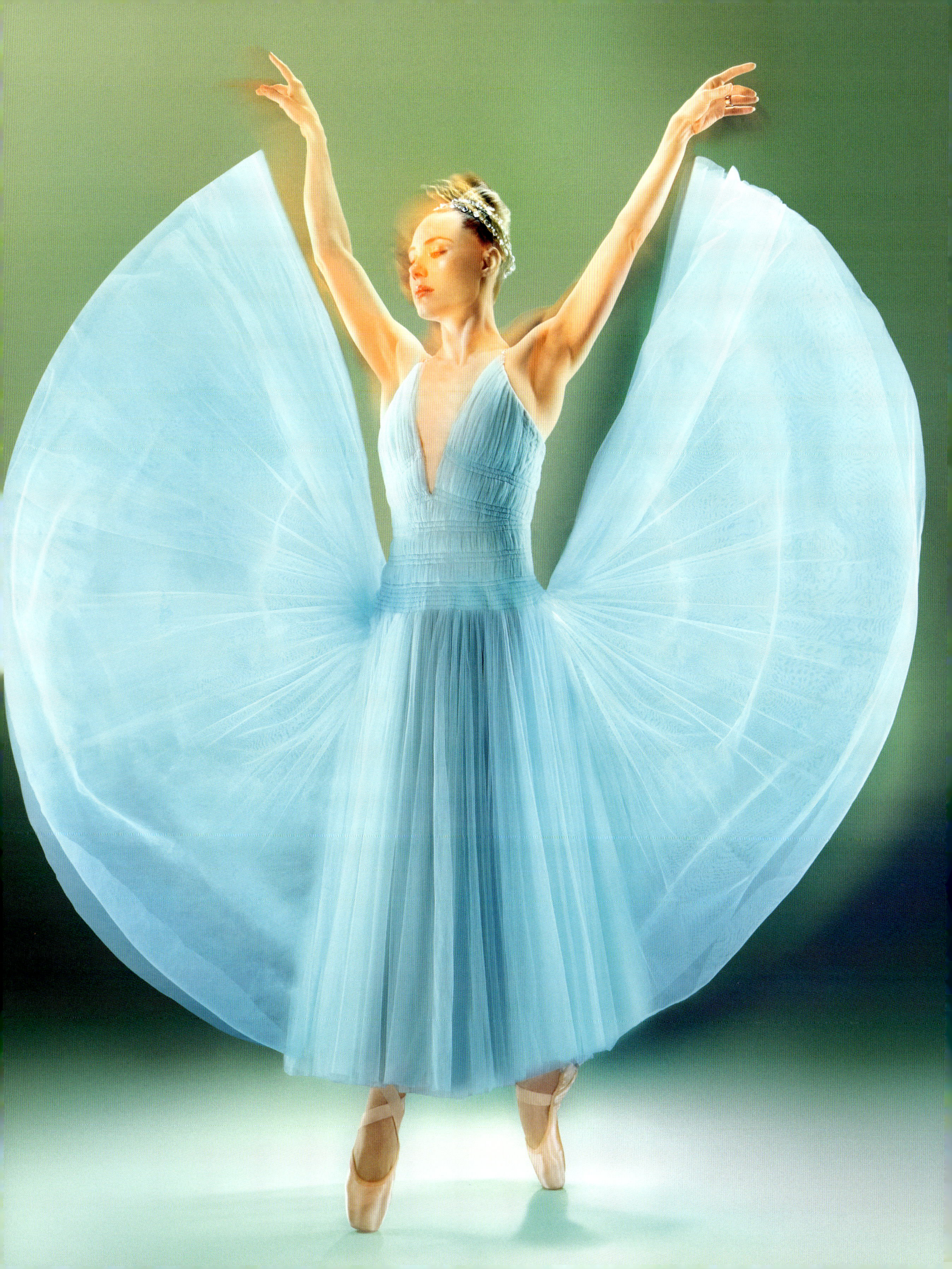

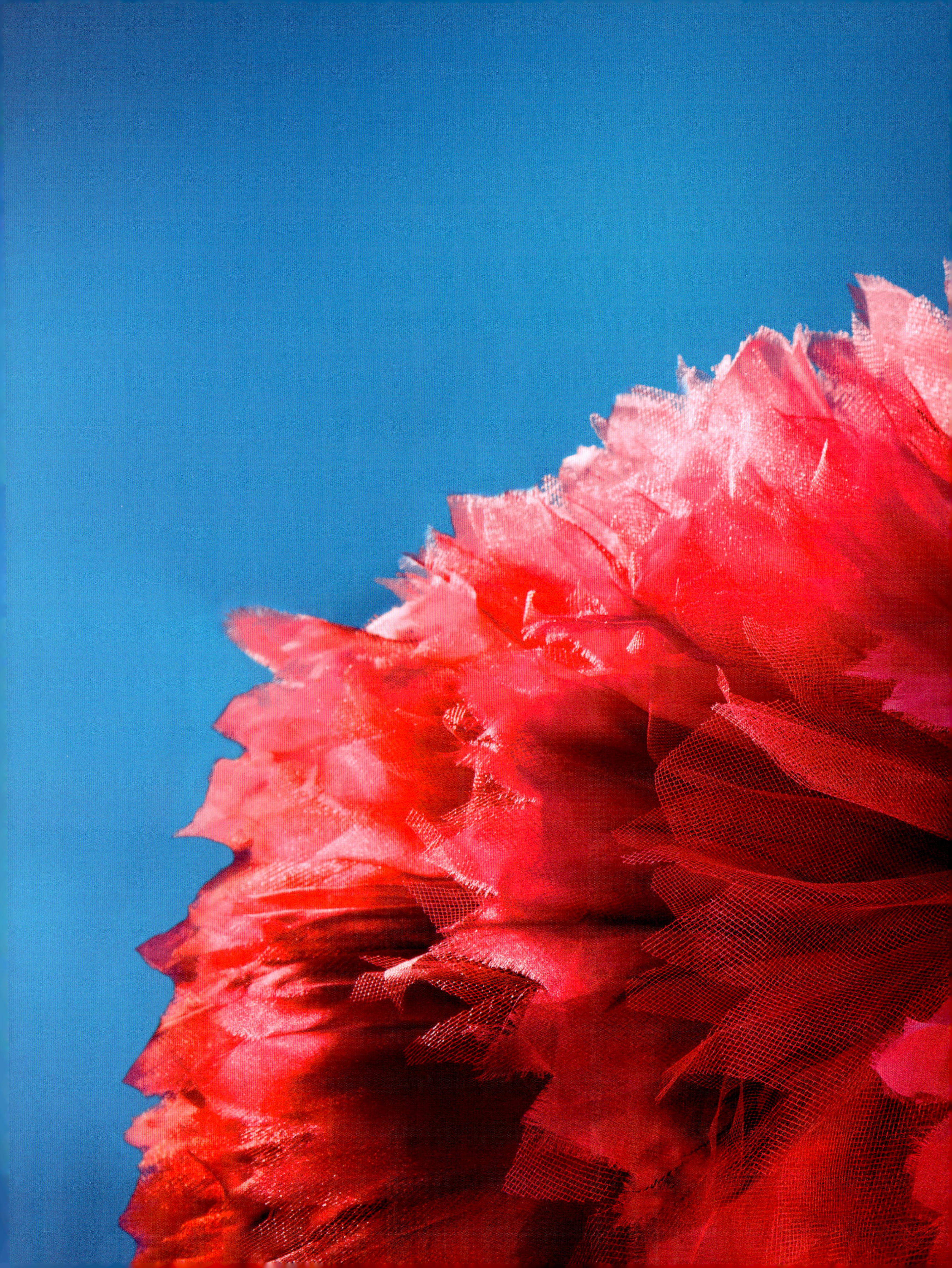

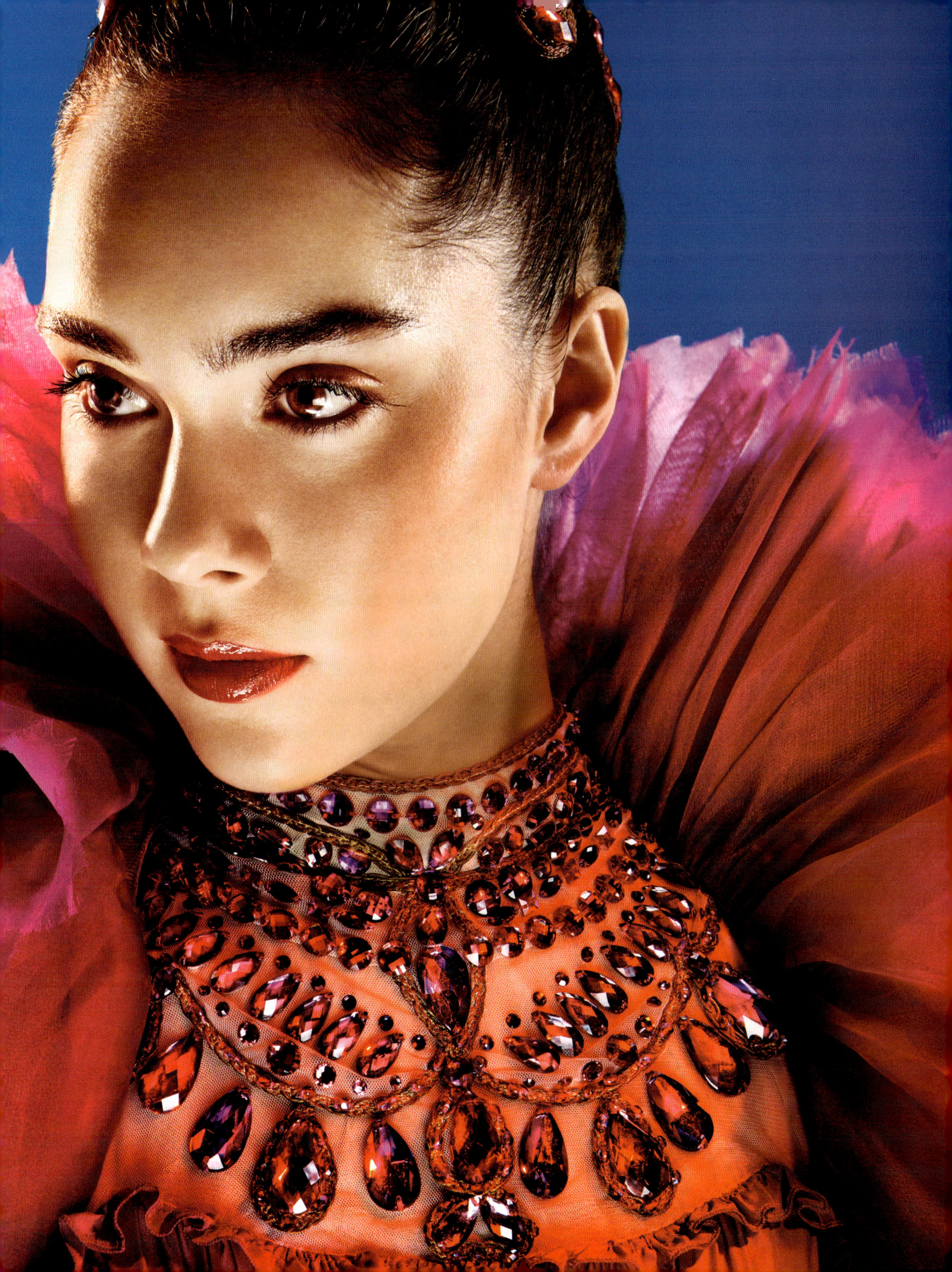

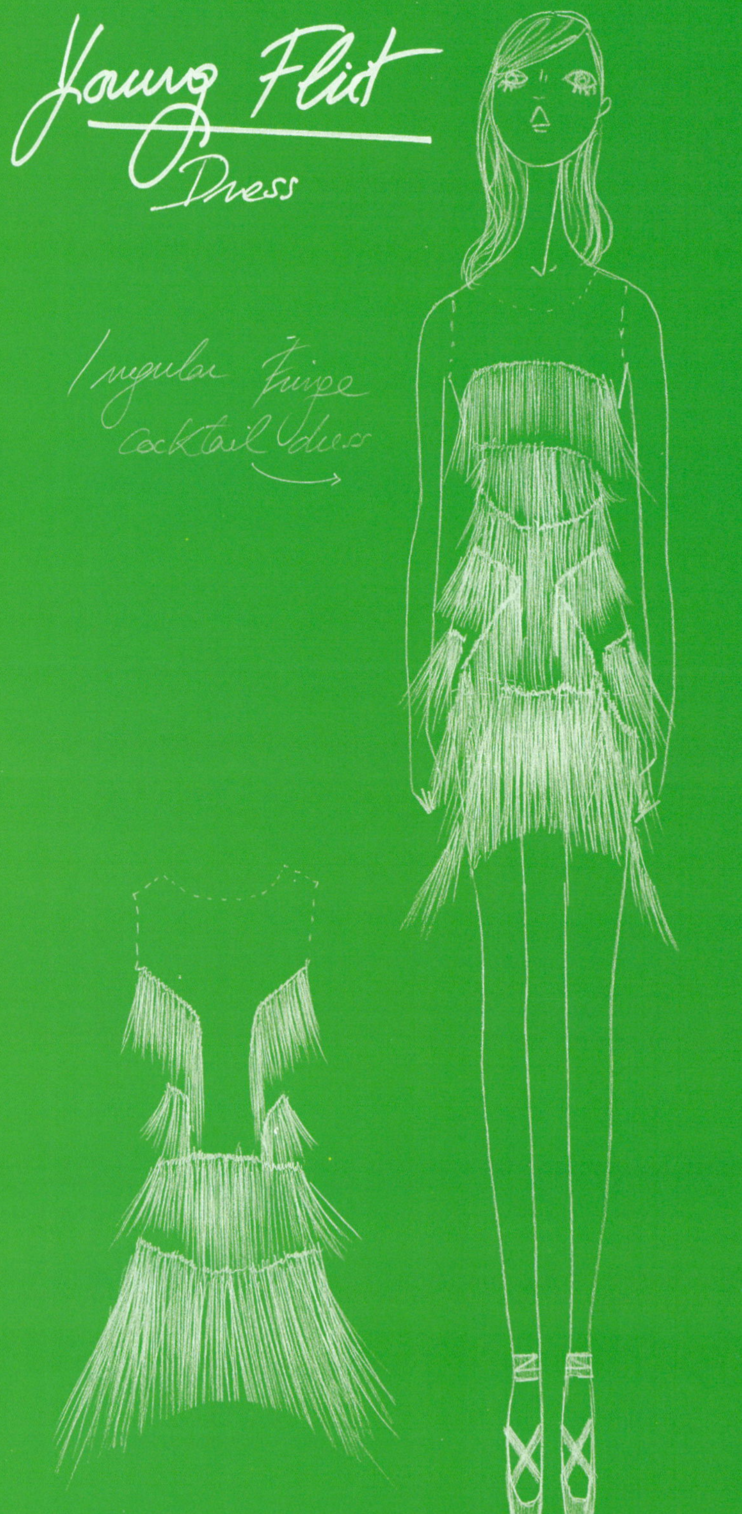

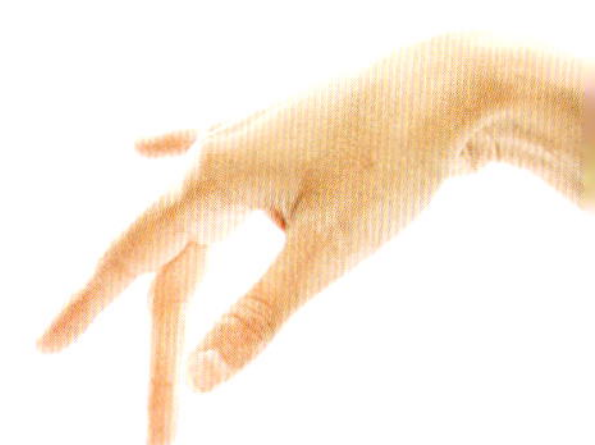

It was a challenge, because I wasn't designing fashion. This had a different set of rules. It was very much a collaboration between Oscar de la Renta and NYCB. I really listened to them and had a lot to learn. I also wanted it to reflect the house of Oscar de la Renta, and all that Oscar loved. —PETER COPPING

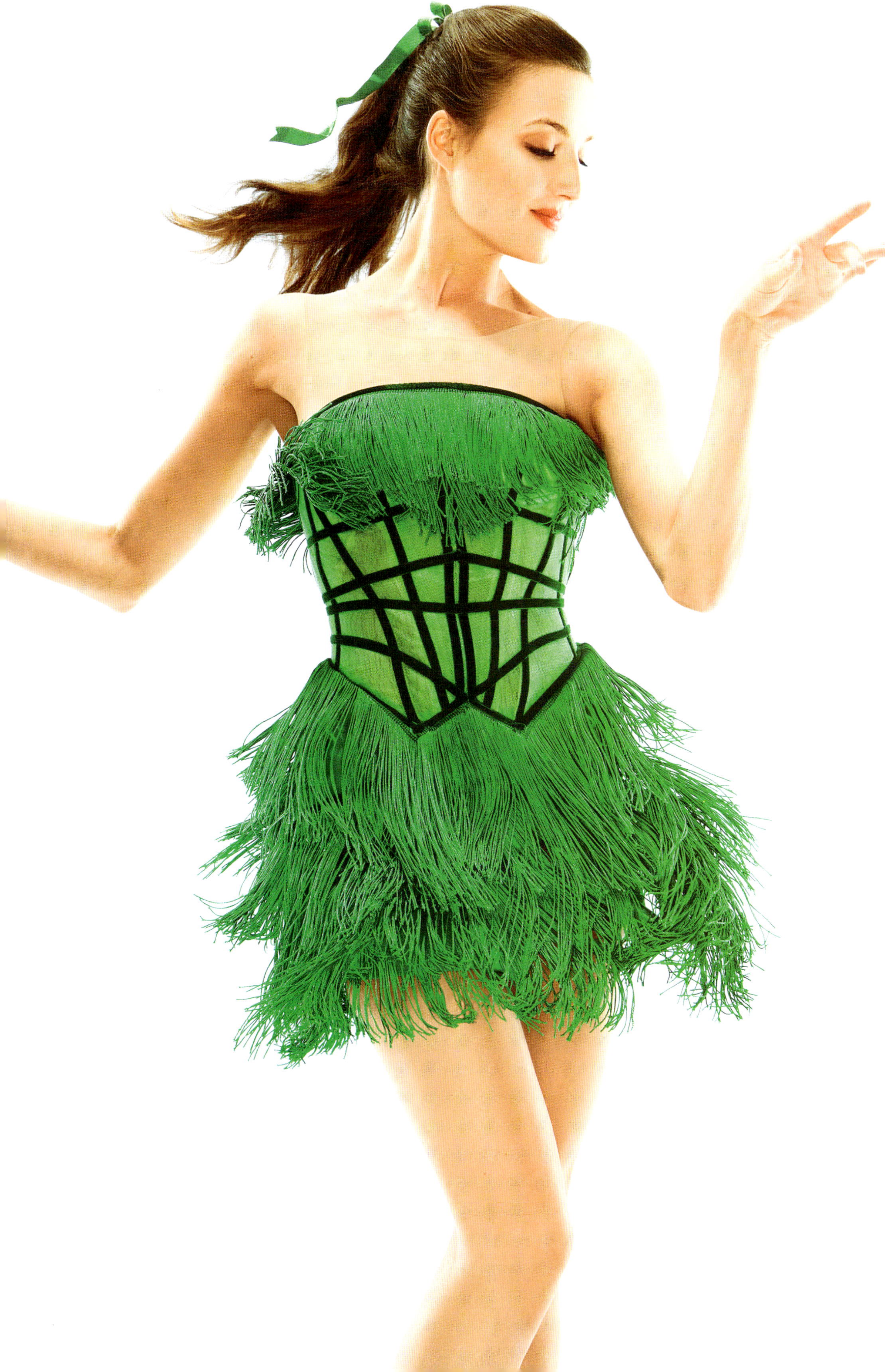

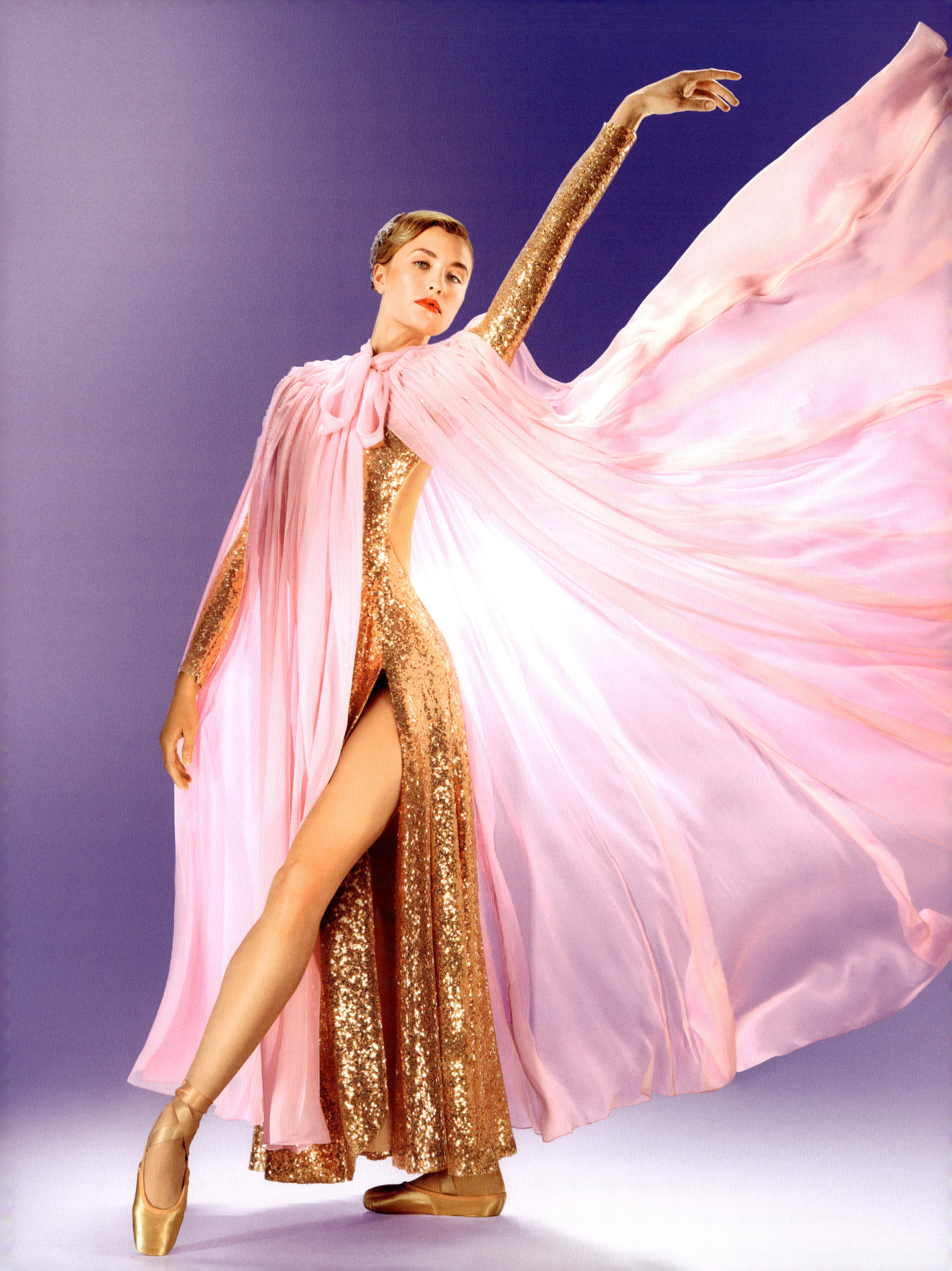

When Peter Copping took over Oscar de la Renta, and his great strength is evening gowns, I thought it would be perfect to re-costume Thou Swell *after all of these years.*

—PETER MARTINS, *Choreographer*

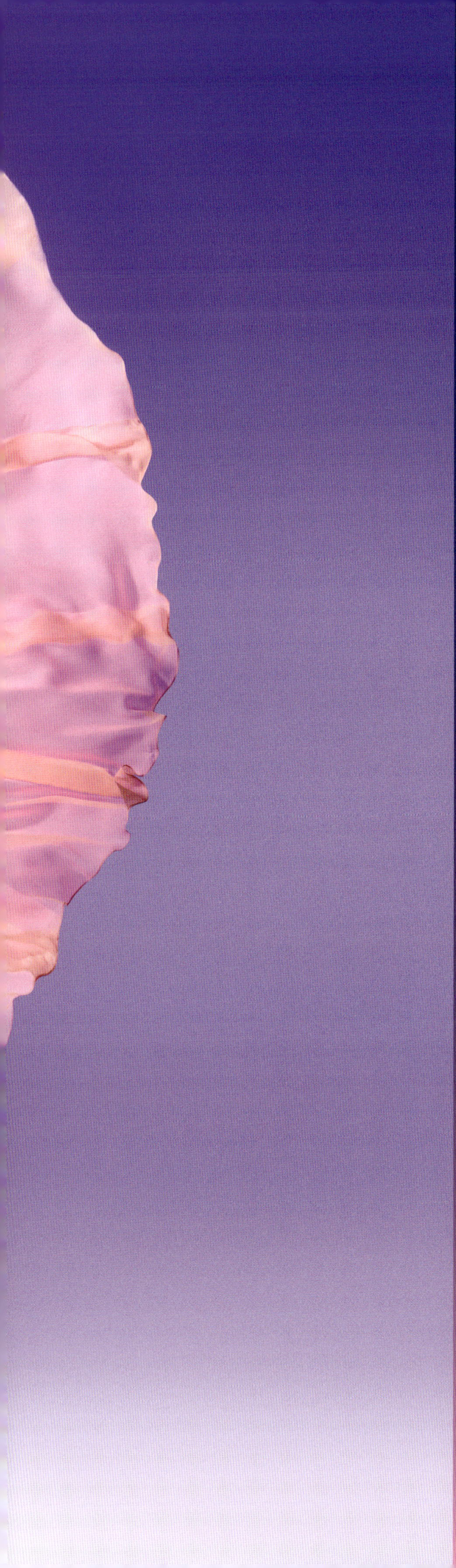

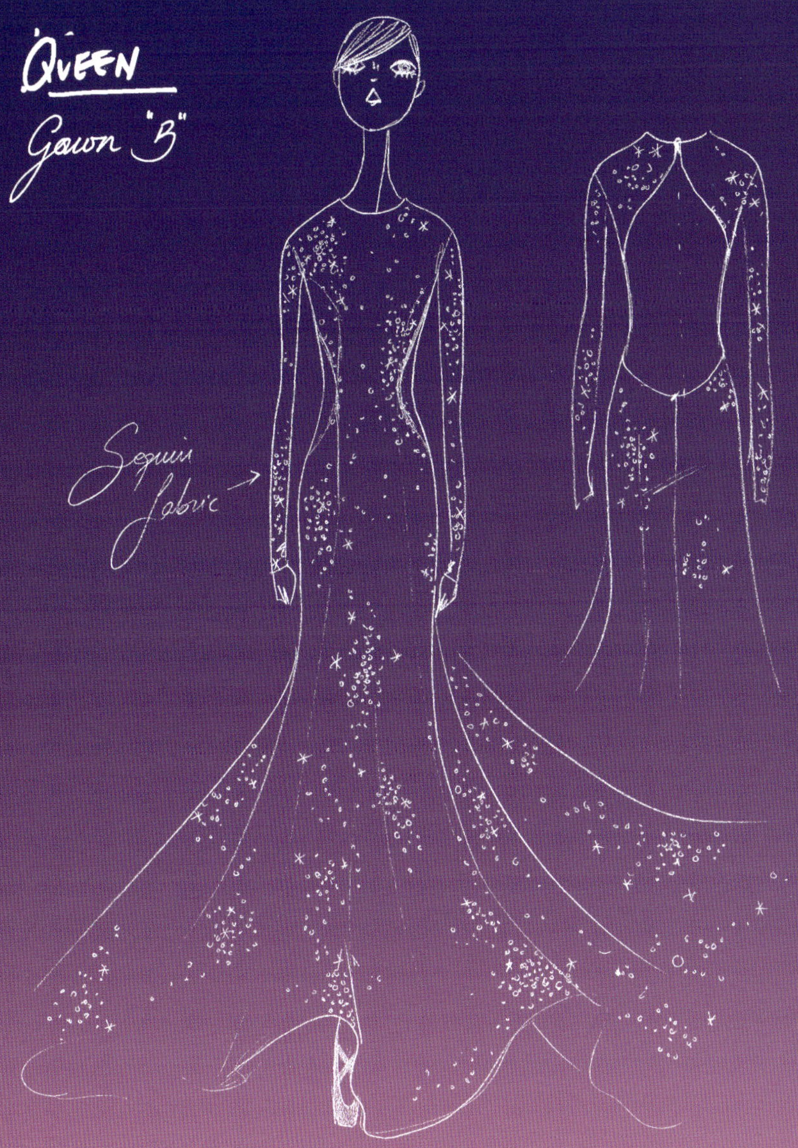

2015

HUMBERTO LEON OF OPENING CEREMONY & KENZO *NEW BLOOD*

When I first spoke to Justin about these constantly connected pas de deux, it dawned on me that I needed each dancer to connect to the next. I wanted to create a gorgeous gradient that would seamlessly flow from person to person. I mapped out these cutouts so every touch of two bodies creates a connection point that celebrates the joining of two people. The electric energy brought by Justin's choreography as well as Steve Reich's music was so special. —HUMBERTO LEON

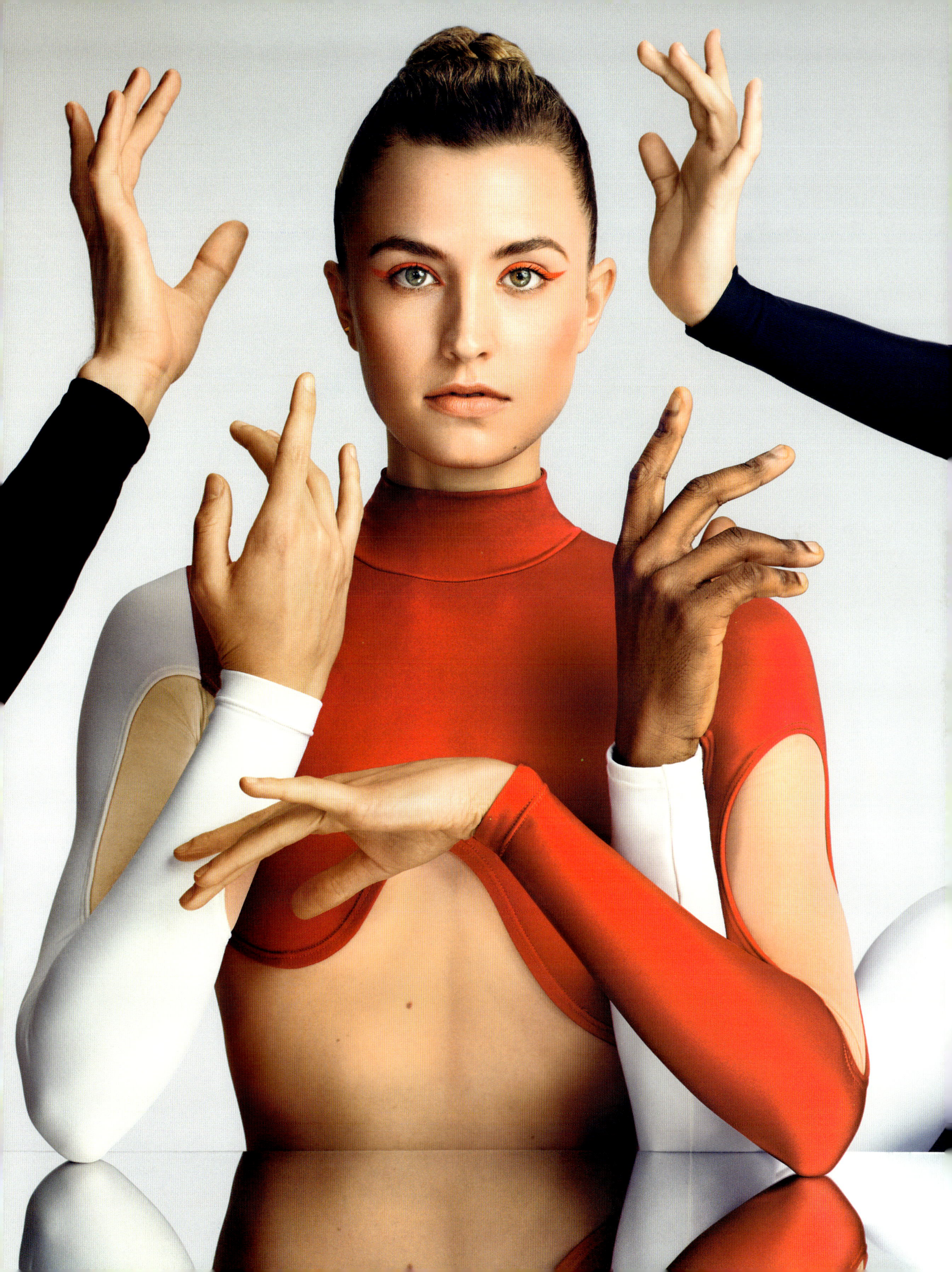

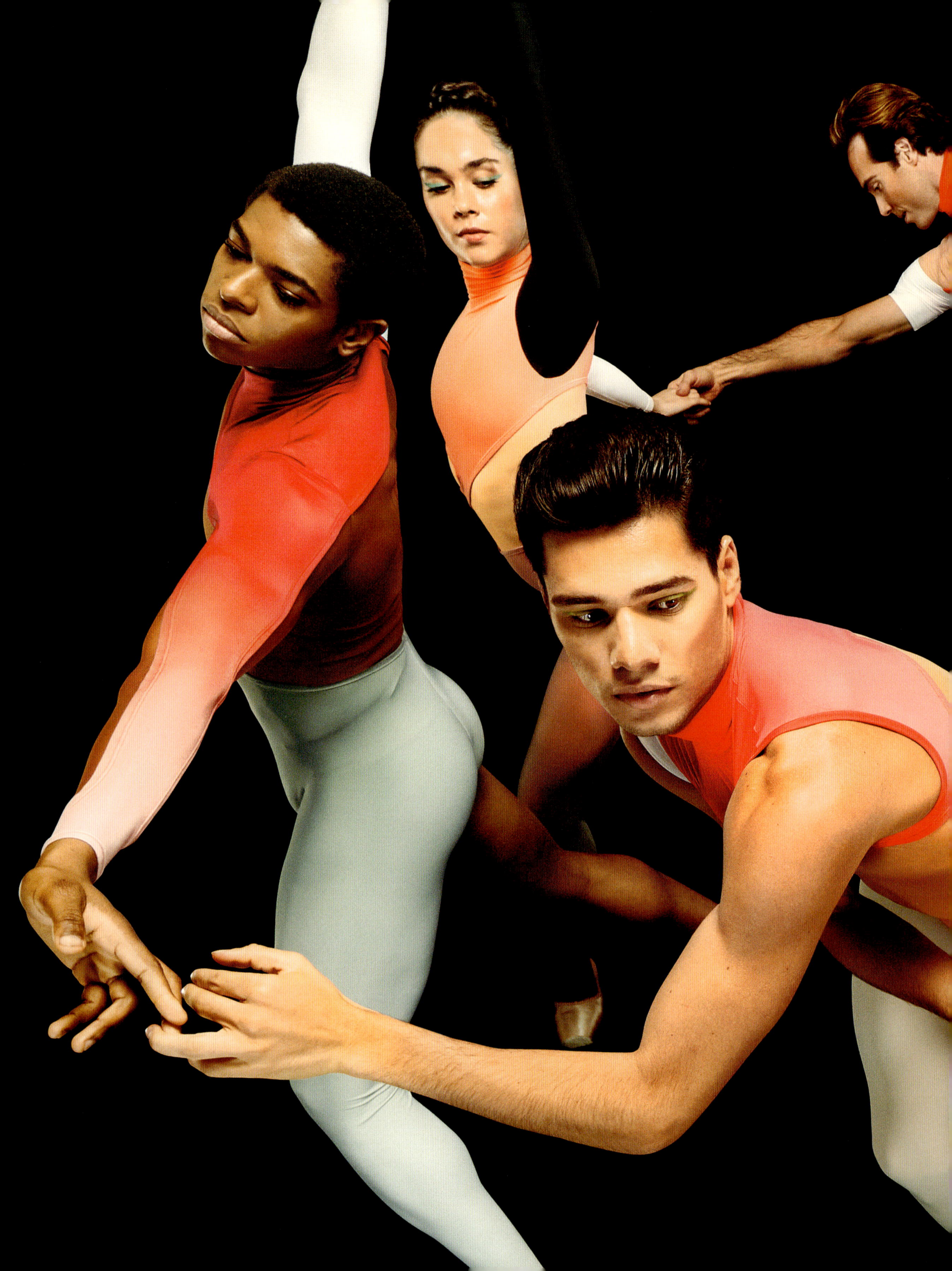

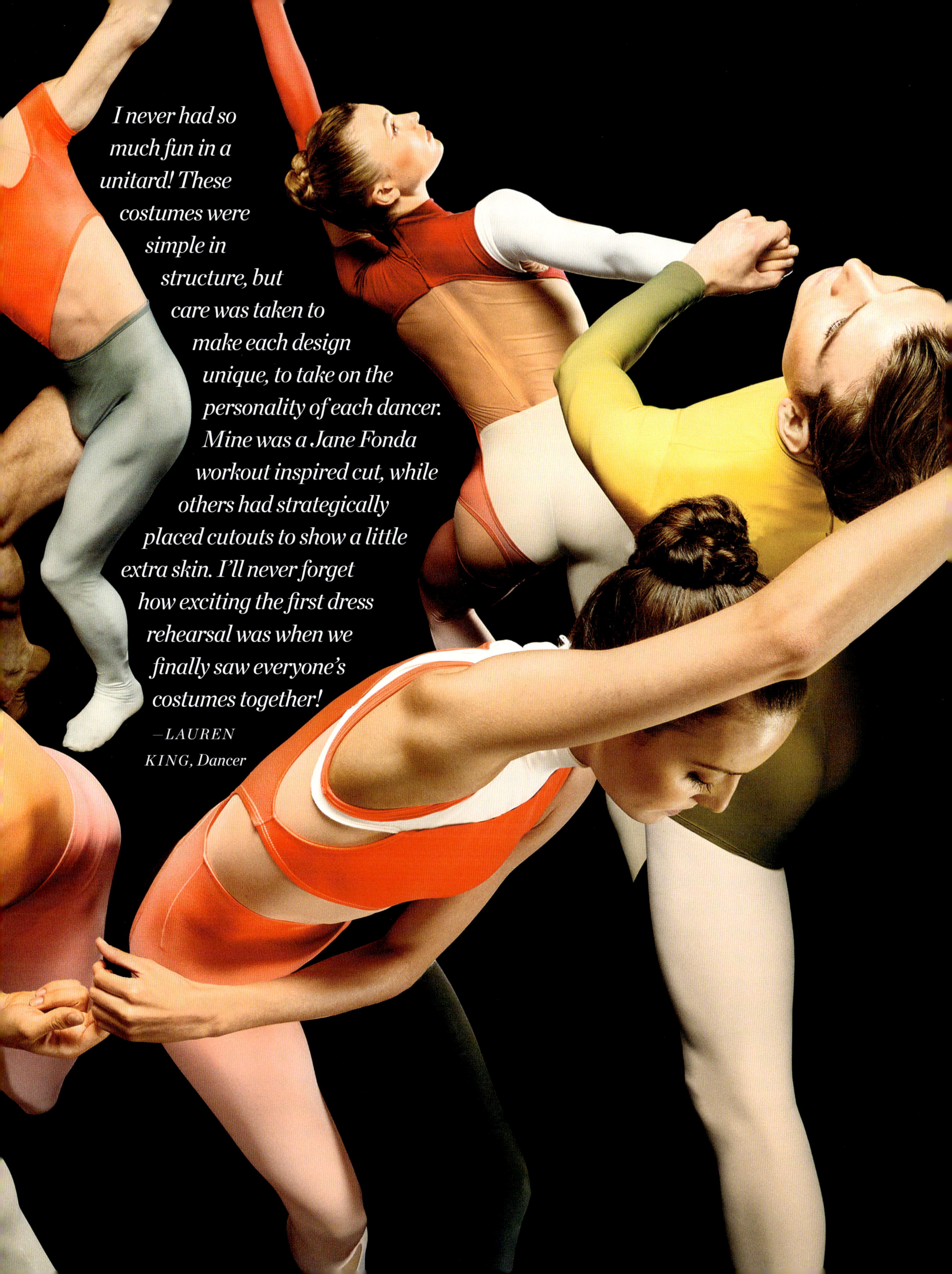

I never had so much fun in a unitard! These costumes were simple in structure, but care was taken to make each design unique, to take on the personality of each dancer. Mine was a Jane Fonda workout inspired cut, while others had strategically placed cutouts to show a little extra skin. I'll never forget how exciting the first dress rehearsal was when we finally saw everyone's costumes together!

—LAUREN KING, *Dancer*

Humberto Leon is one of the most original designers I've ever worked with. I always felt that the way he thinks is not limited to a singular medium, but expands into a fuller realm of creativity.

—JUSTIN PECK, *Choreographer*

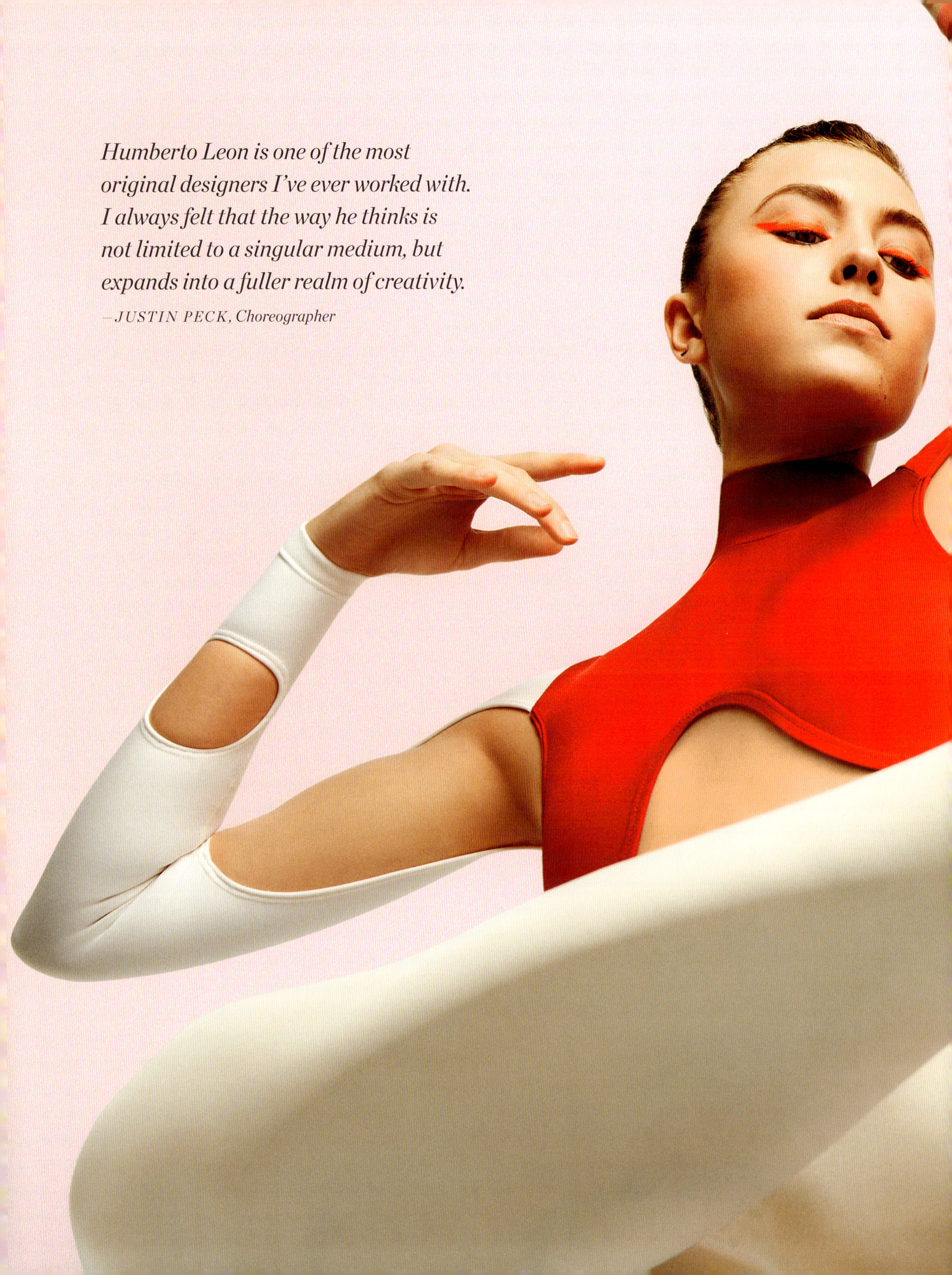

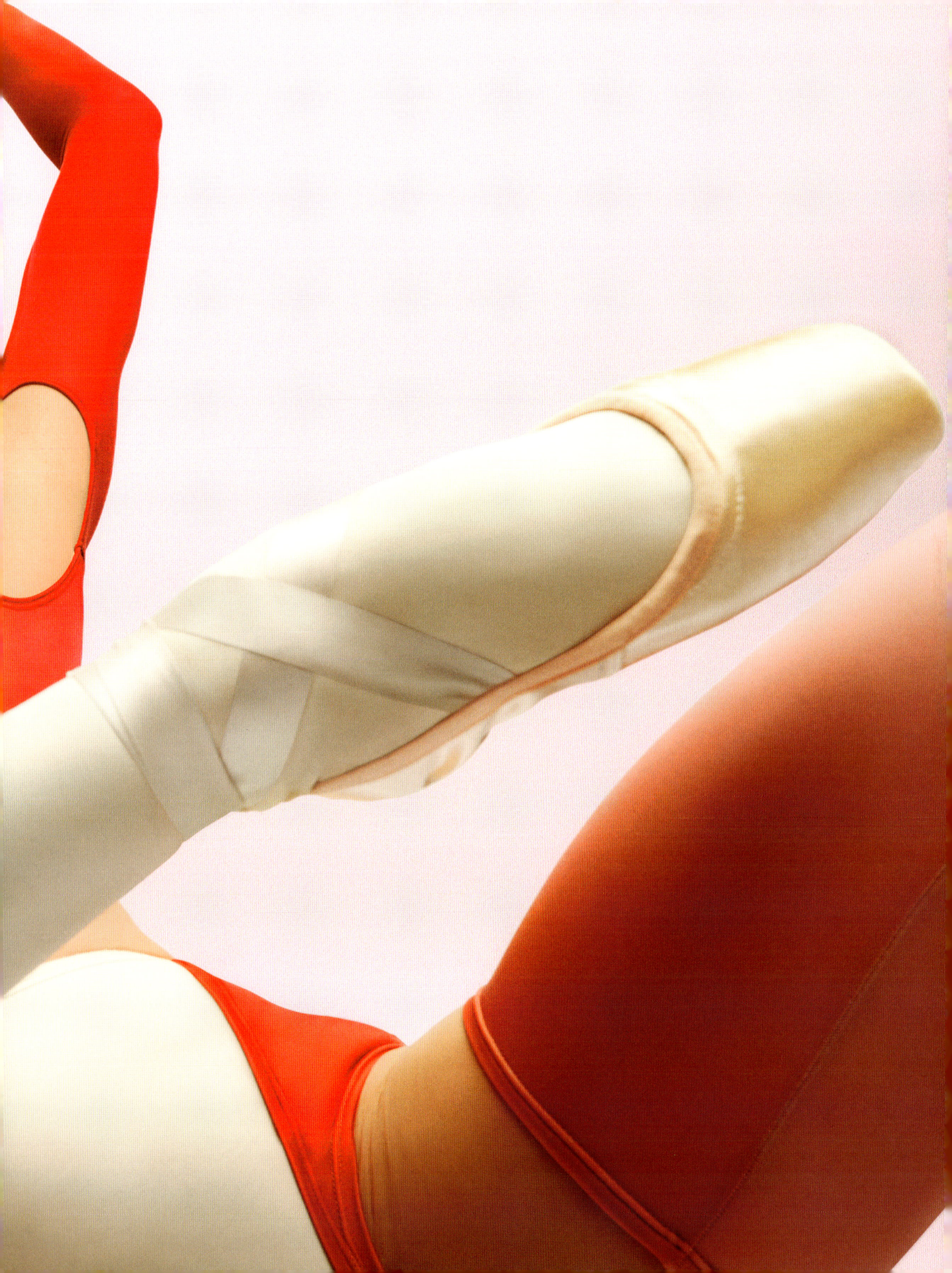

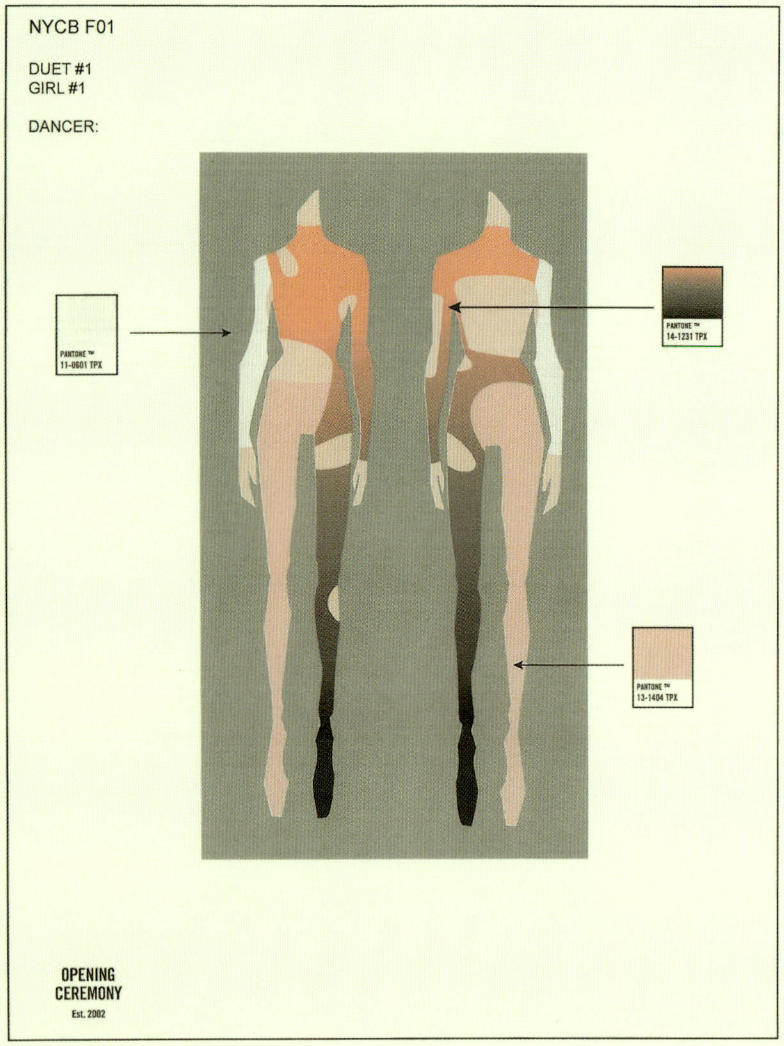
NYCB F01
DUET #1
GIRL #1
DANCER:
PANTONE ™
11-0601 TPX
PANTONE ™
14-1231 TPX
PANTONE ™
13-1404 TPX
OPENING
CEREMONY
Est. 2002

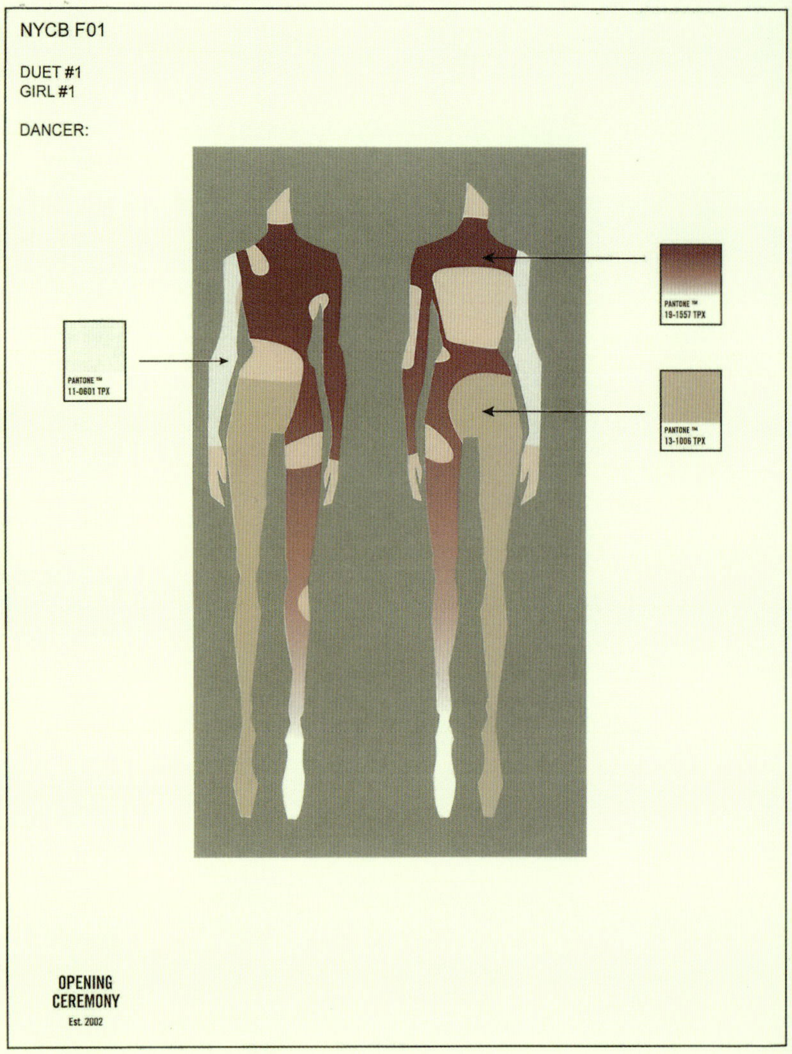
NYCB F01
DUET #1
GIRL #1
DANCER:
PANTONE ™
19-1557 TPX
PANTONE ™
11-0601 TPX
PANTONE ™
13-1006 TPX
OPENING
CEREMONY
Est. 2002

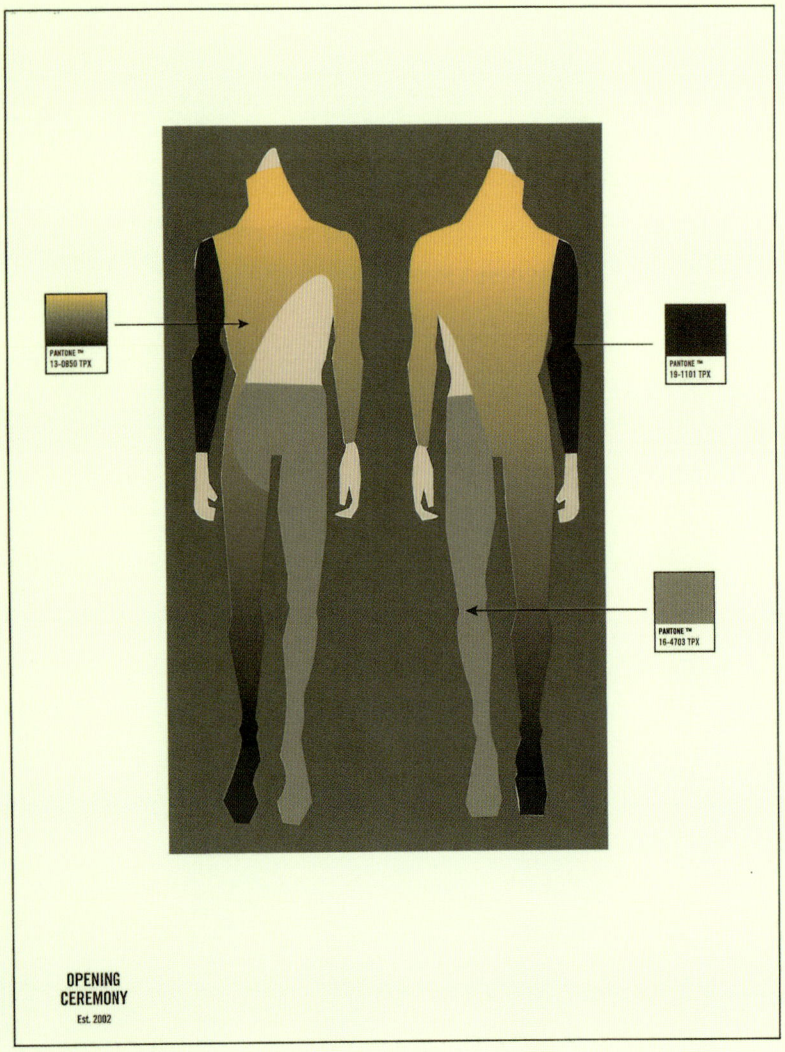
PANTONE ™
13-0850 TPX
PANTONE ™
19-1101 TPX
PANTONE ™
16-4703 TPX
OPENING
CEREMONY
Est. 2002

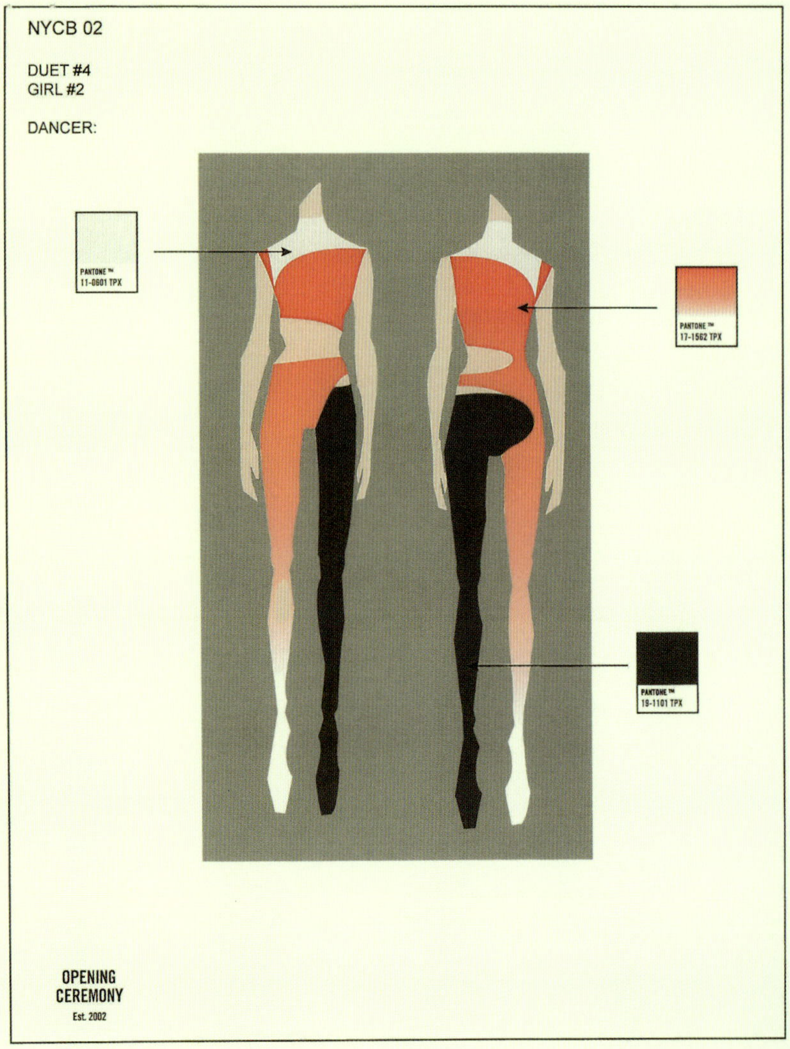
NYCB 02
DUET #4
GIRL #2
DANCER:
PANTONE ™
11-0601 TPX
PANTONE ™
17-1562 TPX
PANTONE ™
19-1101 TPX
OPENING
CEREMONY
Est. 2002

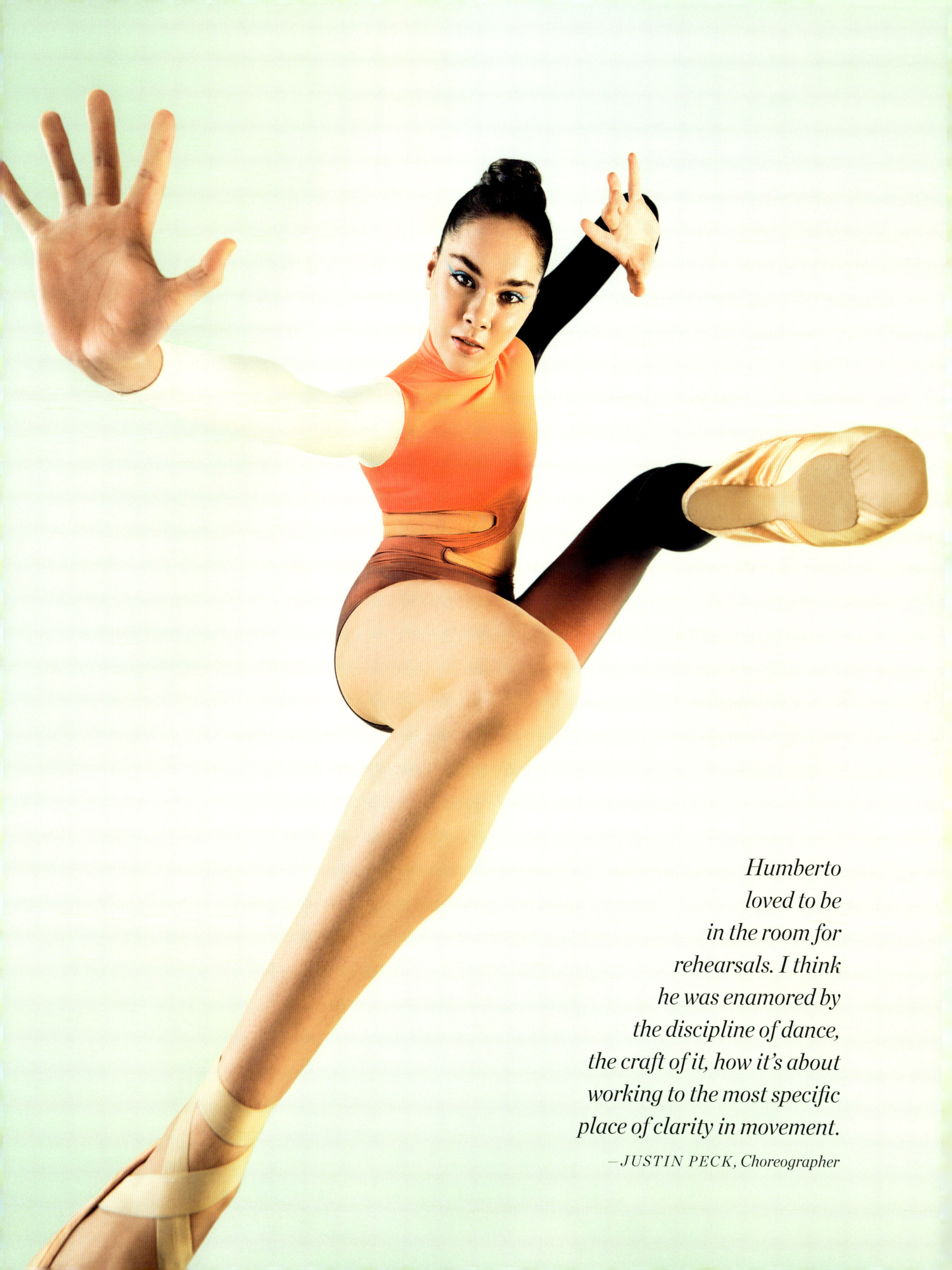

Humberto loved to be in the room for rehearsals. I think he was enamored by the discipline of dance, the craft of it, how it's about working to the most specific place of clarity in movement.

—JUSTIN PECK, *Choreographer*

2015

HANAKO MAEDA OF ADEAM *THE BLUE OF DISTANCE*

When Robert contacted me about his piece, The Blue of Distance, *I was inspired to design costumes that fused traditional and modern concepts, aiming to create pieces that bridged the worlds of fashion and dance. The costumes for this piece had an aquatic mood, I felt like I was being embraced by the ocean when I listened to the music. This led to the idea of creating embroidery that replicated fish scales. I decided to use blue fabric in different shades and the embroidery was on top of nude mesh, so it looked like the scales were growing on the dancers' bodies. I also wanted to create this look of the dancers glistening like they're emerging from under water, so we applied crystals on top of the fish scales, which were dégradé—they went from dark to light blue and faded into white.* – HANAKO MAEDA

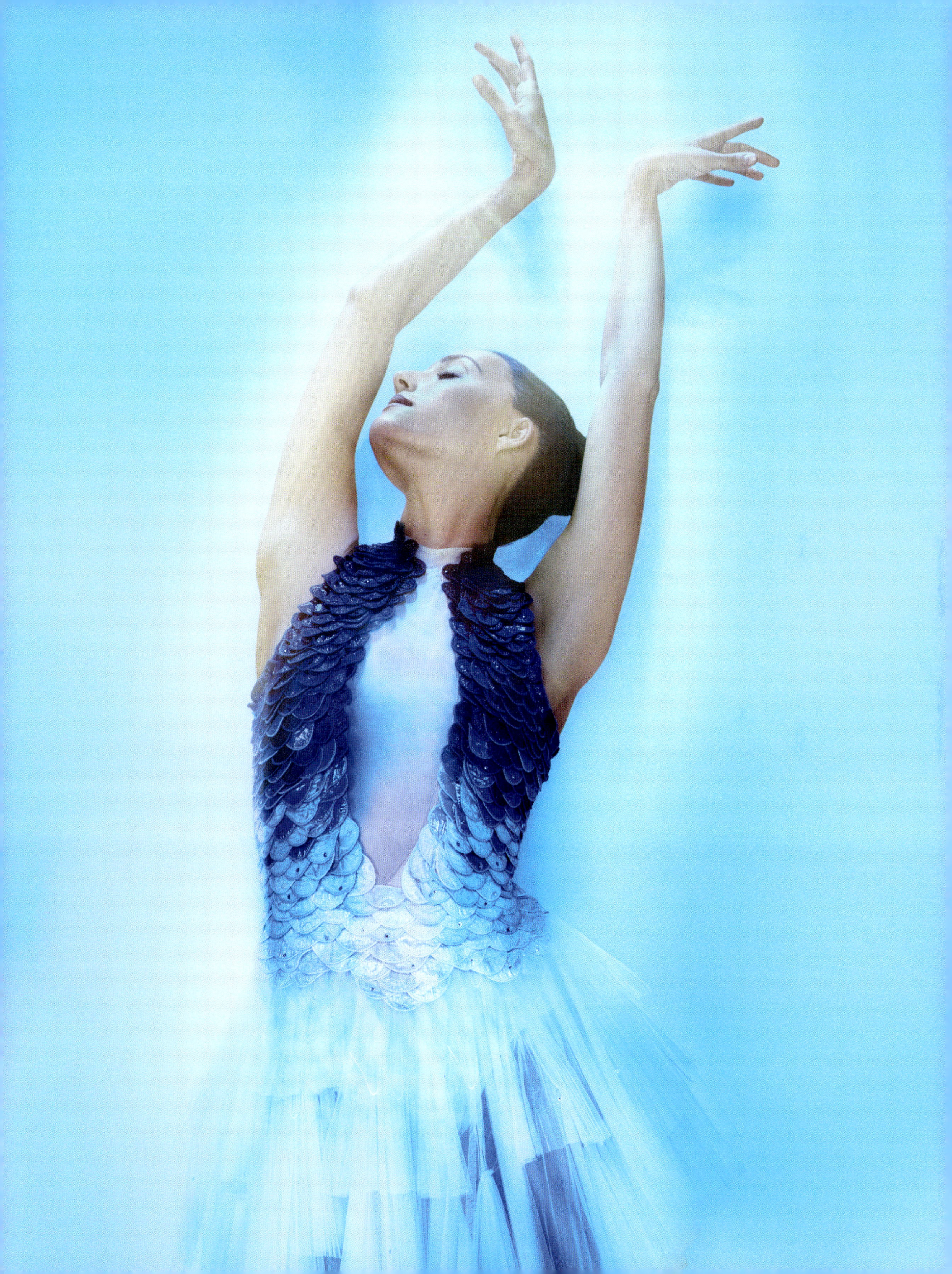

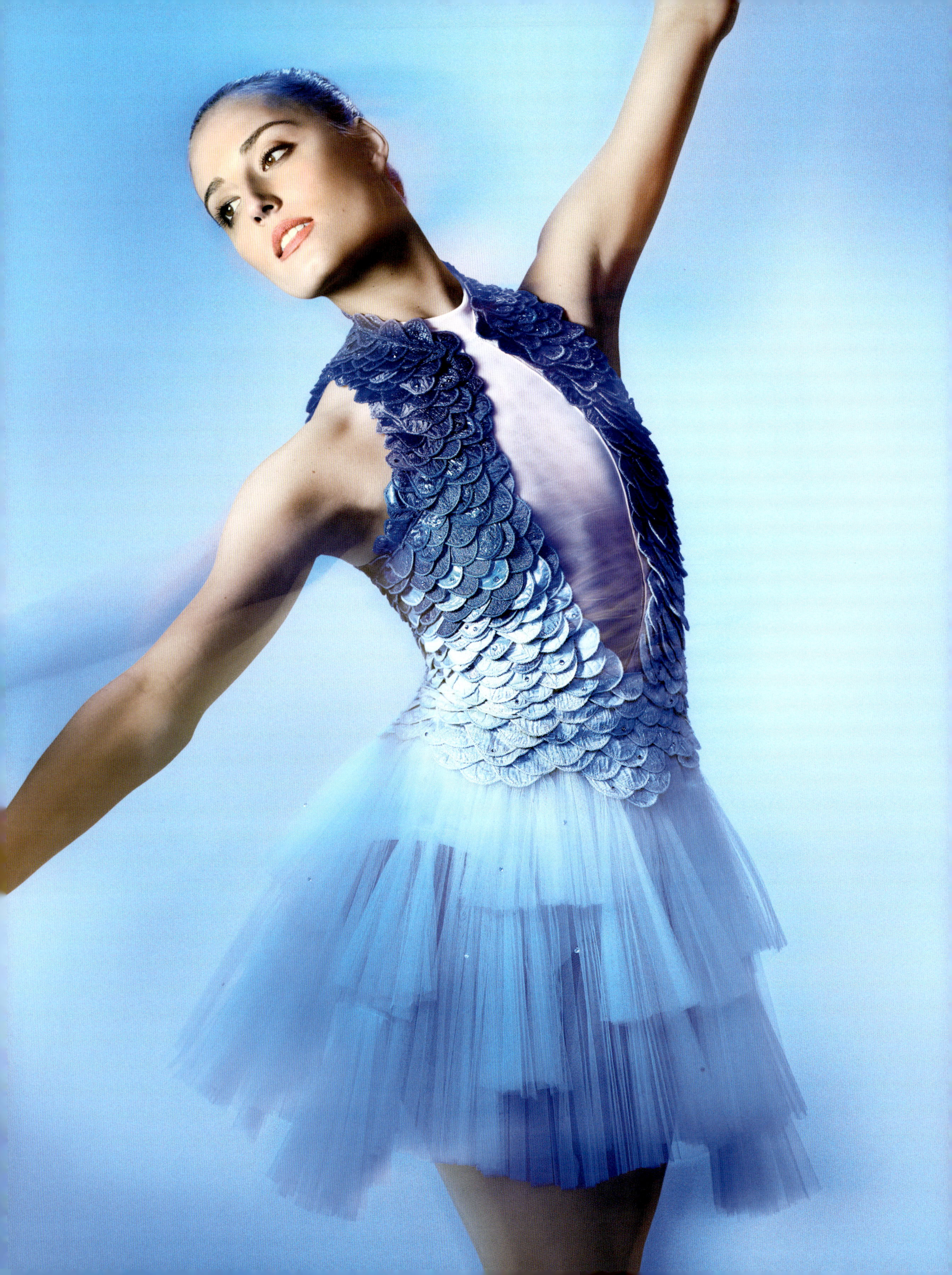

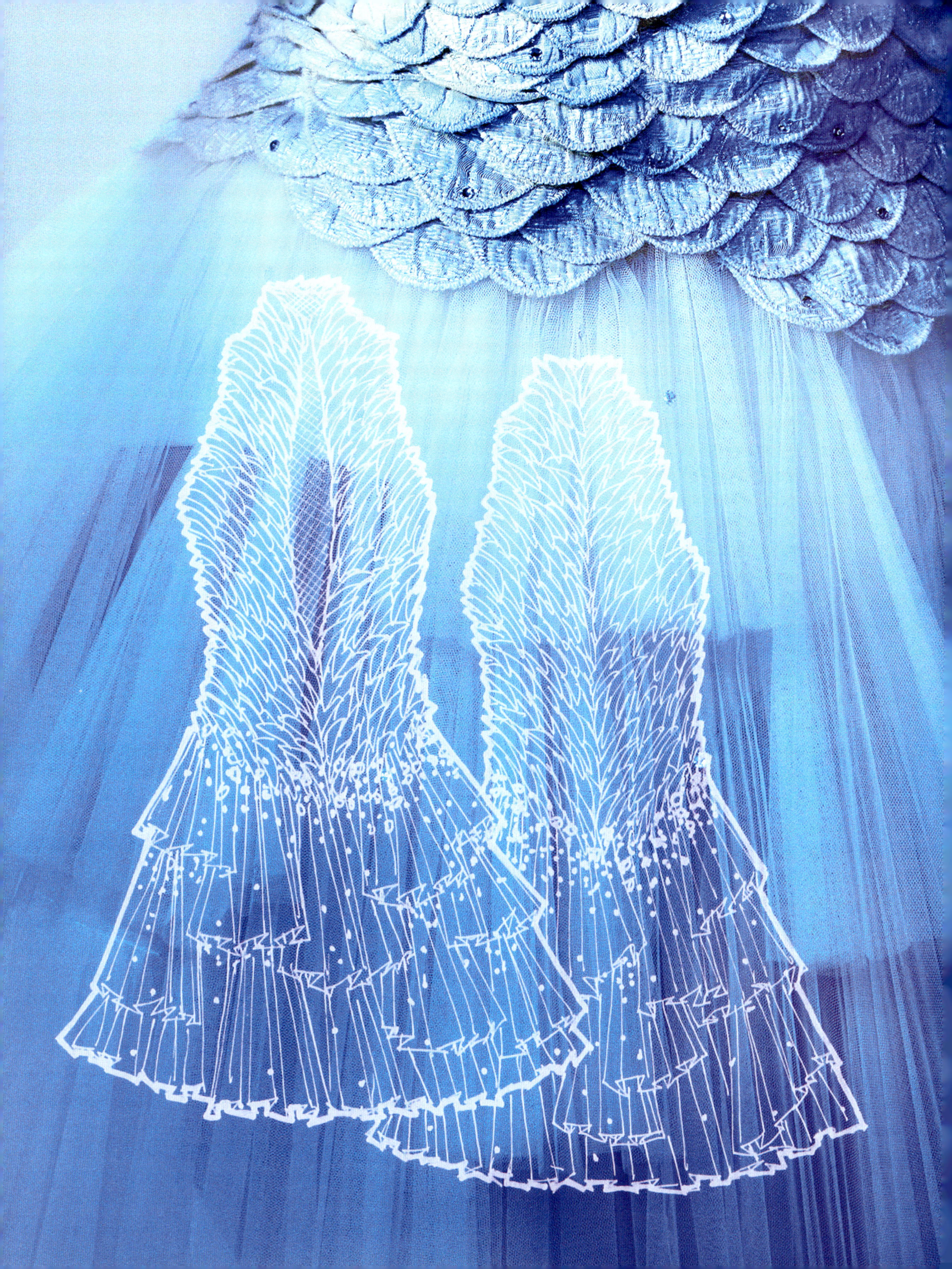

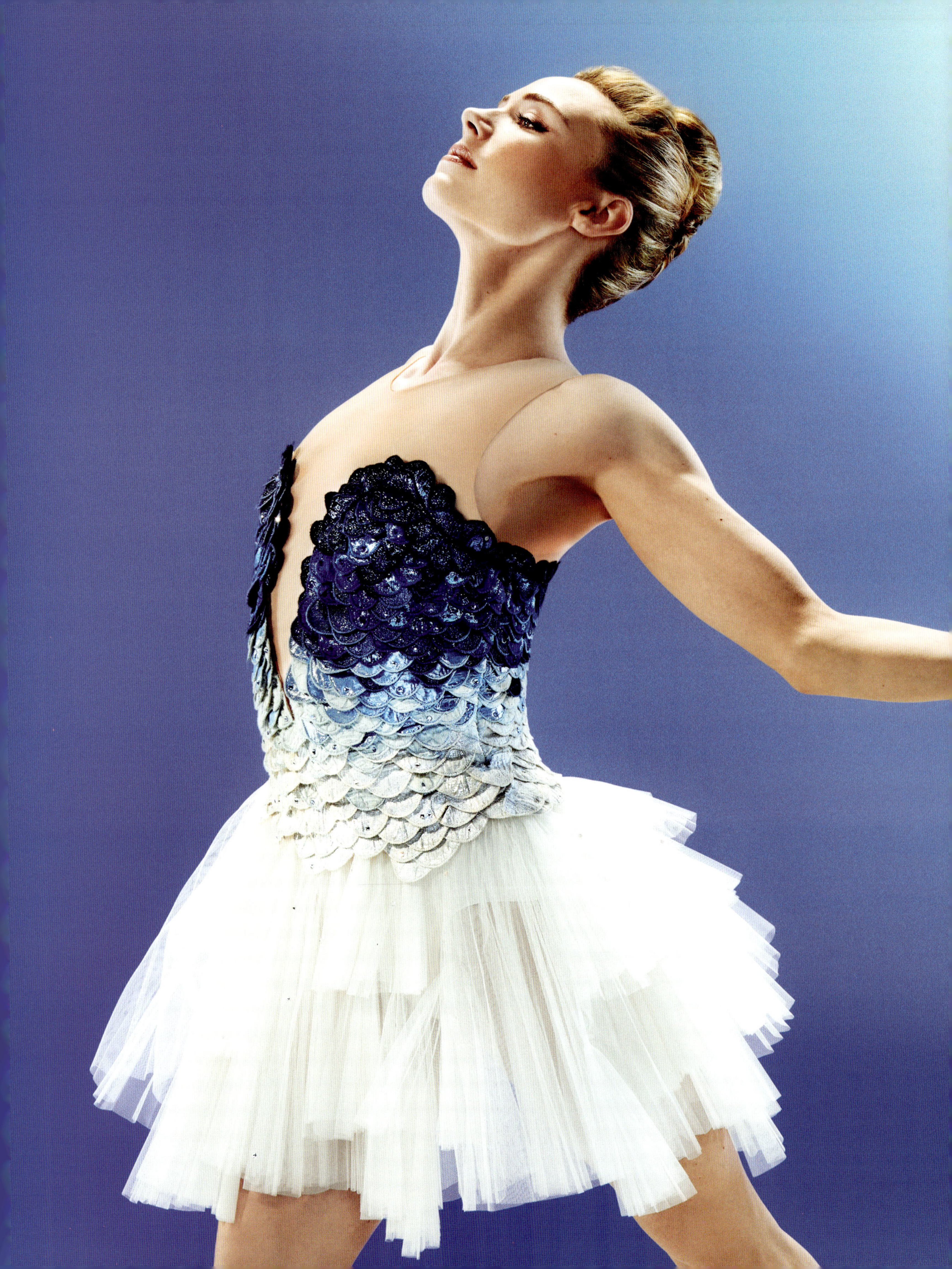

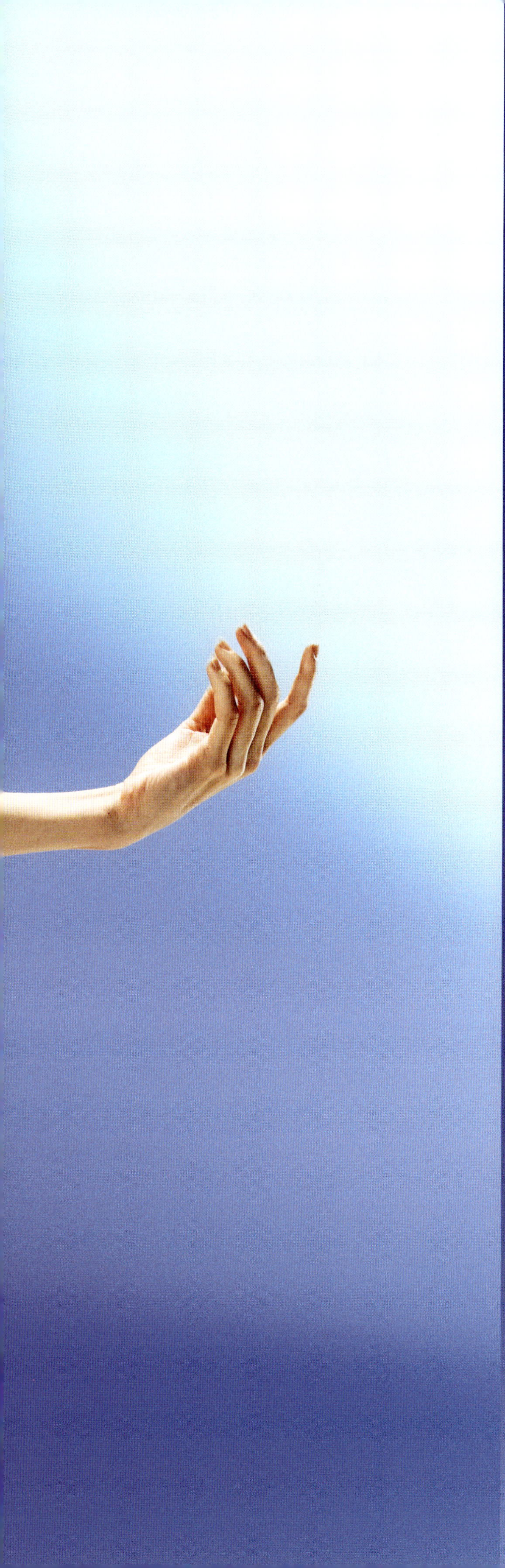

Hanako captured the detail of Ravel's piano music in the stunning scales of fabric that ran up the women's costumes, and created designs that had so much rippling movement even before the dancers took a step. Hanako was incredibly collaborative, constantly fine-tuning the designs to flatter the choreography and reflect our shared vision for the ballet.

—ROBERT BINET, *Choreographer*

2015

MARTA MARQUES & PAULO ALMEIDA OF MARQUES'ALMEIDA *COMMON GROUND*

We're very interested in the way that the dancers are as individuals, so Troy was kind enough to send us pictures of all the dancers and rehearsals, which we had stuck up on the mood board. We felt super connected to them and identified with the idea of effortless, raw imagery. We wanted to bring the realism to the stage.

—*MARTA MARQUES*

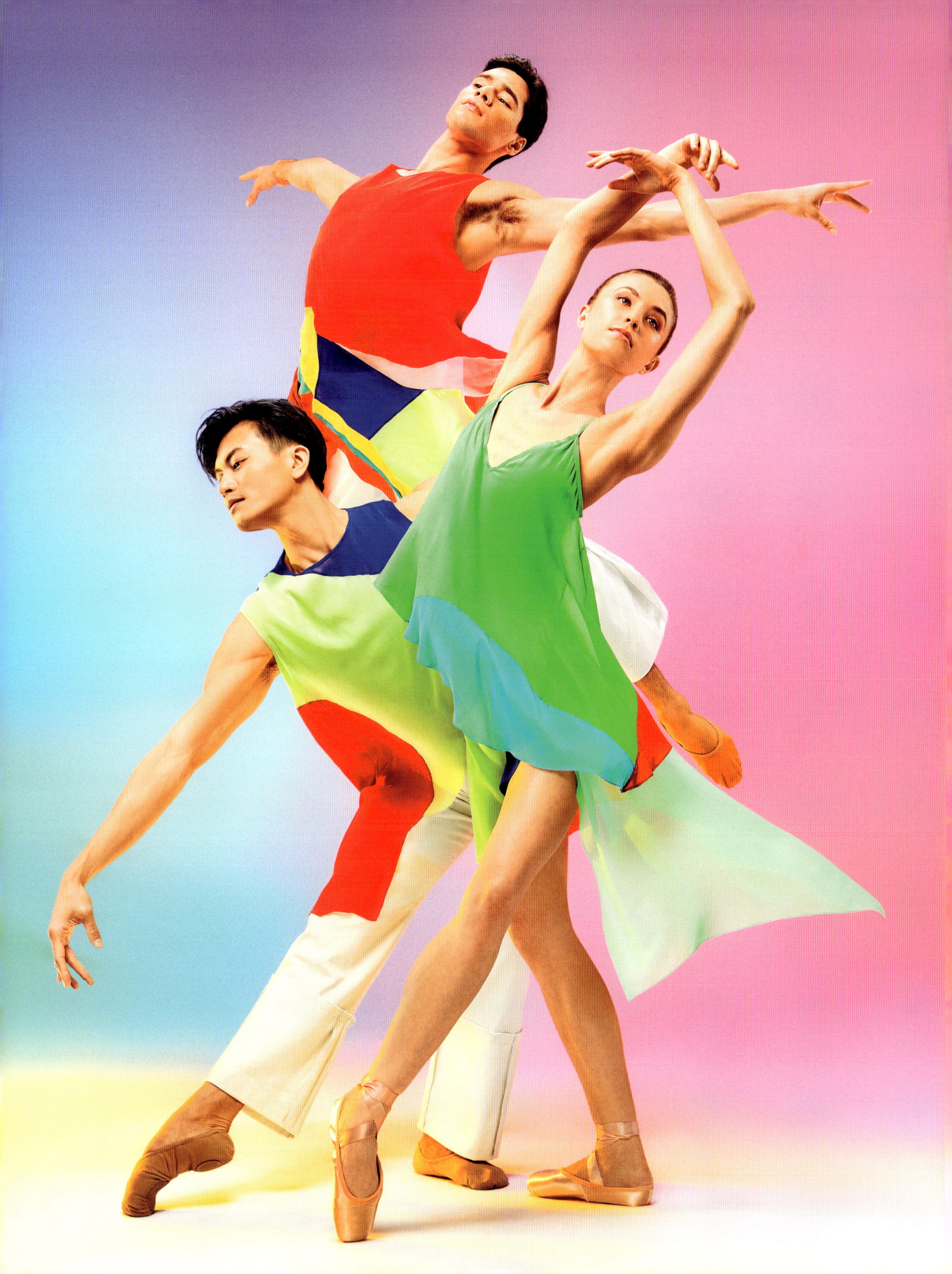

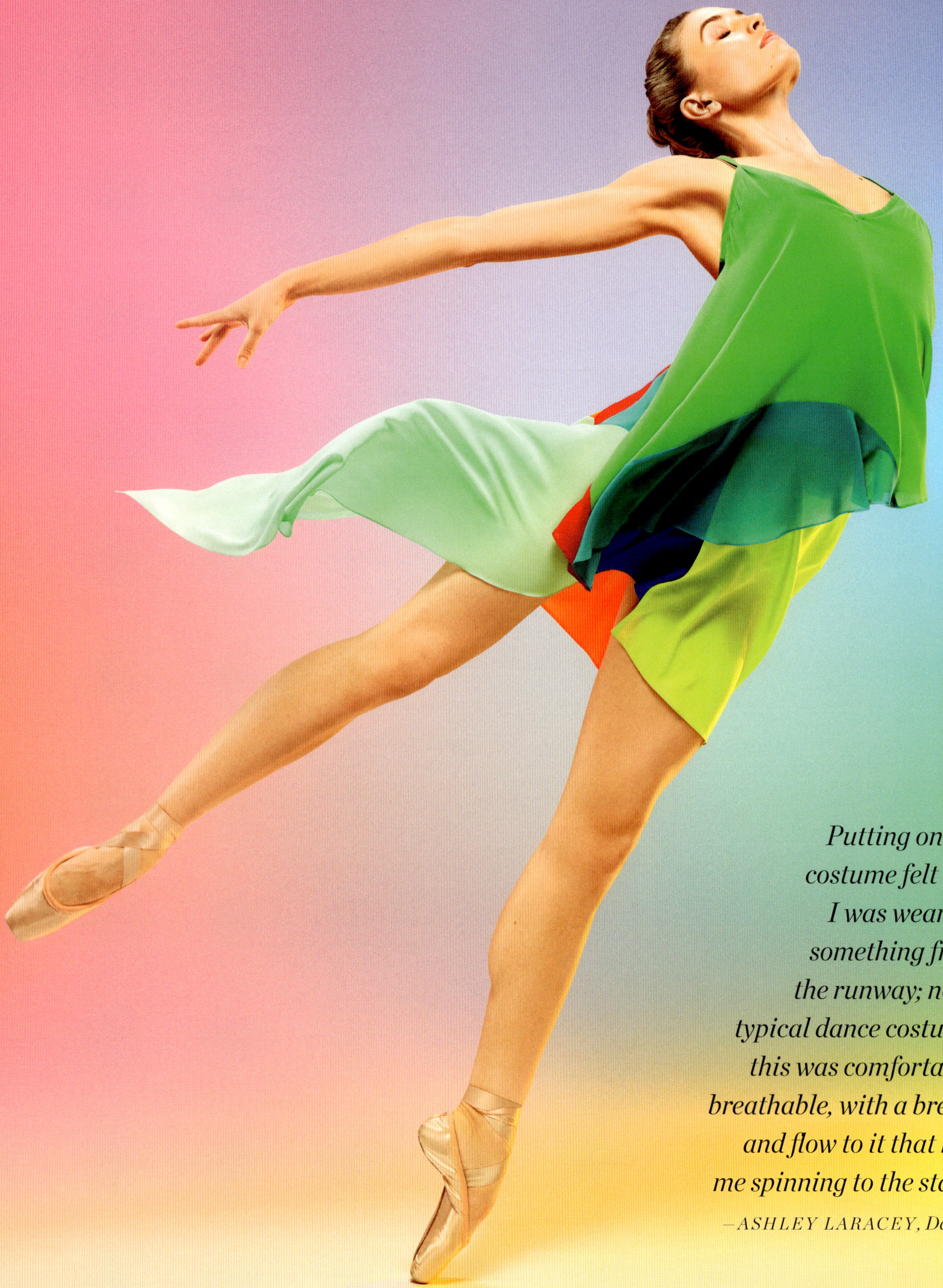

Putting on the costume felt like I was wearing something from the runway; not a typical dance costume, this was comfortable, breathable, with a breeze and flow to it that had me spinning to the stage.

—ASHLEY LARACEY, *Dancer*

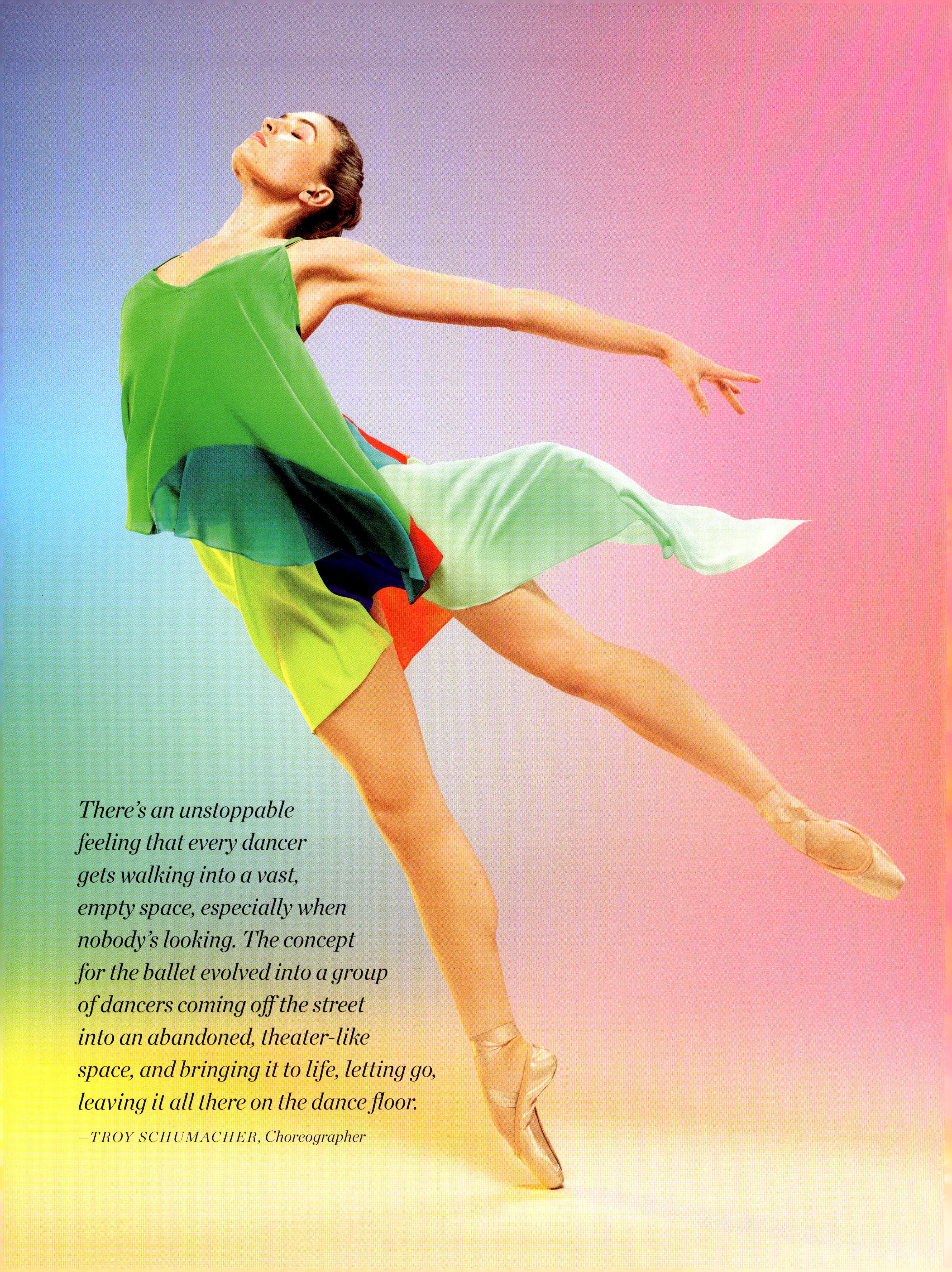

There's an unstoppable feeling that every dancer gets walking into a vast, empty space, especially when nobody's looking. The concept for the ballet evolved into a group of dancers coming off the street into an abandoned, theater-like space, and bringing it to life, letting go, leaving it all there on the dance floor.

—TROY SCHUMACHER, *Choreographer*

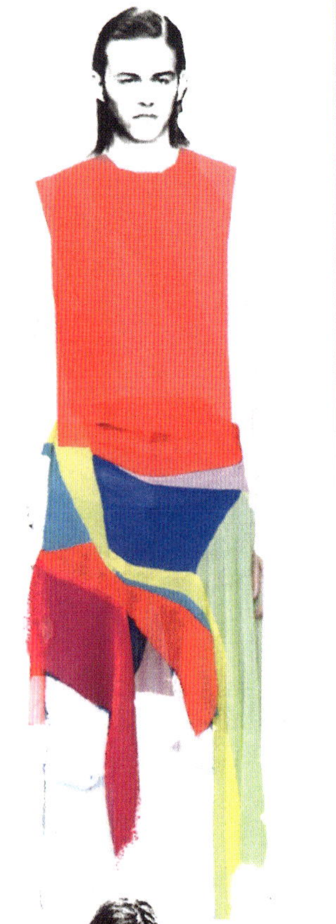

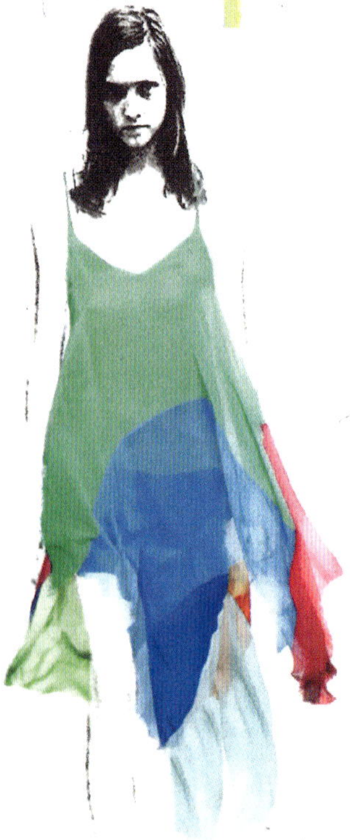

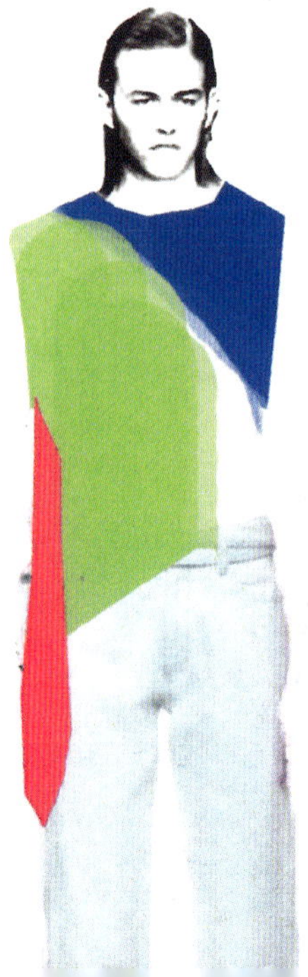

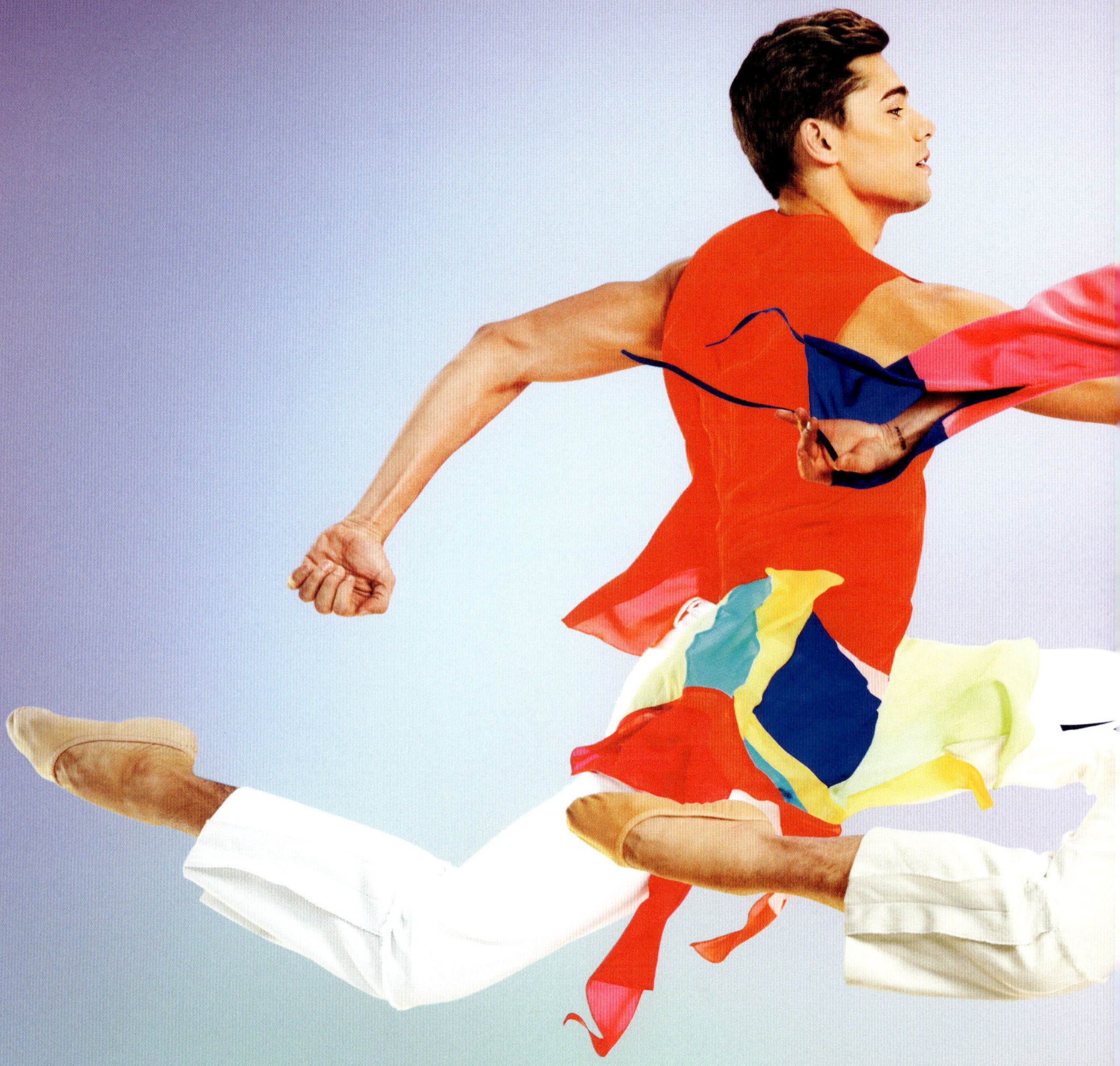

I wore a sheer patchwork shirt with long strings trailing from the sleeves. I wasn't in tights or a fitted jacket as I typically am onstage. My body wasn't hidden, but it also wasn't shaped by the costume I wore. I didn't look like a cavalier or like any of the idealized versions of men I'd long seen and embodied in ballet. My costume's colors were vibrant, almost tropical.

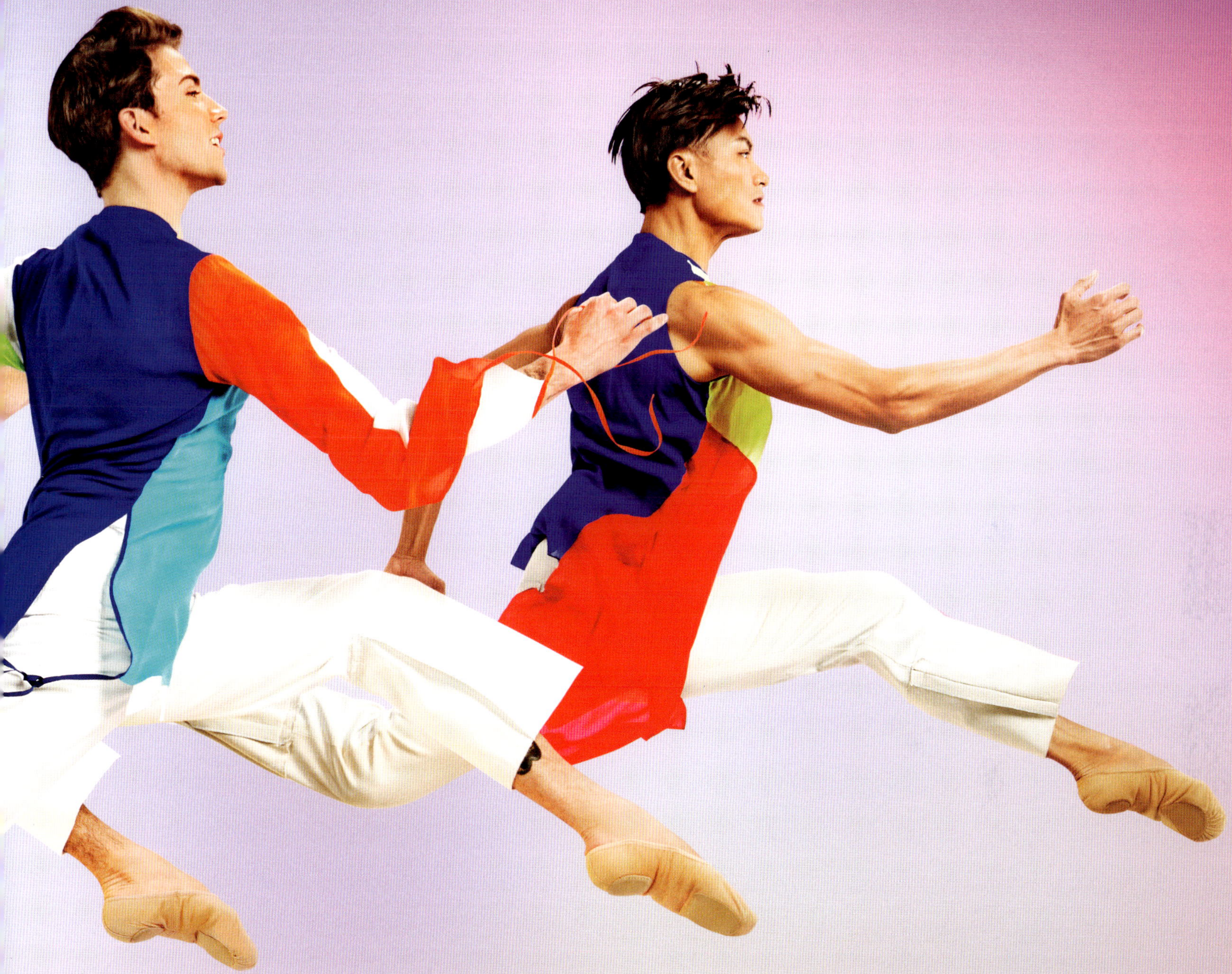

There was a breeze when I moved. I'd seen a photo of a gorgeous model, hair teased, eyes darkened, walking the runway in my same garment. I stepped out onstage dressed as I'd never been before, and the costume gave me permission to dance with a kind of unrestricted joy and flamboyance I don't often find on our stage. It was freeing. —RUSSELL JANZEN, *Dancer*

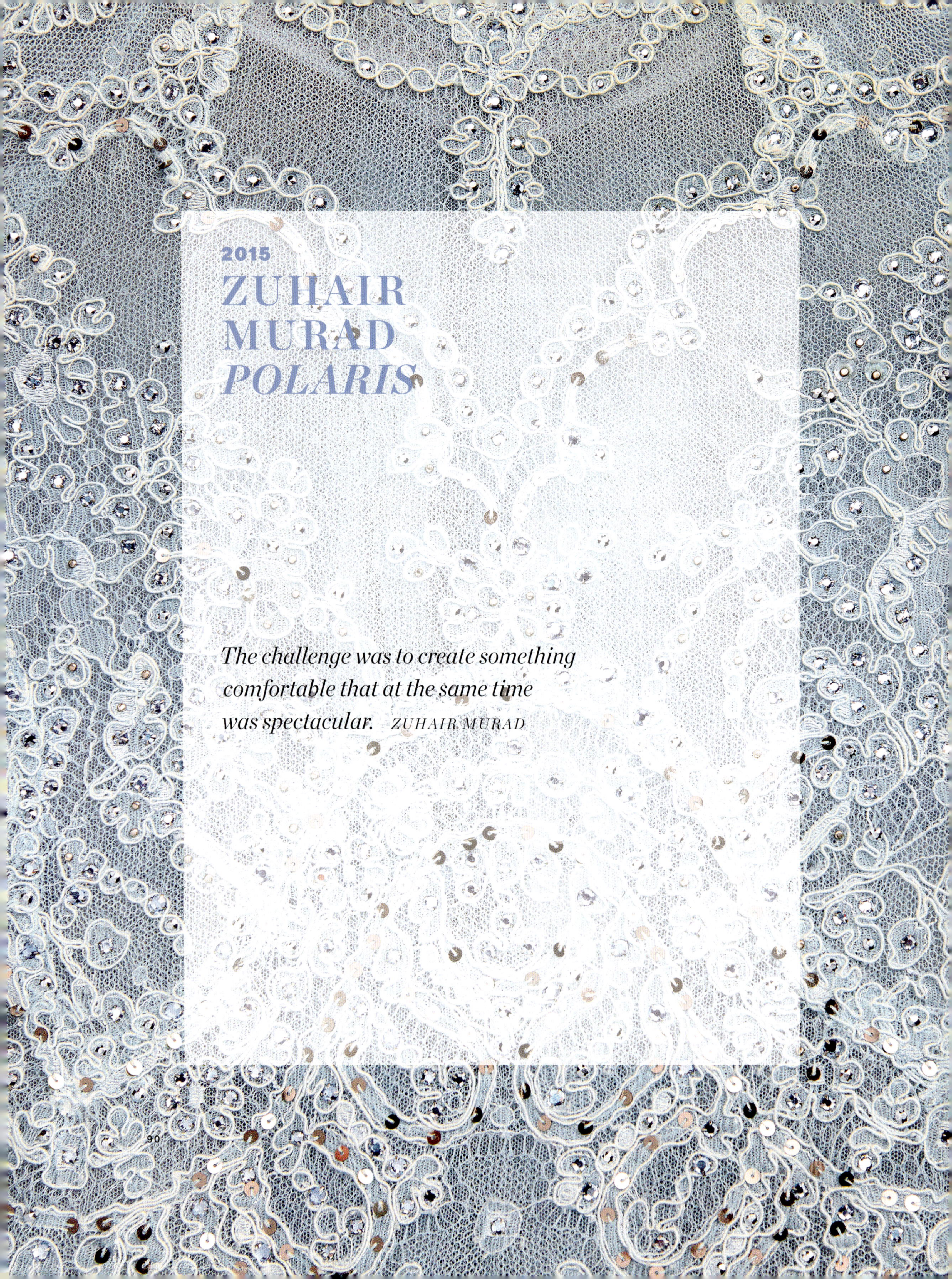

2015

ZUHAIR MURAD *POLARIS*

The challenge was to create something comfortable that at the same time was spectacular. –ZUHAIR MURAD

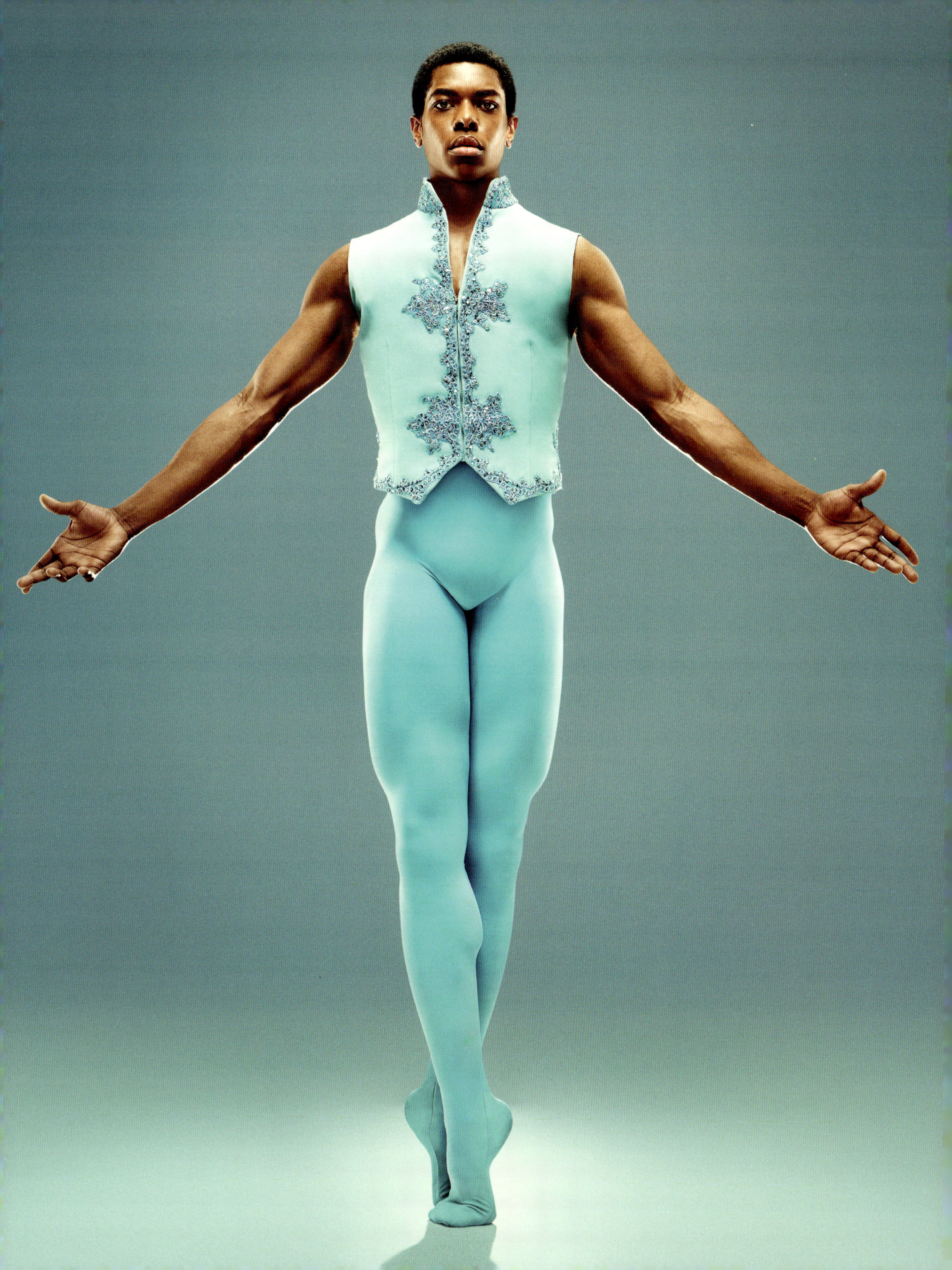

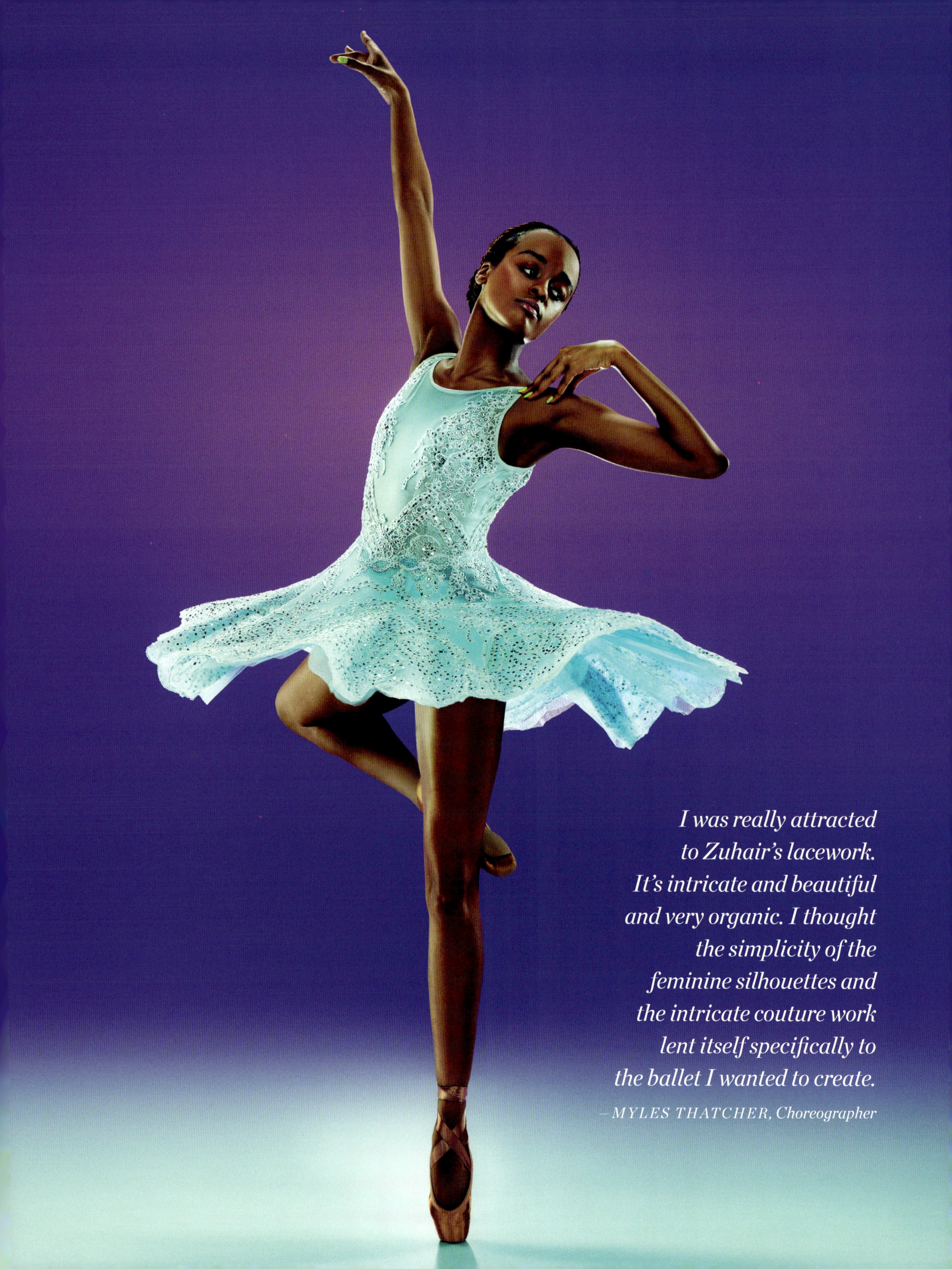

I was really attracted to Zuhair's lacework. It's intricate and beautiful and very organic. I thought the simplicity of the feminine silhouettes and the intricate couture work lent itself specifically to the ballet I wanted to create.

—MYLES THATCHER, *Choreographer*

ZUHAIR MURAD

LEAD FEMALE DANCER'S OUTFIT
(lace placement)

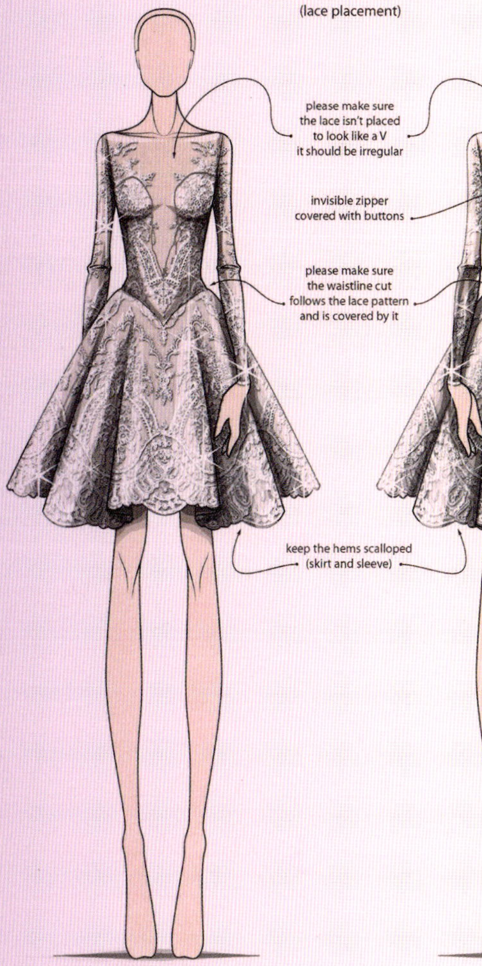

ZUHAIR MURAD

LEAD FEMALE DANCER'S OUTFIT
(color codes)

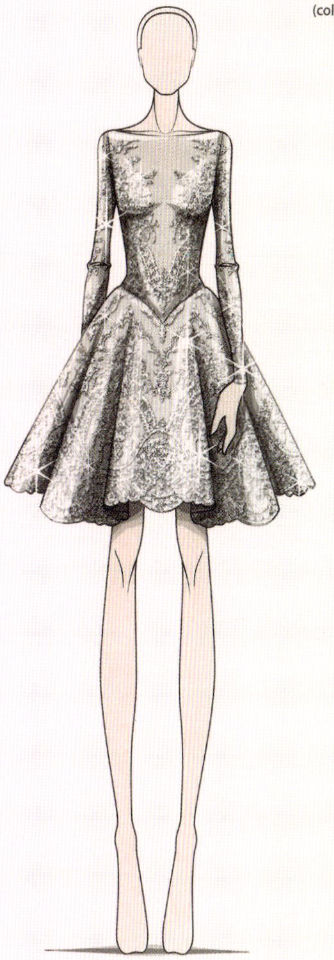

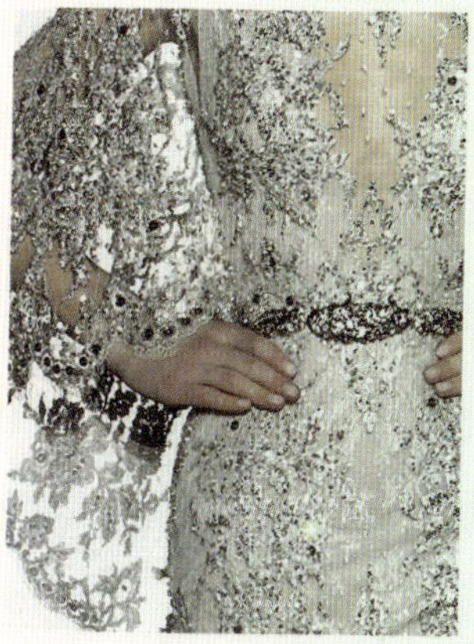

color combination as seen
on the SS15 runway

LACE
TULLE

PANTONE®
SILVER

PANTONE®
14-4002TPX

ZUHAIR MURAD

ACCOMPANYING FEMALE DANCERS' OUTFIT
(color codes)

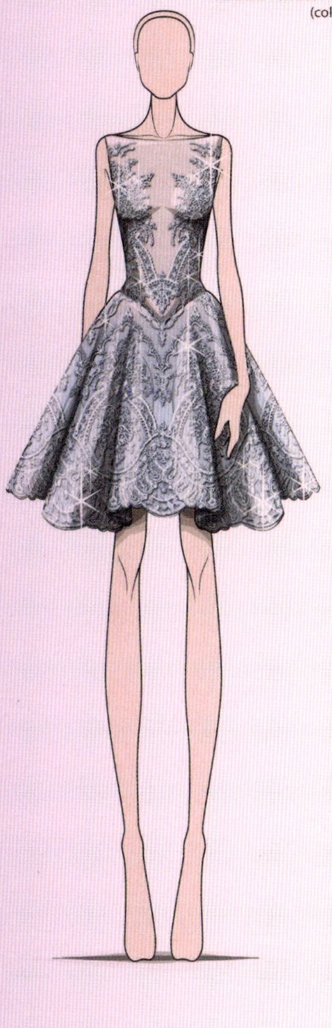

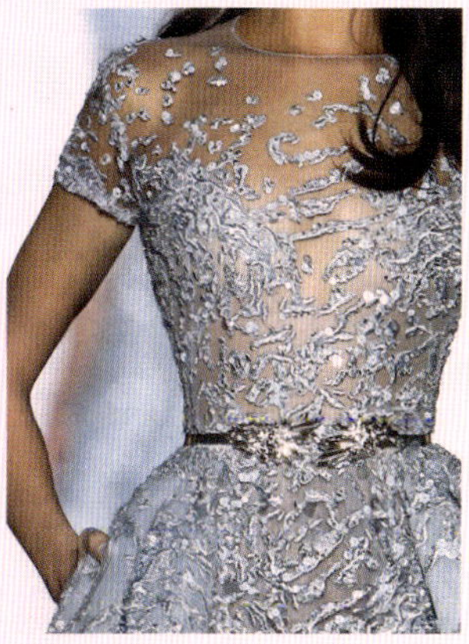

color combination as seen
on the SS15 runway

PANTONE®
14-4005TPX

ZUHAIR MURAD

MALE DANCERS' OUTFIT
(lace placement)

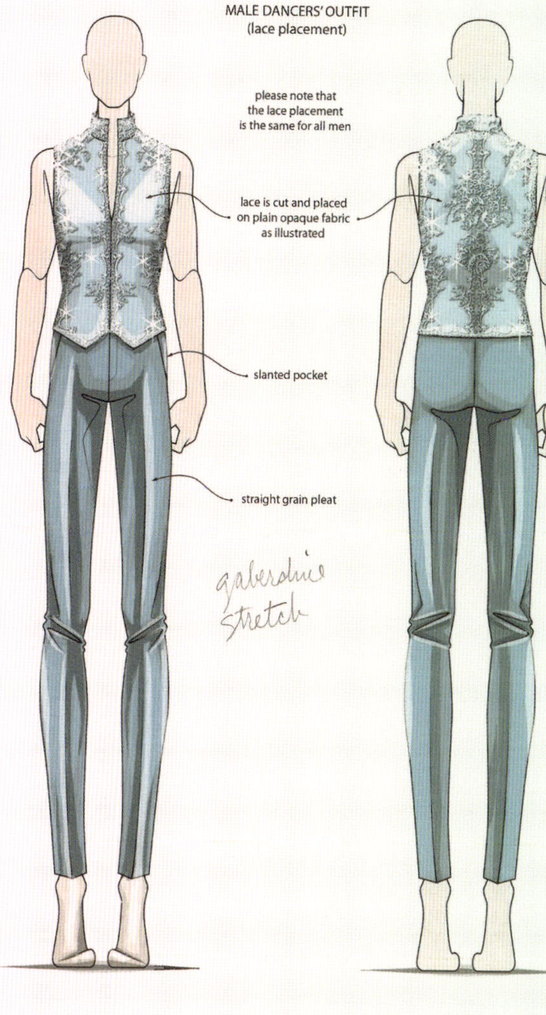

TONNE GOODMAN

I HAVE BEEN A FASHION EDITOR for many years, and I've been a diehard fan of ballet for many, *many* years, since I was a child growing up in New York, privileged by cultural exposure. As a child I was delighted by the fantasy of ballet and the spectacle of extraordinary beauty in motion. As an editor, I remain awed by that beauty but I understand and appreciate the creative challenge, hours, and consideration behind it. The challenge to move the dancer effortlessly, to tell a particular story visually, and to command that presence within an enormous theater.

Since 2012 New York City Ballet has championed the conversation between fashion designers and their visions for the ballet. At times, there is an obvious connection. At other times, it is a stretch of possibility. Whichever, the work involved is like no other.

What goes into each and every costume, even if it is a very simple costume, is formidable. My good friend Marc Happel, the Company's Director of Costumes, has collaborated with over two dozen designers and has overseen all of the intense production that is involved. For the Fall Fashion Gala, when the collaboration involves more than one designer, four or five different designers perhaps, that is equivalent to the costume department doing four or five different collections that are on par with couture.

The distinction with couture is significant. Ready to wear is fashion that is *ready to wear*. Costume for the ballet is fashion that is exclusively *made to order* for the dancer, and for the particular role the dancer is dancing. The variety is astounding in the vision, approach, and materials. Some echo what is considered ballet fare—dresses in tulle, fluttering silk, and fluid chiffon. There are others that are just the opposite, ones that seem to totally contradict what a dancer can move in! Case in point: Iris van Herpen, the extraordinary Dutch designer renowned for her otherworldly fashion visions using original innovative technique and fabrications. Her costumes for Benjamin Millepied's 2013 work *Neverwhere* are composed of individually cut slices of shiny ebony plastic that scale and overlap into place over the body. For the audience, they are provocative and astounding sensations. For the dancers, they are anatomical wonders.

Fashion as Costume. Costume as Fashion. This has never been more true than when these fashion designers have lent their hands to NYCB's stage. I am grateful that New York City Ballet began this conversation ten years ago. It is magic, a true delight, a joy, and a remarkable gift.

TONNE GOODMAN
Sustainability Editor, *Vogue*

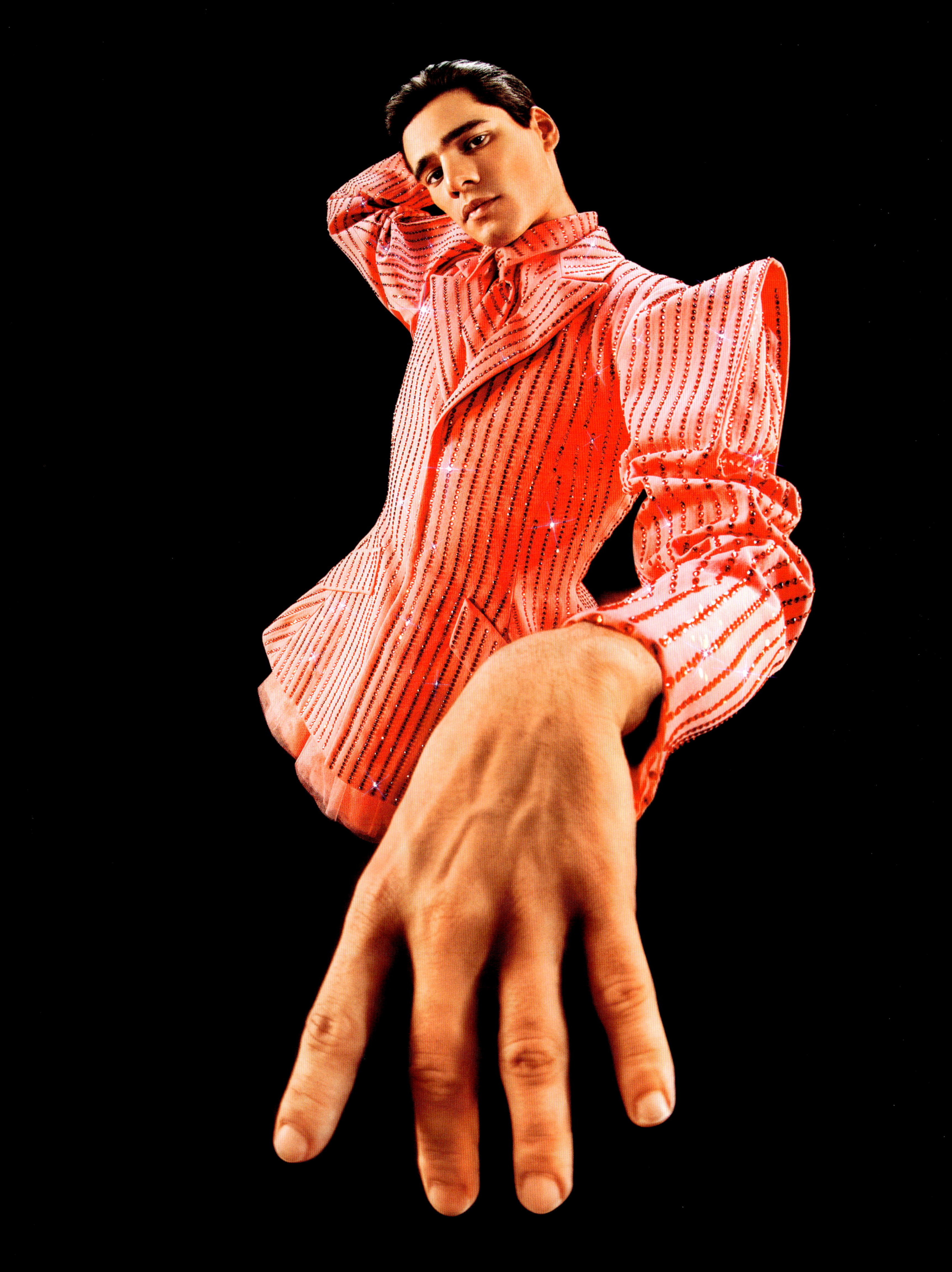

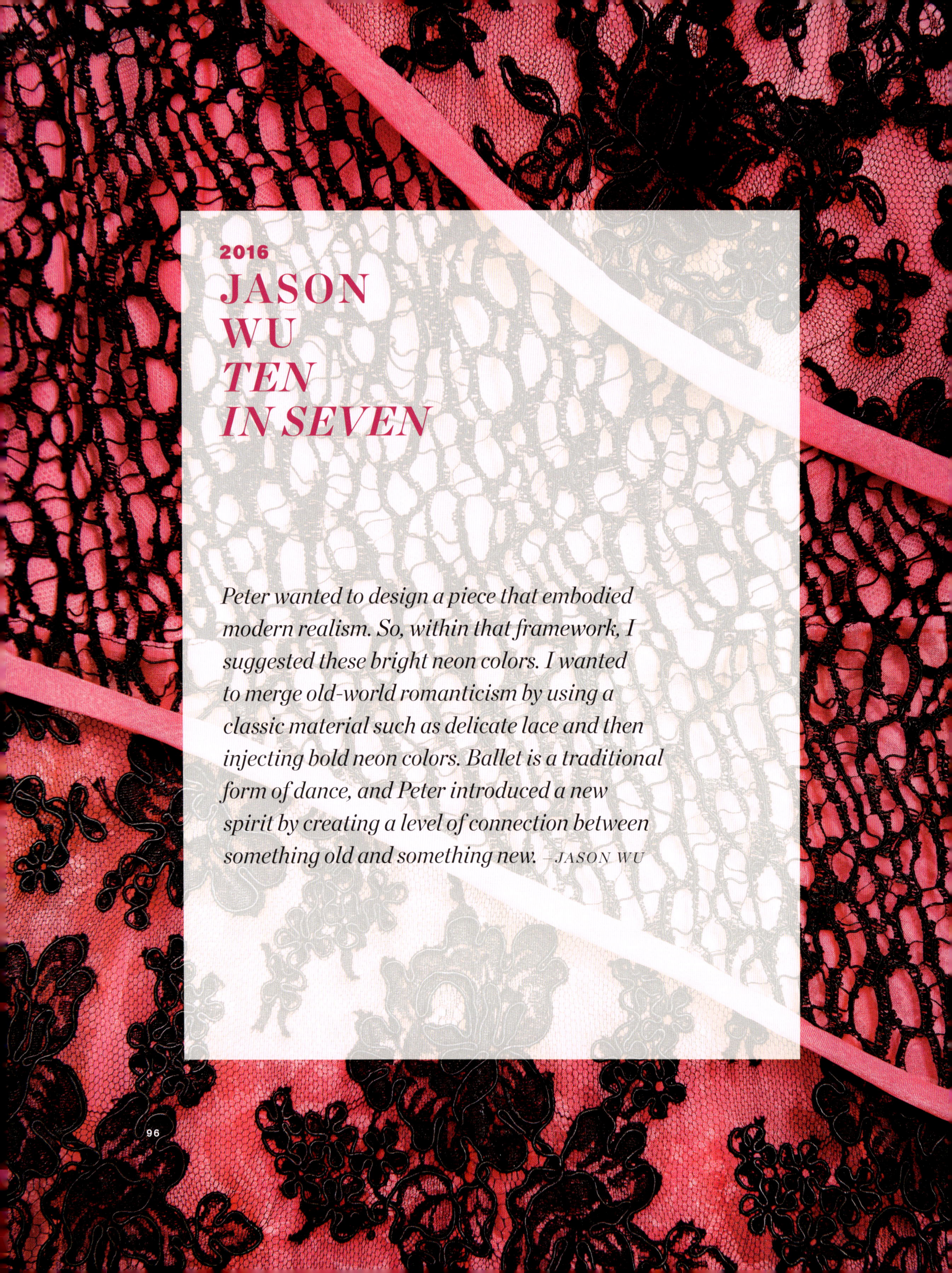

2016

JASON WU *TEN IN SEVEN*

Peter wanted to design a piece that embodied modern realism. So, within that framework, I suggested these bright neon colors. I wanted to merge old-world romanticism by using a classic material such as delicate lace and then injecting bold neon colors. Ballet is a traditional form of dance, and Peter introduced a new spirit by creating a level of connection between something old and something new. —JASON WU

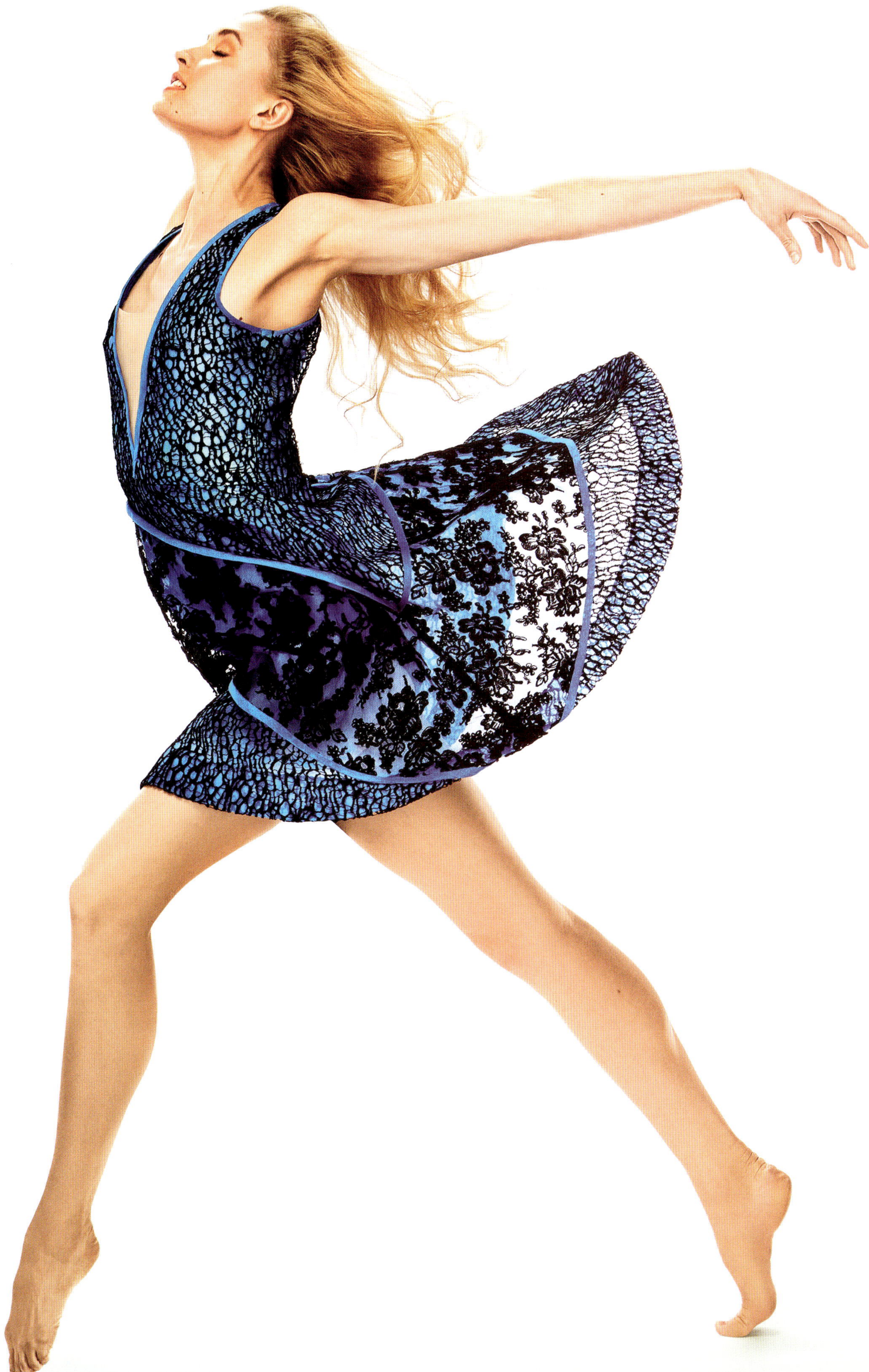

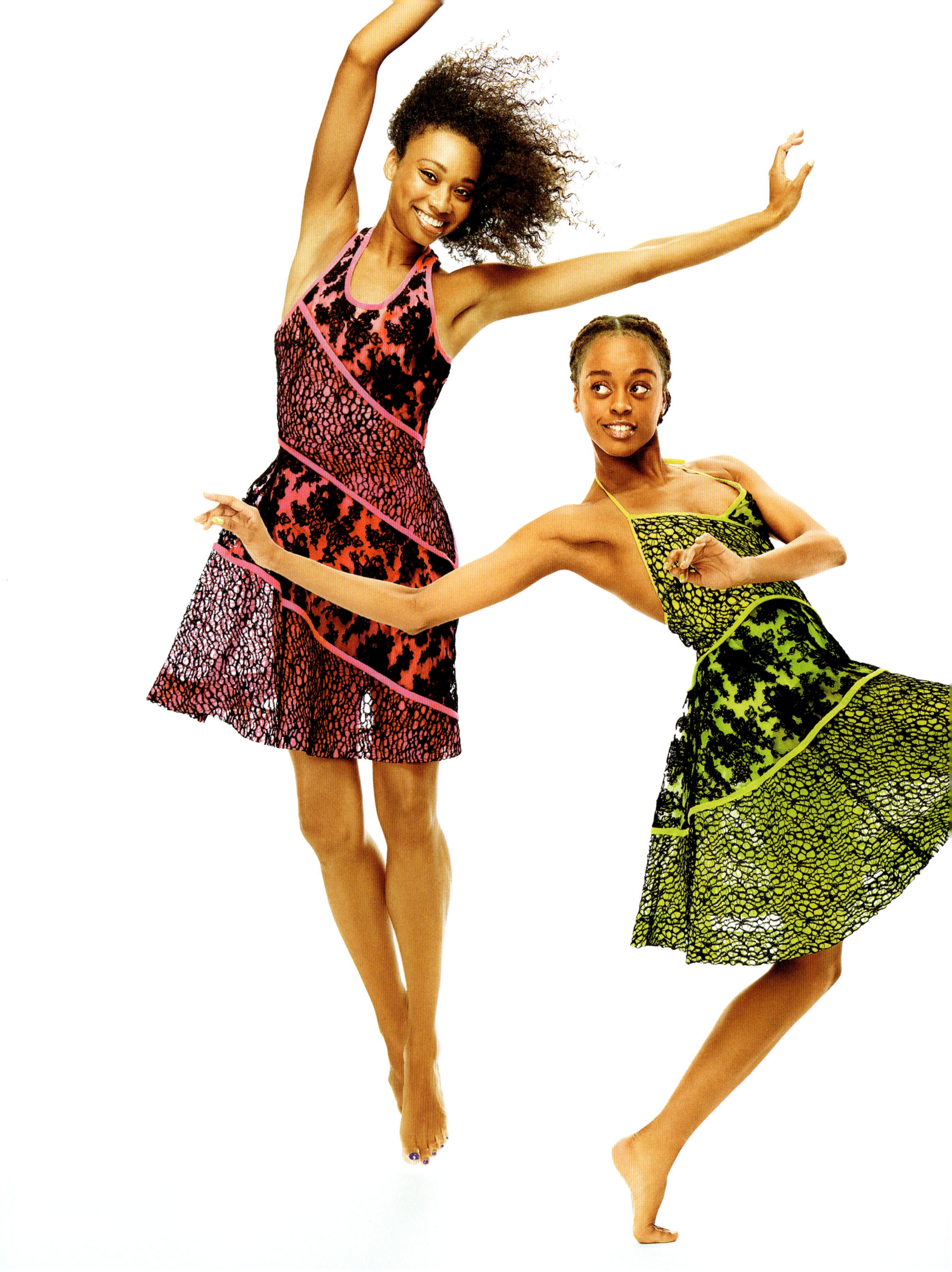

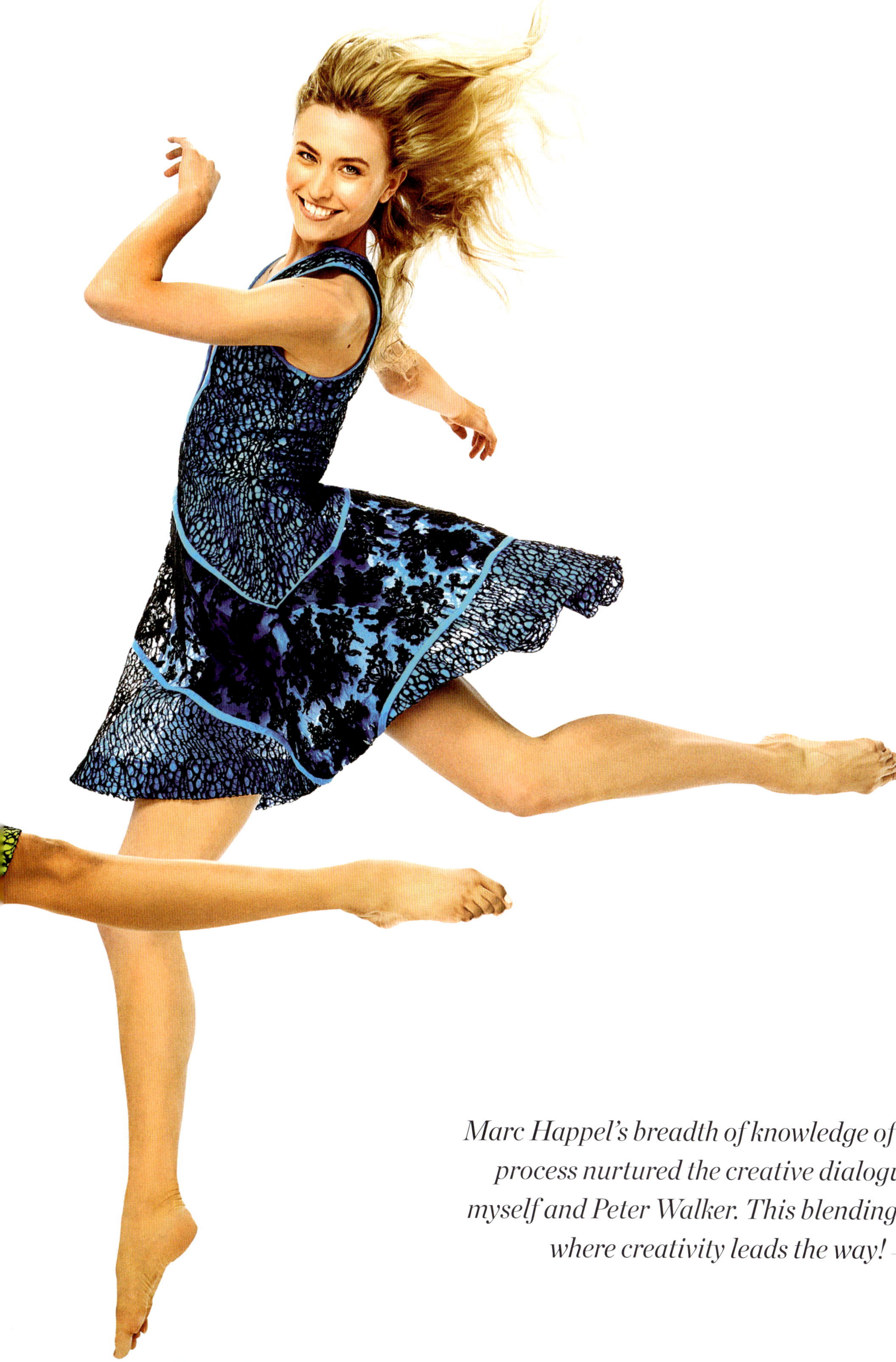

Marc Happel's breadth of knowledge of the design process nurtured the creative dialogue between myself and Peter Walker. This blending of ideas is where creativity leads the way! —JASON WU

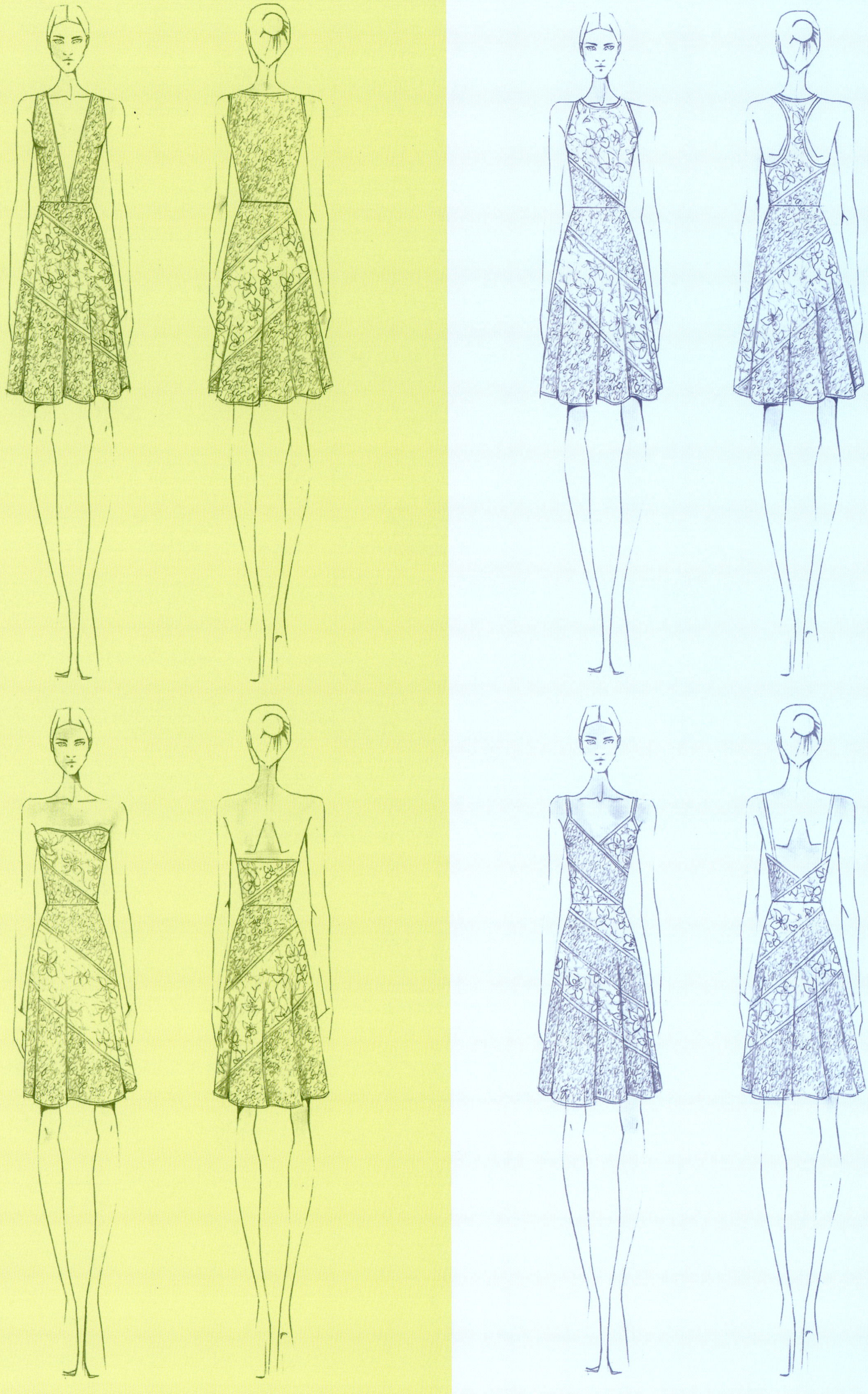

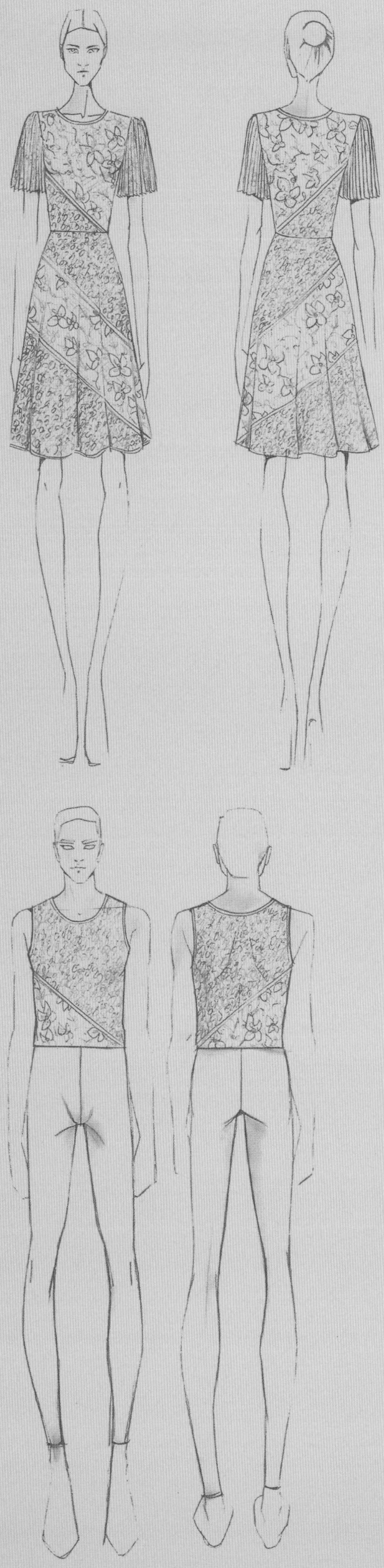

The cool thing about collaborations is you're able to work off of other people's ideas. Once Jason and I got the color scheme, it was so clear to me that this movement would be these colors and this movement would be these colors, and I think having those specific color swatches from the beginning took my choreography in a direction that I hadn't originally intended. —PETER WALKER, *Choreographer*

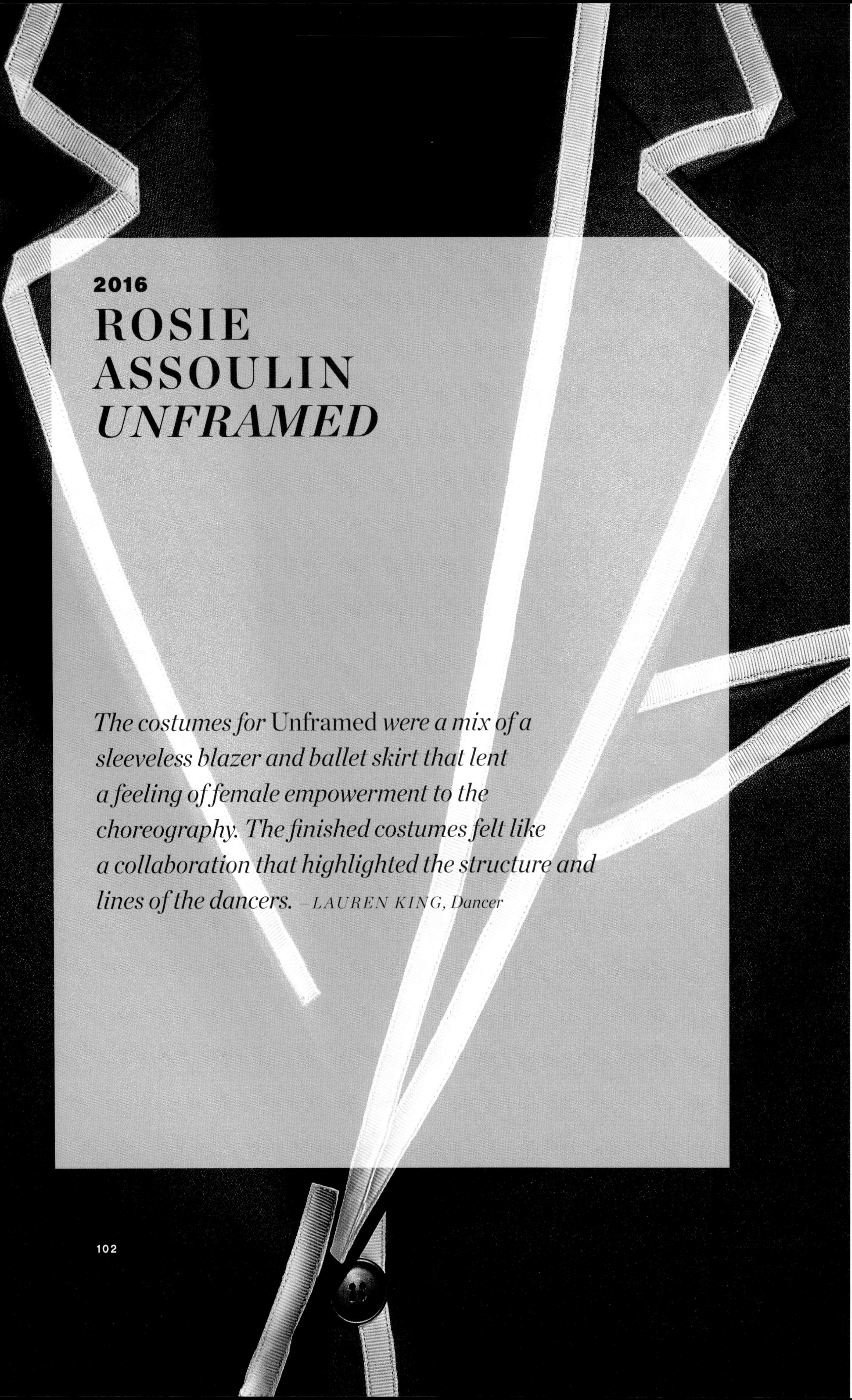

2016

ROSIE ASSOULIN *UNFRAMED*

The costumes for Unframed *were a mix of a sleeveless blazer and ballet skirt that lent a feeling of female empowerment to the choreography. The finished costumes felt like a collaboration that highlighted the structure and lines of the dancers.* —*LAUREN KING, Dancer*

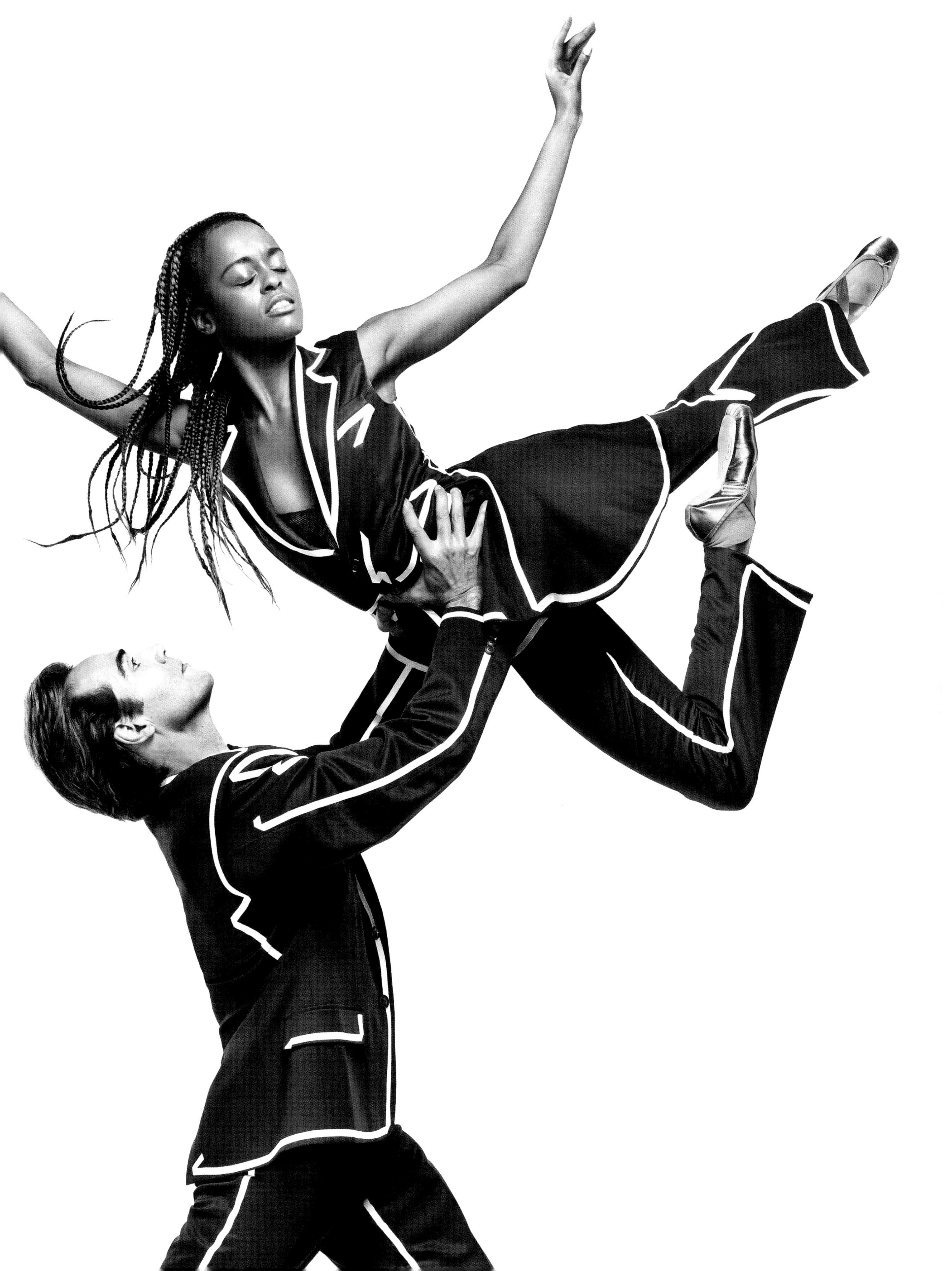

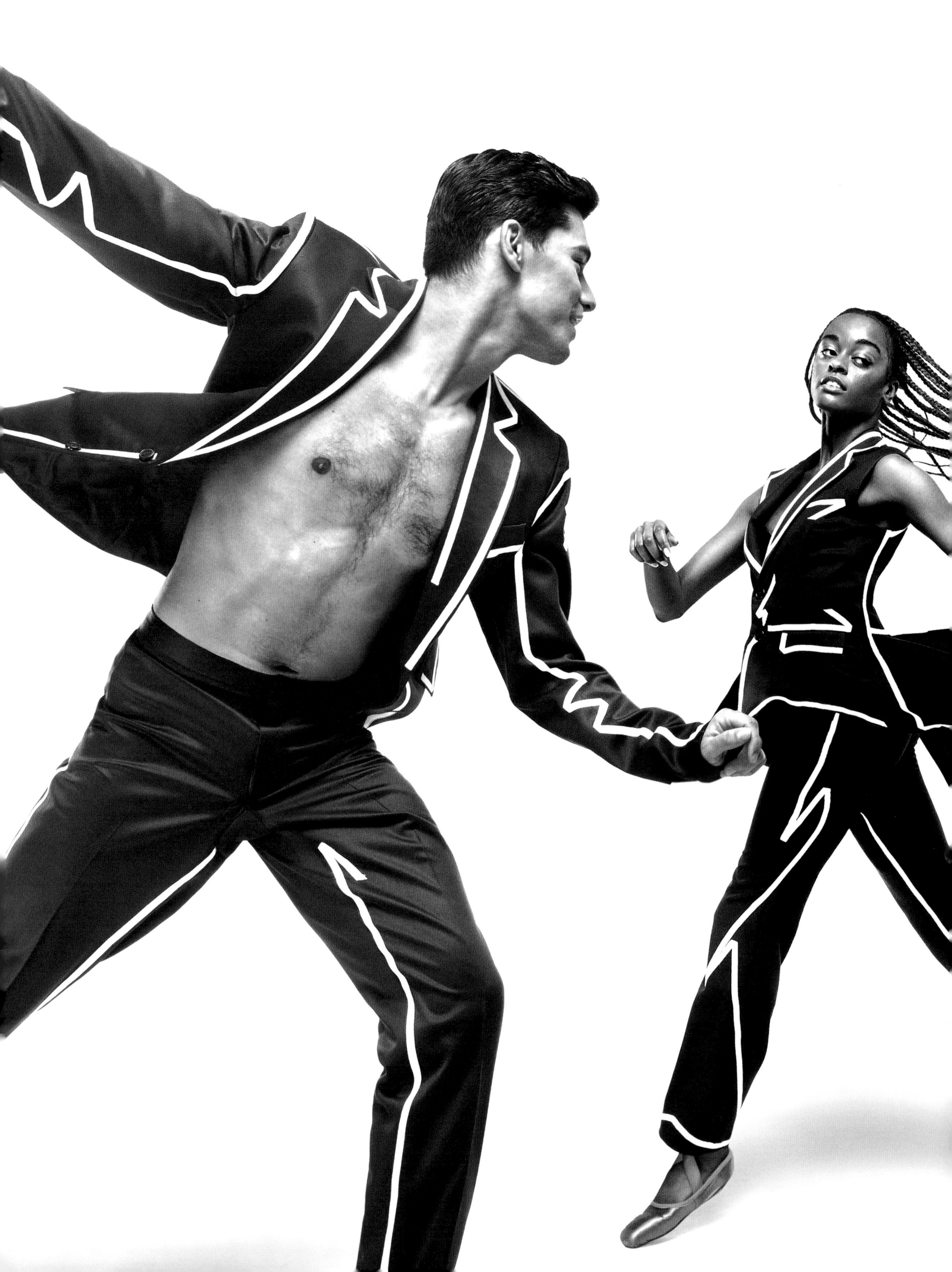

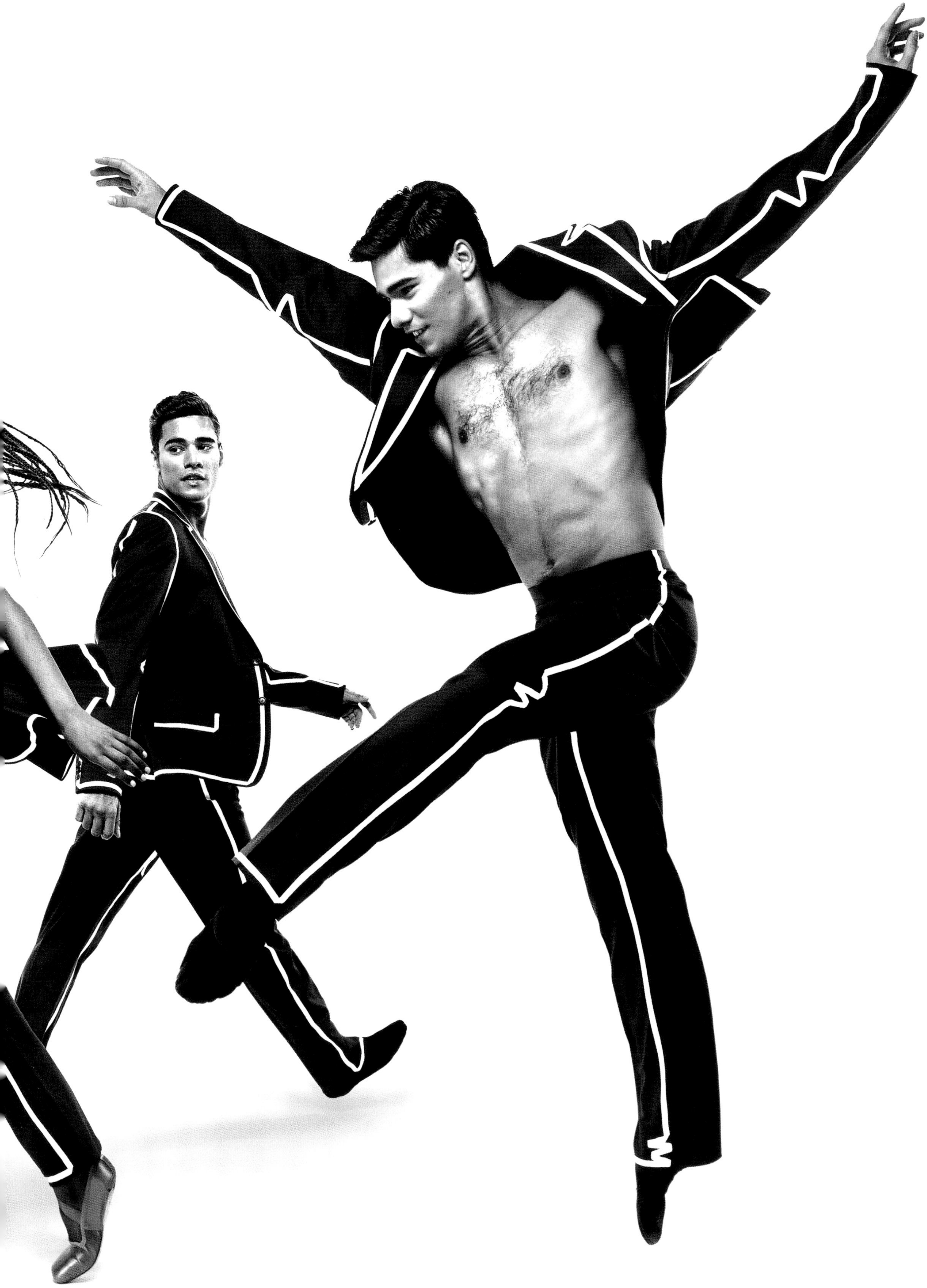

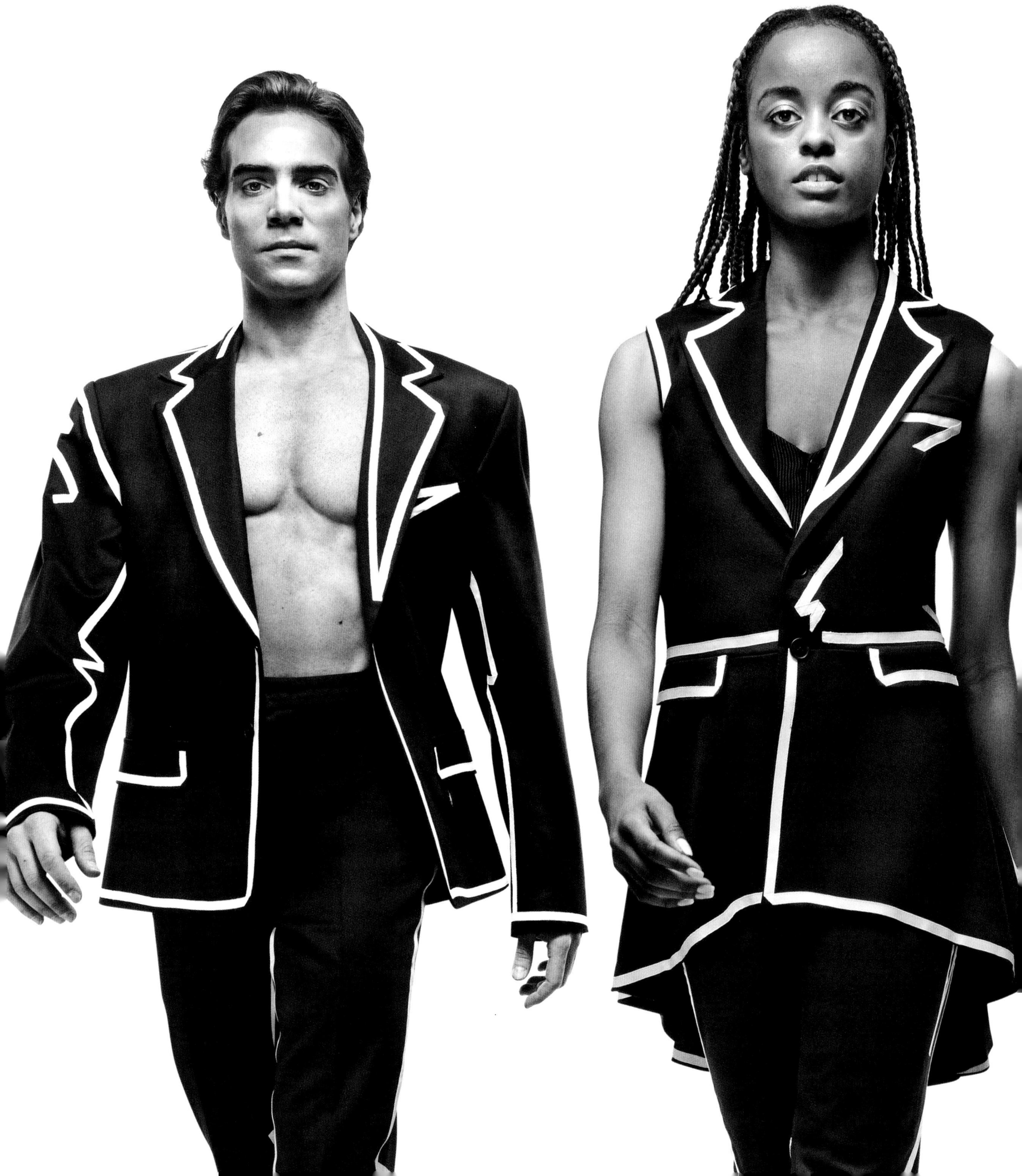

When thinking of fashion and dance, I can't help but see their similarities and discrepancies side by side. One of the discrepancies is that in fashion the garment expresses what the person wants to be. In dance, the body is the dancer's instrument of expression. Therefore dressing a dancer's body sometimes hides their most vulnerable emotions. So I came up with a concept that would undress the dancers as the dance evolved. The armor of the garments got shed and the bodies of the performers were revealed to their purest form. The musculature of the dancers created new energies and revealed hidden emotions. By the end of the piece, the female dancers wore their hair down to express the escape of the rigid ballet bun, and the dance was finally unframed and free on all fronts.

—ANNABELLE LOPEZ OCHOA, Choreographer

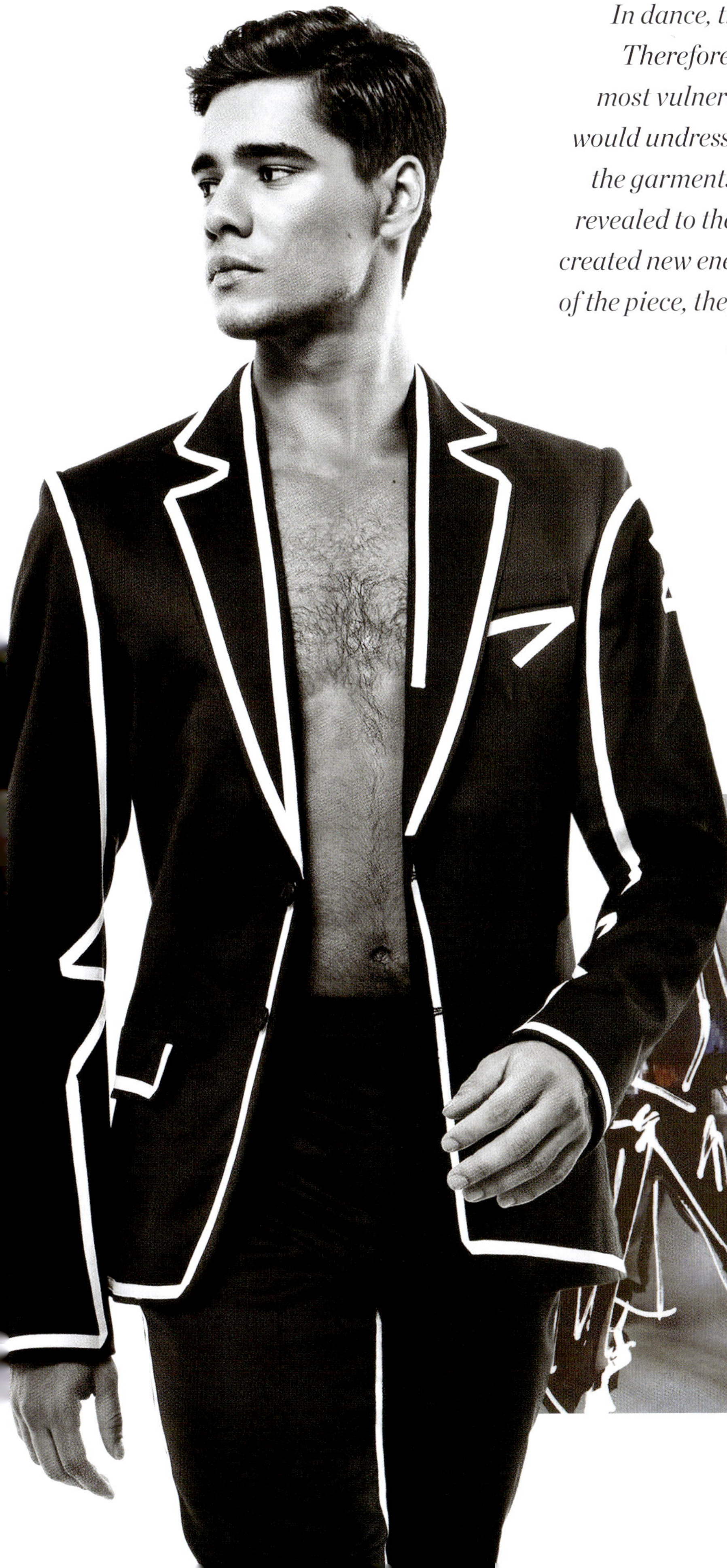

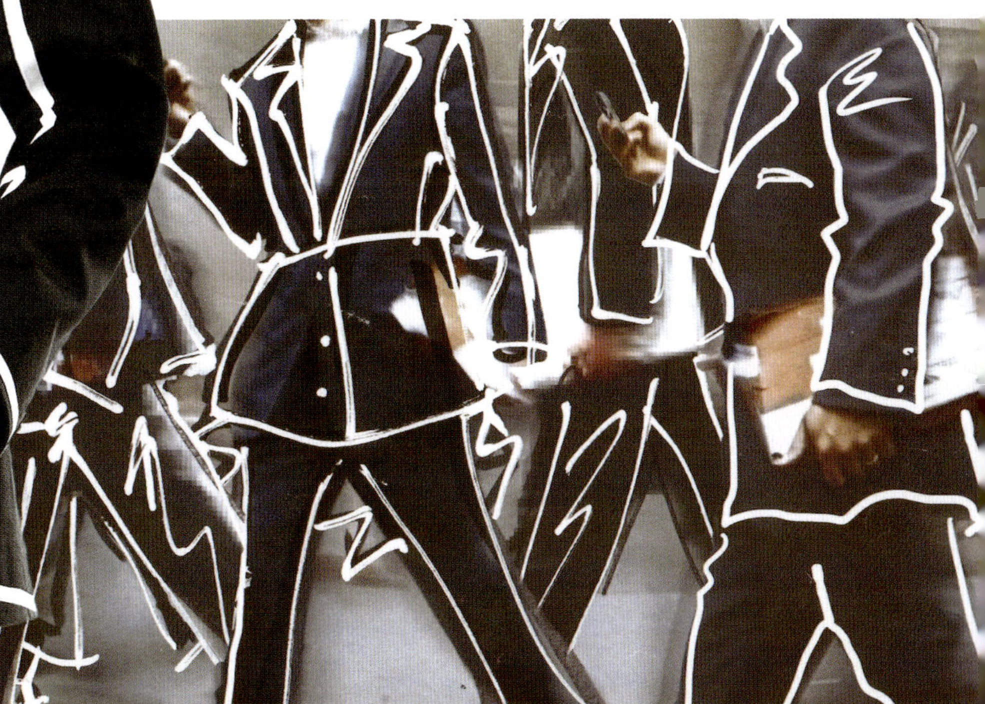

2016

NARCISO RODRIGUEZ *FOR CLARA*

My goal was to trace the dancers' movements while keeping the attention on the original piece Lauren Lovette had created for her passionate choreographic debut.

—NARCISO RODRIGUEZ

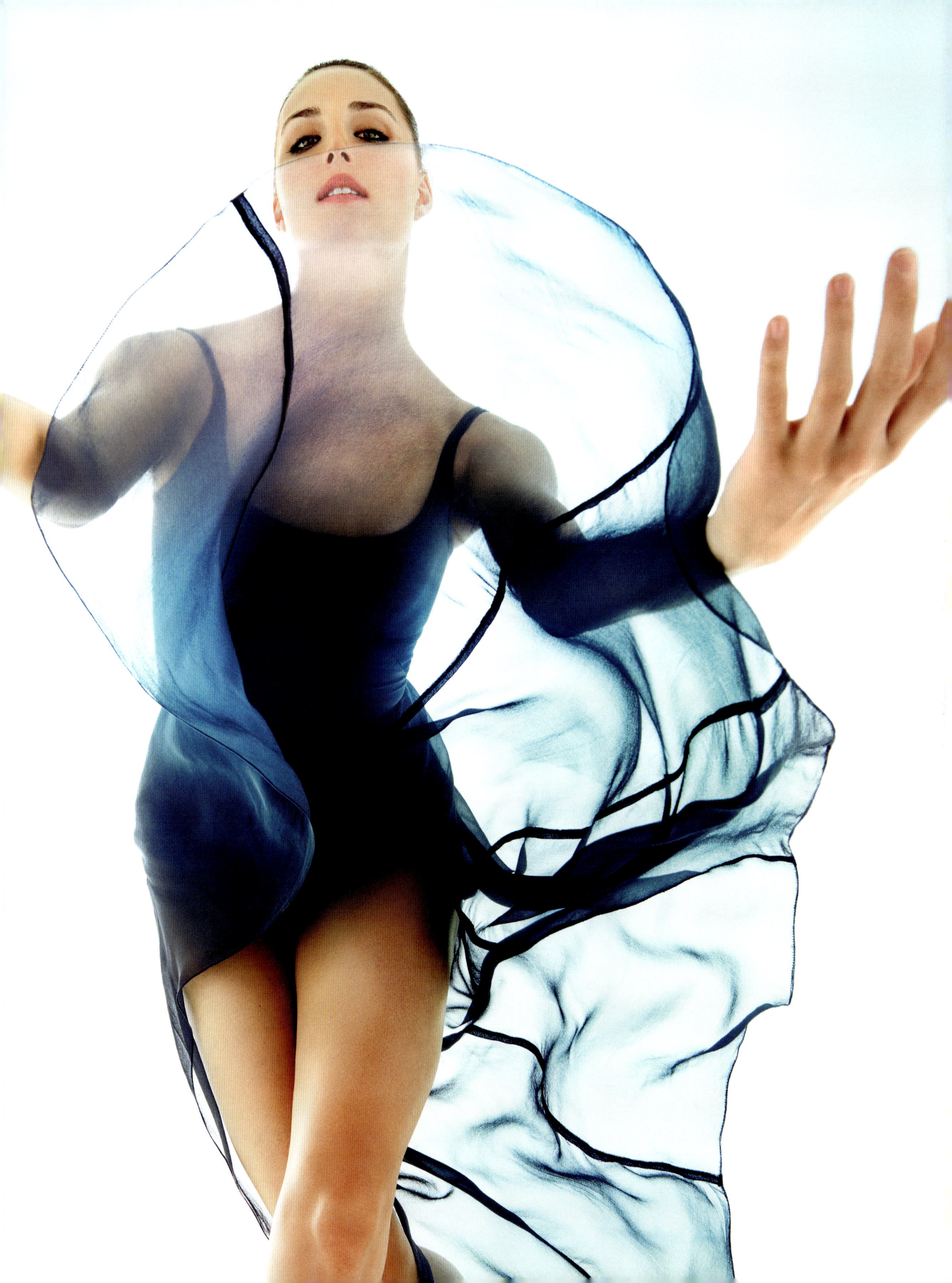

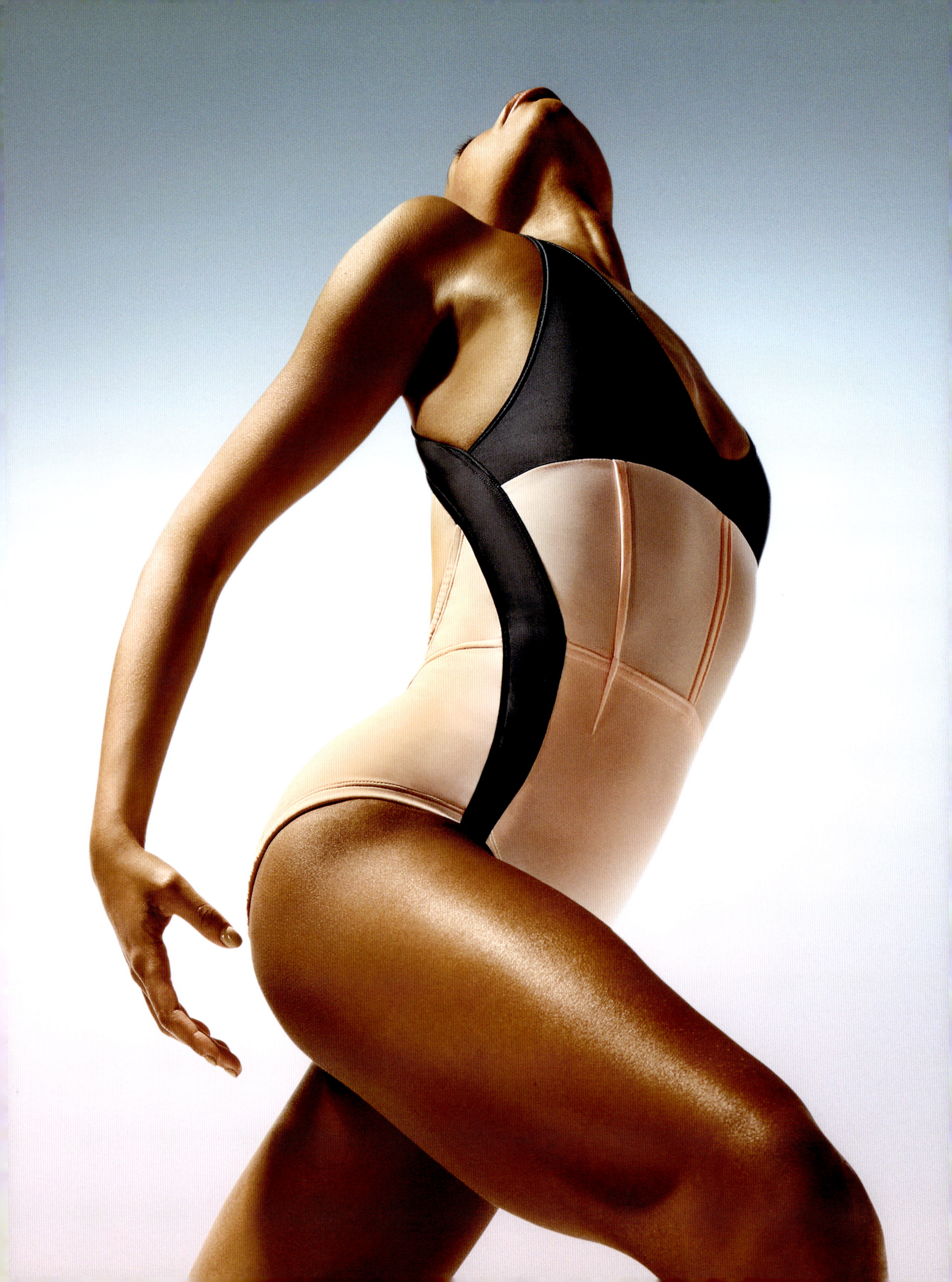

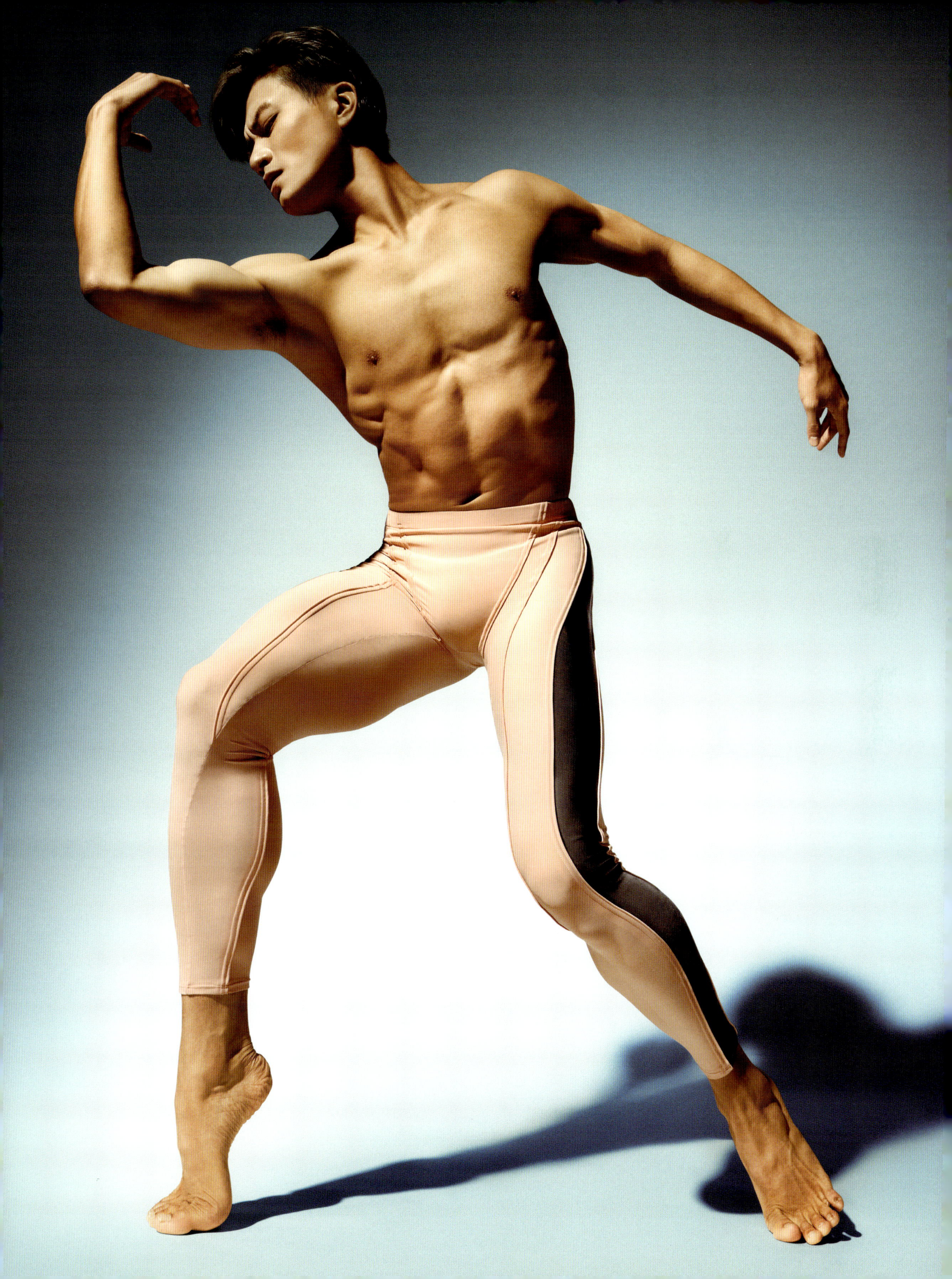

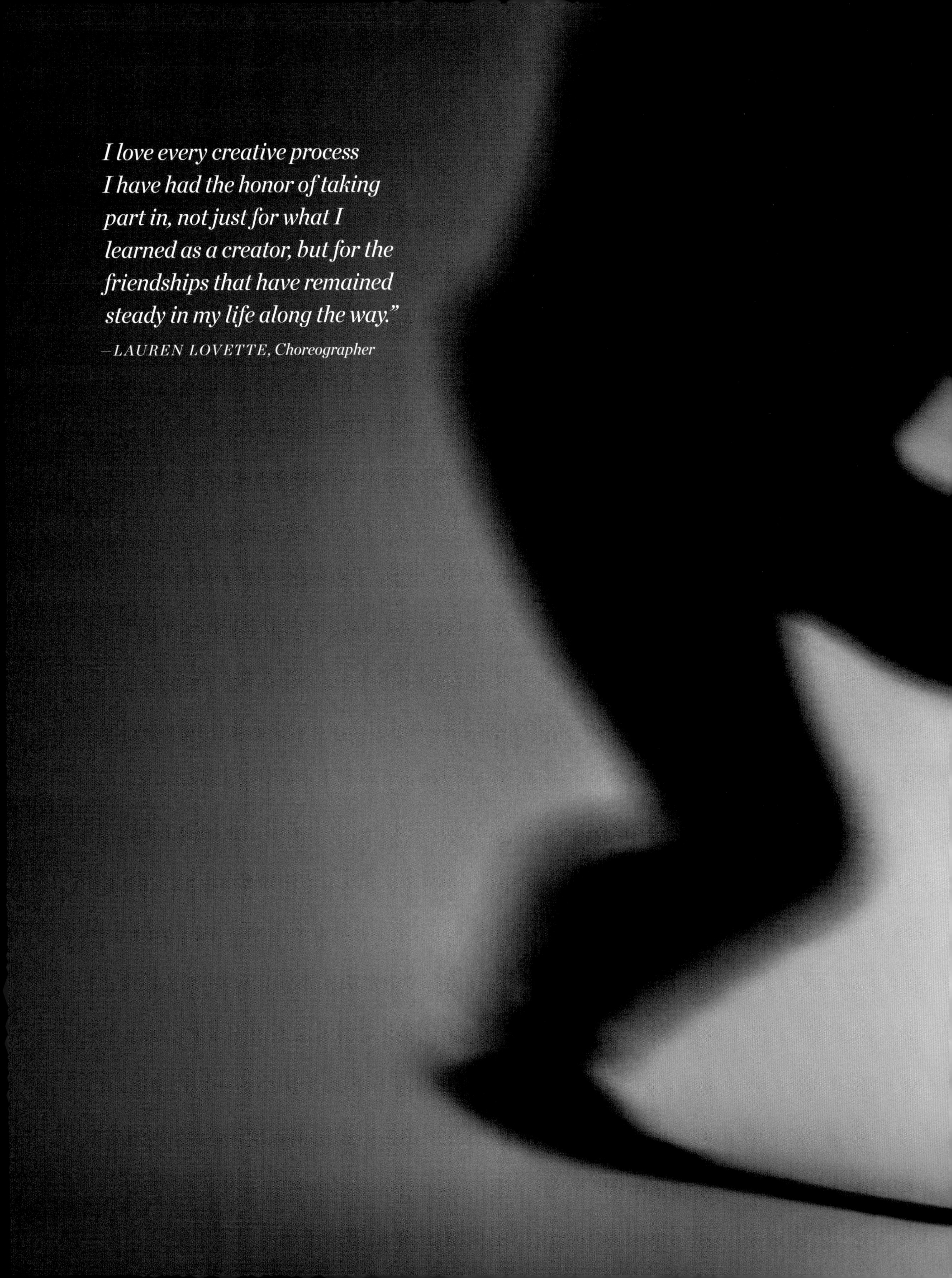

I love every creative process I have had the honor of taking part in, not just for what I learned as a creator, but for the friendships that have remained steady in my life along the way."

—*LAUREN LOVETTE, Choreographer*

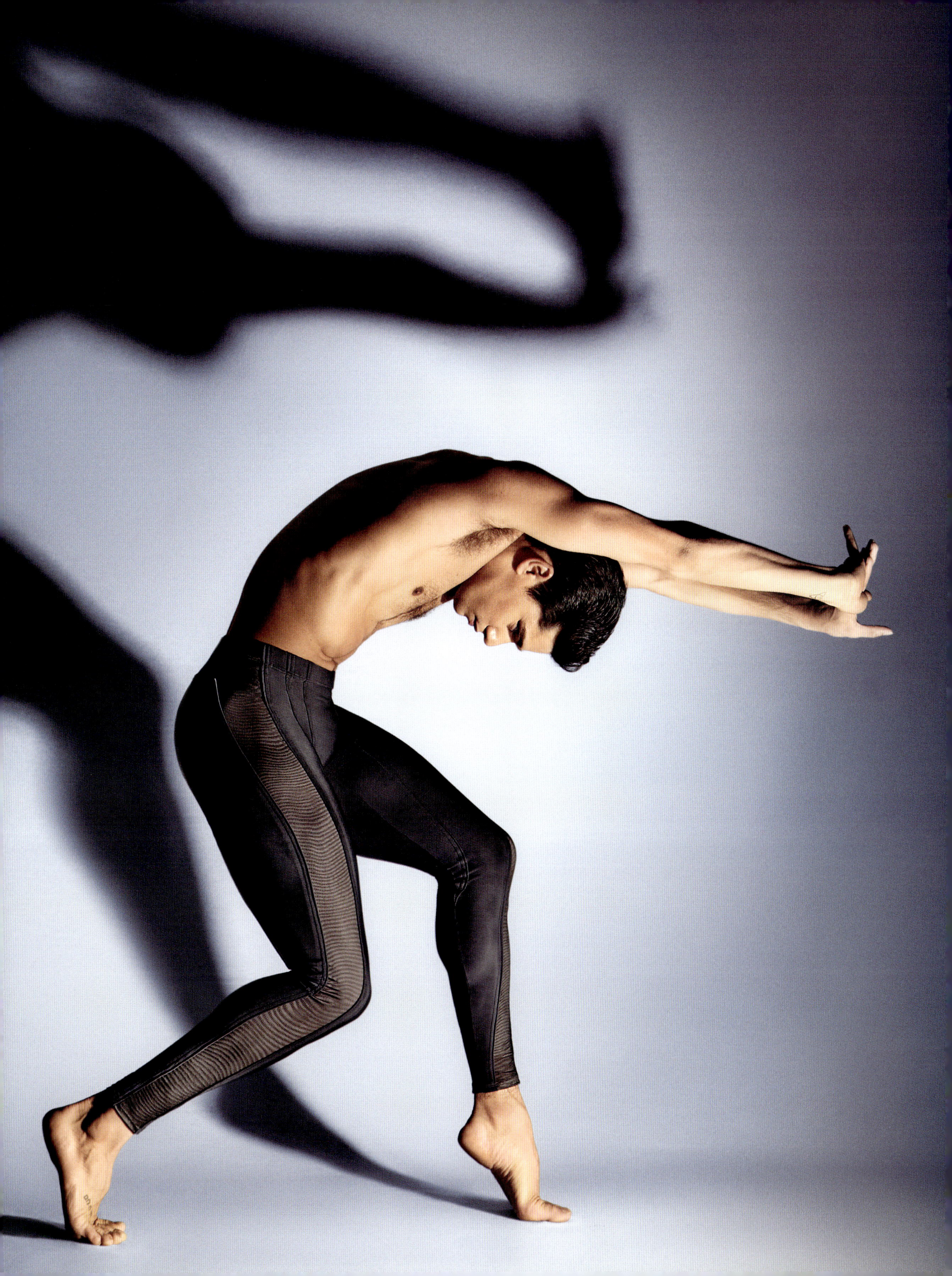

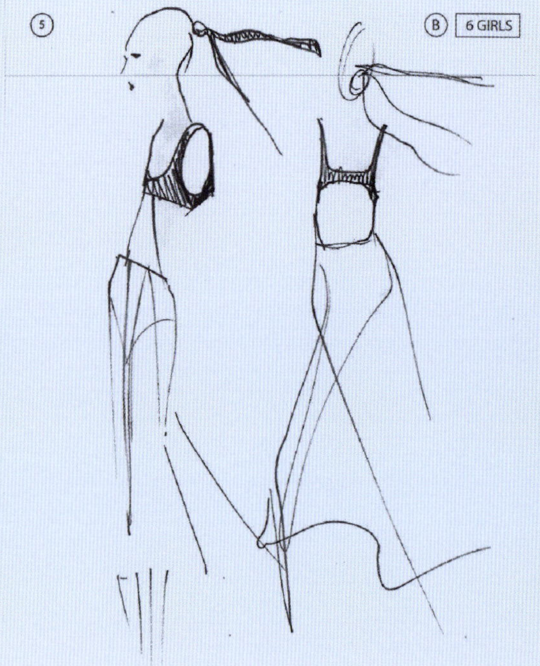
5
B
6 GIRLS

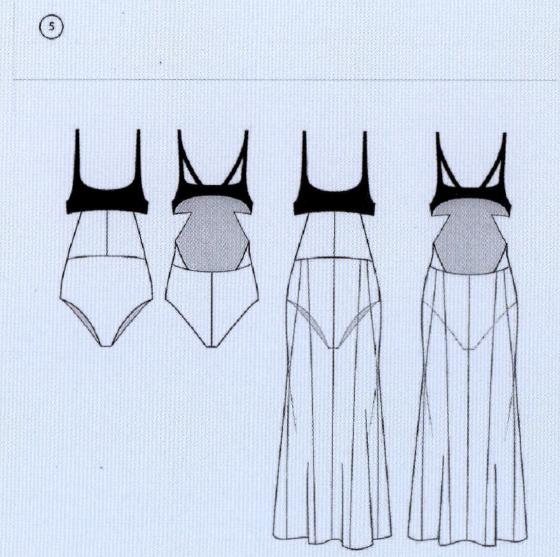
5

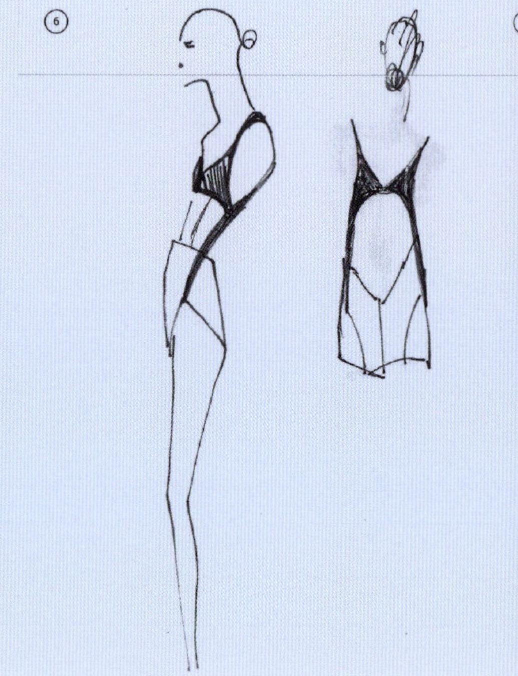
6
A

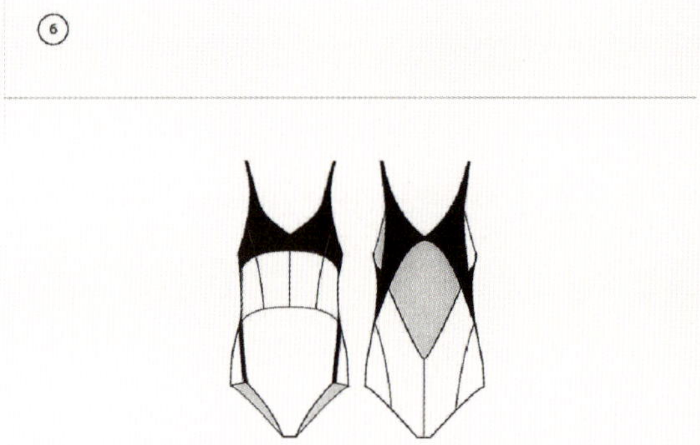
6

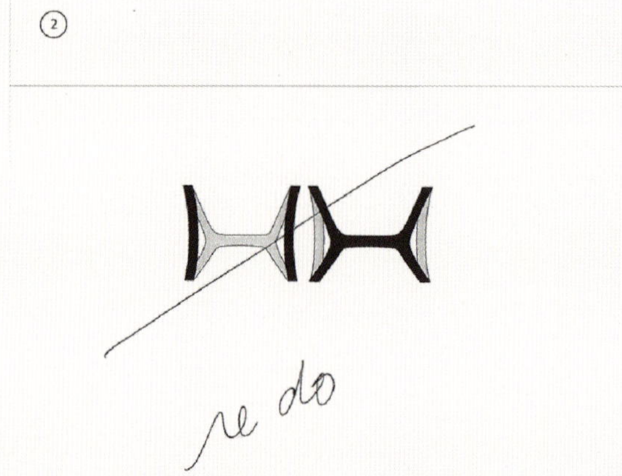
2
re do

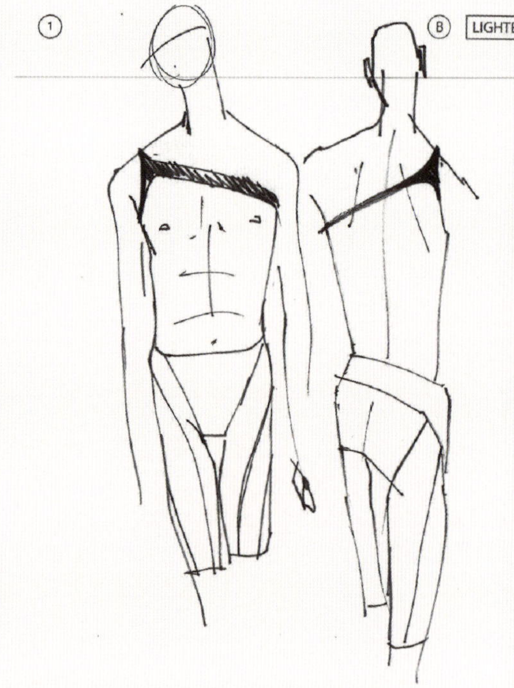
1
B
LIGHTER

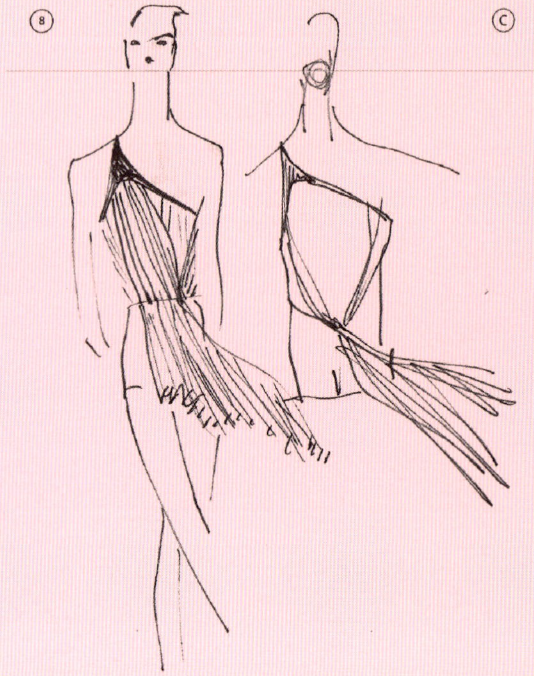
8
C

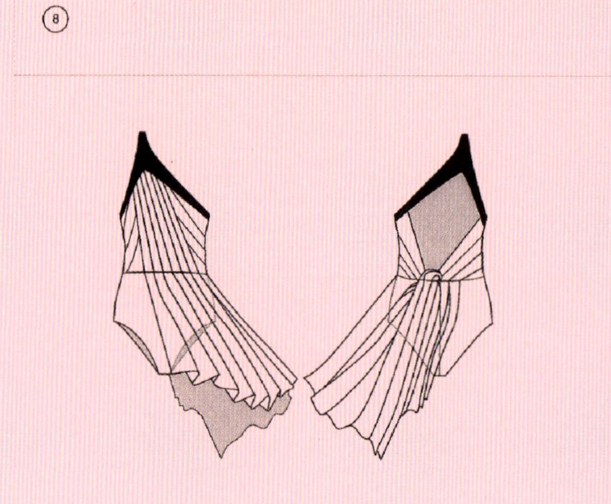
8

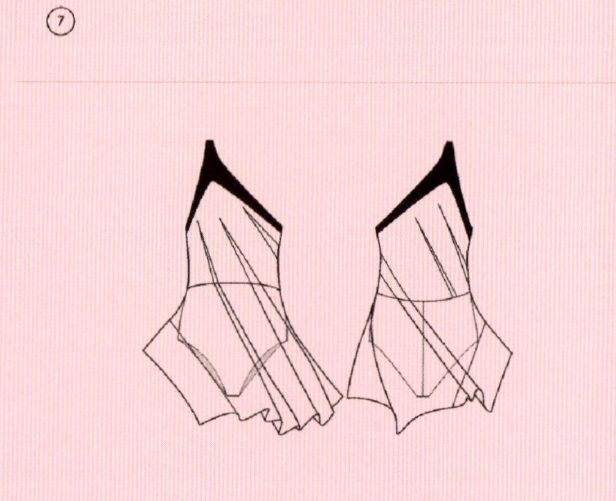
7

①

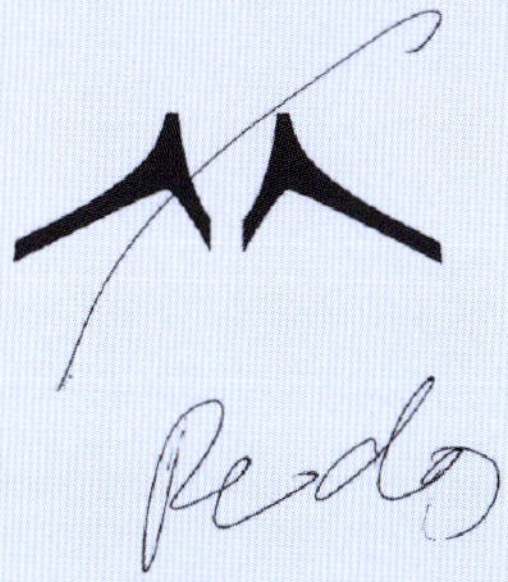

②

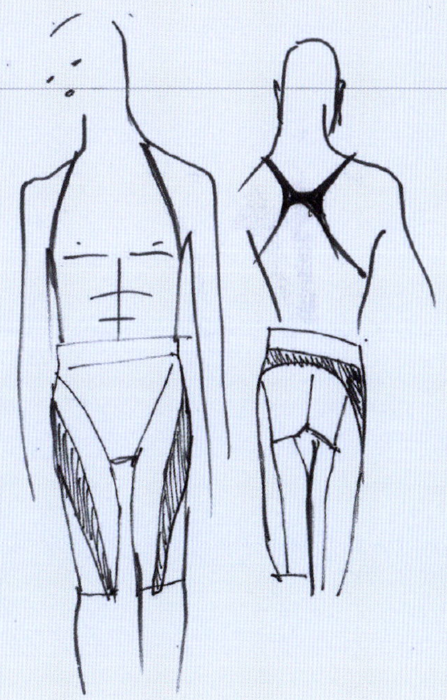

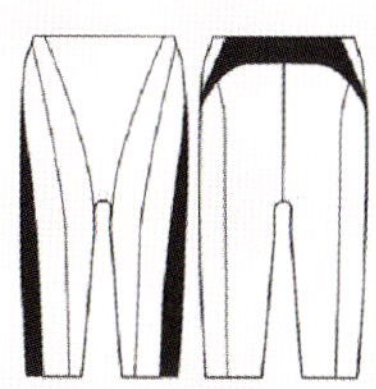

③ Ⓐ

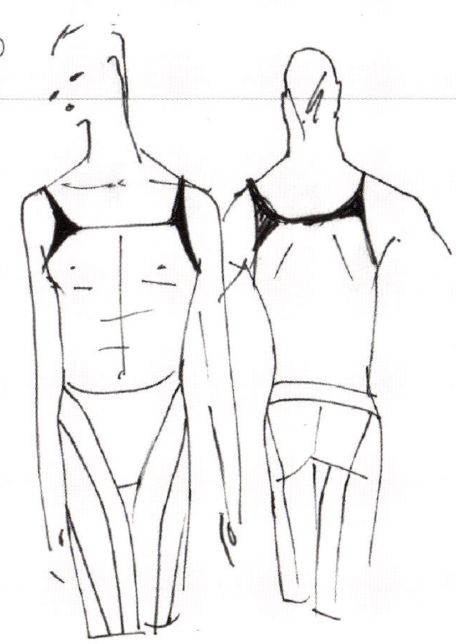

Part of what is exciting about the annual collaborations with fashion designers is the transgression and exploration, the flaunting of the traditions and dictums of ballet.

—RUSSELL JANZEN, *Dancer*

④

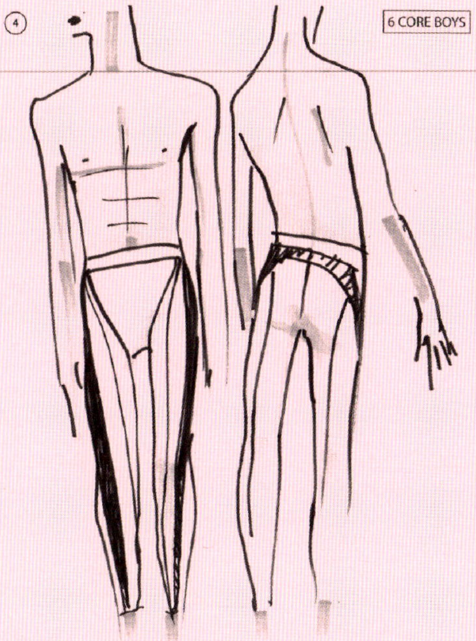

④

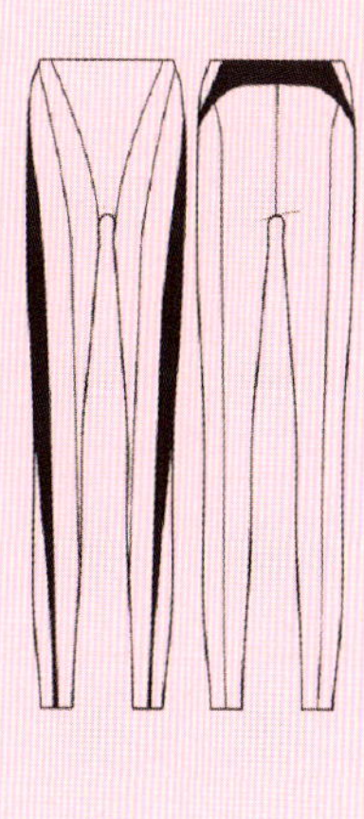

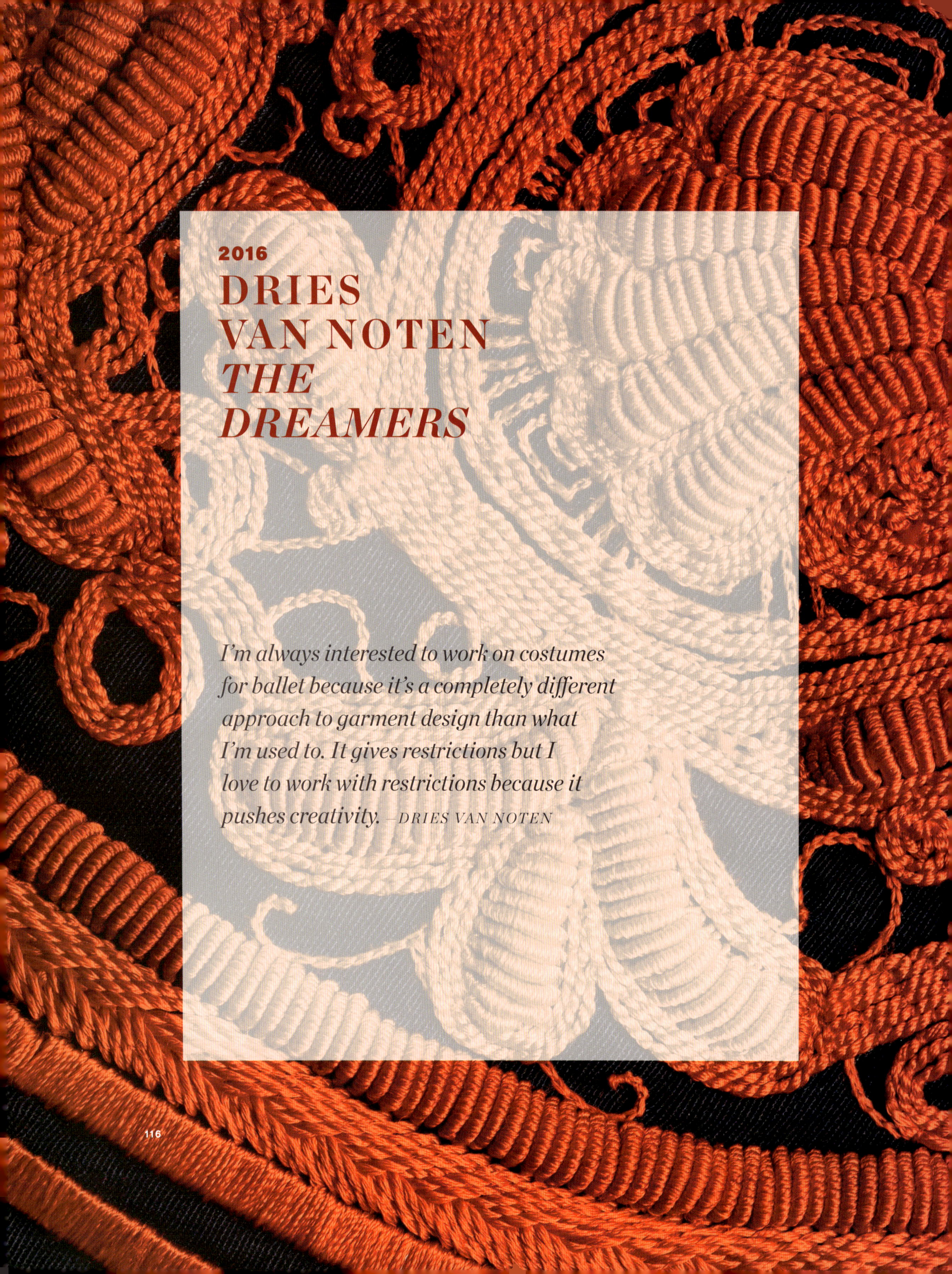

2016

DRIES VAN NOTEN *THE DREAMERS*

I'm always interested to work on costumes for ballet because it's a completely different approach to garment design than what I'm used to. It gives restrictions but I love to work with restrictions because it pushes creativity. —DRIES VAN NOTEN

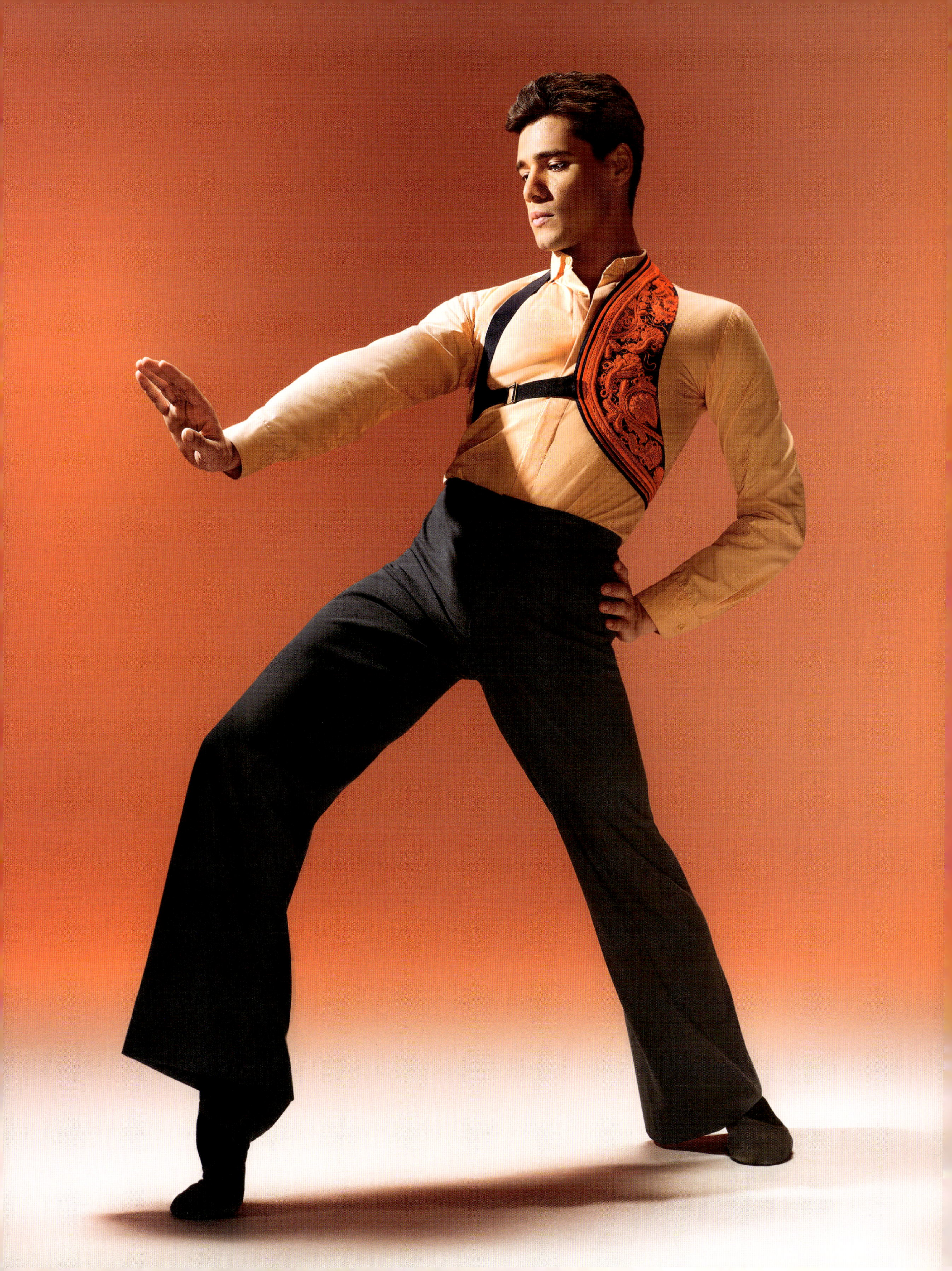

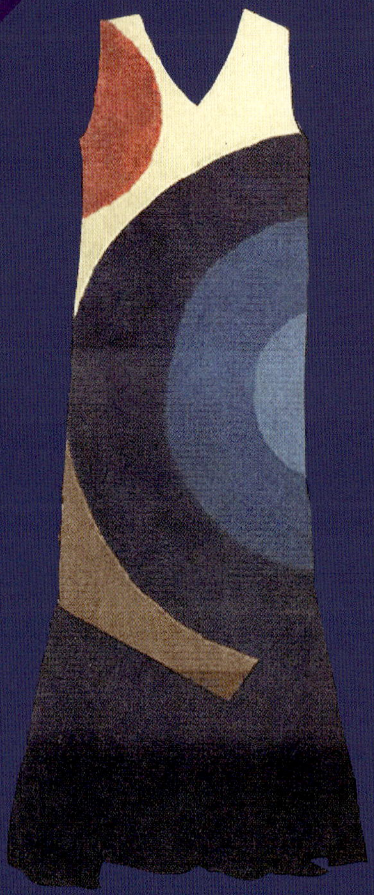

We talked a lot about art. Rothko was a major point of reference because of his use of color and the meditative feeling that comes from his abstract work.

—*JUSTIN PECK, Choreographer*

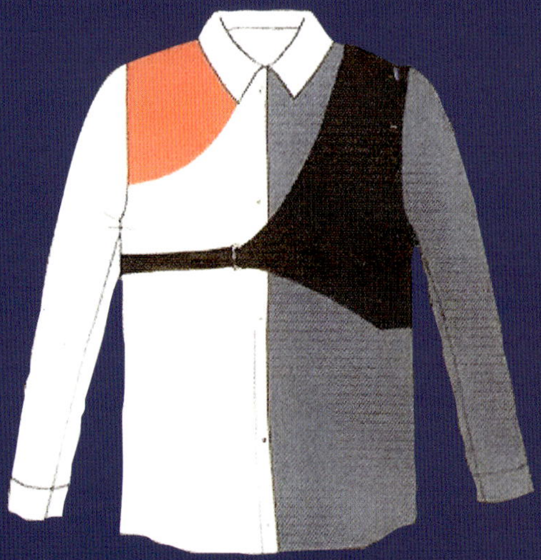

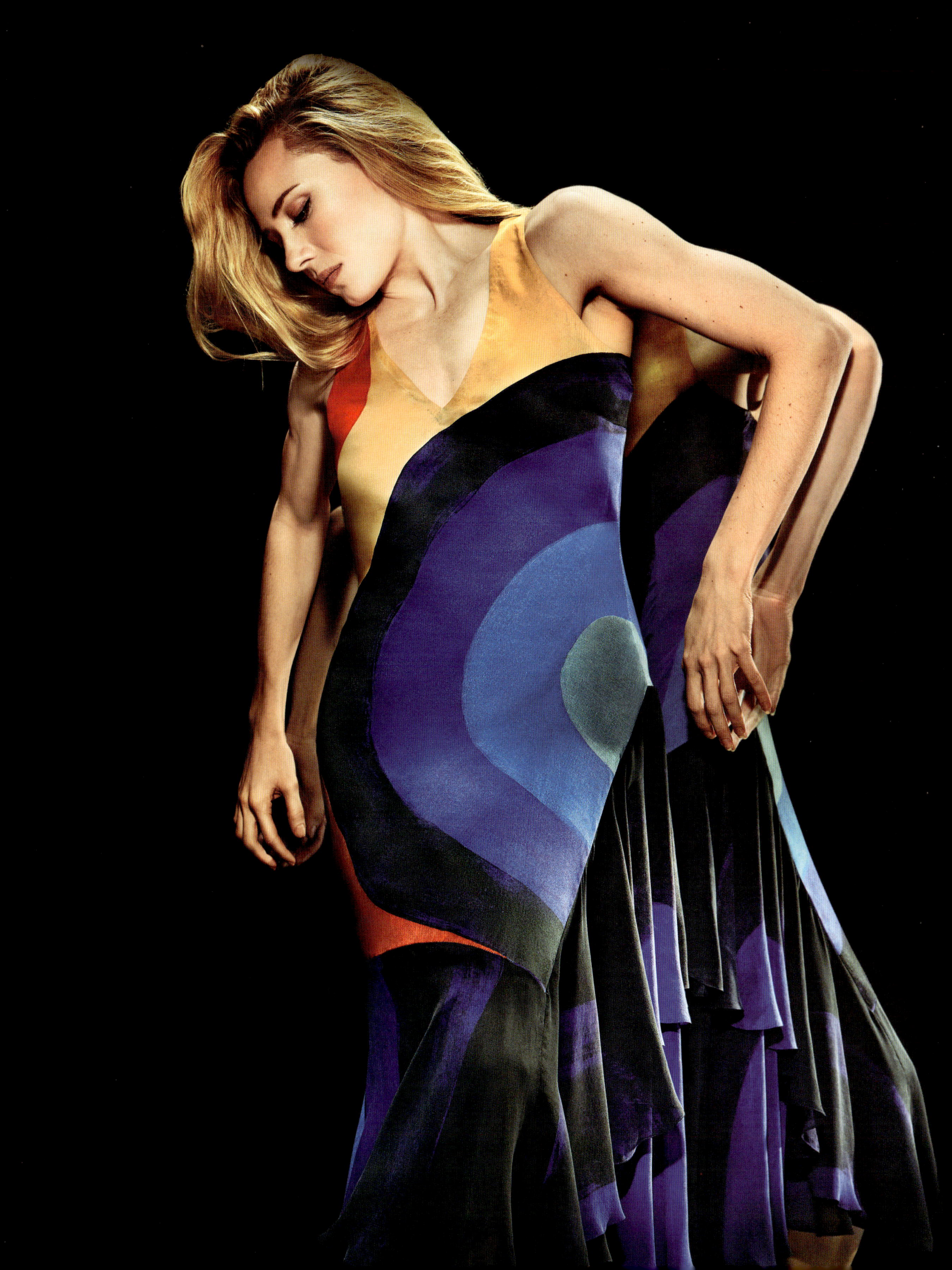

2017

JONATHAN SAUNDERS

THE WIND STILL BRINGS

My most important consideration was movement. It is, after all, the essence of what dance is about. Cutting fabric on the bias gave the designs fluidity and a sense of ease. Wrap skirts could move freely in a sensual way. Overall, the graphic simplicity brought focus to, not distraction from, the dancer.

Color and graphic pattern are tools that I have always used in my work. I was imagining the combination of cold and warm tones, the clash of cold blues with warm caramel. Contrasting elements—earth and water. I then broke this down into a simplistic and bold stripe, and used it together as color blocked tones to create the final designs. —JONATHAN SAUNDERS

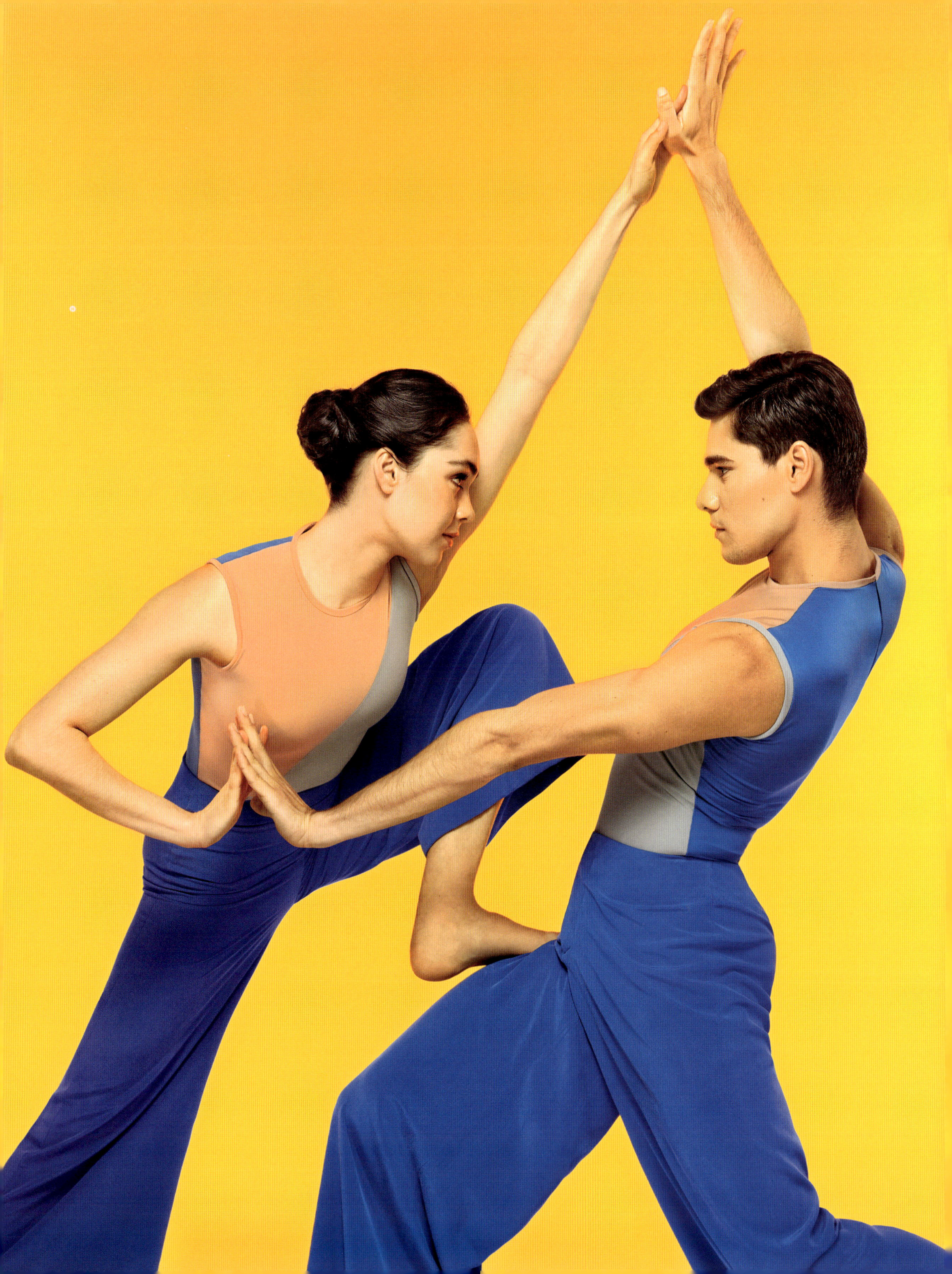

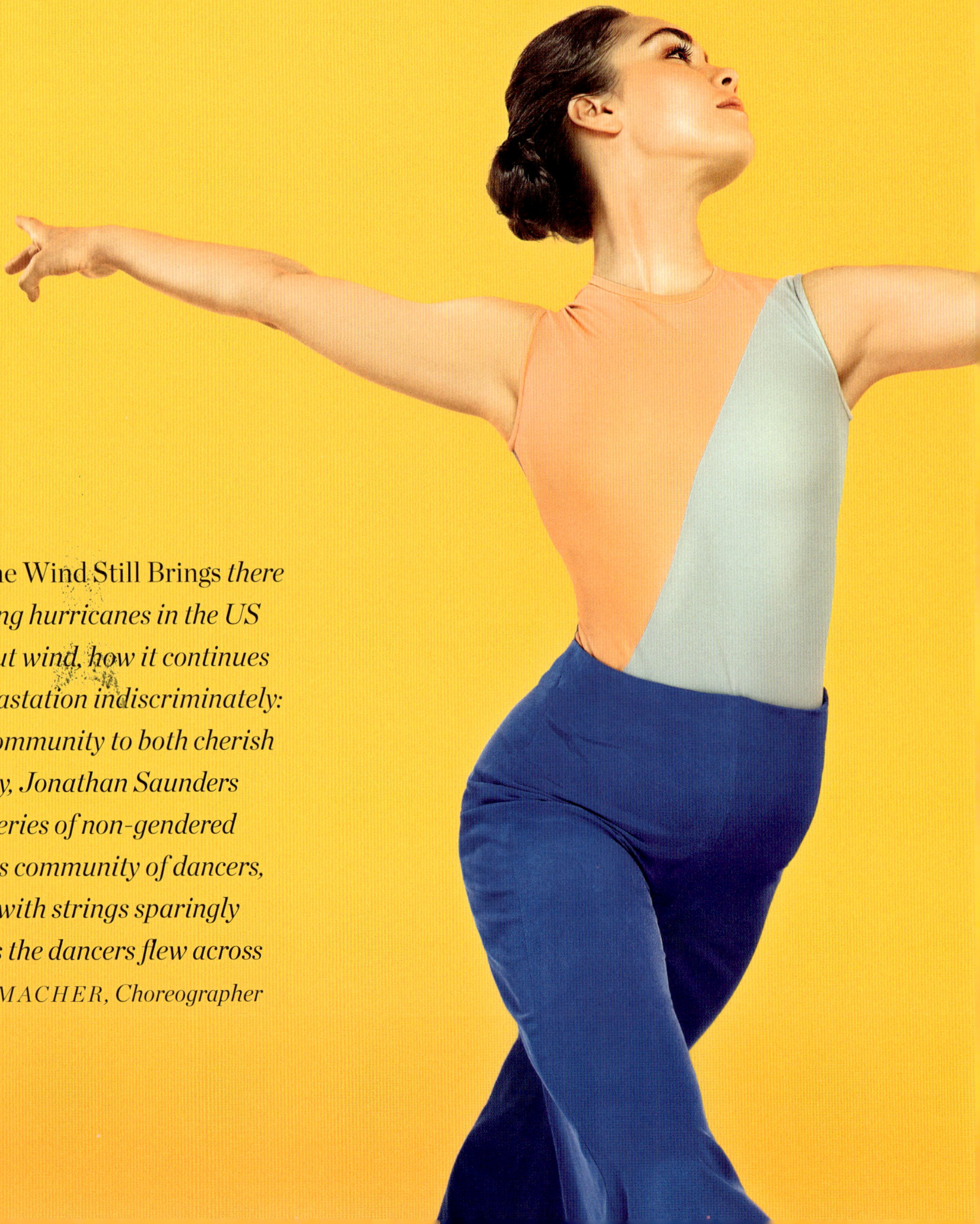

During the creation of The Wind Still Brings *there were a series of devastating hurricanes in the US that got me thinking about wind, how it continues to bring both life and devastation indiscriminately: two things that require community to both cherish and rebuild. Conceptually, Jonathan Saunders and I set out to create a series of non-gendered costumes that formed this community of dancers, featuring blues and tans with strings sparingly attached that fluttered as the dancers flew across the stage.* —TROY SCHUMACHER, *Choreographer*

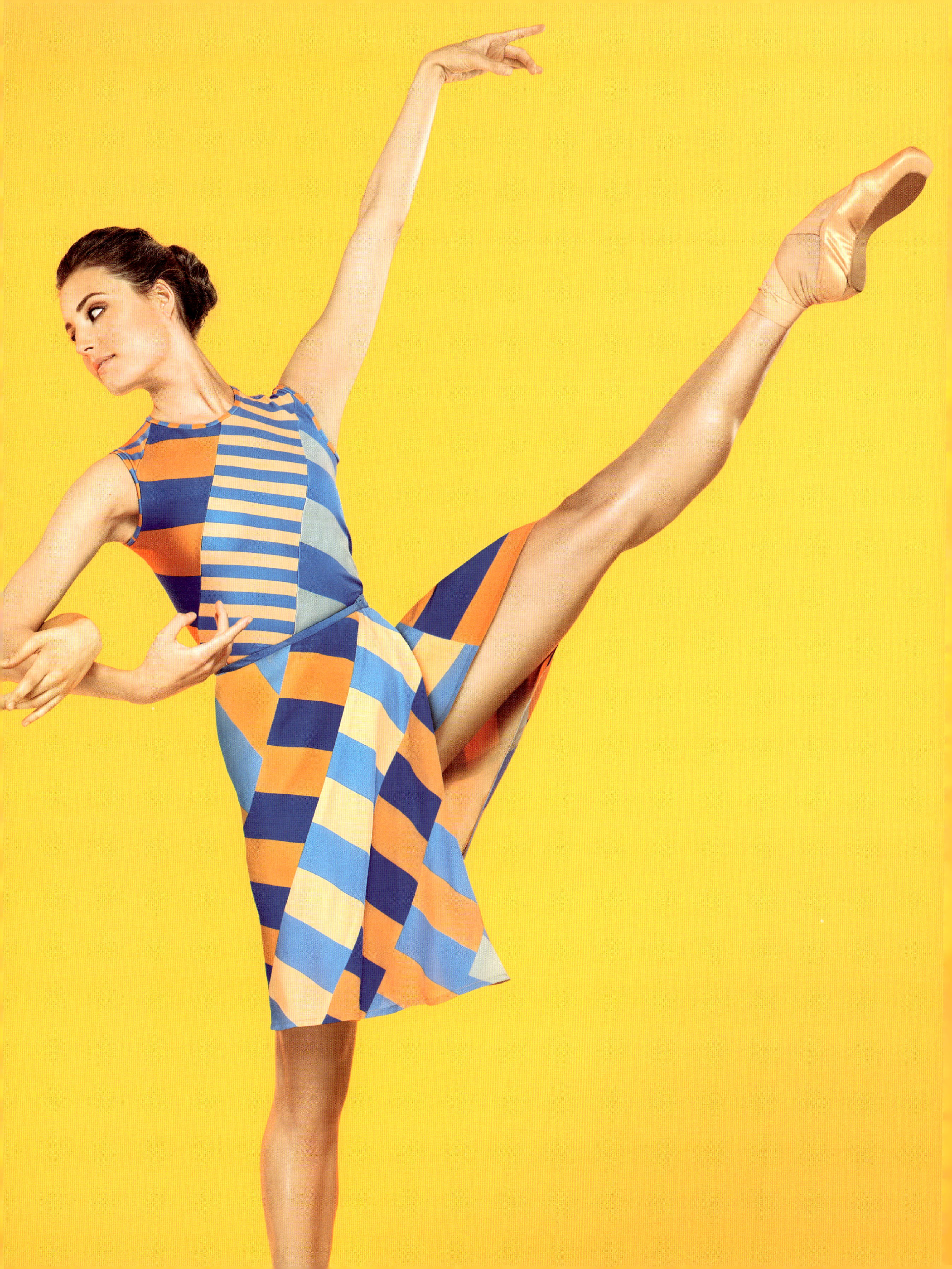

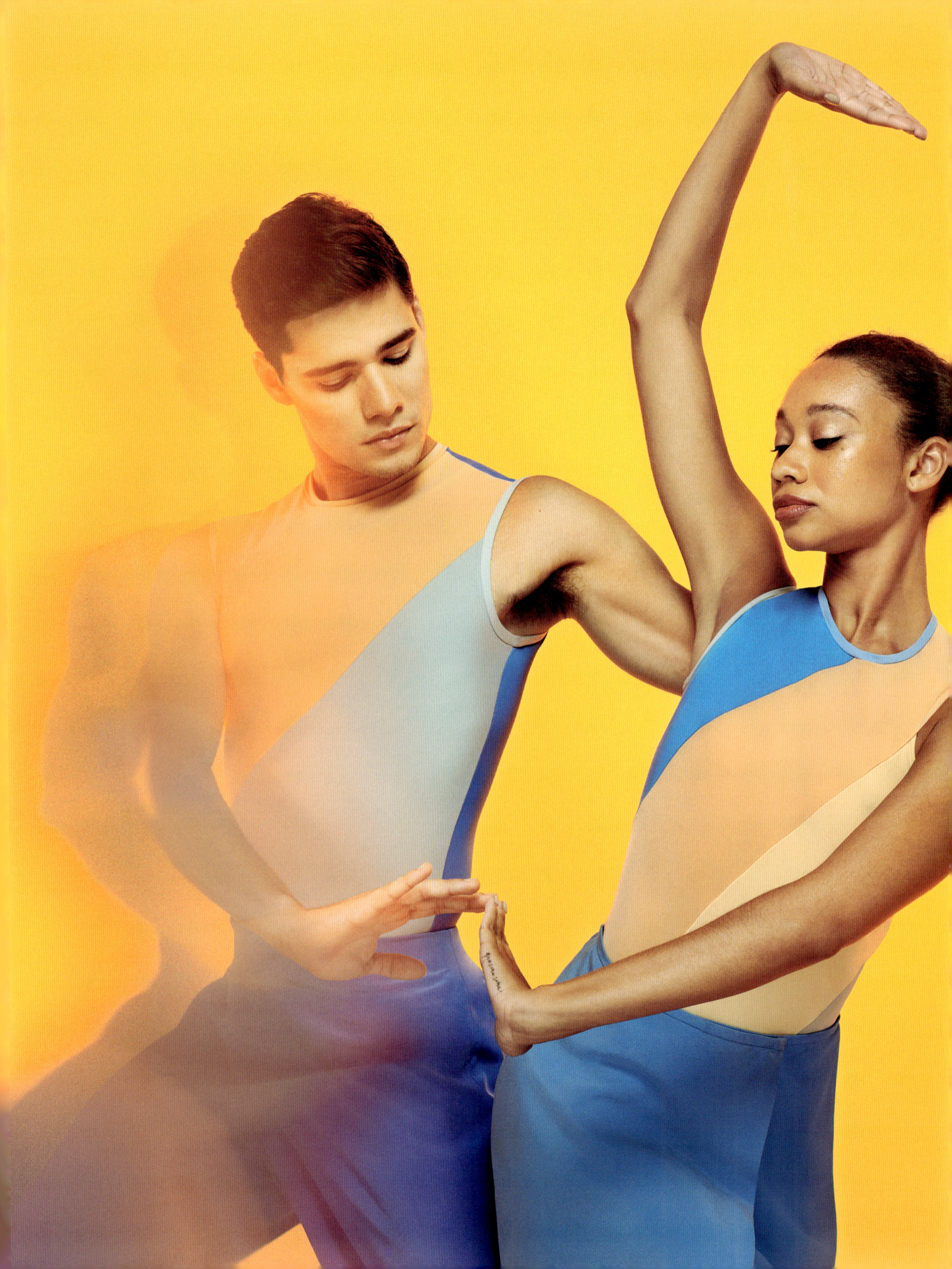

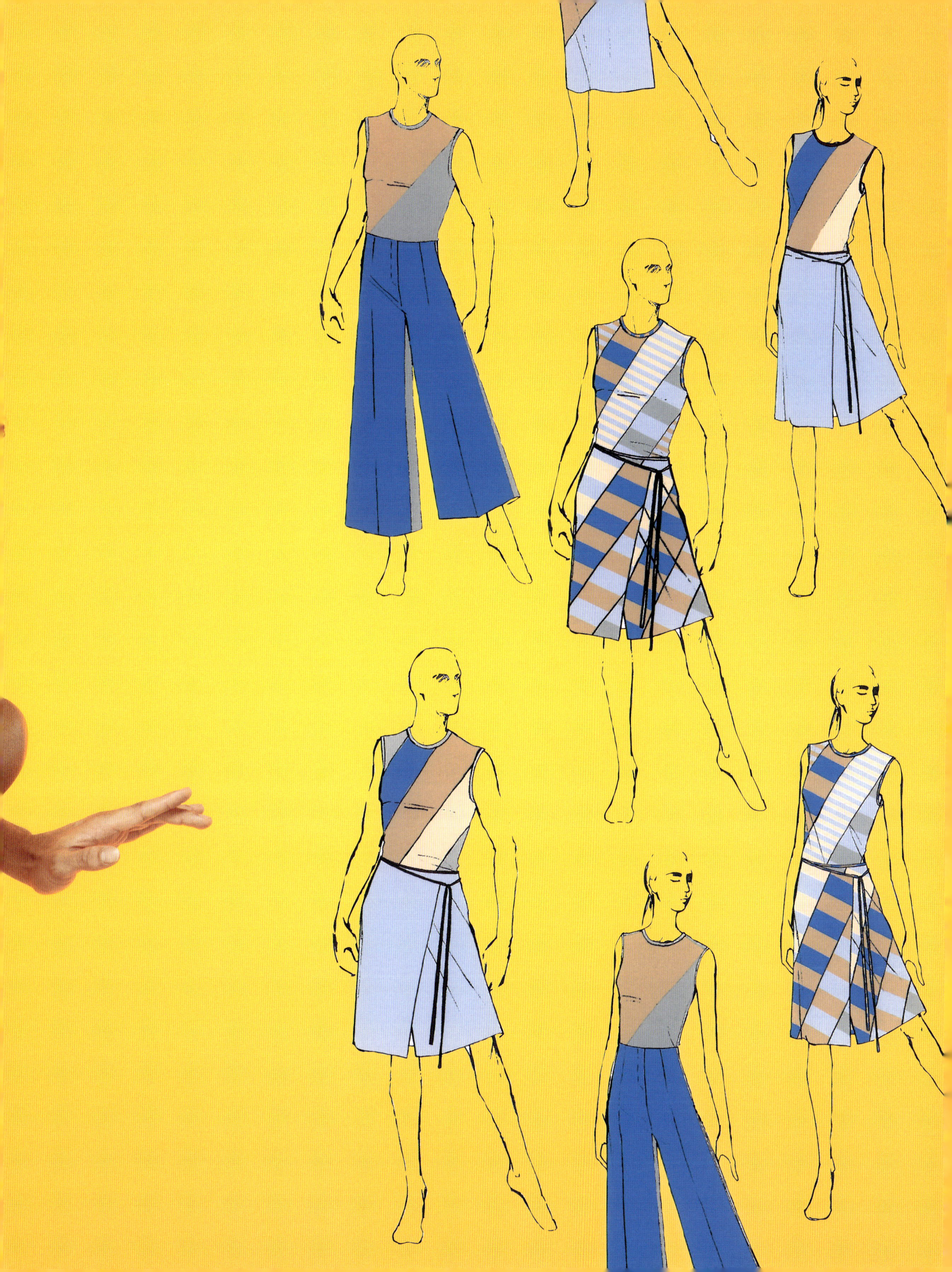

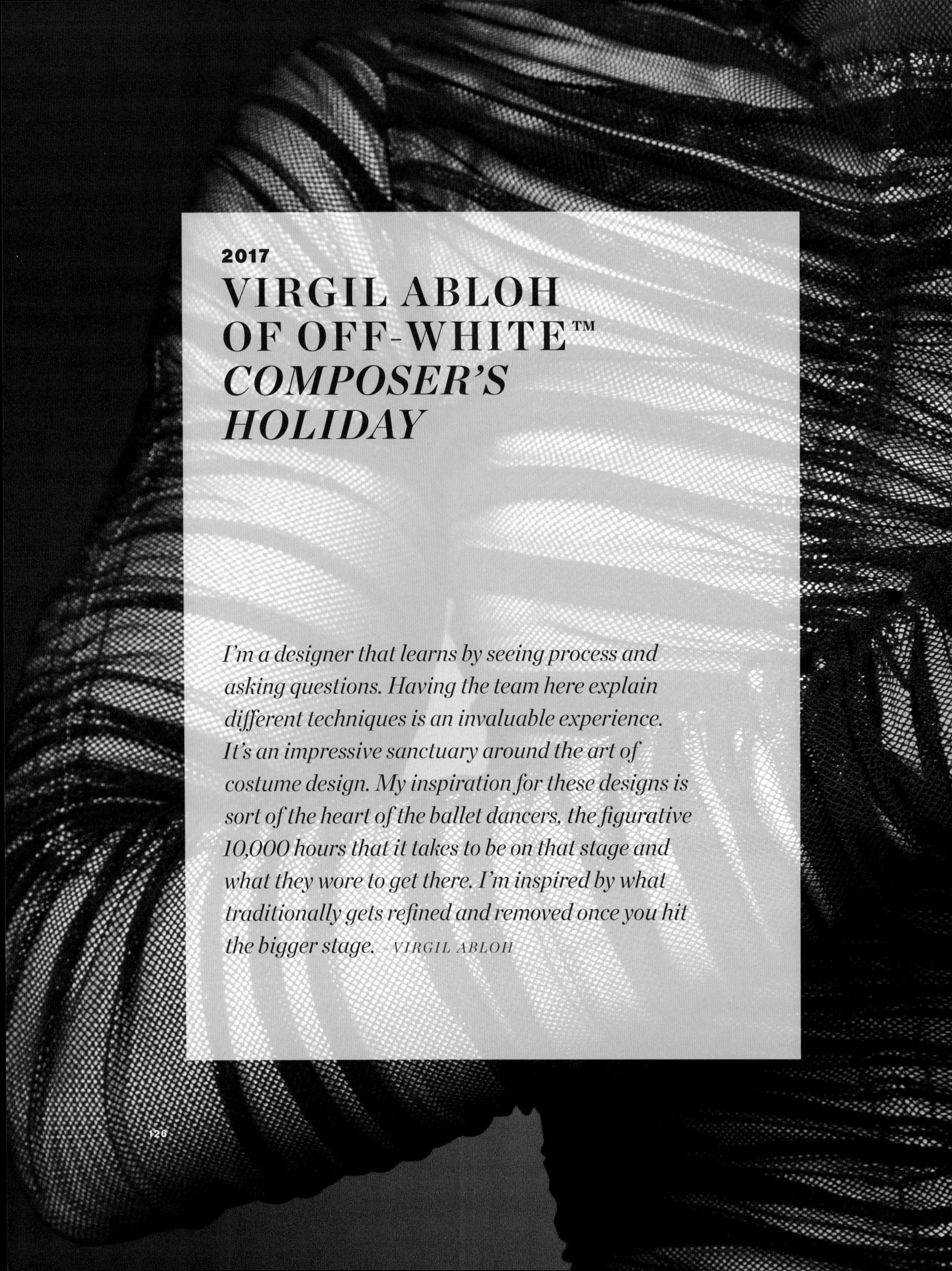

2017

VIRGIL ABLOH OF OFF-WHITE™ *COMPOSER'S HOLIDAY*

I'm a designer that learns by seeing process and asking questions. Having the team here explain different techniques is an invaluable experience. It's an impressive sanctuary around the art of costume design. My inspiration for these designs is sort of the heart of the ballet dancers, the figurative 10,000 hours that it takes to be on that stage and what they wore to get there. I'm inspired by what traditionally gets refined and removed once you hit the bigger stage. —VIRGIL ABLOH

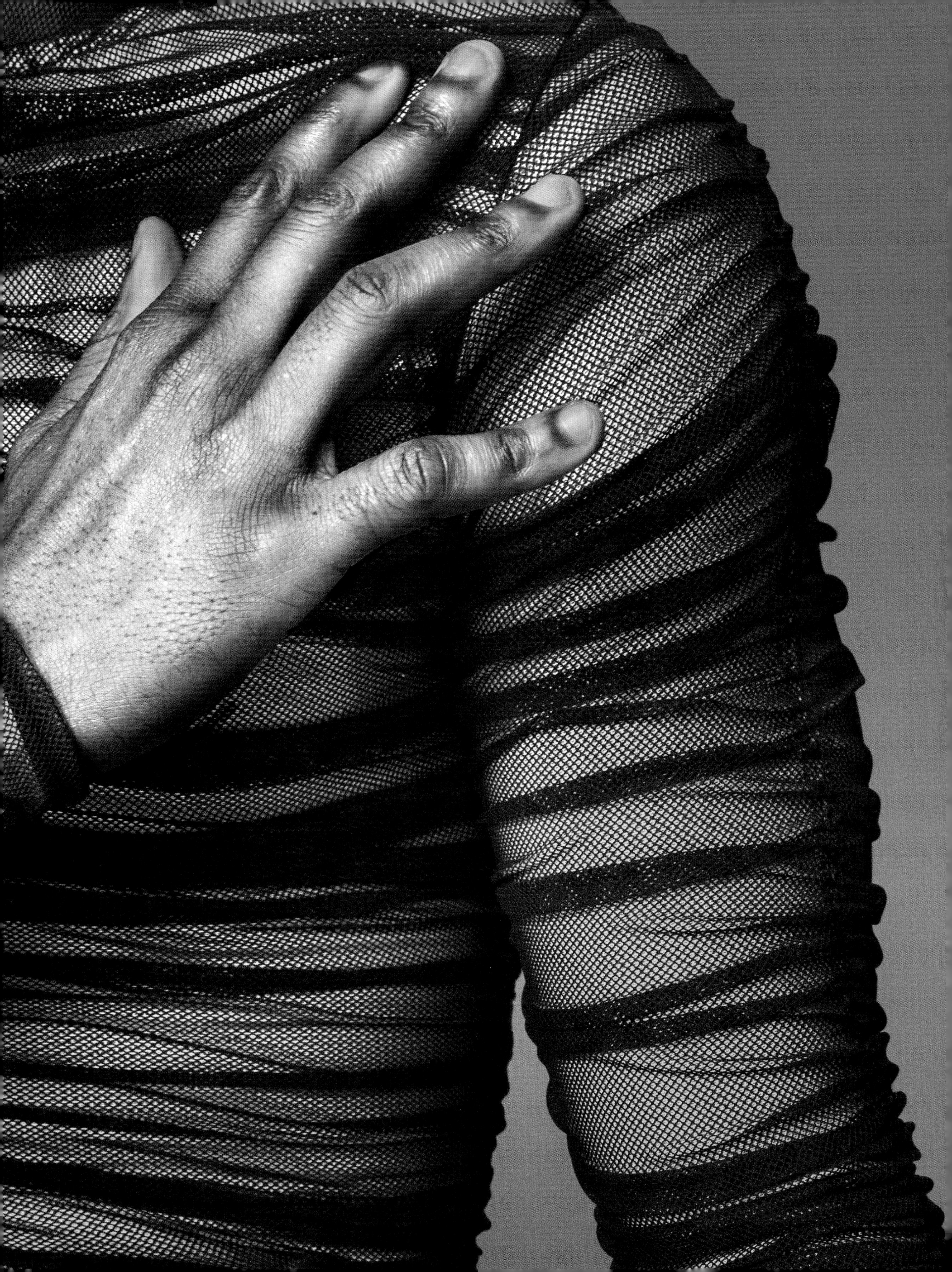

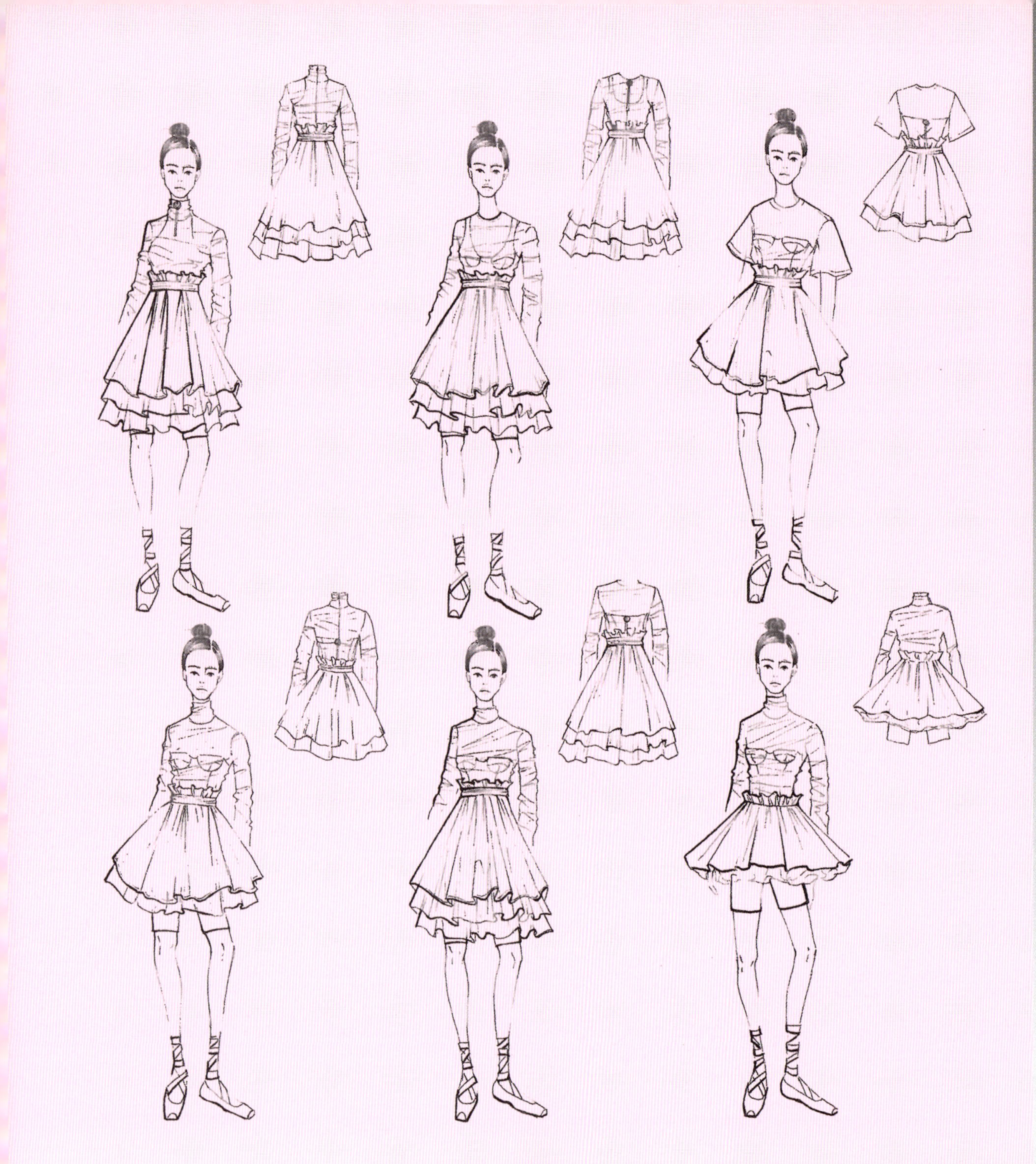

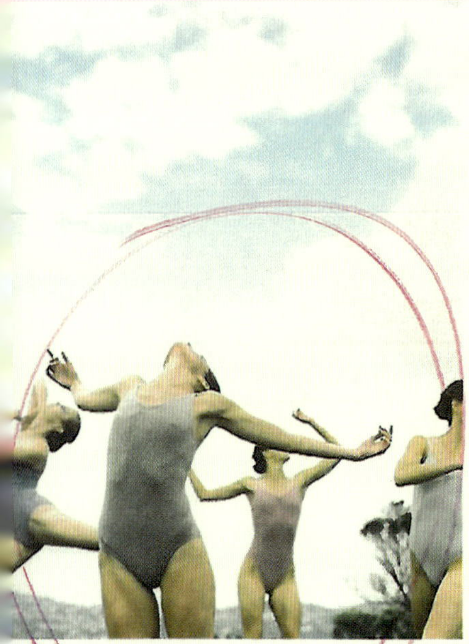

"COLOR"

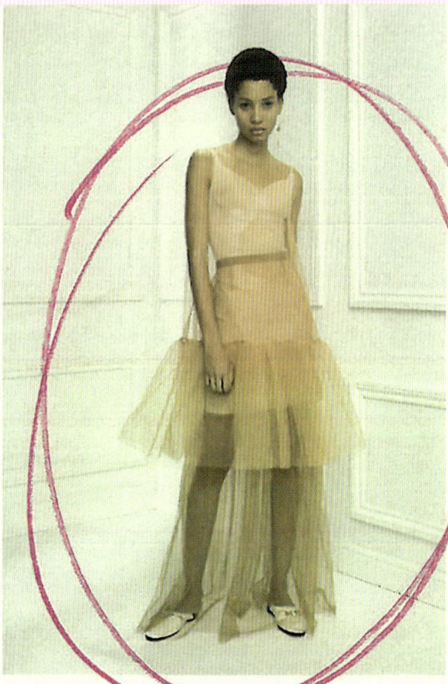

"TEXTURE"

Off-White™

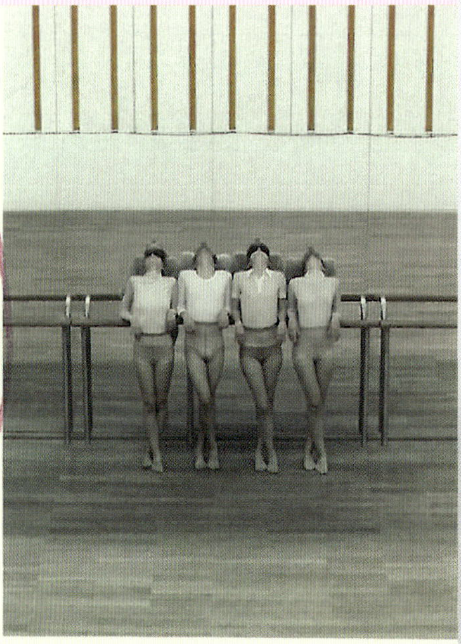

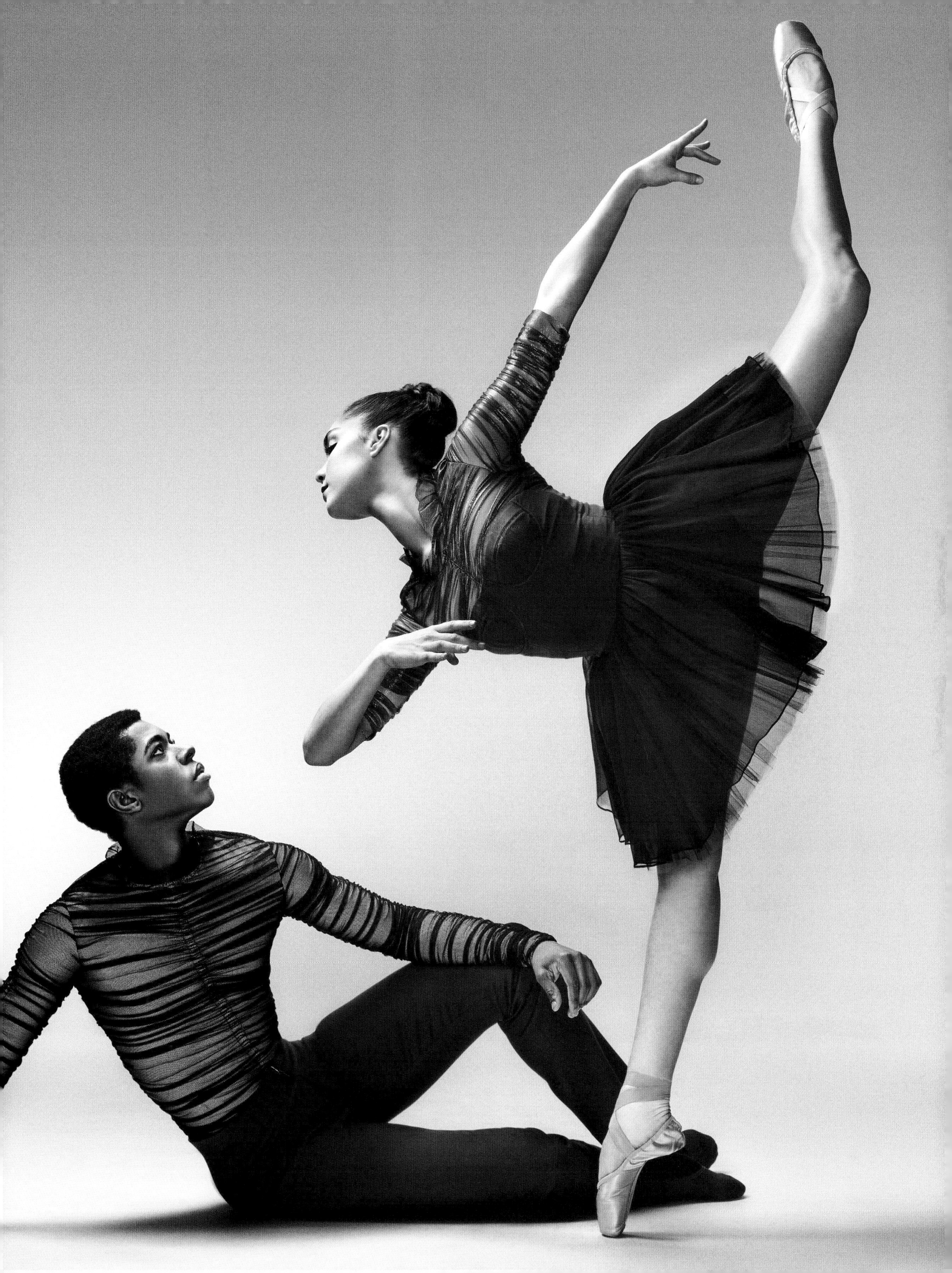

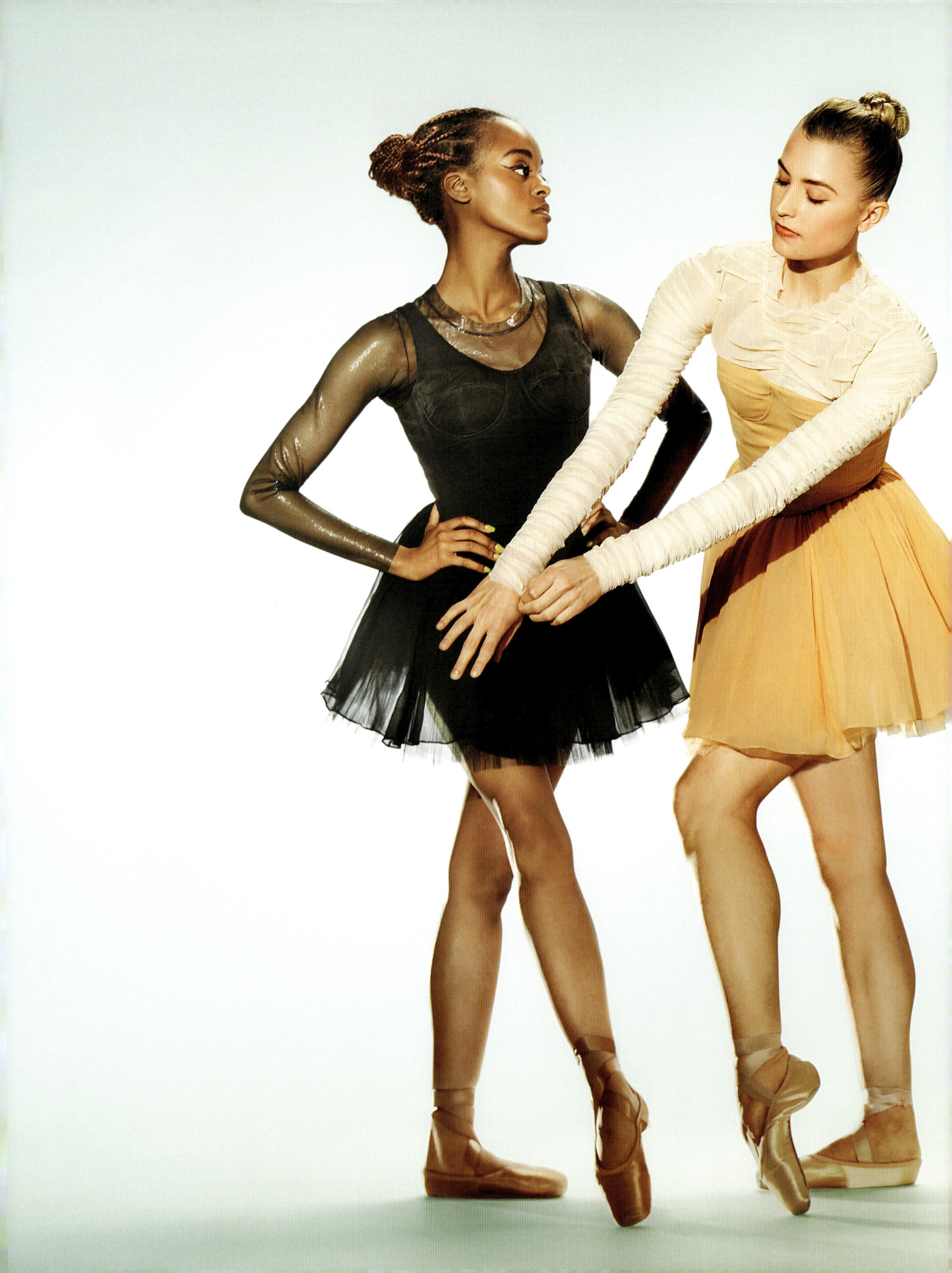

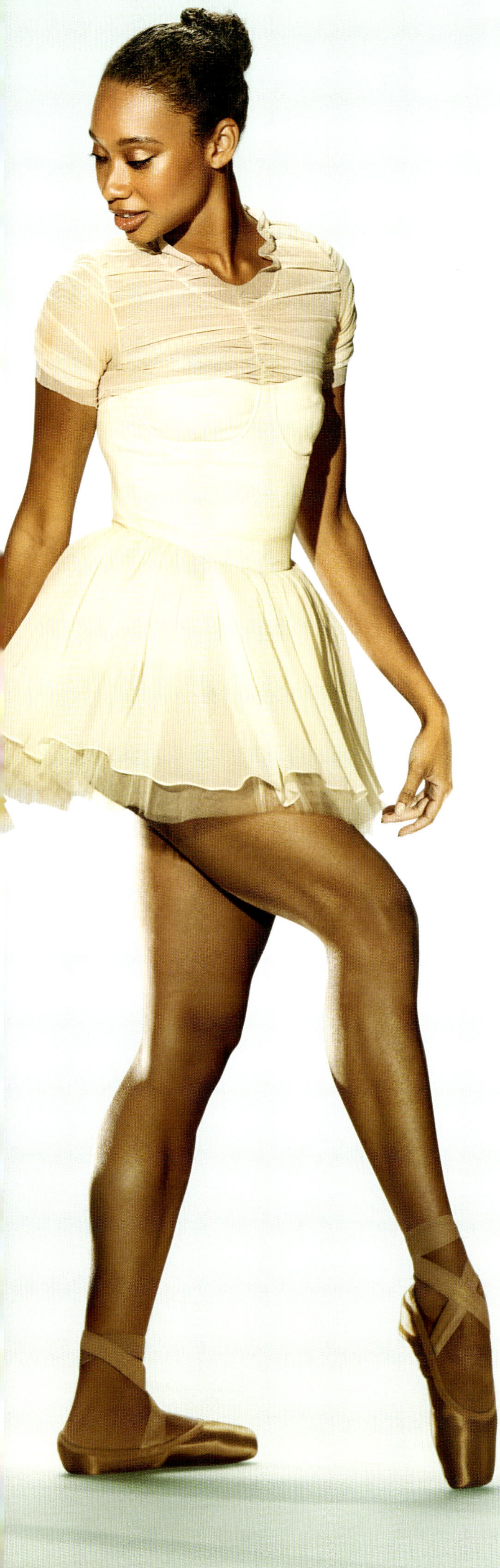

Virgil liked to push boundaries, and I tend to gravitate toward simplicity, so together, we were able to come to a unique middle ground in regards to our ideas. It was such a special collaboration because he widened my perspective on fashion and challenged me with his inventiveness, while embracing the process of theatrical costuming and classical ballet. Virgil appreciated, yet enhanced the traditional "ballerina look" with his designs for Composer's Holiday.

—GIANNA REISEN, Choreographer

2017

FERNANDO GARCIA & LAURA KIM OF MONSE & OSCAR DE LA RENTA *NOT OUR FATE*

We wanted the pieces for Lauren Lovette's Not Our Fate *to feel like they were made specific to the dancers and to move with their bodies. This was a key element for us. We combined our (now staple) lacing detail with another one of our staples, the asymmetrical hemline.*

—*FERNANDO GARCIA & LAURA KIM*

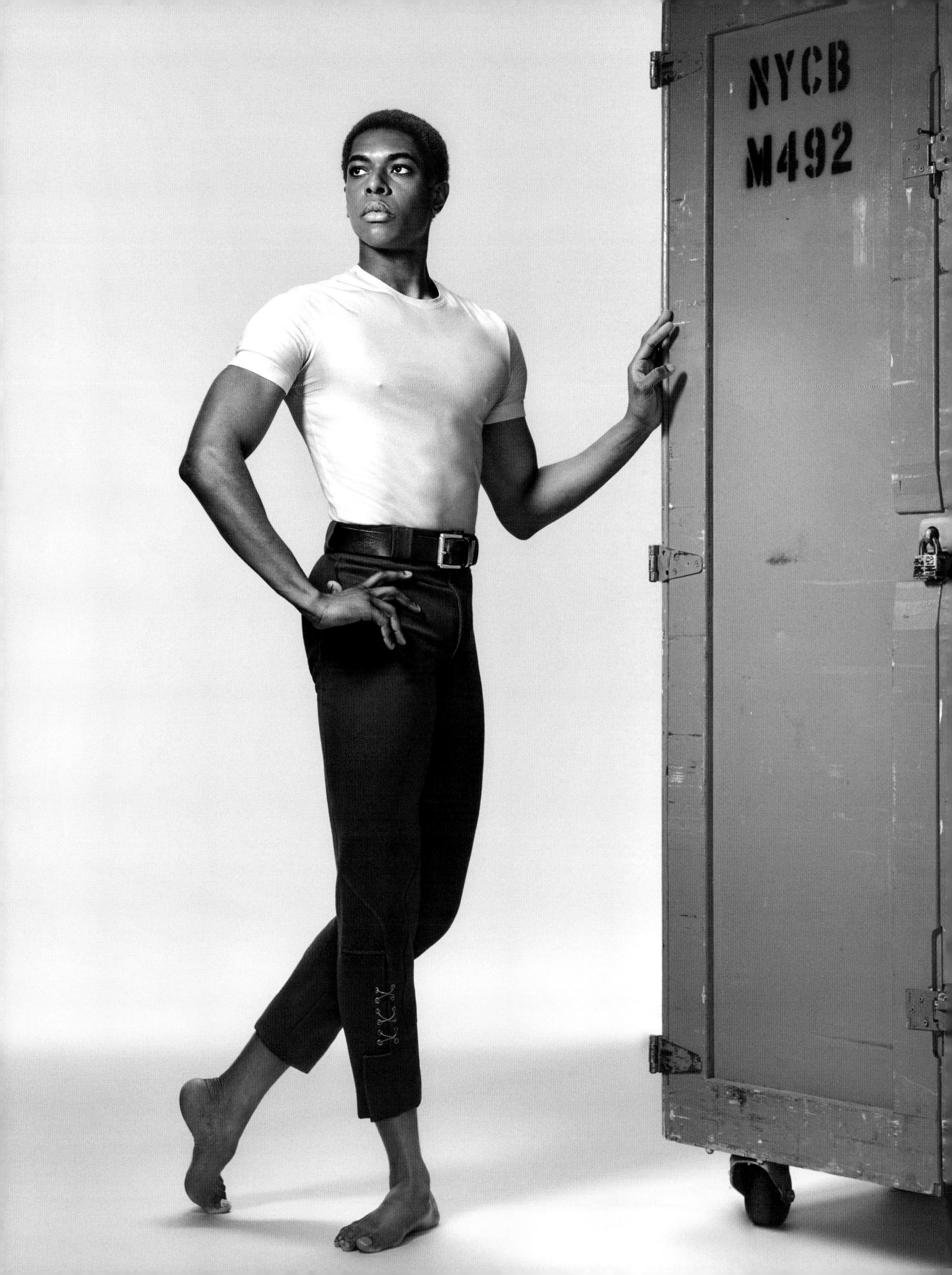
NYCB
M492

It's always exciting to see how the designer's ideas come together and how the costumes end up impacting the ballets. Sometimes a costume can completely change the tone of a ballet and the way the steps are danced.

—*MIRA NADON, Dancer*

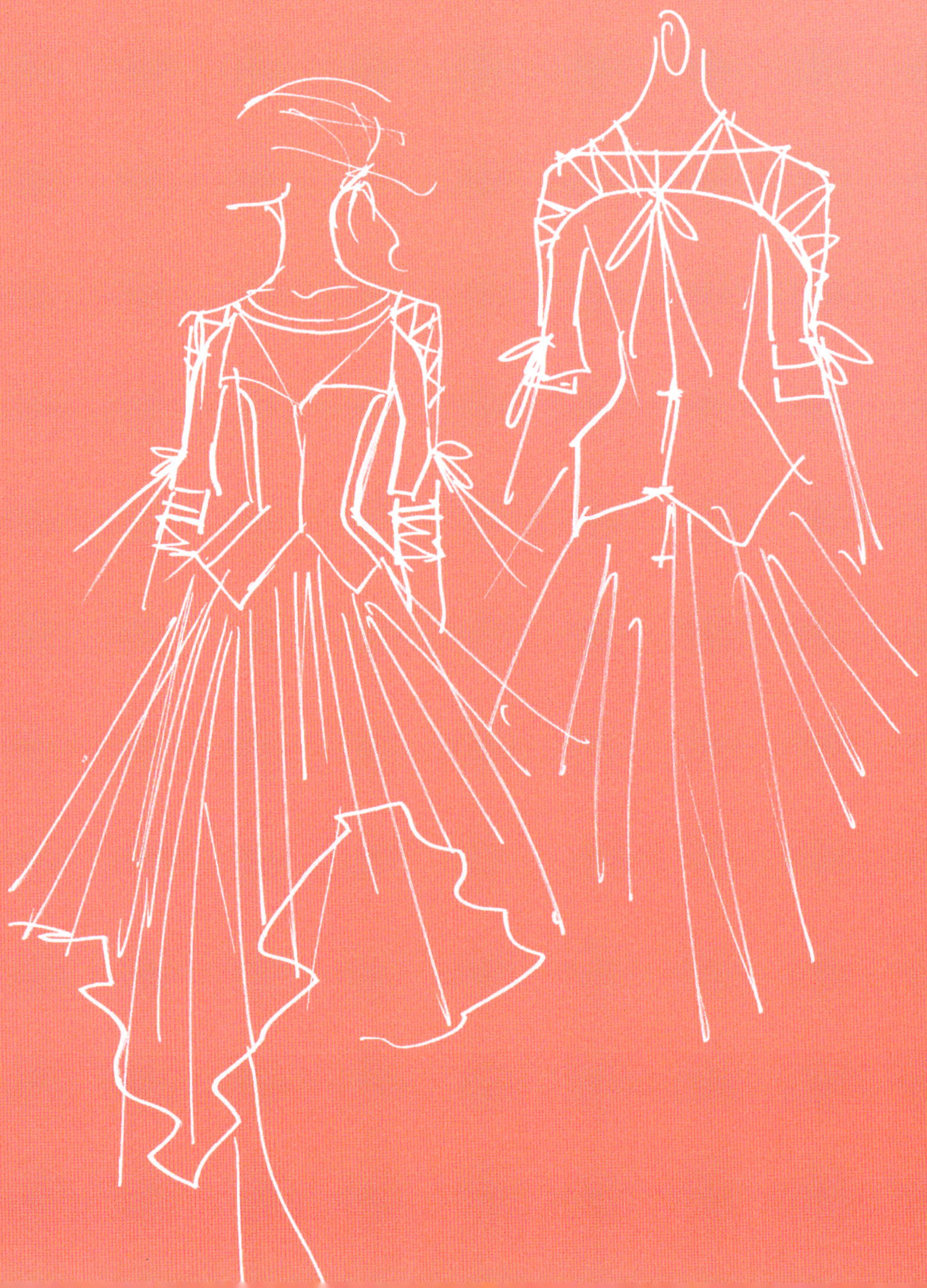

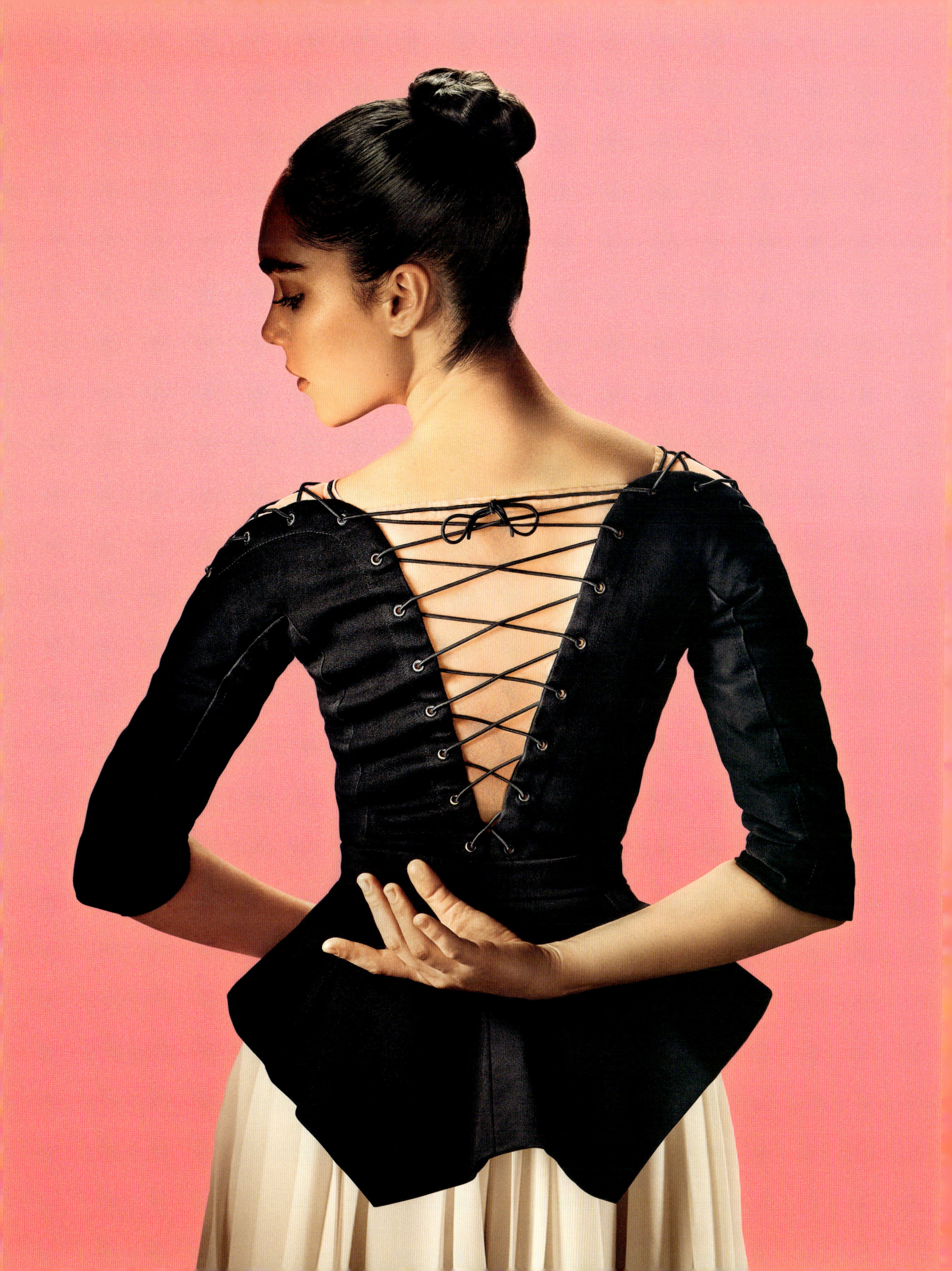

2017

TSUMORI CHISATO *PULCINELLA VARIATIONS*

In July, I visited the New York atelier. I started design drawings while listening to music and discussing with Justin so that I could follow his wonderful vision as much as possible. I thought the image of Bauhaus was perfect. Very rich time passed in a blink of an eye and the design picture was completed. After that, I worked with Marc, who considered the length and recommended various techniques to make it easier for dancers to dance. It was a very exciting day in New York for me. —TSUMORI CHISATO

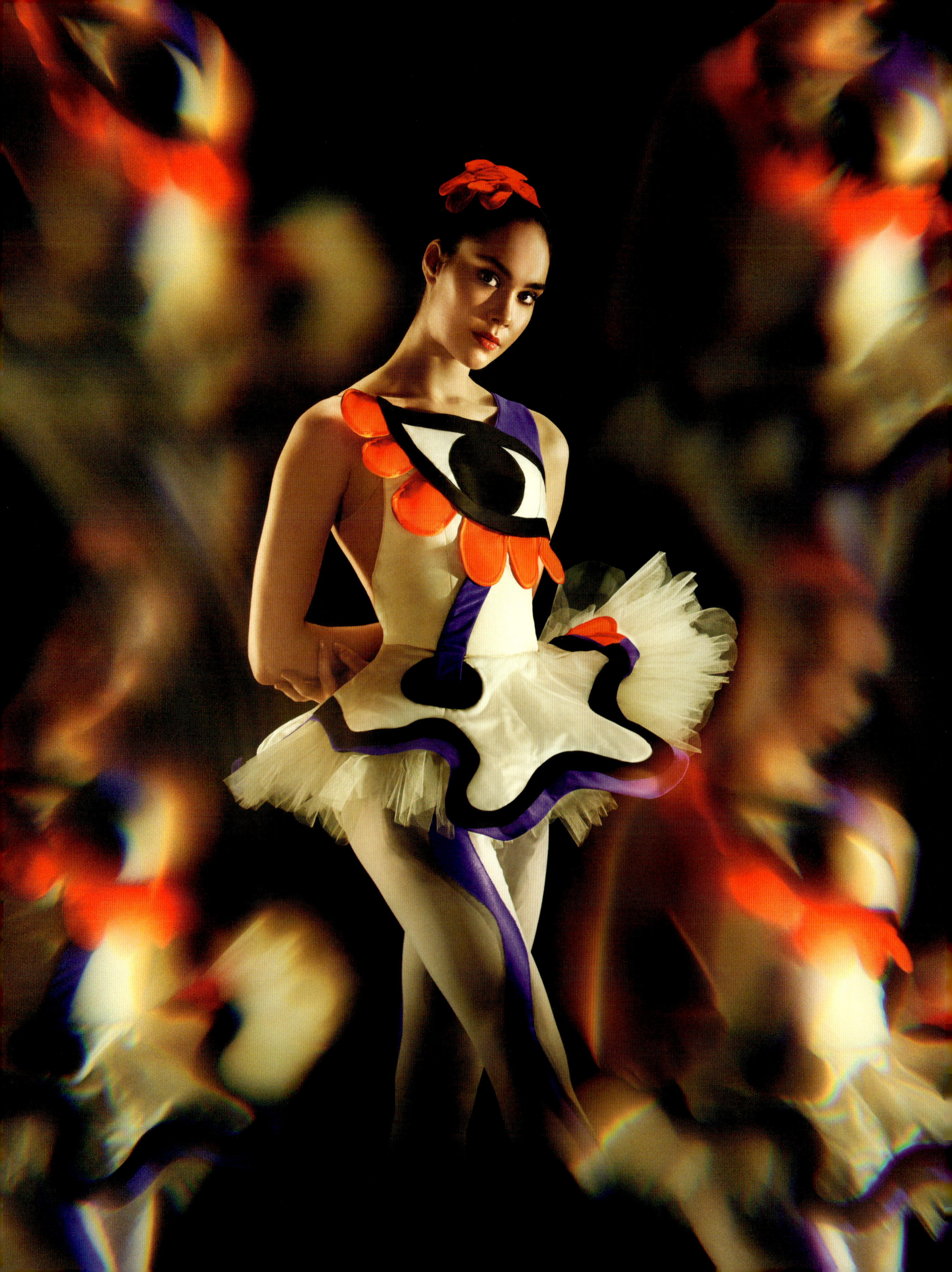

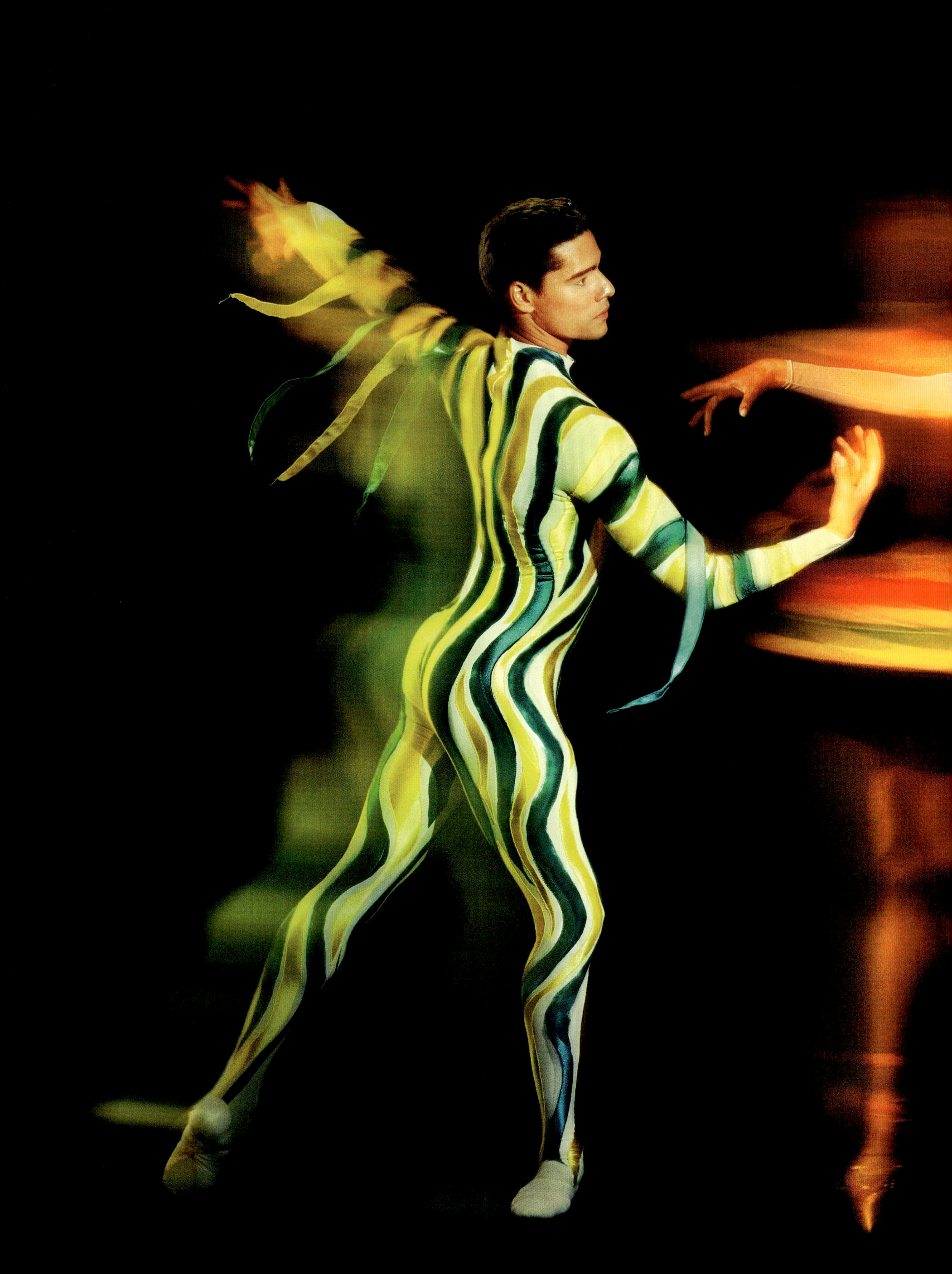

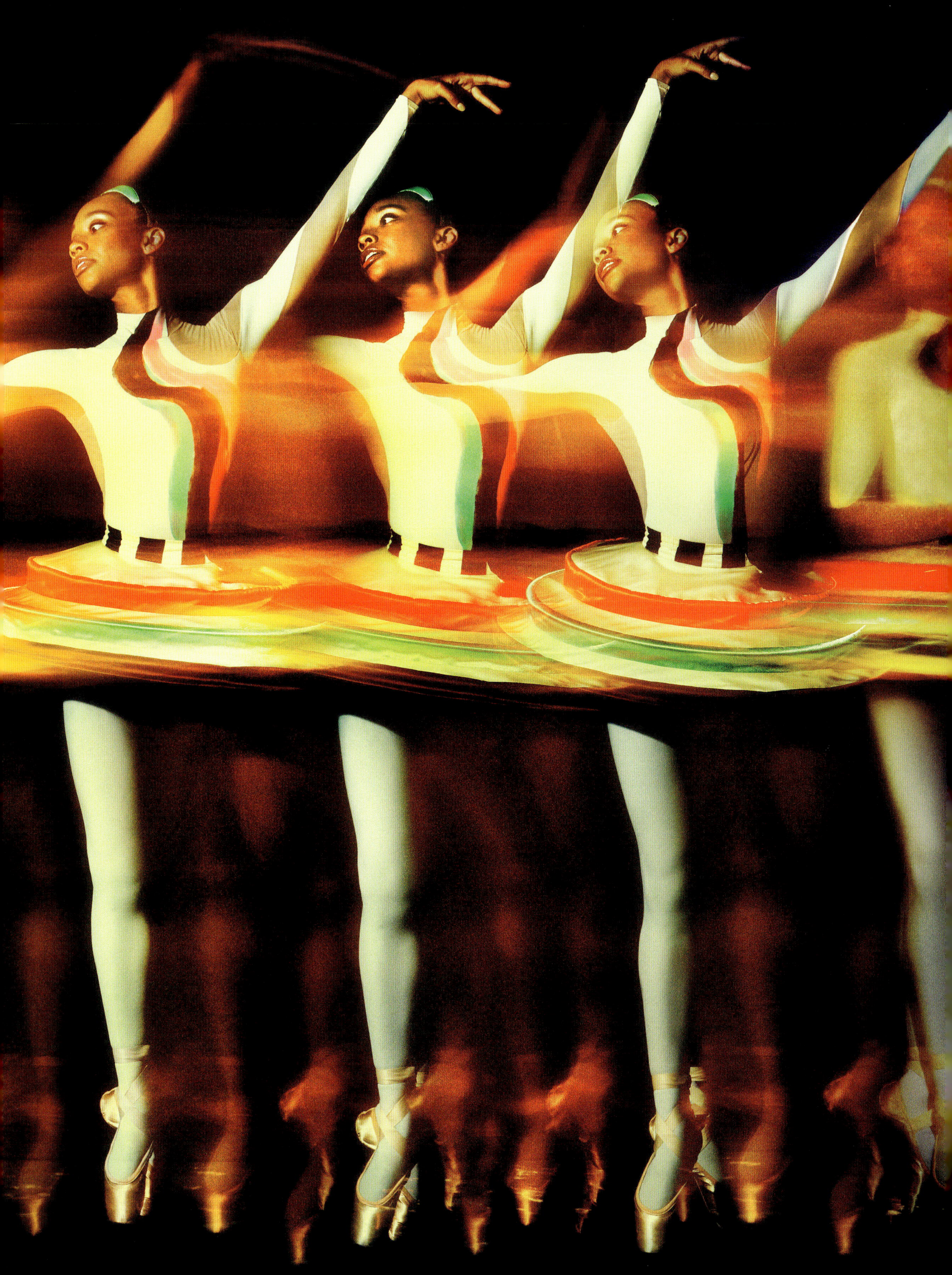

I first met Tsumori Chisato in our NYCB costume shop, and we immediately embarked upon a creative collaboration. We spoke about influence, color, shape, tone, and a kind of whimsical style inspired by Commedia Dell'Arte. I was astonished when she took out some watercolor pens from her bag and began sketching several costume design ideas right there on the spot. The visual world that she designed came forward with such ease and assurance.

— *JUSTIN PECK, Choreographer*

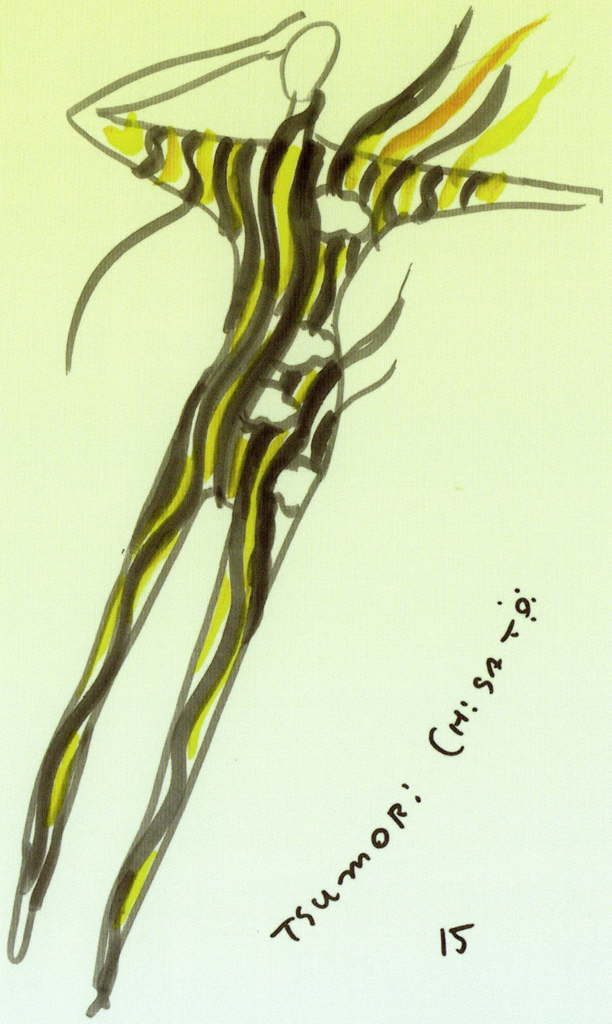

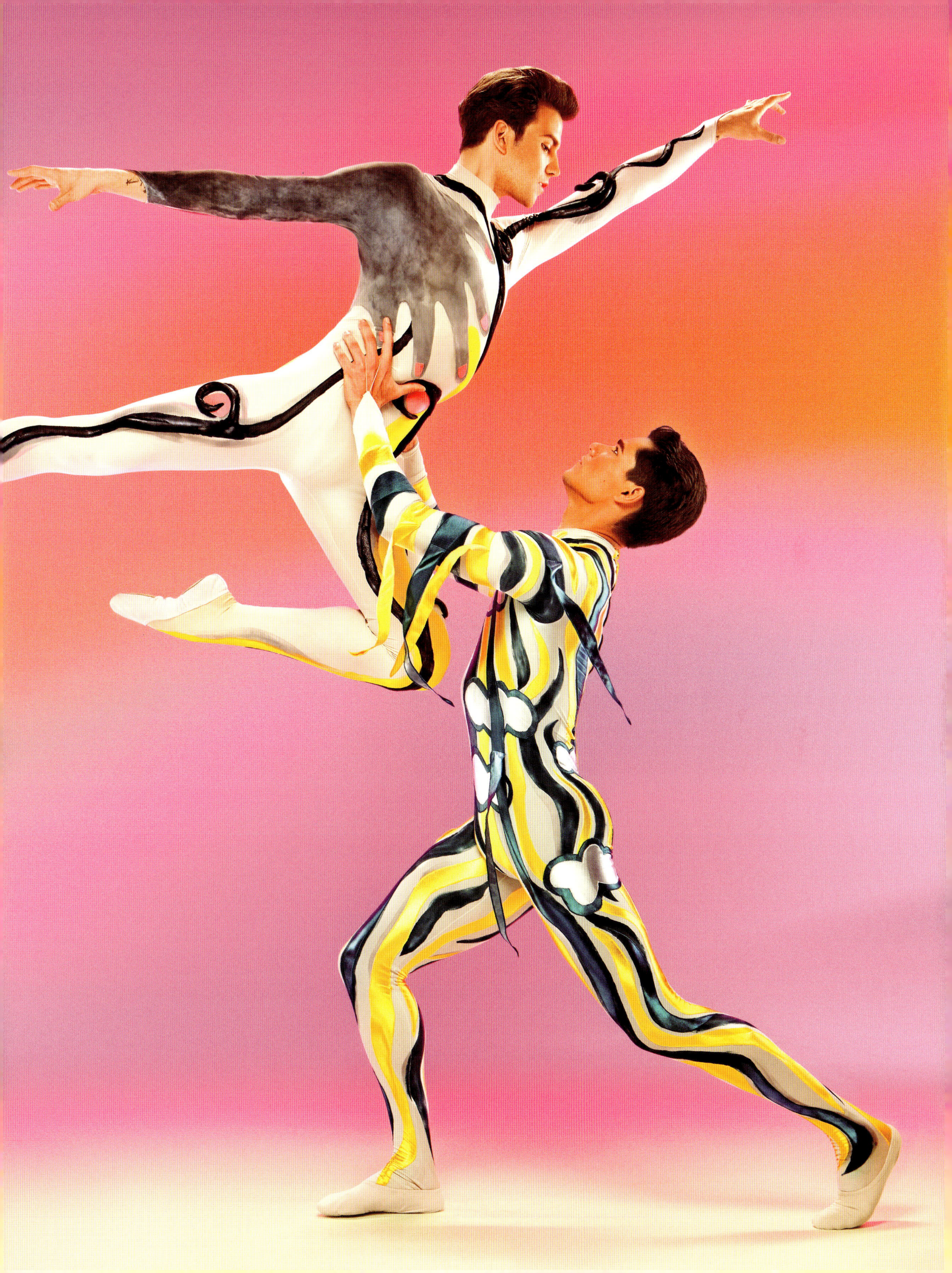

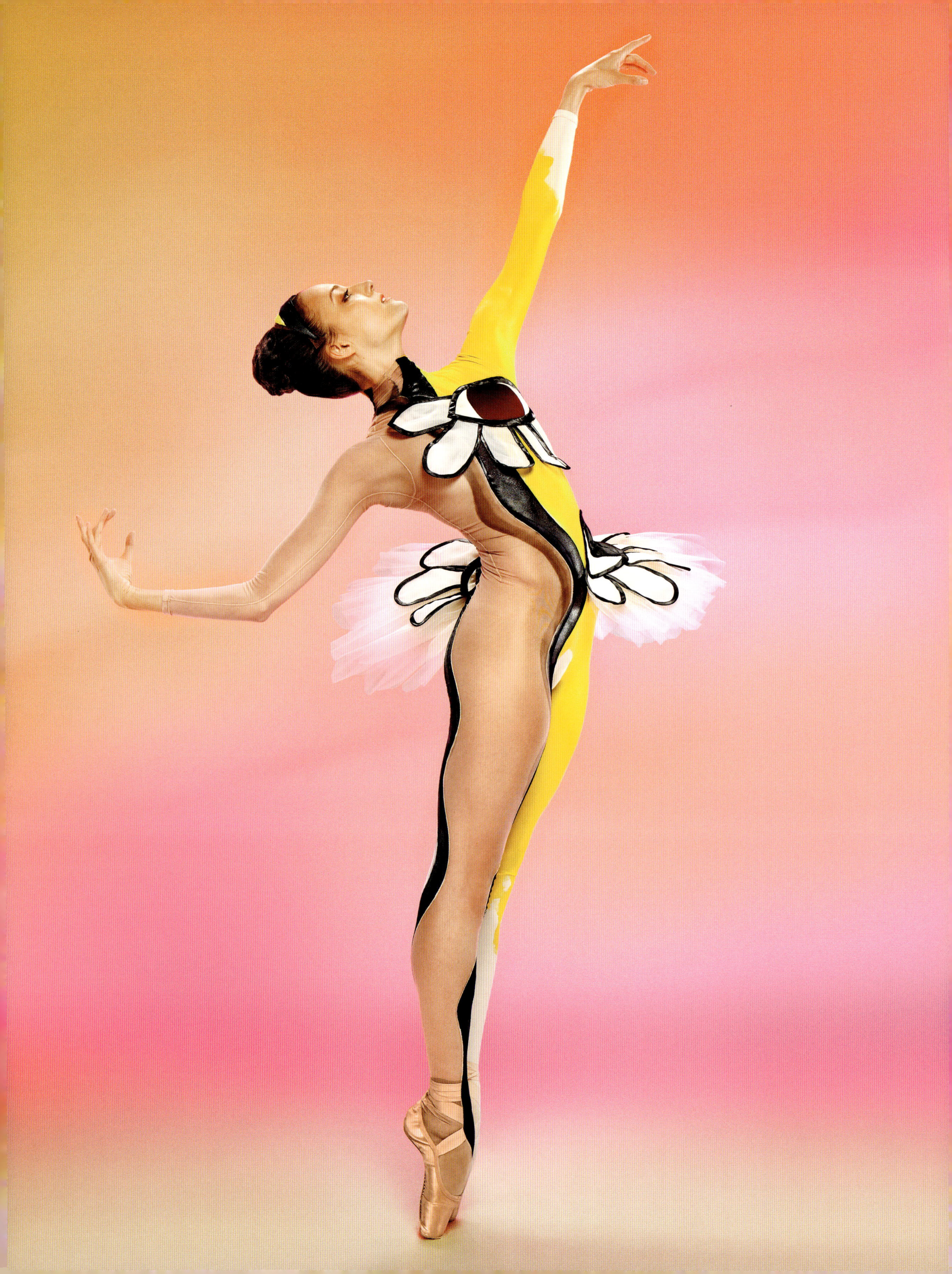

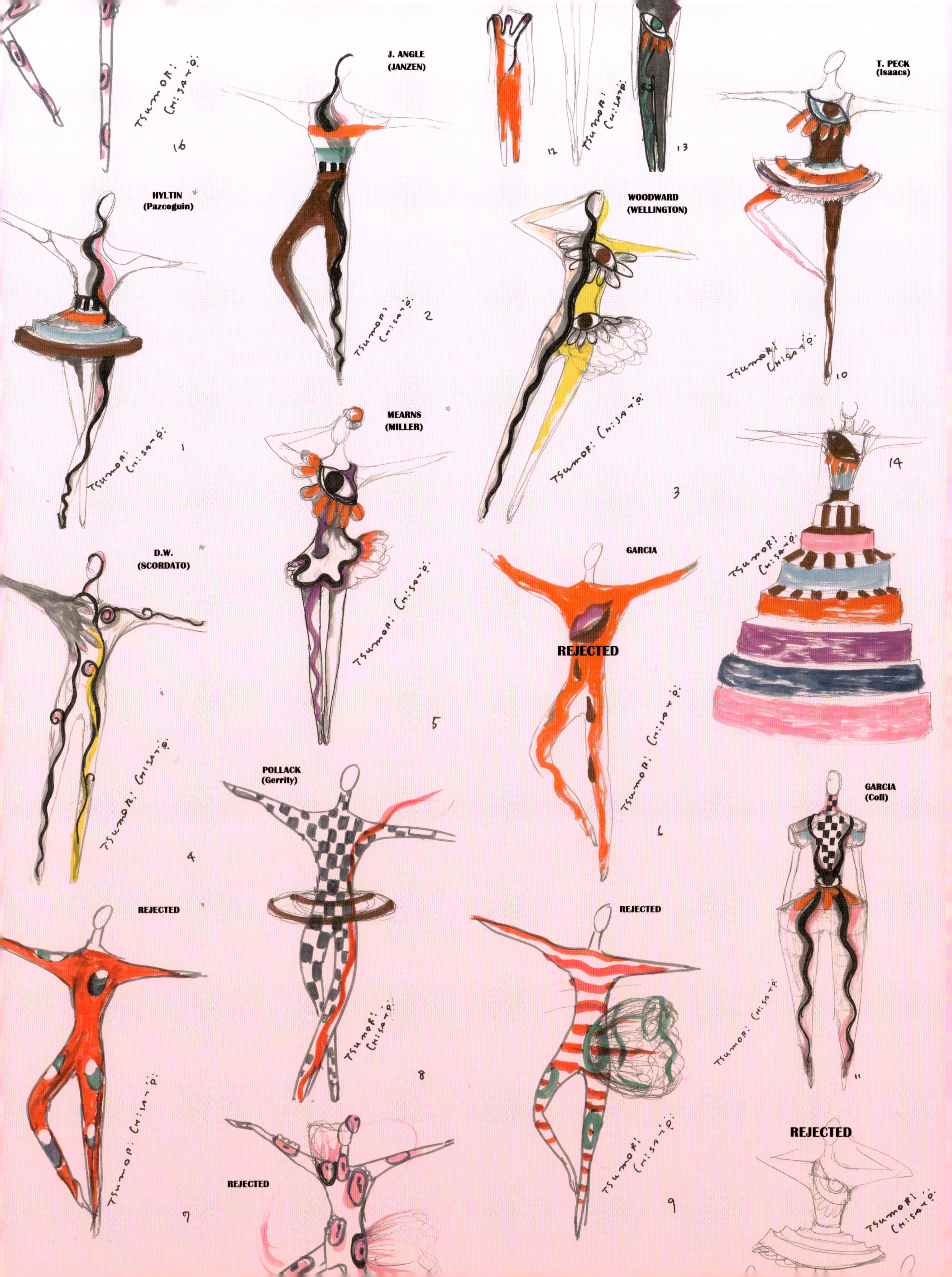
J. ANGLE
(JANZEN)
T. PECK
(Isaacs)
HYLTIN
(Pazcoguin)
WOODWARD
(WELLINGTON)
MEARNS
(MILLER)
D.W.
(SCORDATO)
GARCIA
REJECTED
POLLACK
(Gerrity)
GARCIA
(Coll)
REJECTED
REJECTED
REJECTED
REJECTED

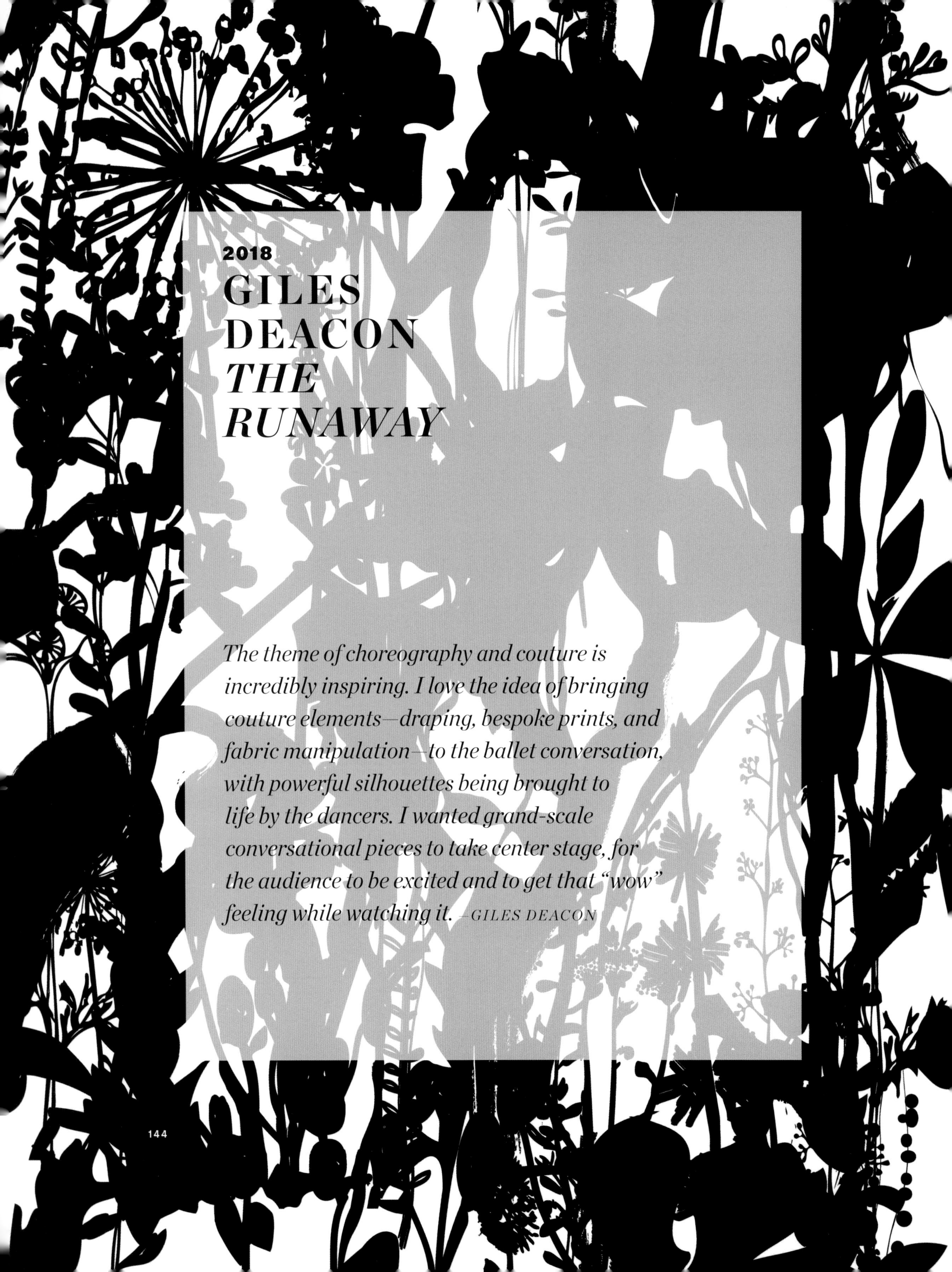

2018

GILES DEACON
THE RUNAWAY

The theme of choreography and couture is incredibly inspiring. I love the idea of bringing couture elements—draping, bespoke prints, and fabric manipulation—to the ballet conversation, with powerful silhouettes being brought to life by the dancers. I wanted grand-scale conversational pieces to take center stage, for the audience to be excited and to get that "wow" feeling while watching it. —GILES DEACON

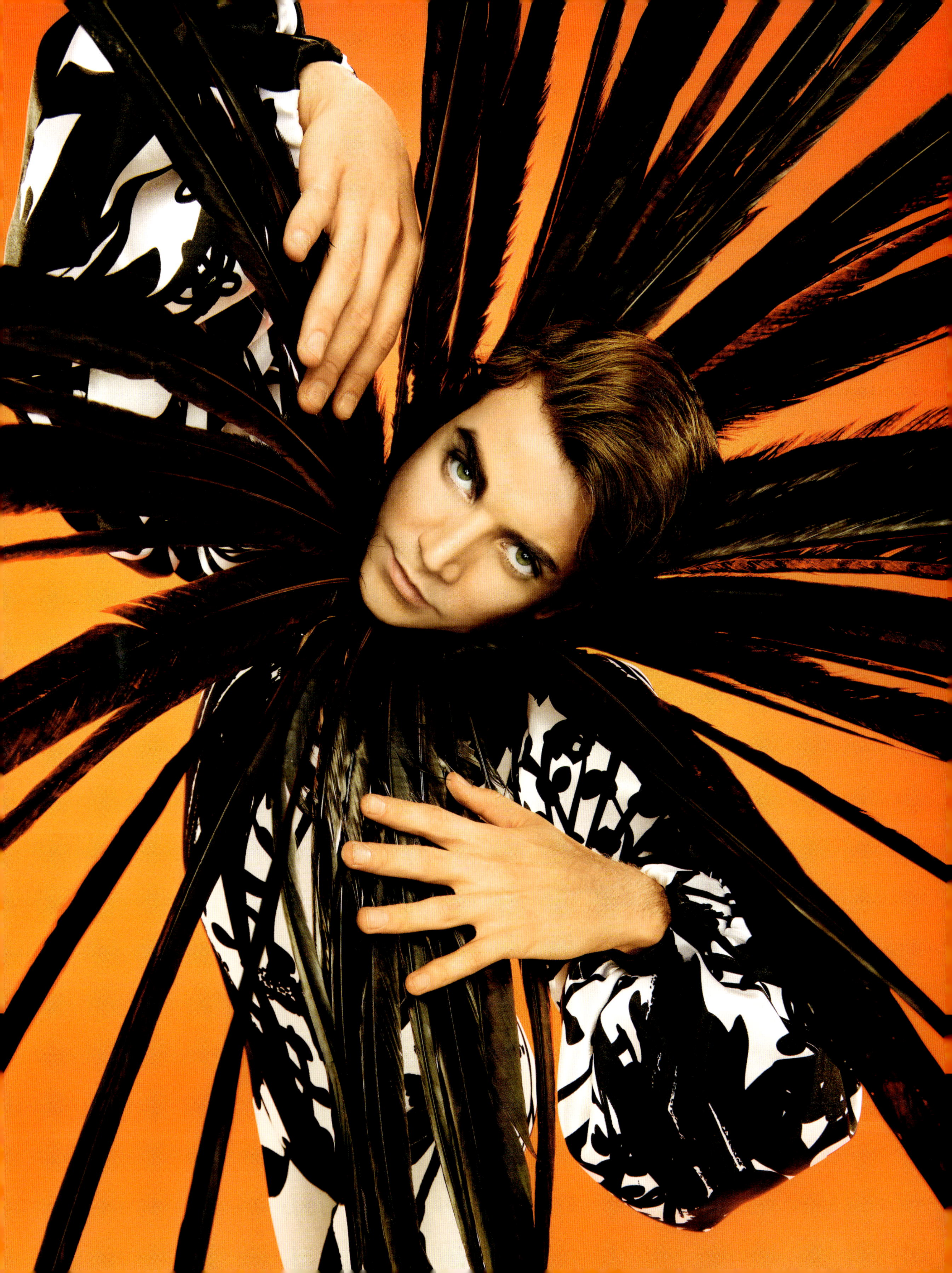

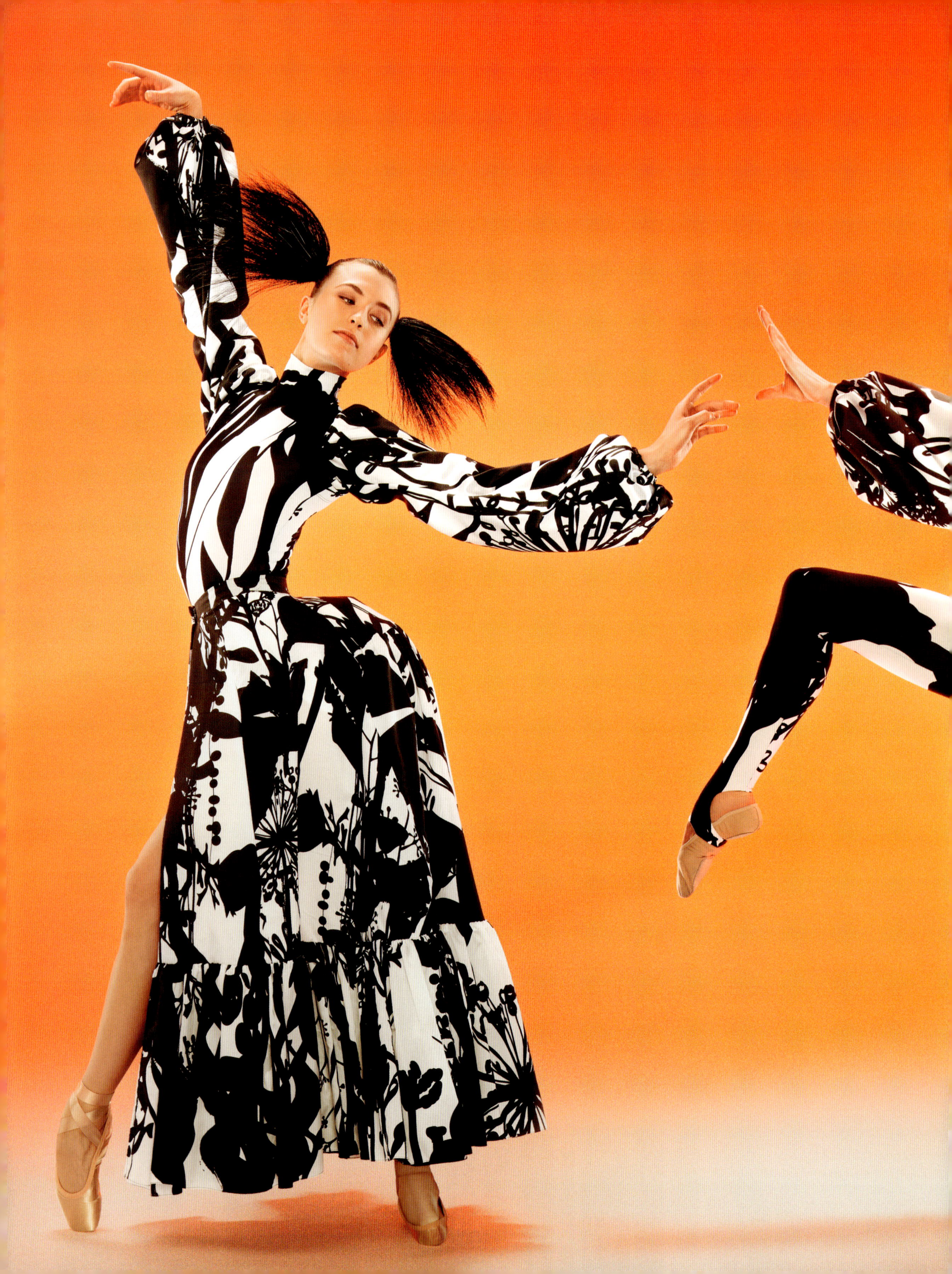

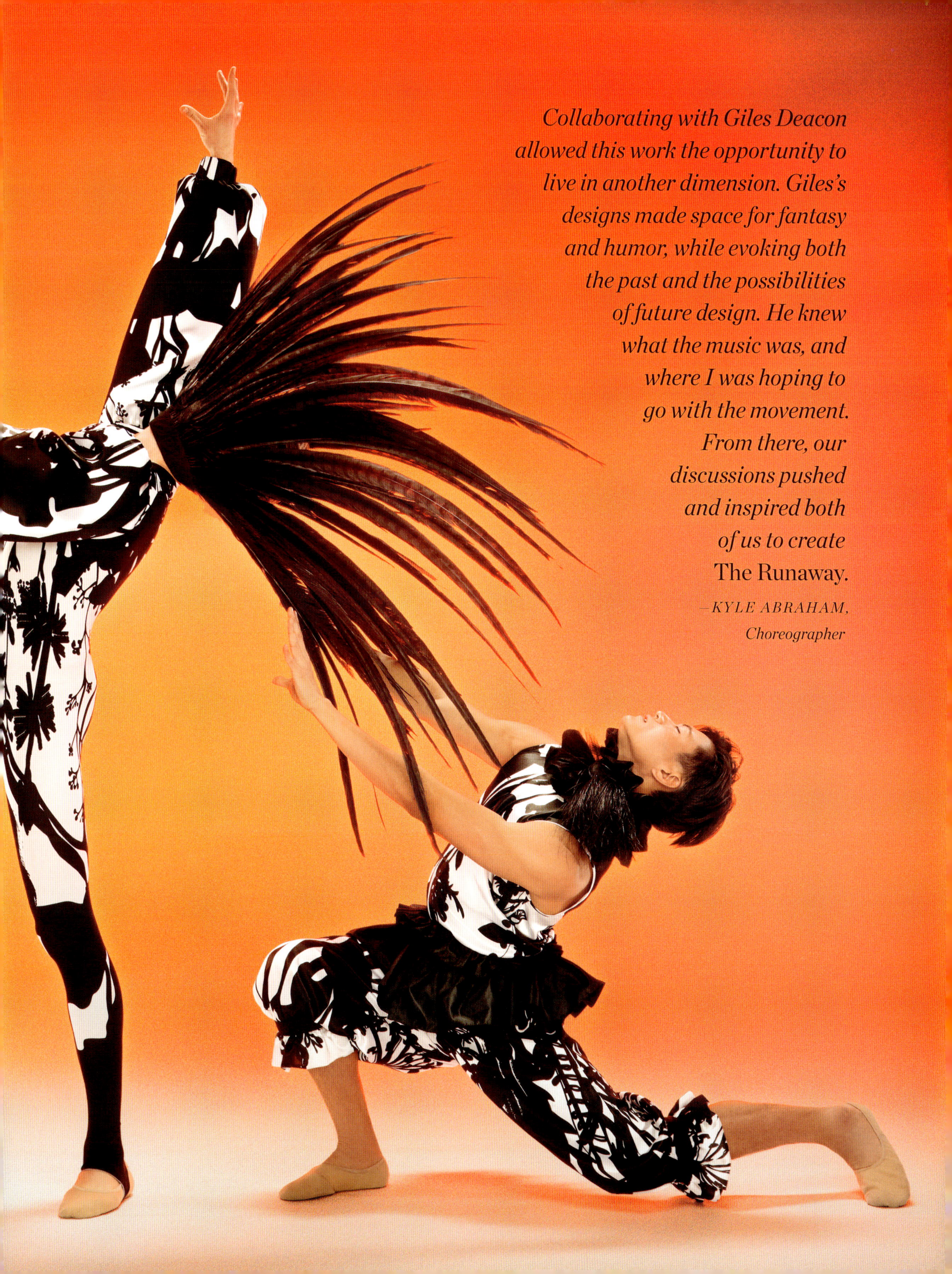

Collaborating with Giles Deacon allowed this work the opportunity to live in another dimension. Giles's designs made space for fantasy and humor, while evoking both the past and the possibilities of future design. He knew what the music was, and where I was hoping to go with the movement. From there, our discussions pushed and inspired both of us to create The Runaway.

—*KYLE ABRAHAM,*
Choreographer

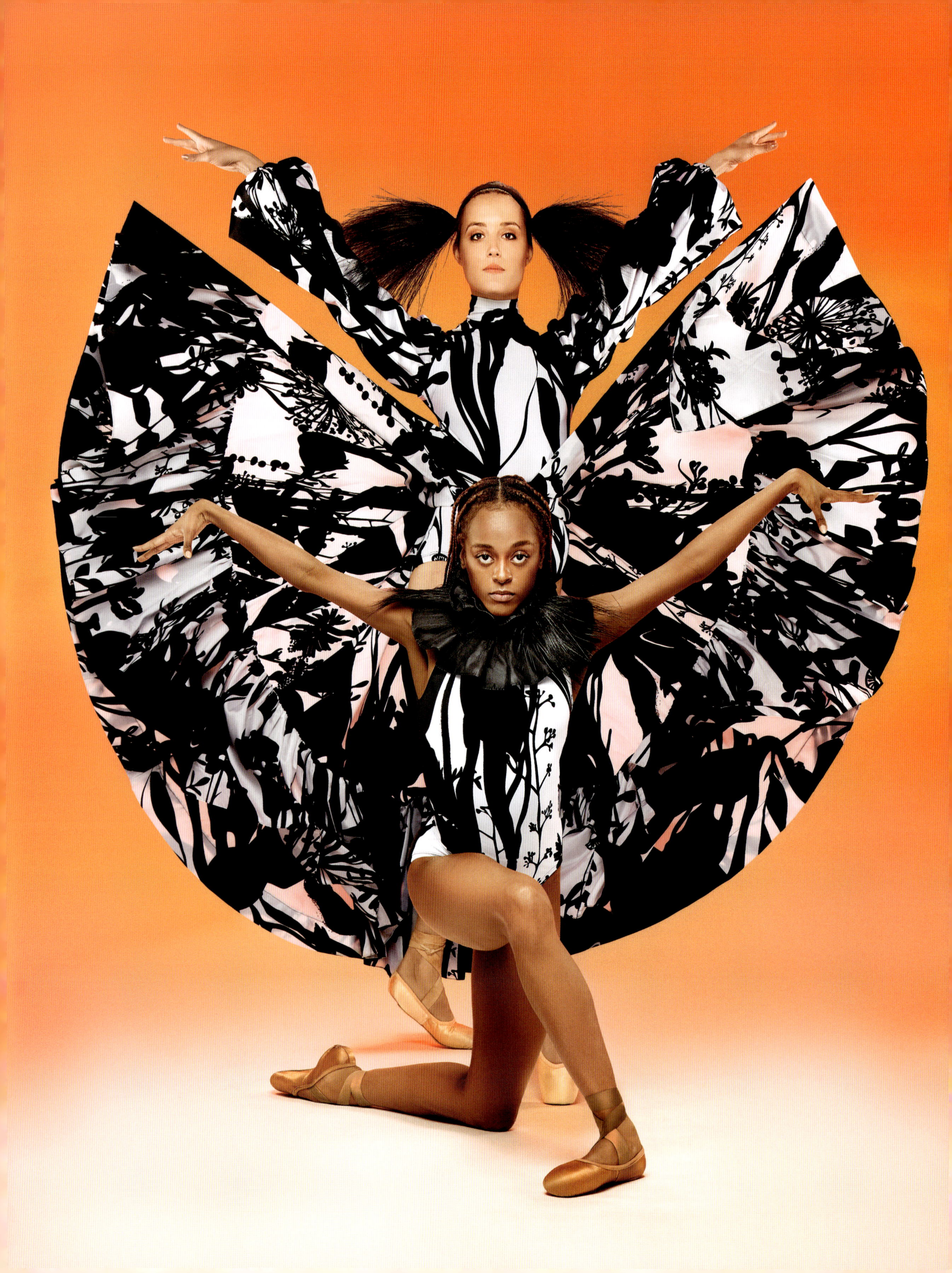

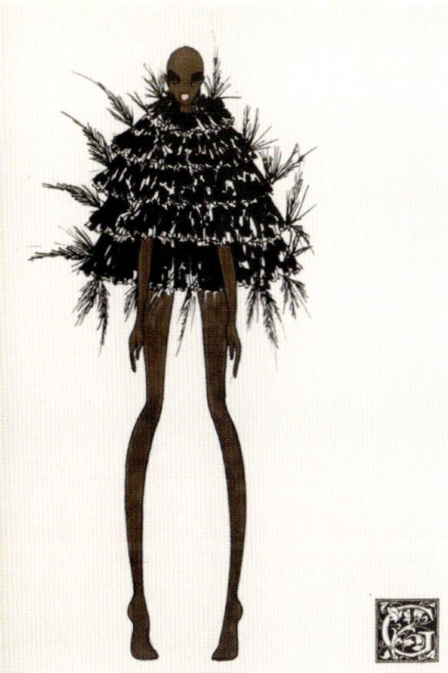
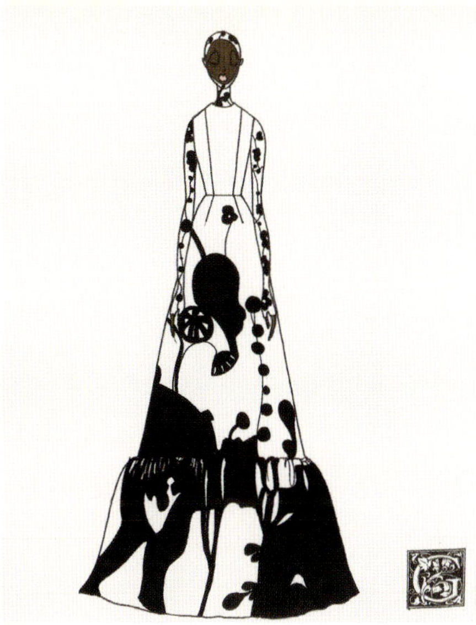
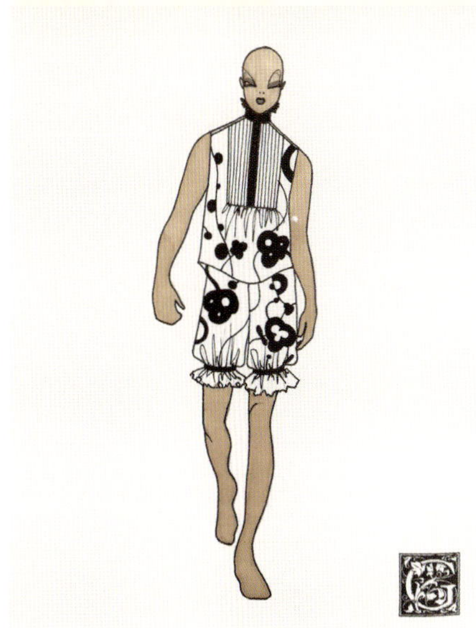
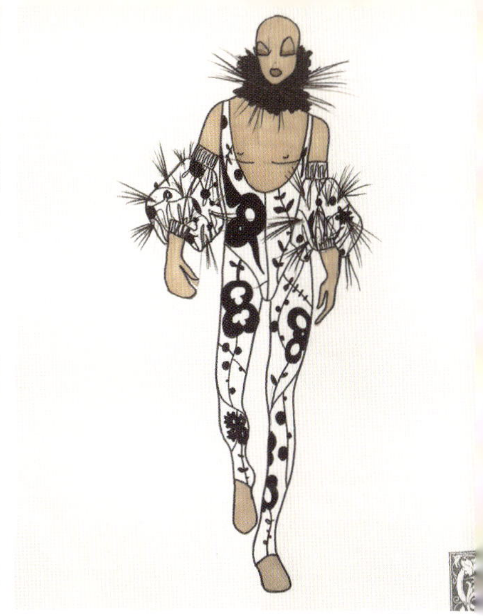
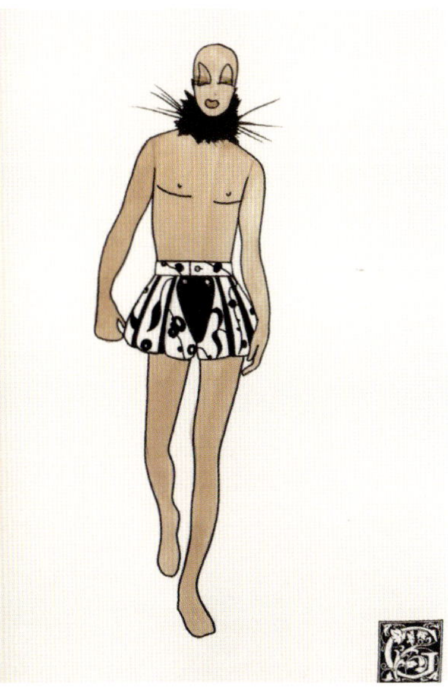
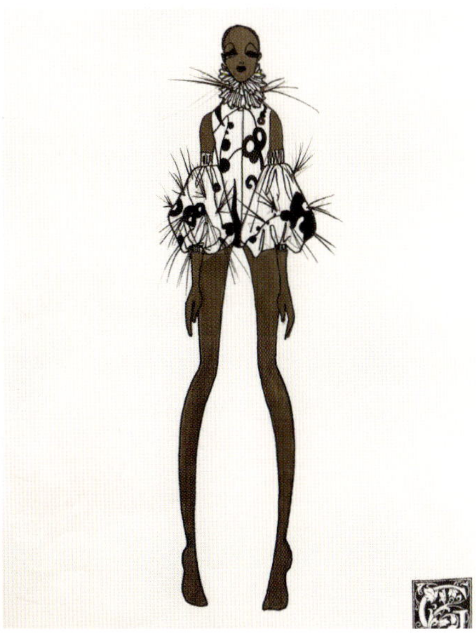
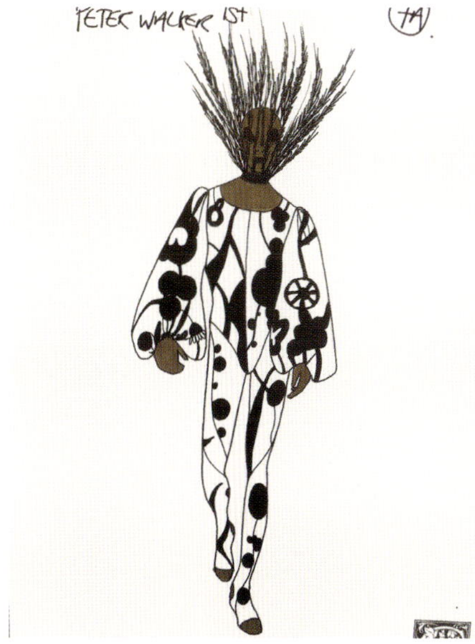
PETER WALKER 1st (7A)
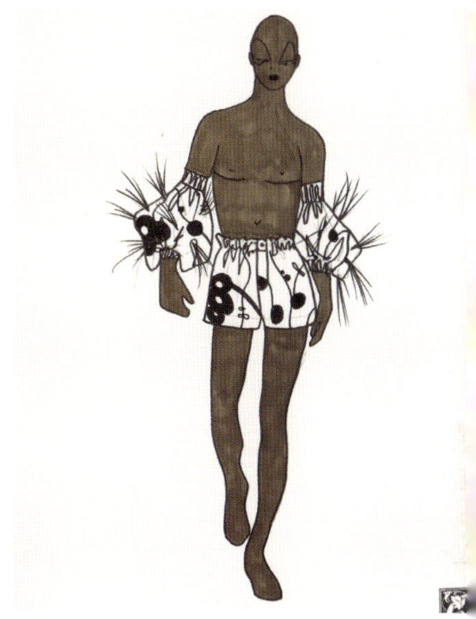
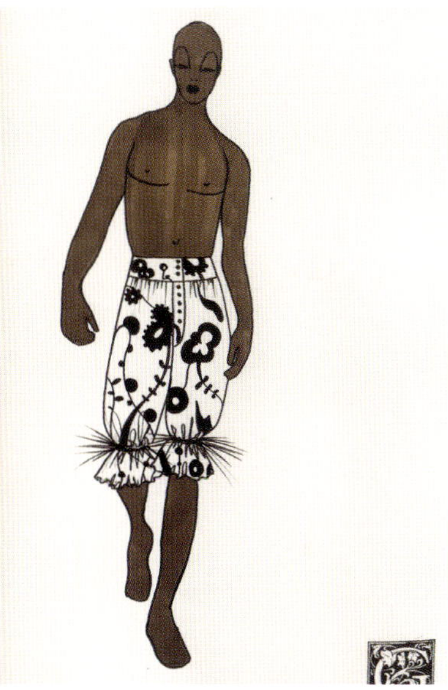
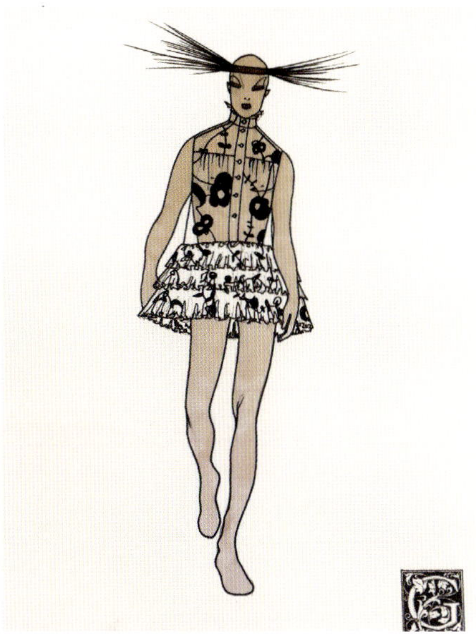
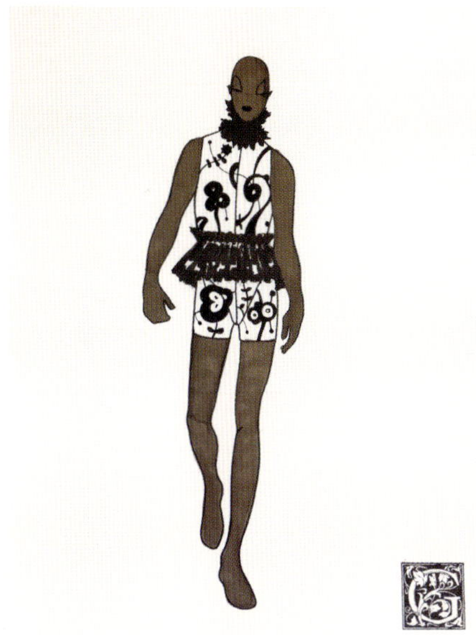
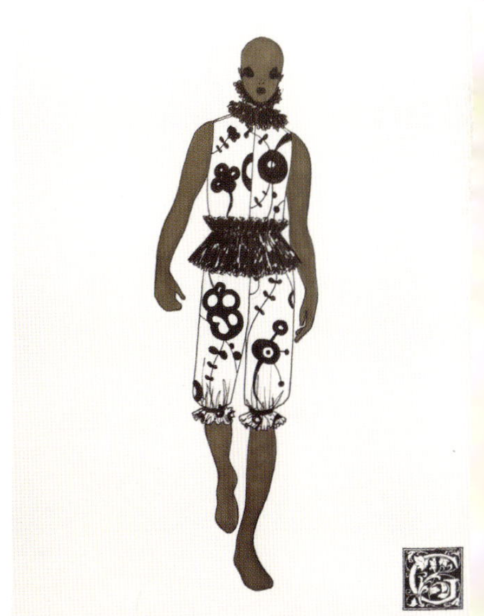
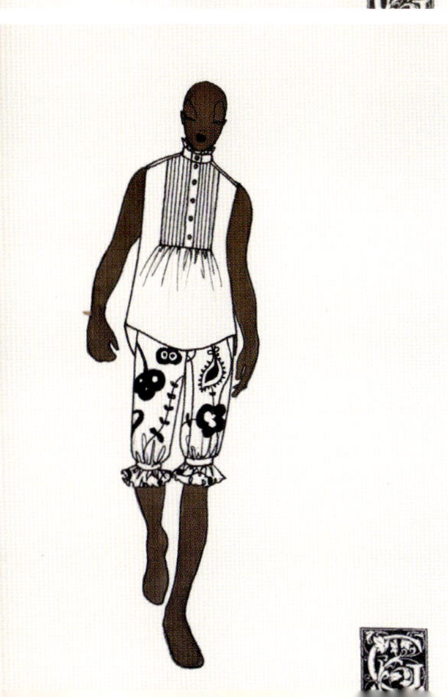
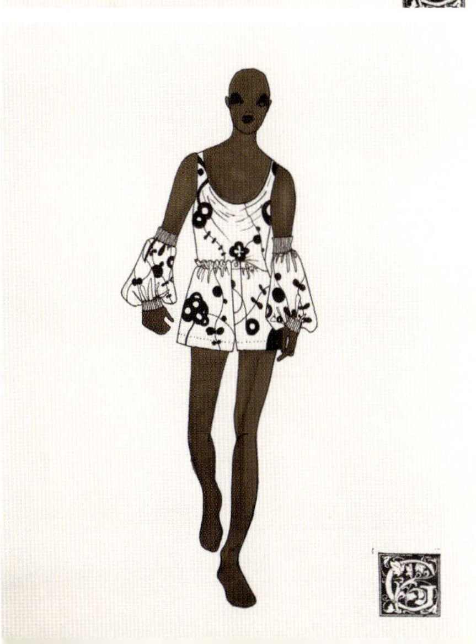
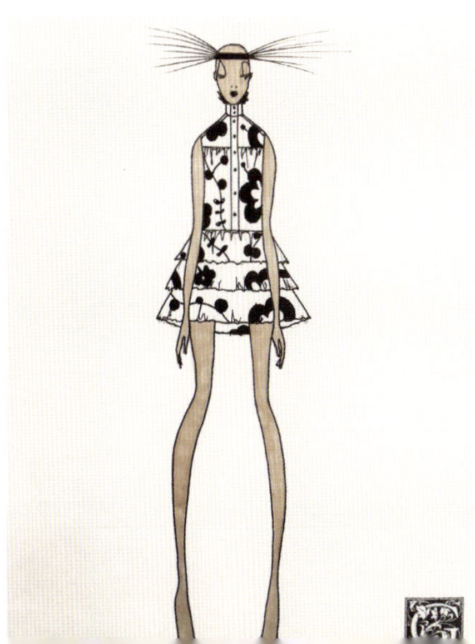
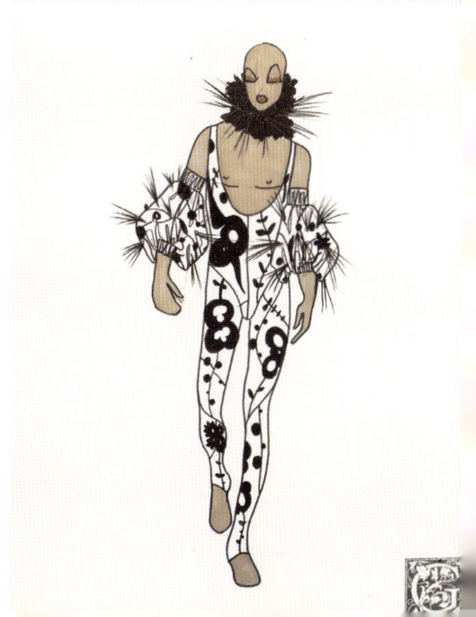

2018

GARETH PUGH *THE EXCHANGE*

Ballet can be quite fluffy and quite frilly, and the idea was to try and inject a little bit of Brutalism. –GARETH PUGH

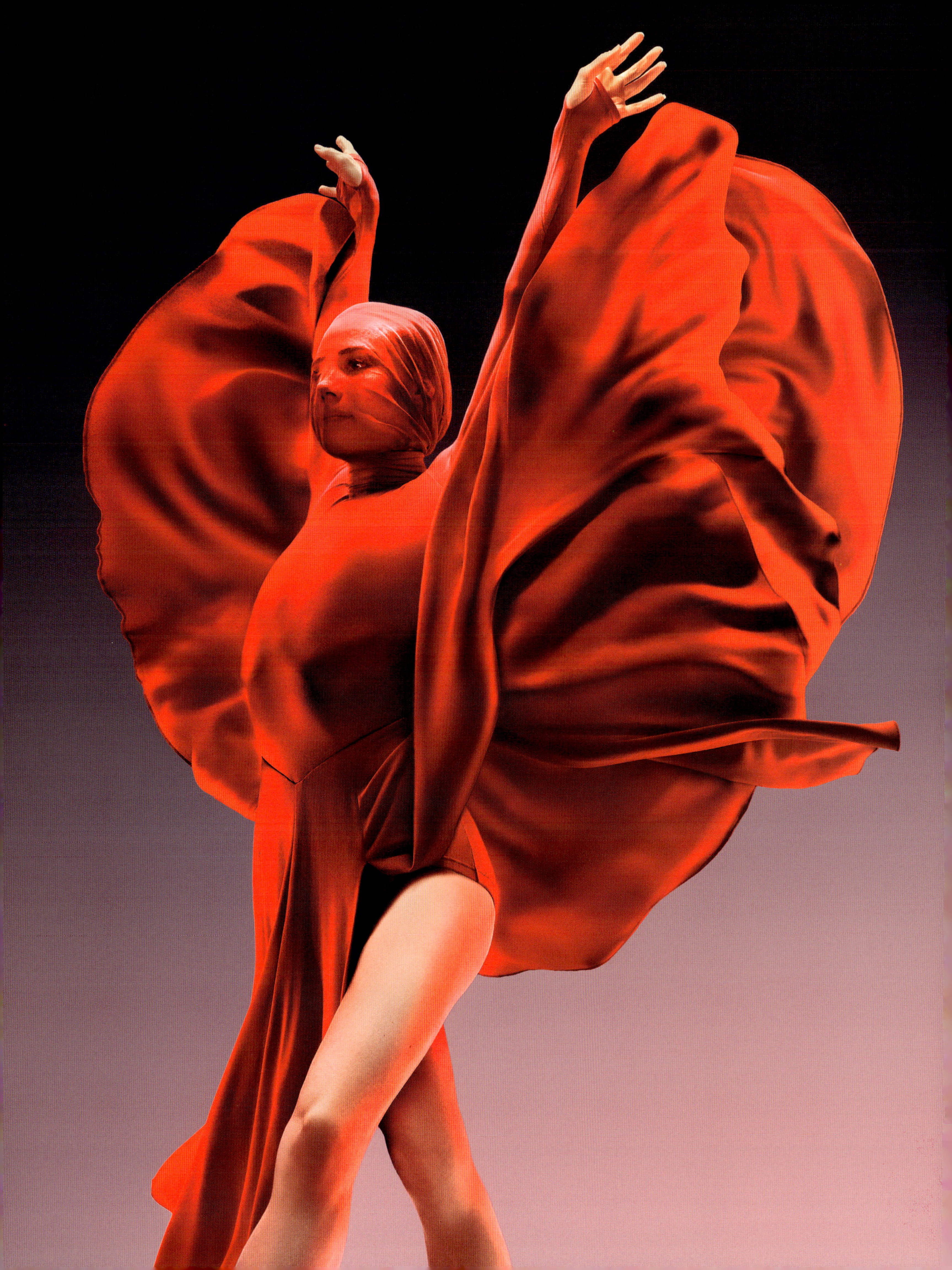

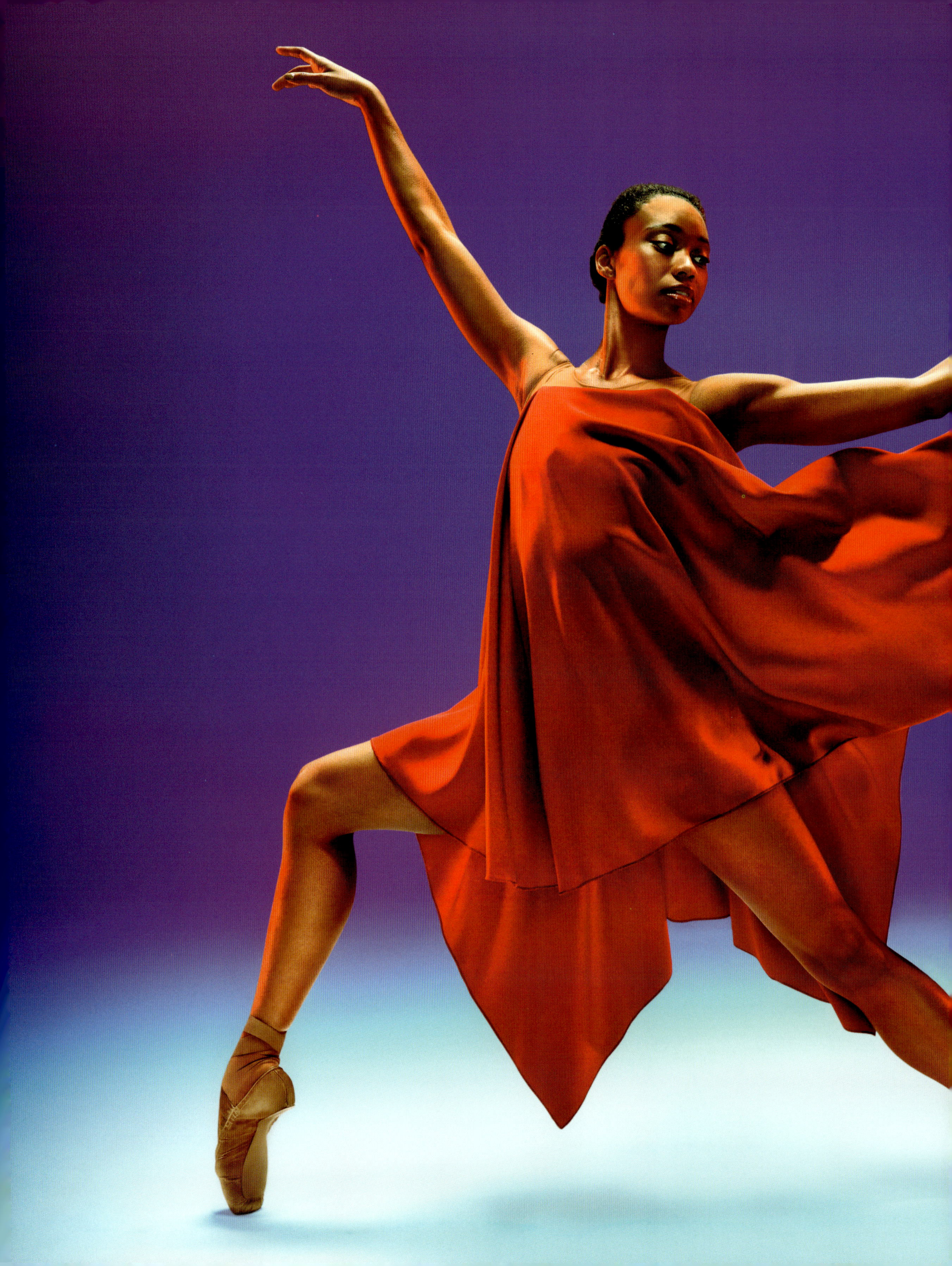

Collaborating with Gareth Pugh and the amazing team at New York City Ballet's costume department was an exhilarating experience, and definitely a career highlight. At first I was skeptical about the red cocktail dress he designed for Tiler Peck in her initial fitting. But once it was constructed I was blown away by how it moved so freely and how much it added to the movement. It's certainly one of my favorite costumes ever.

—*MATTHEW NEENAN, Choreographer*

I love getting to see how each designer's creative idea, sketched, designed, and discussed in passionate detail, suddenly appears and is translated onto a moving body.

—TAYLOR STANLEY, Dancer

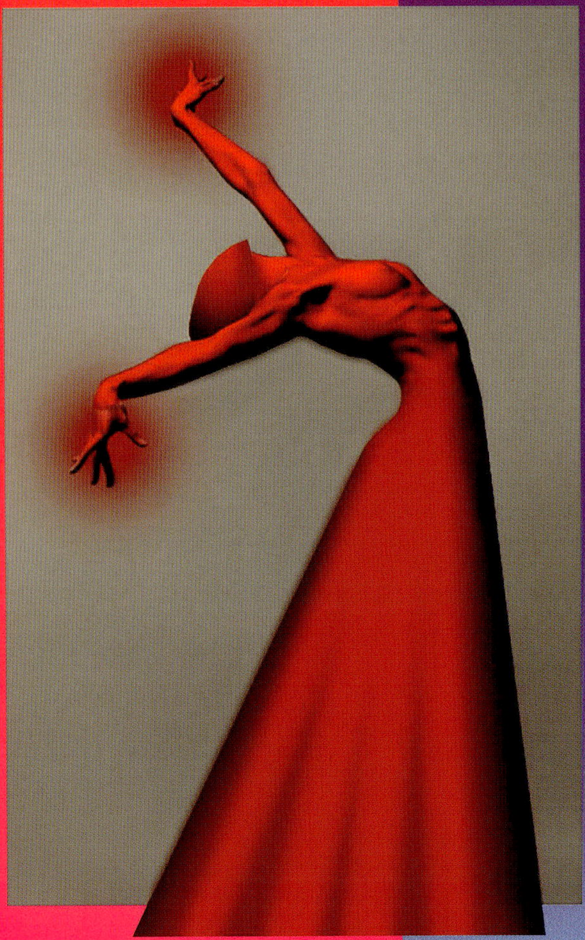

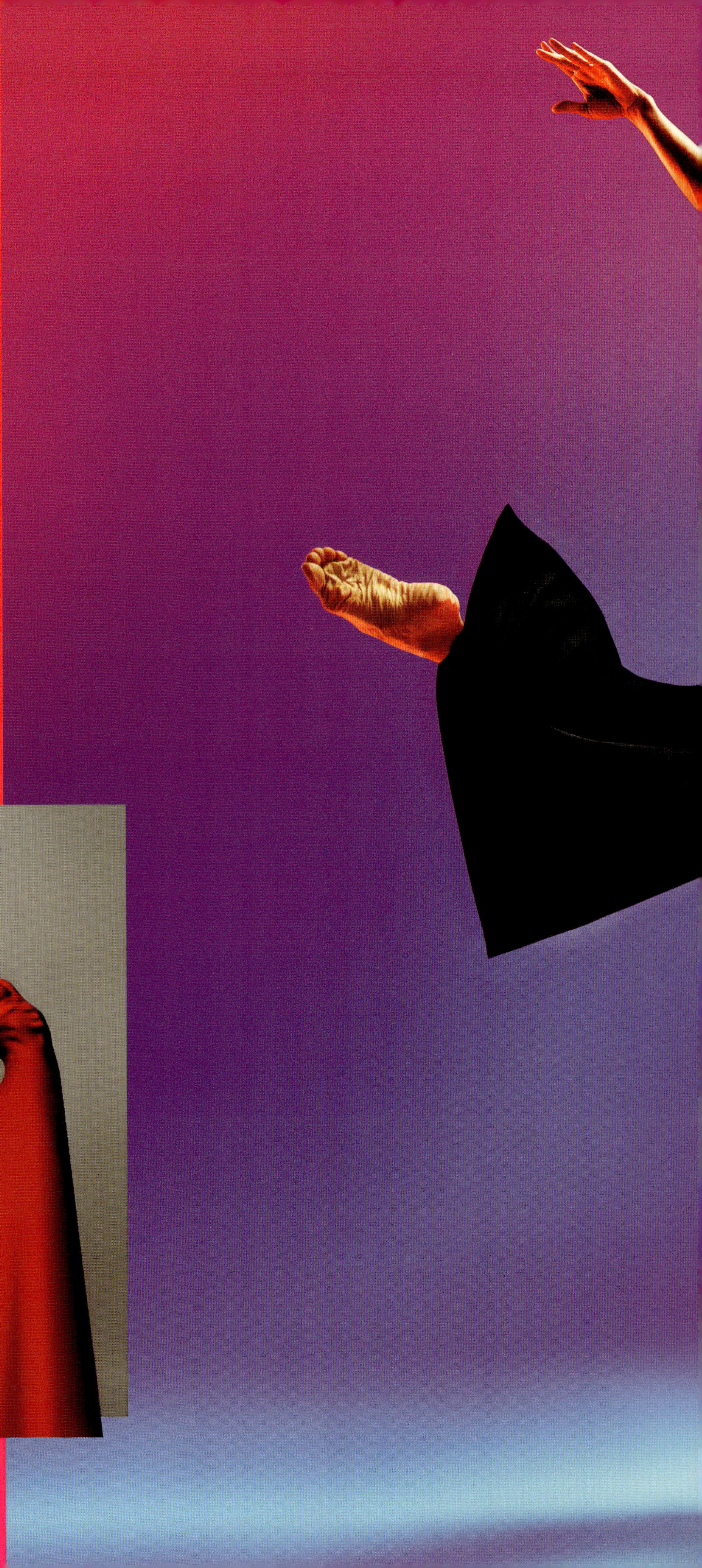

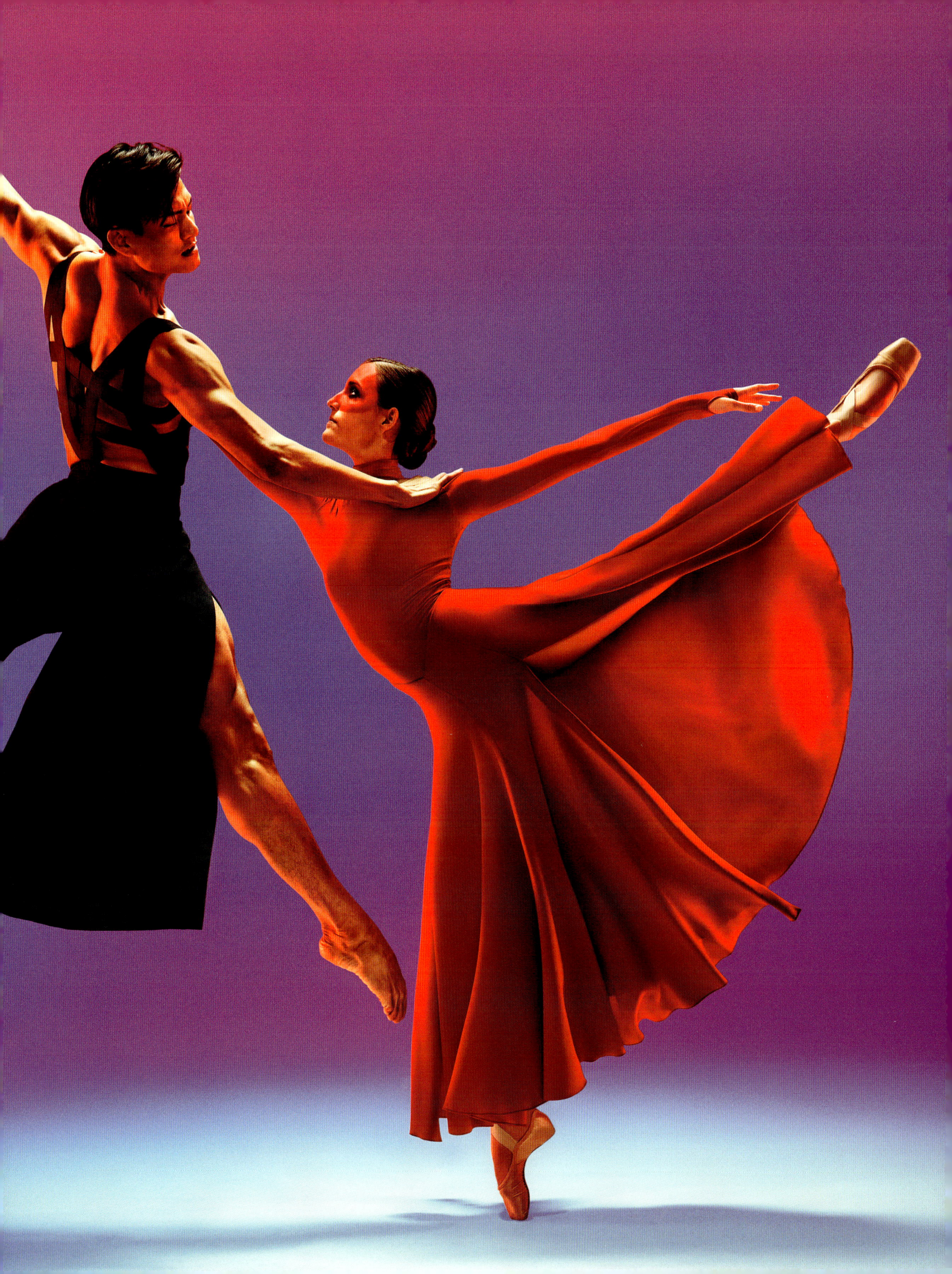

2018

ALBERTA FERRETTI *JUDAH*

For me it's the first time I've contributed to a contemporary composition, and with an American institution. Seeing my ethereal costumes for Gianna Reisen's Judah *move and come to life on stage brought me a huge amount of joy. Unforgettable.*

—*ALBERTA FERRETTI*

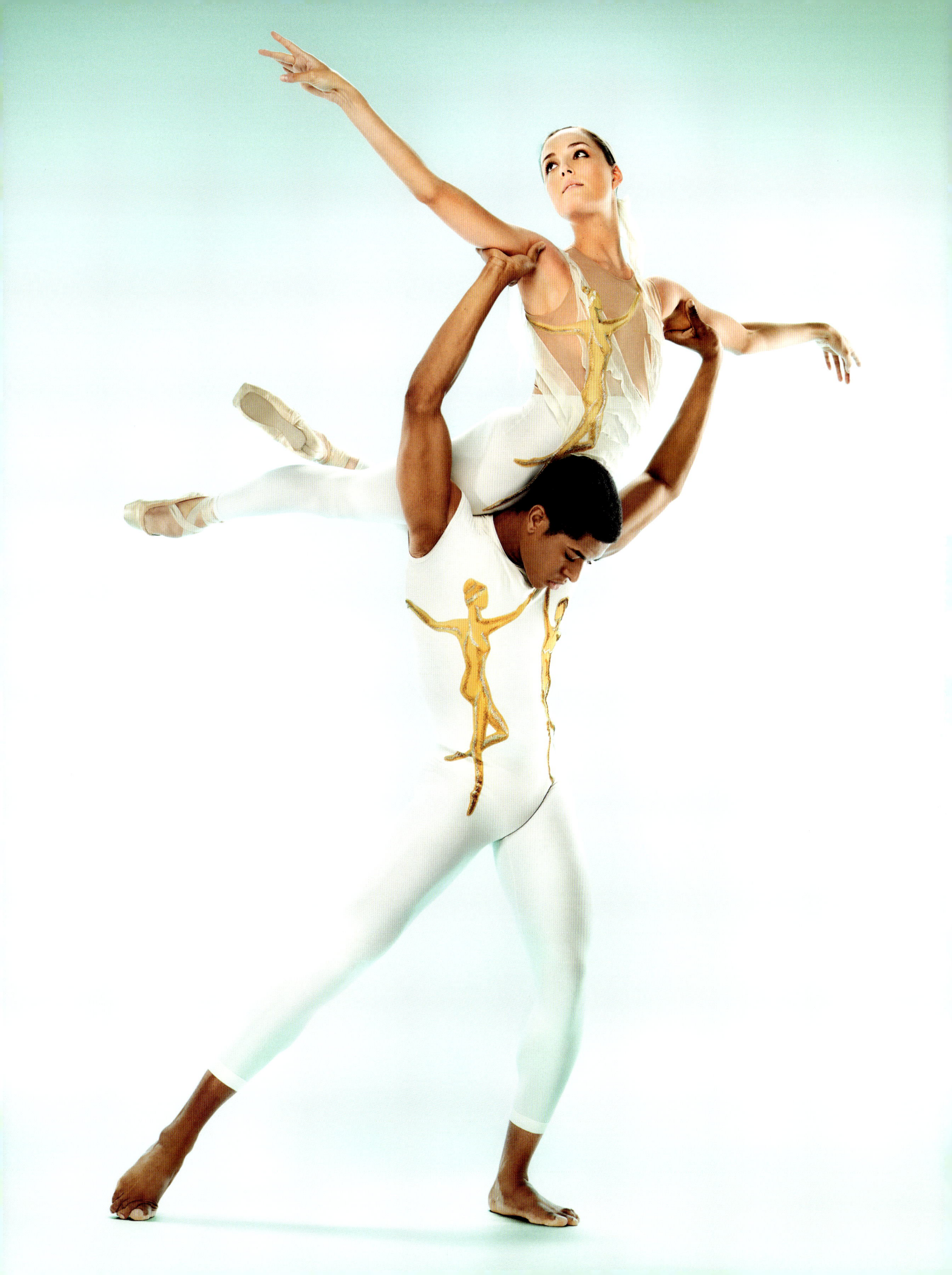

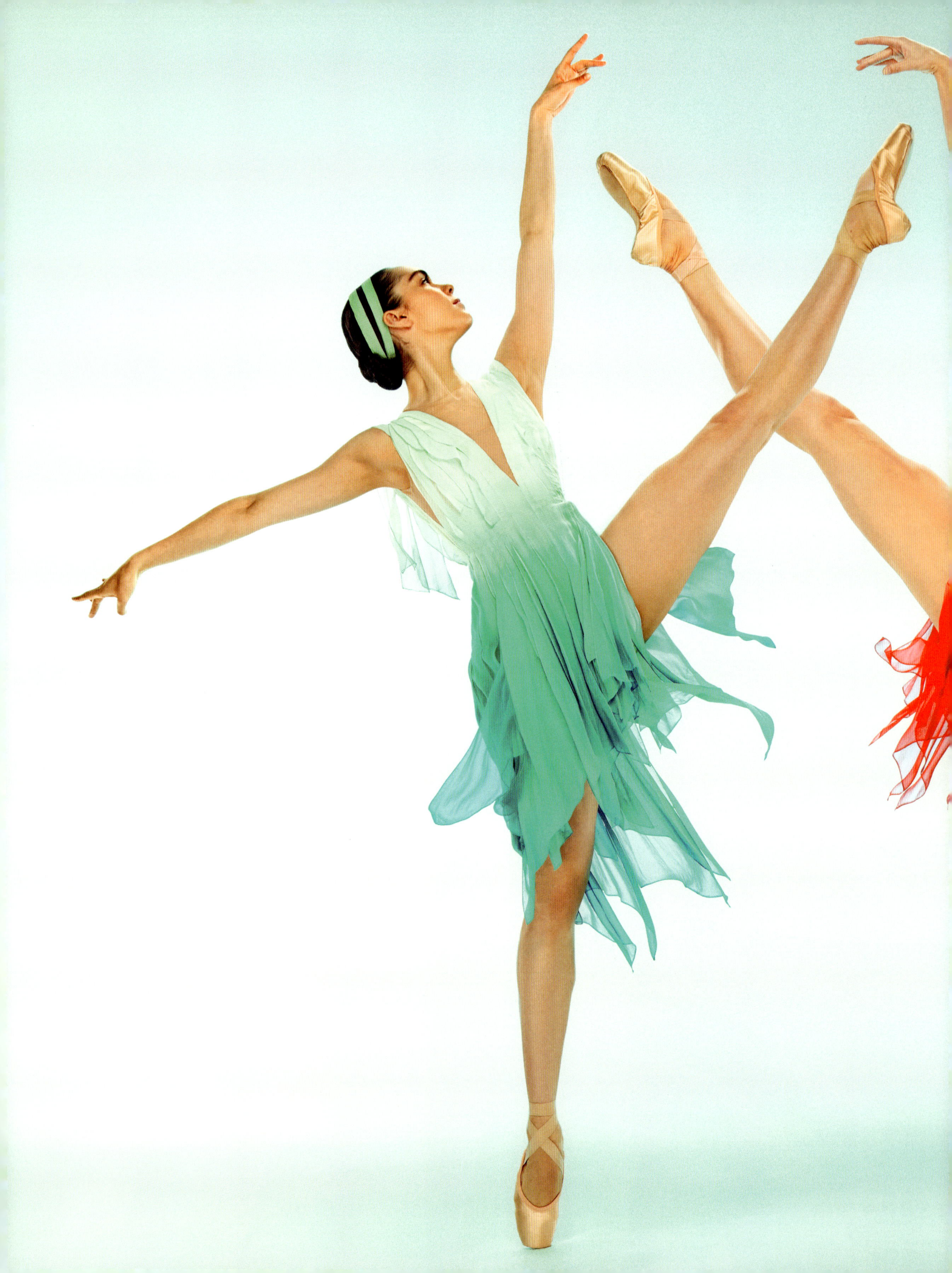

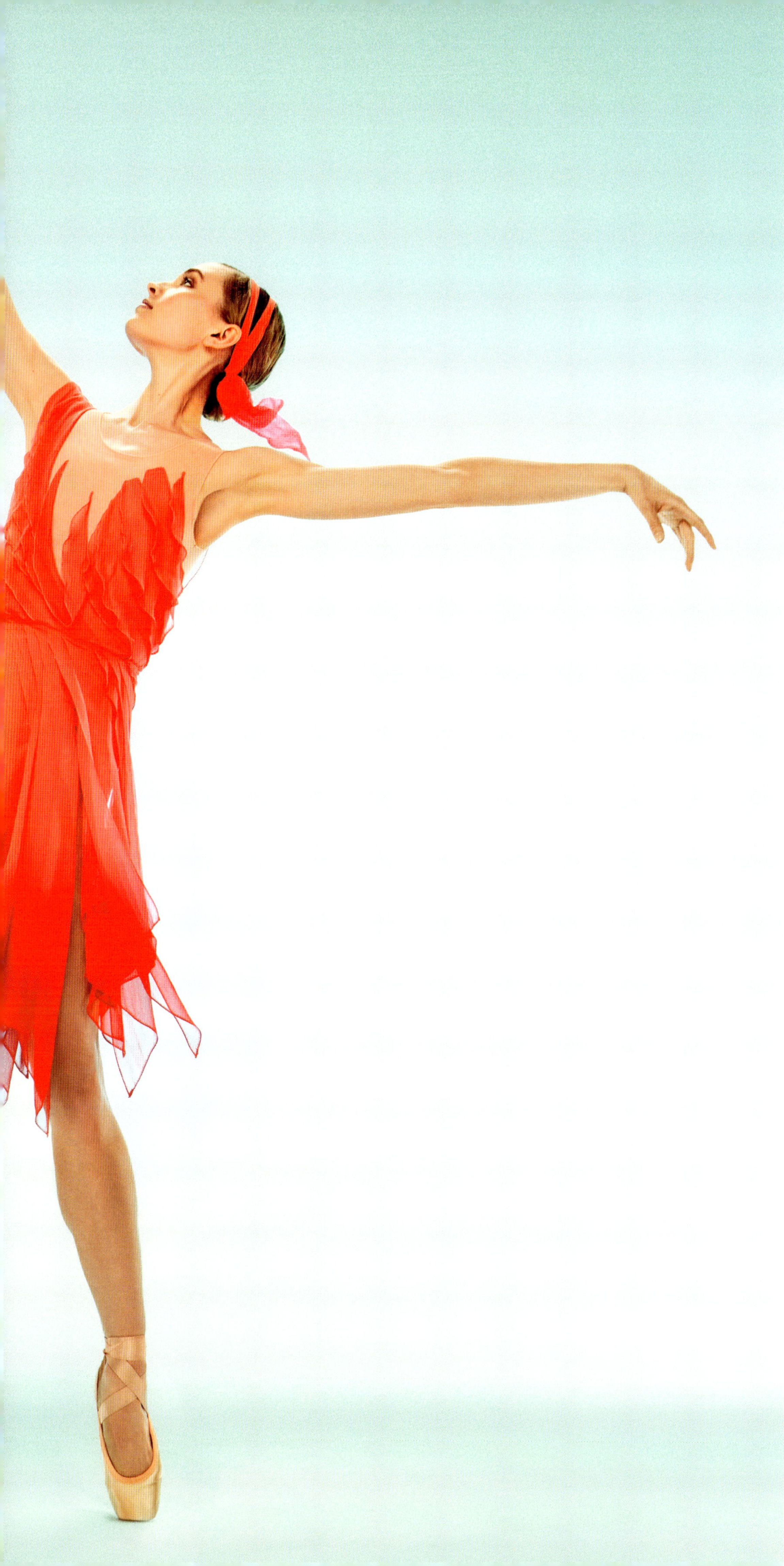

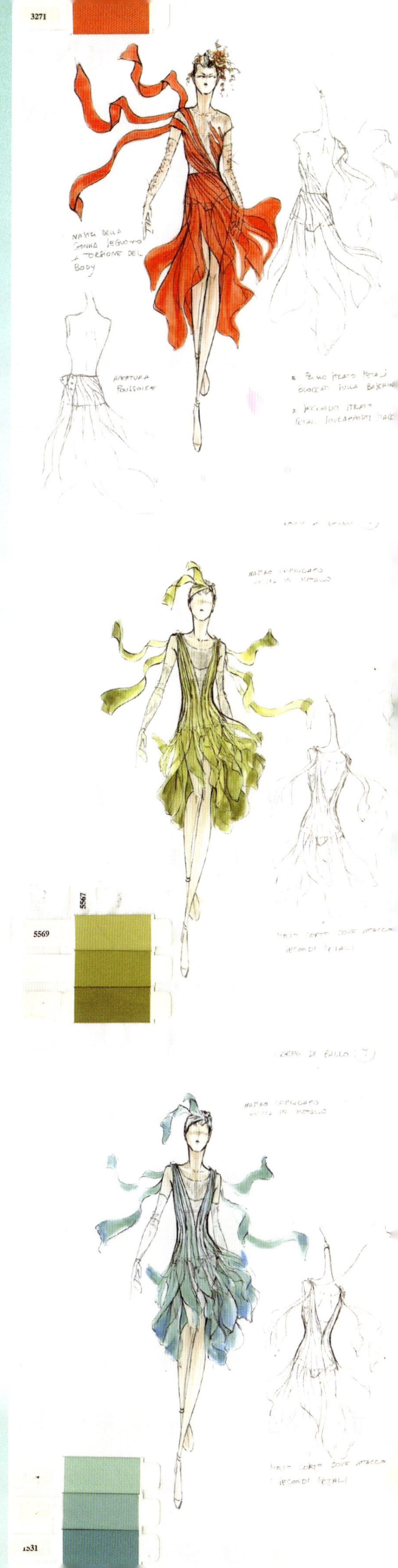
3271
5567
5569

2019

ANNA SUI *LINEAGE*

We began the project by listening to the new music composed by Oliver Davis for the new ballet, choreographed by Edwaard Liang. I immediately felt a folkloric image. I love the Ballet Russes' Rite of Spring *by Igor Stravinsky, and could picture the folkloric costumes and pagan dances.*

I was so happy when Edwaard said he felt something folkloric about this ballet too. I imagined beautiful peasant tops and skirts. It was so fun working with Marc Happel and his amazing team, finding trims for the peasant tops and using one of the prints from my collection, with roses printed on lurex chiffon. This gave a dazzling effect in movement. —ANNA SUI

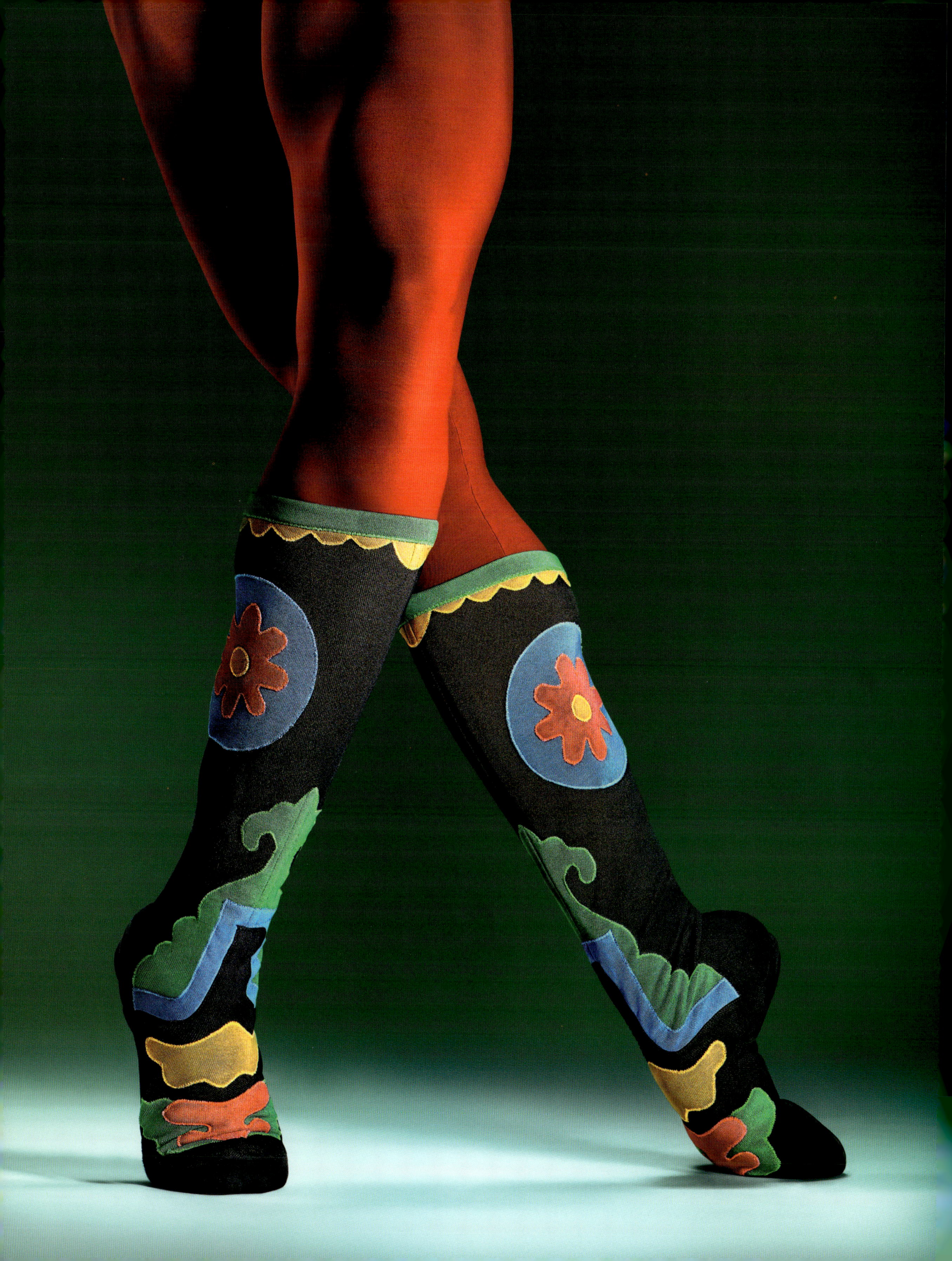

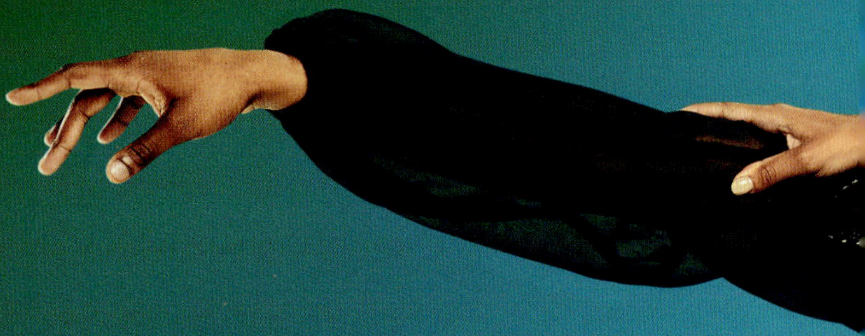

The most exciting day was the first fitting. My assistant Thomas, an avid ballet fan, and I rode up in the elevator with two principal dancers. The look on his face was like if I saw David Bowie or Keith Richards. It was priceless to see him so enthralled. —ANNA SUI

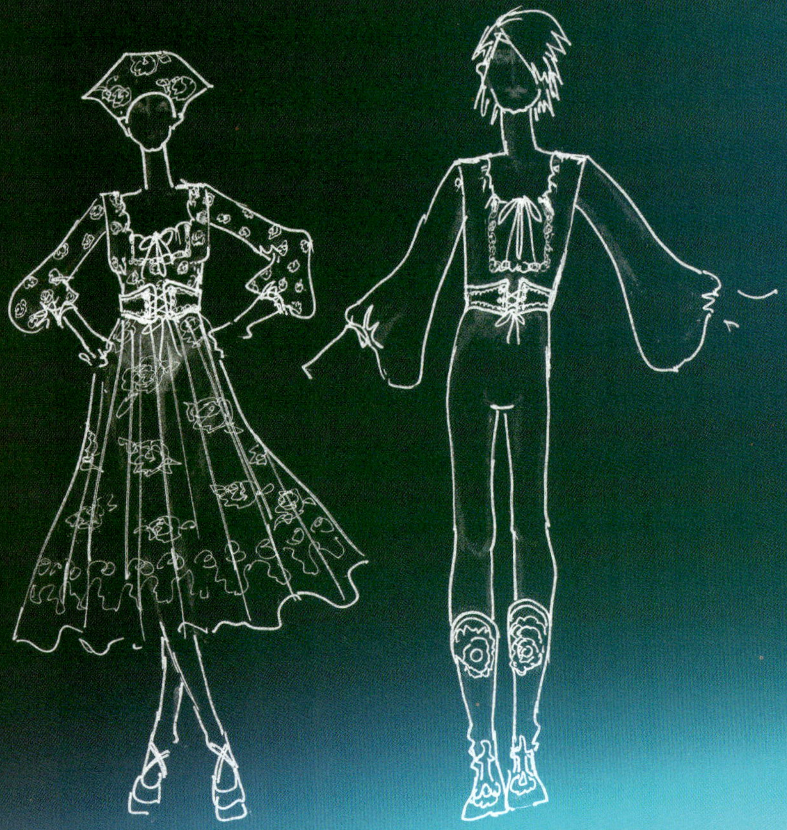

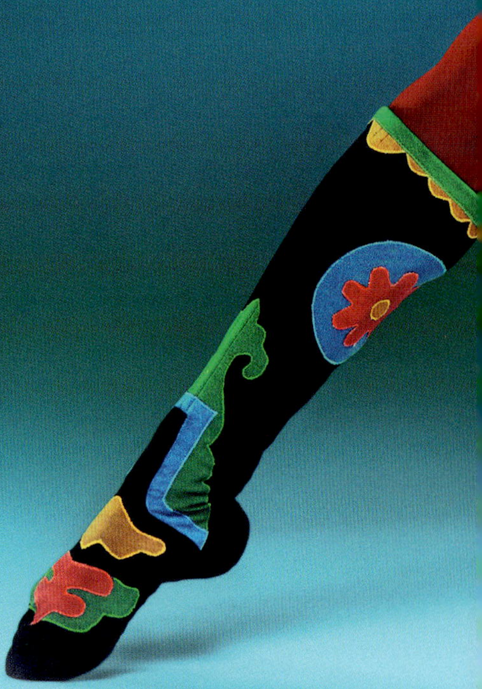

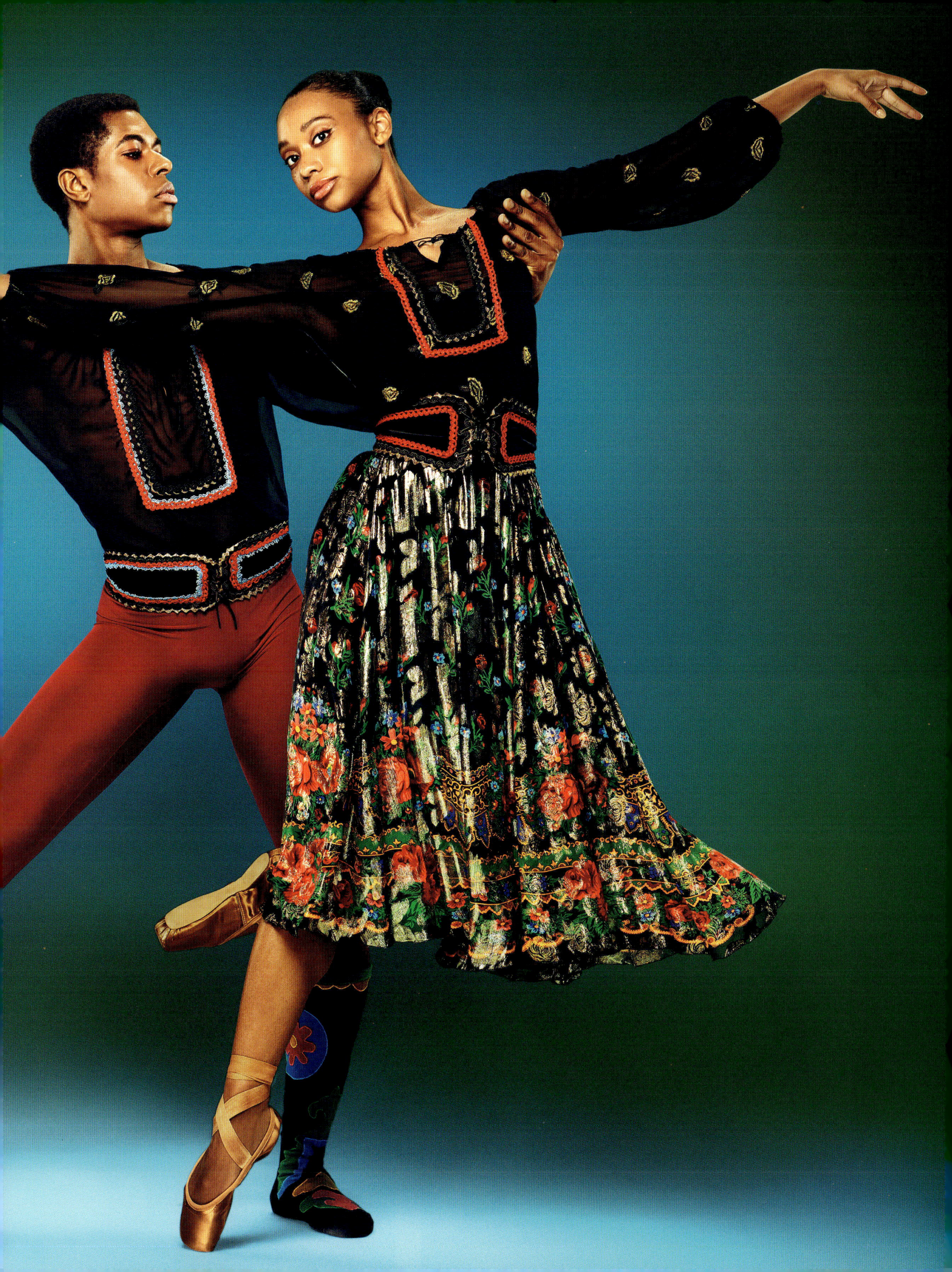

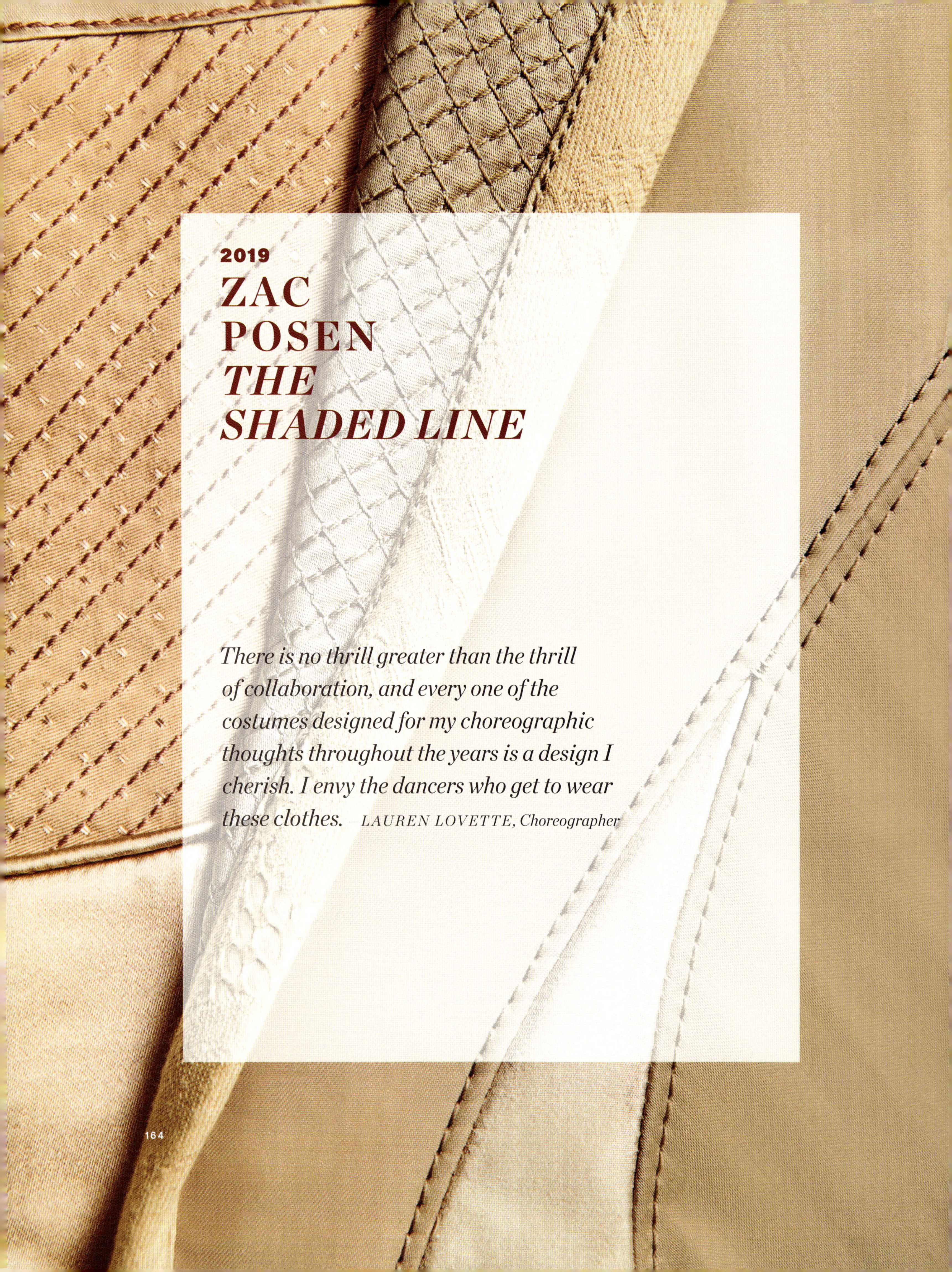

2019

ZAC POSEN *THE SHADED LINE*

There is no thrill greater than the thrill of collaboration, and every one of the costumes designed for my choreographic thoughts throughout the years is a design I cherish. I envy the dancers who get to wear these clothes. —LAUREN LOVETTE, *Choreographer*

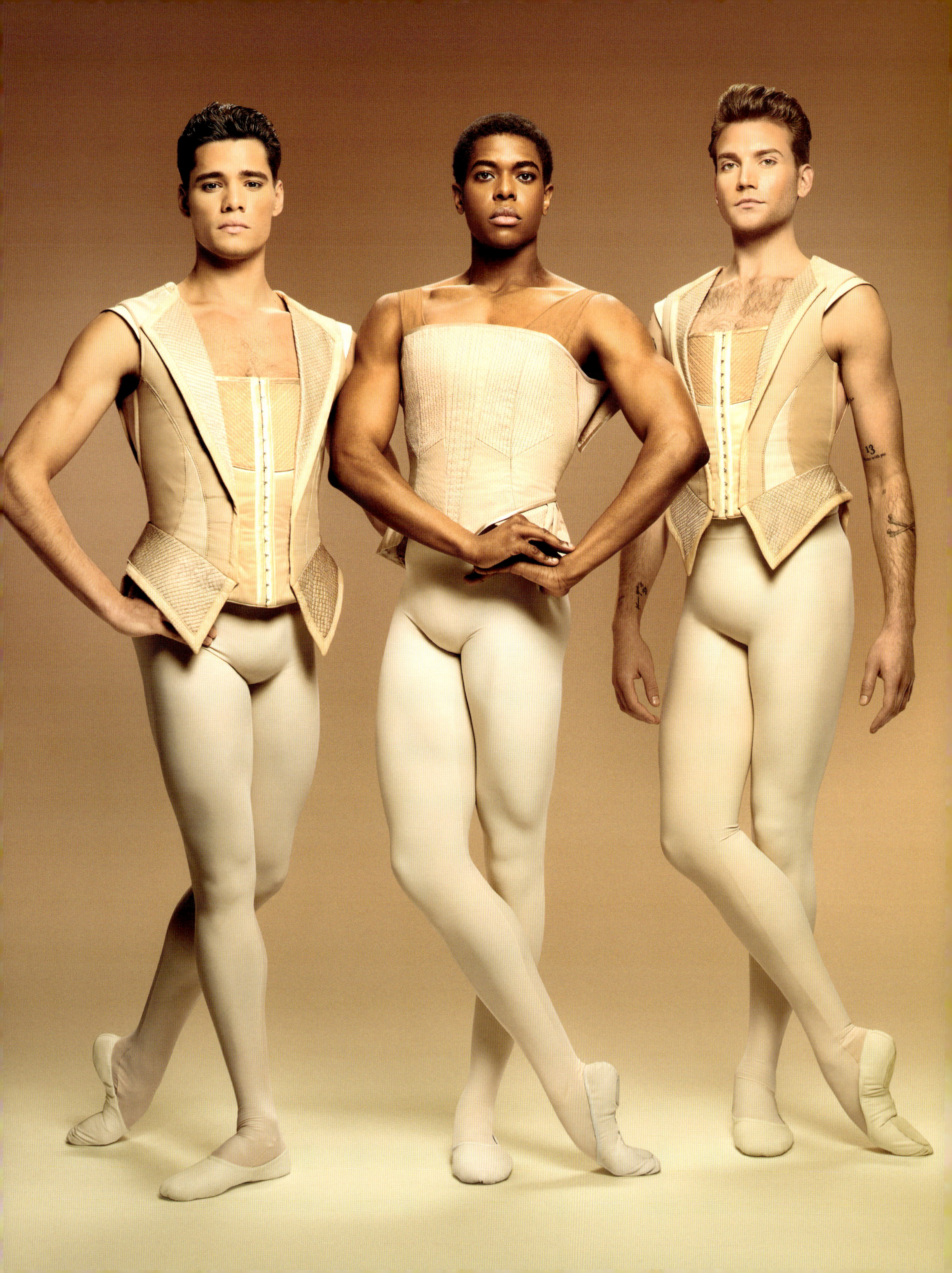

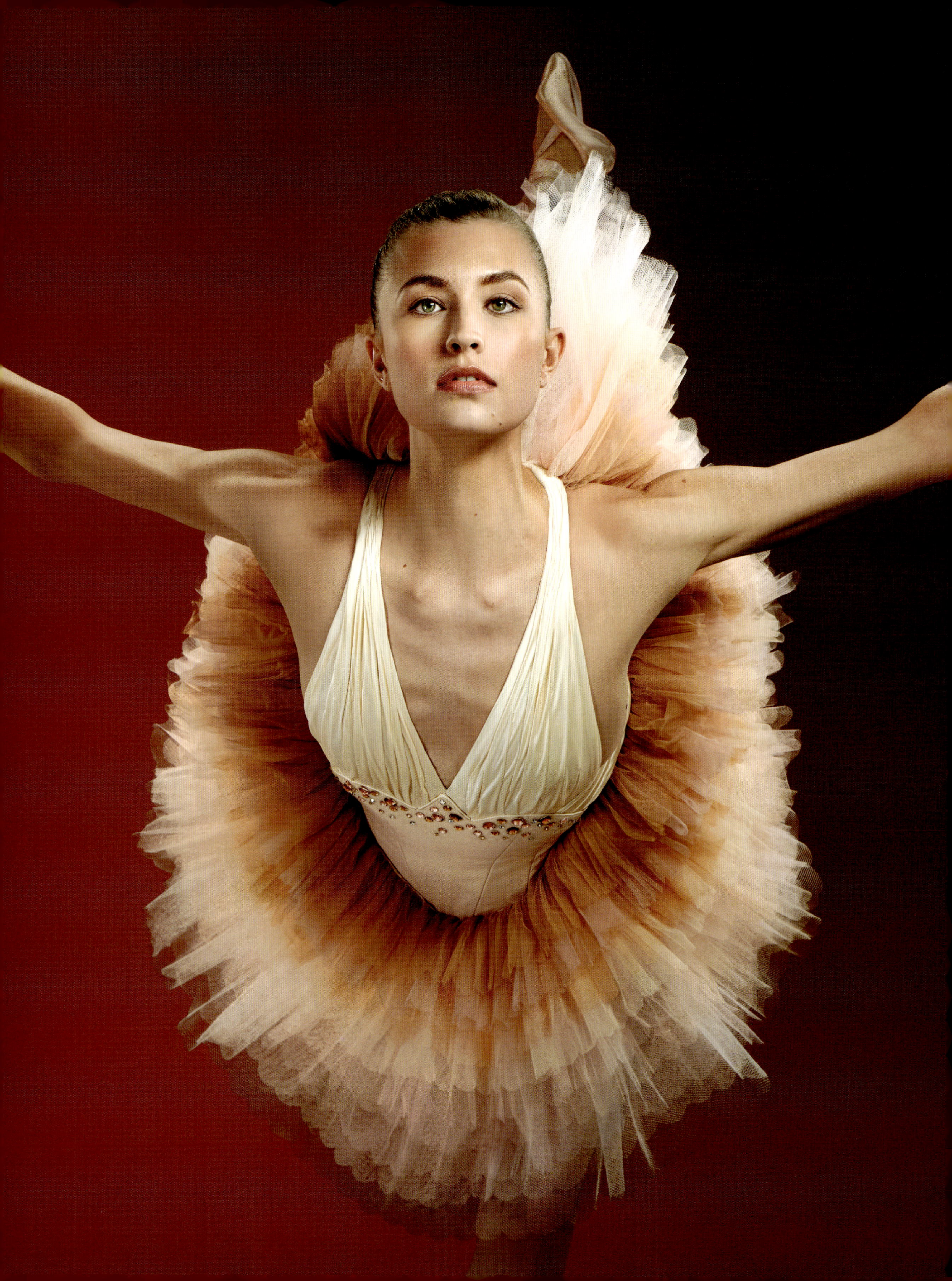

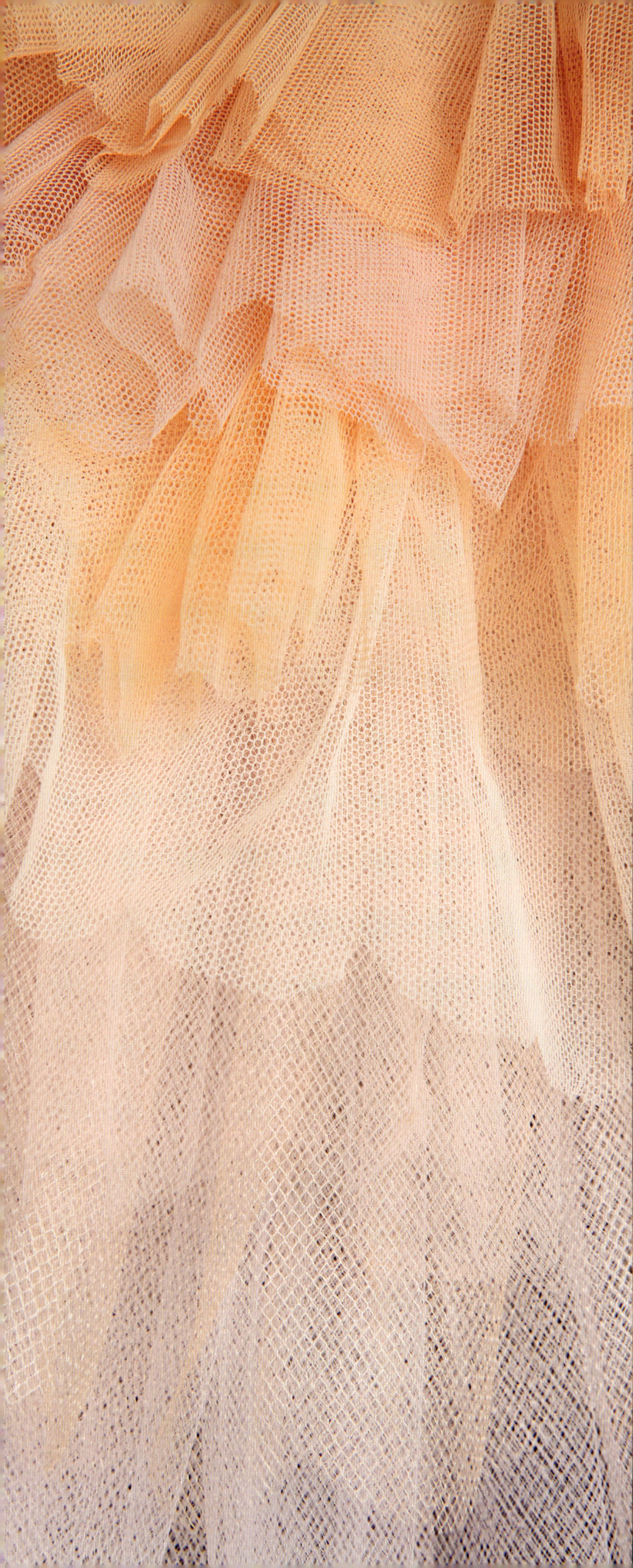
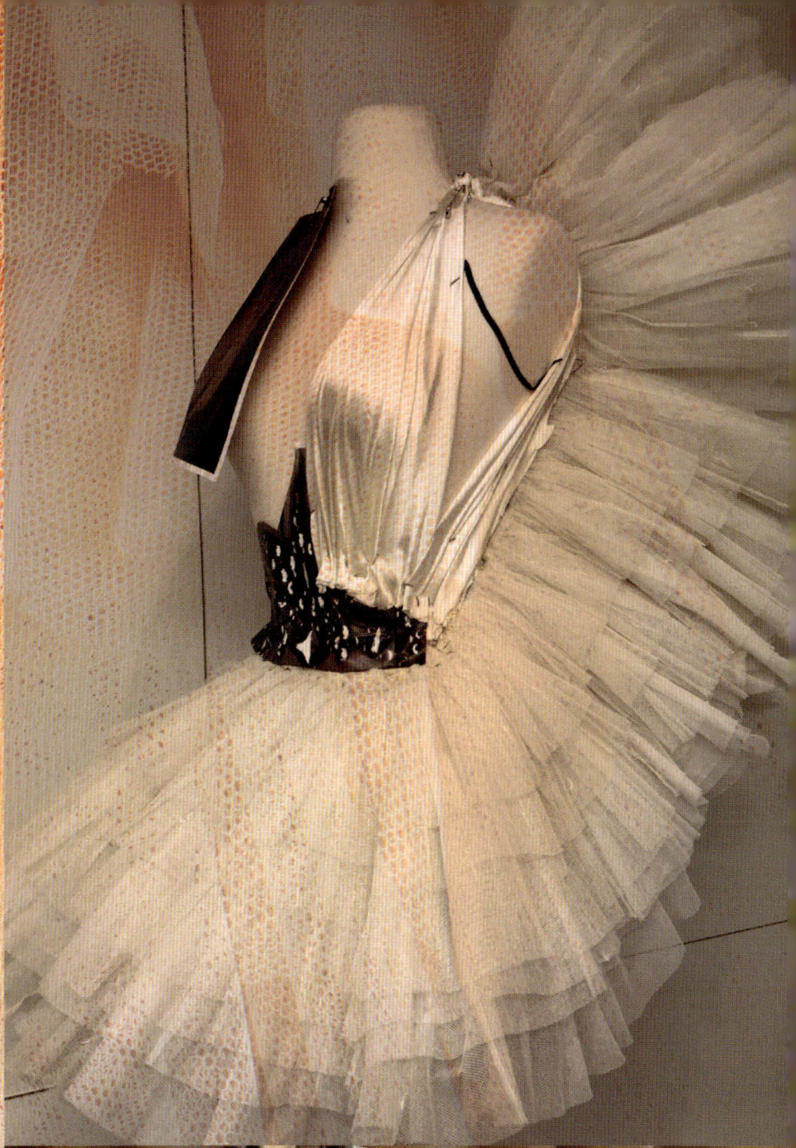
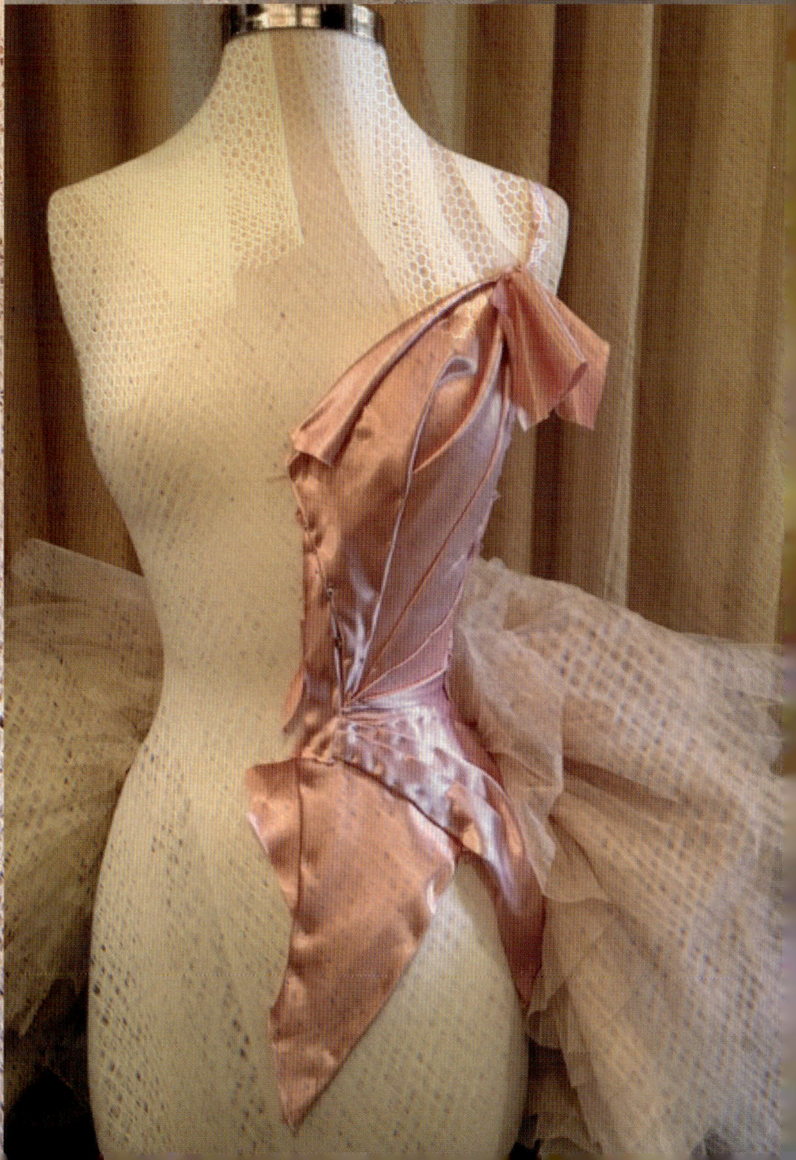

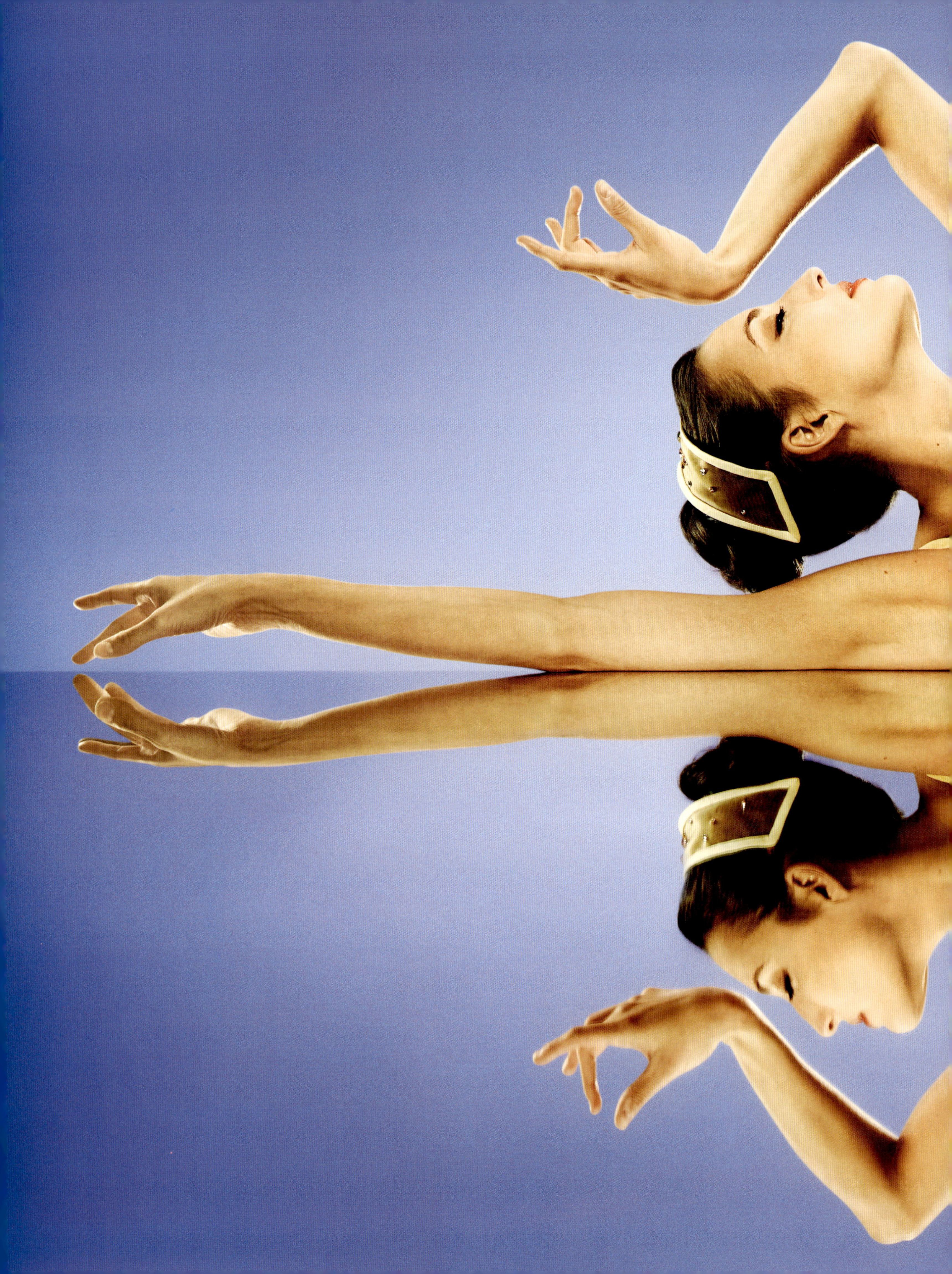

Designing costumes for Lauren's ballet The Shaded Line *became a life-changing project. As I'm drawn to the history of NYCB, and George Balanchine's collaboration with the great costume designer Barbara Karinska, my process in designing the costumes involved researching NYCB itself. I inquired if there were any old ballet costumes from her classics that I could take a look at and, magically, Marc had some incredible Karinska costumes delivered to my office so I could delve into them deeply. I was so fortunate to physically study these original, iconic costumes. I was inspired by them and how the*

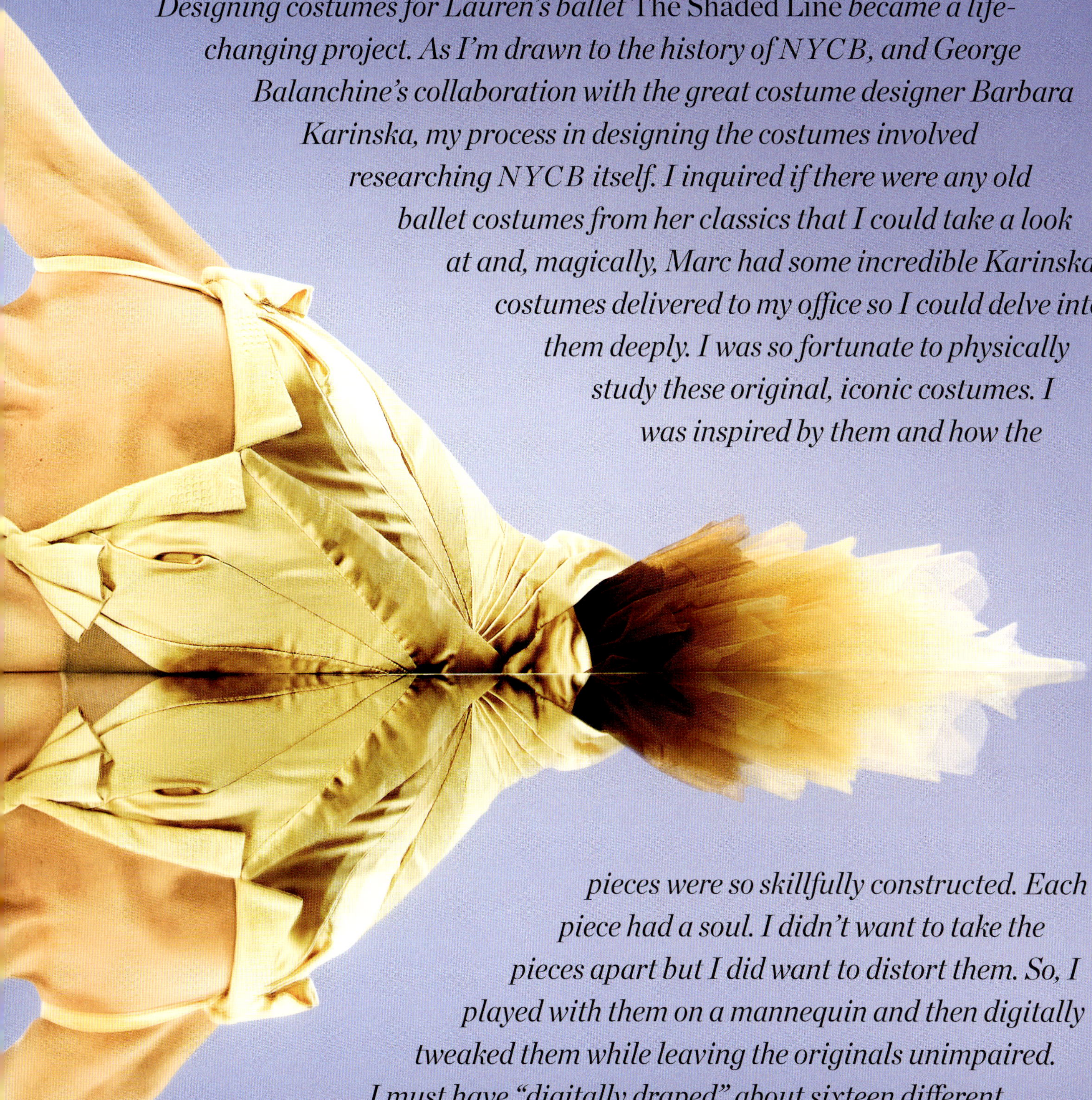

pieces were so skillfully constructed. Each piece had a soul. I didn't want to take the pieces apart but I did want to distort them. So, I played with them on a mannequin and then digitally tweaked them while leaving the originals unimpaired. I must have "digitally draped" about sixteen different variations of the costumes in order to satisfy myself with the final versions. On first glance my choices seem traditional but gradually reveal powdery-colored skirts ever so slightly subverted with off-kilter orientations, uneven like the earth on its axis. –ZAC POSEN

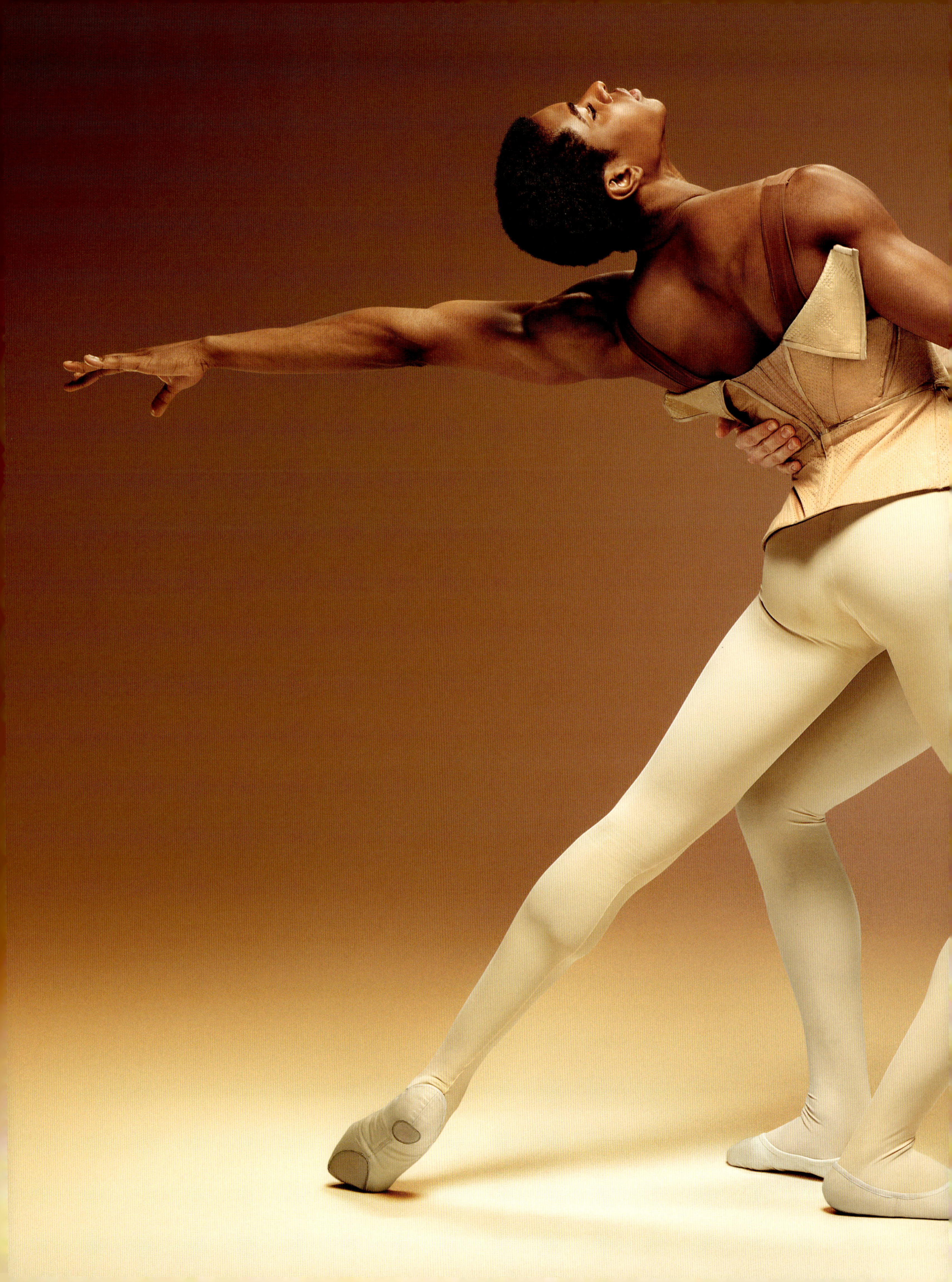

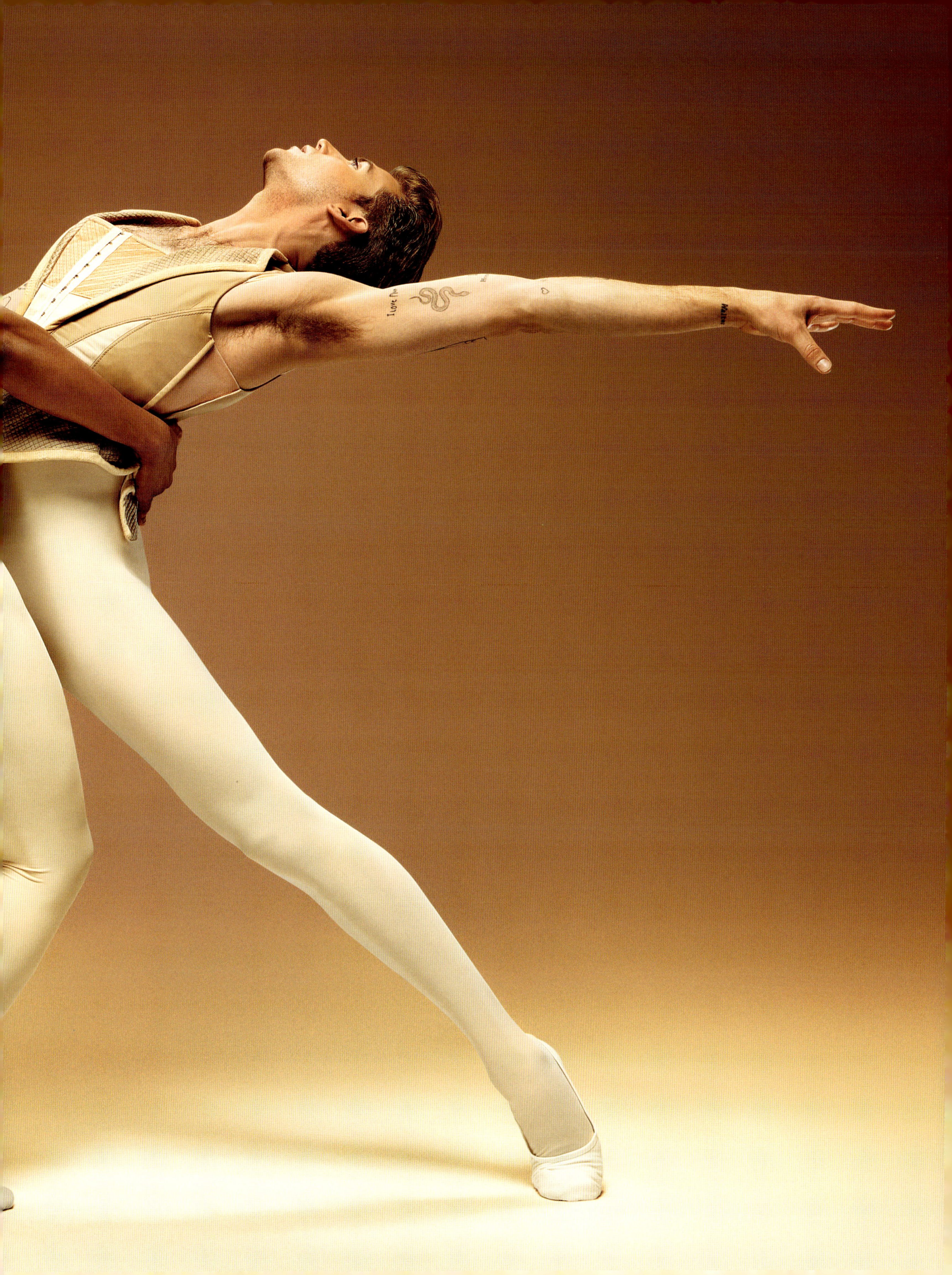

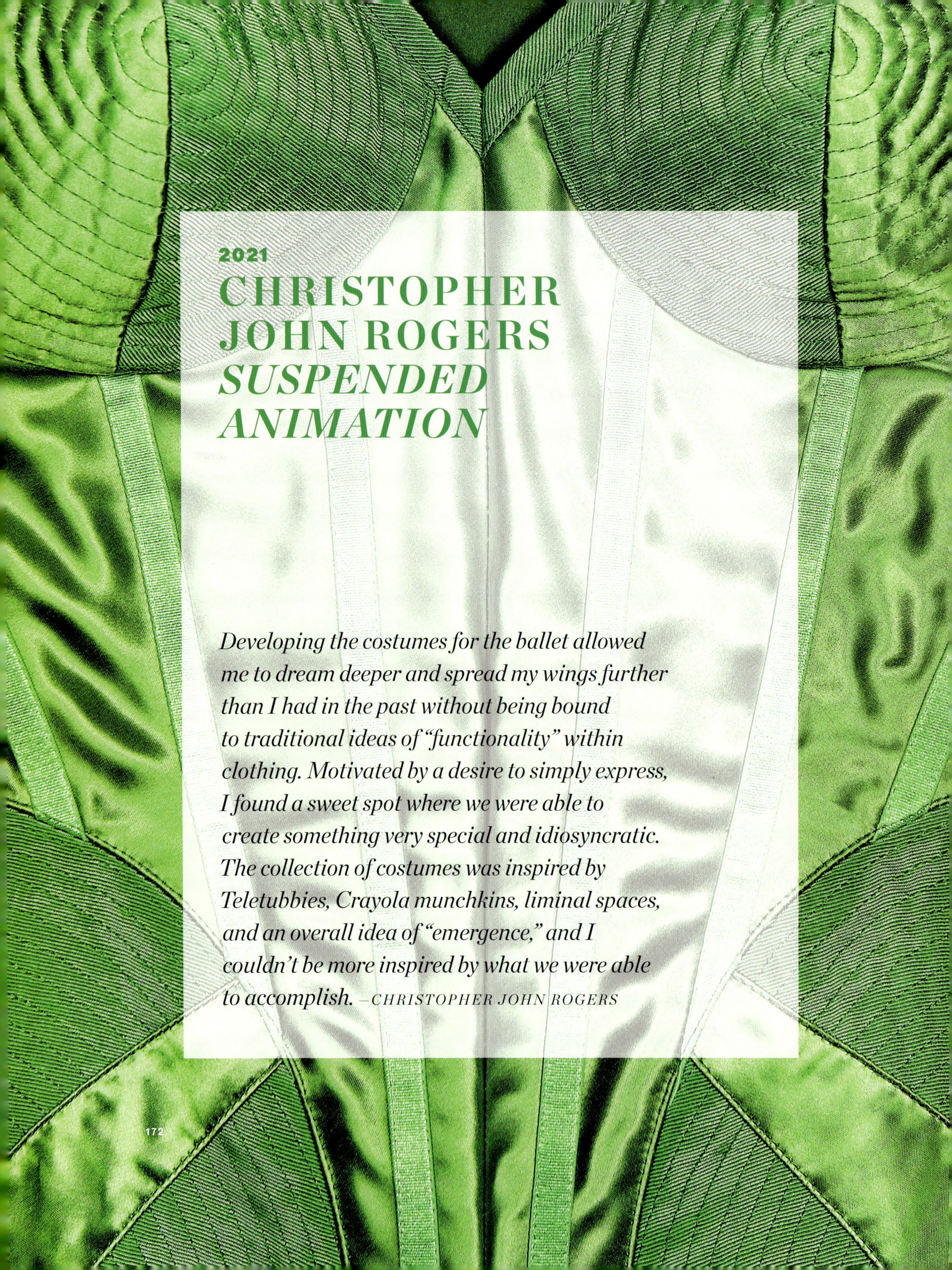

2021

CHRISTOPHER JOHN ROGERS *SUSPENDED ANIMATION*

Developing the costumes for the ballet allowed me to dream deeper and spread my wings further than I had in the past without being bound to traditional ideas of "functionality" within clothing. Motivated by a desire to simply express, I found a sweet spot where we were able to create something very special and idiosyncratic. The collection of costumes was inspired by Teletubbies, Crayola munchkins, liminal spaces, and an overall idea of "emergence," and I couldn't be more inspired by what we were able to accomplish. —CHRISTOPHER JOHN ROGERS

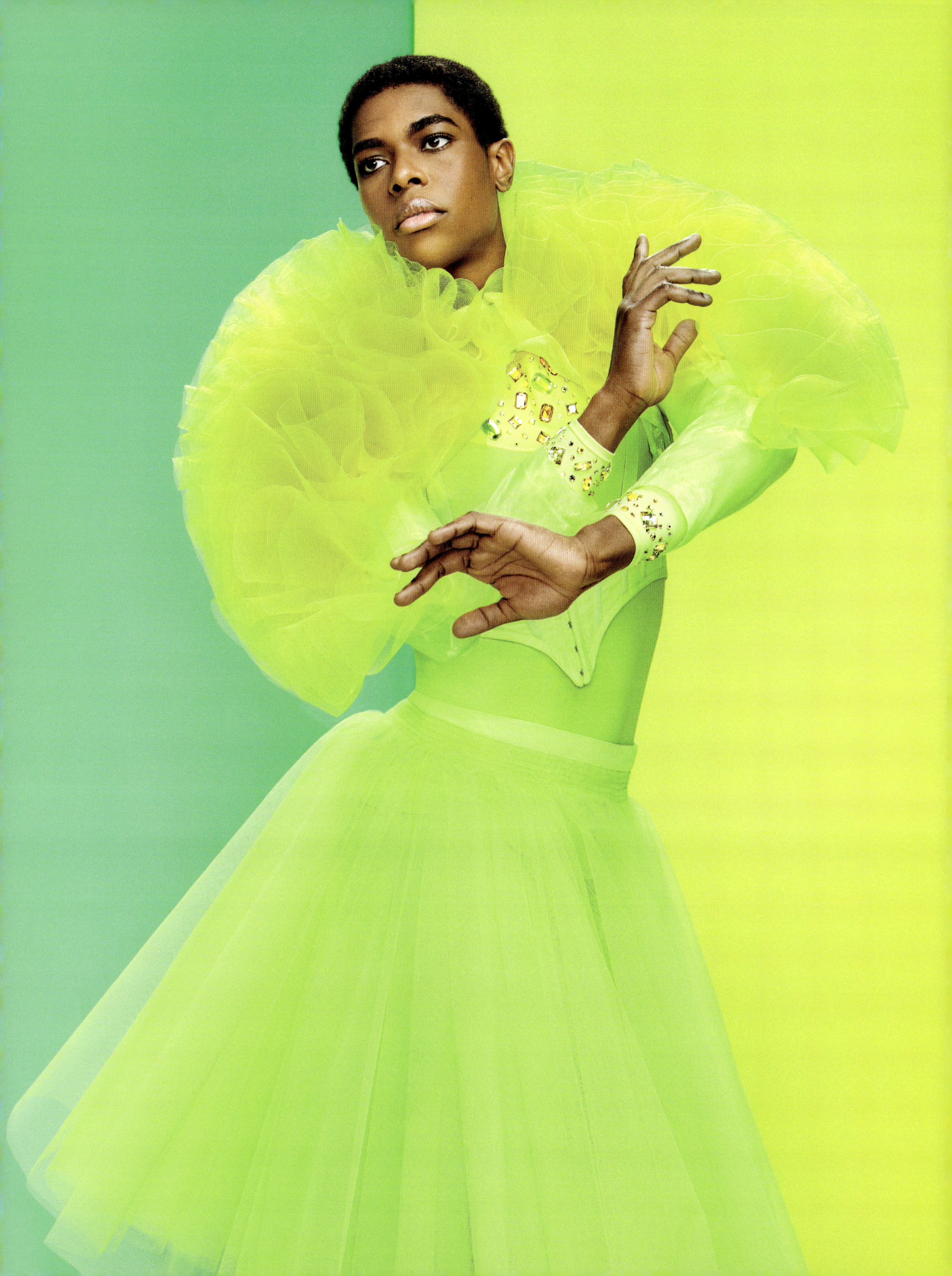

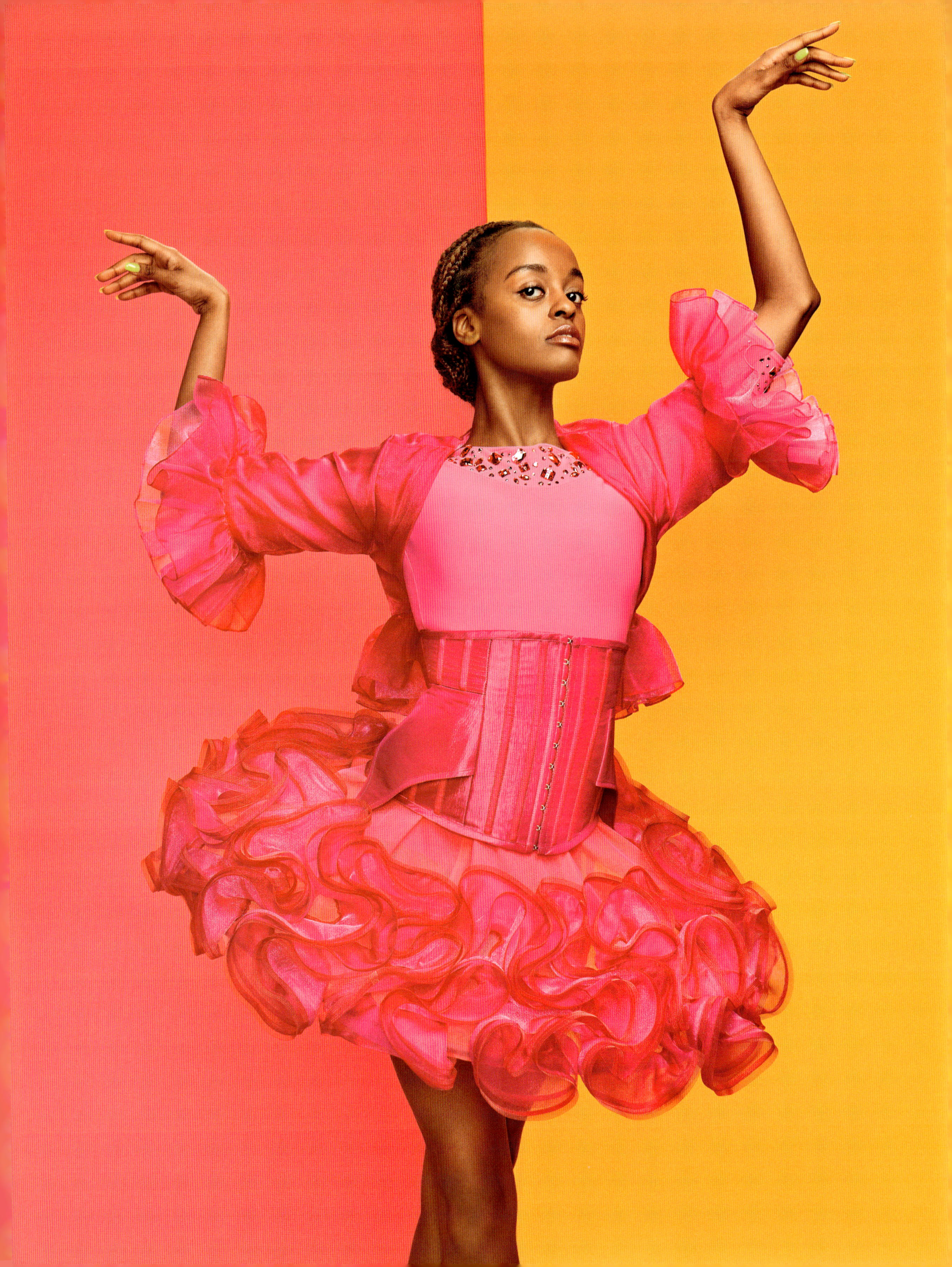

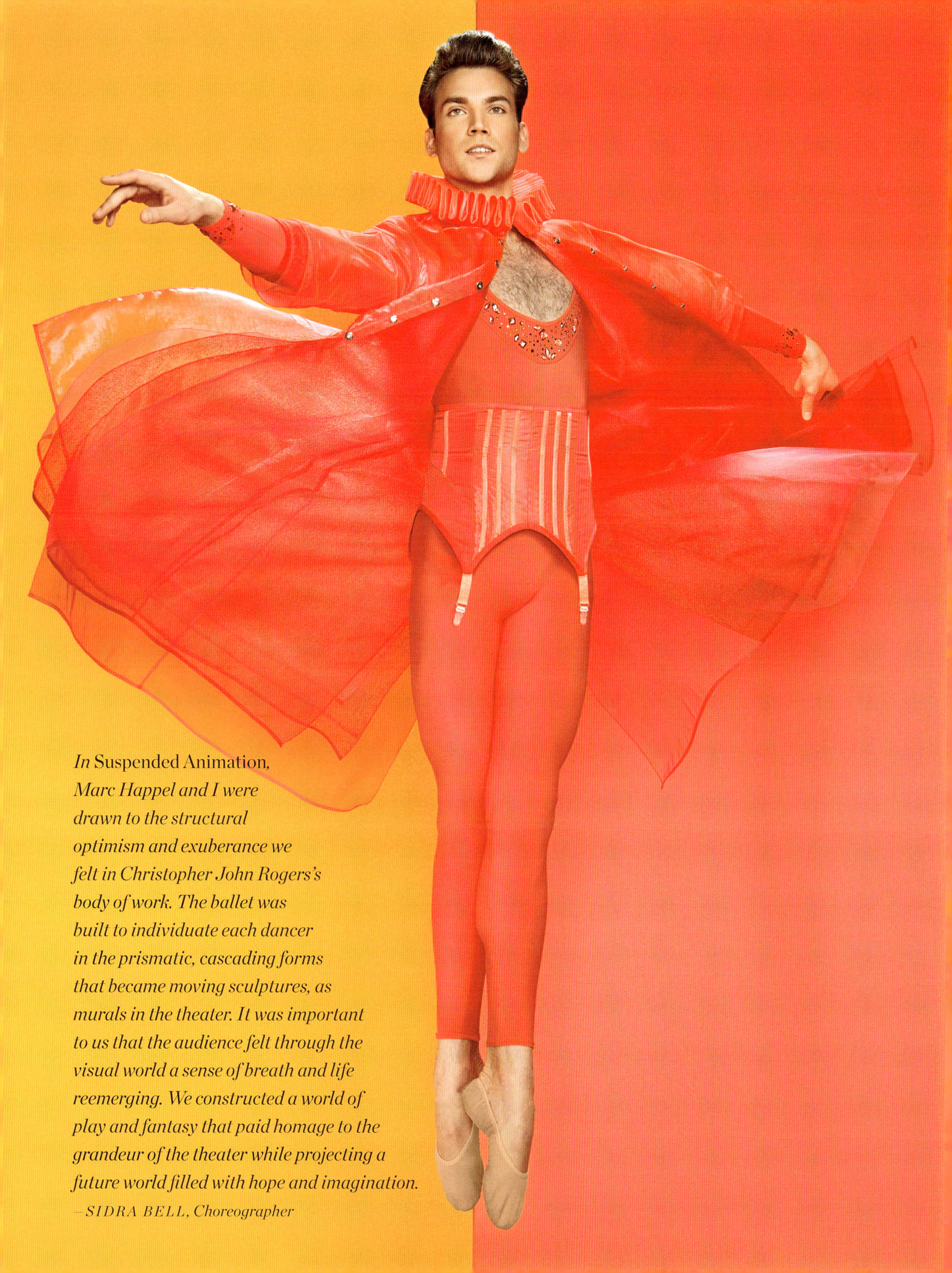

In Suspended Animation, *Marc Happel and I were drawn to the structural optimism and exuberance we felt in Christopher John Rogers's body of work. The ballet was built to individuate each dancer in the prismatic, cascading forms that became moving sculptures, as murals in the theater. It was important to us that the audience felt through the visual world a sense of breath and life reemerging. We constructed a world of play and fantasy that paid homage to the grandeur of the theater while projecting a future world filled with hope and imagination.*

—SIDRA BELL, Choreographer

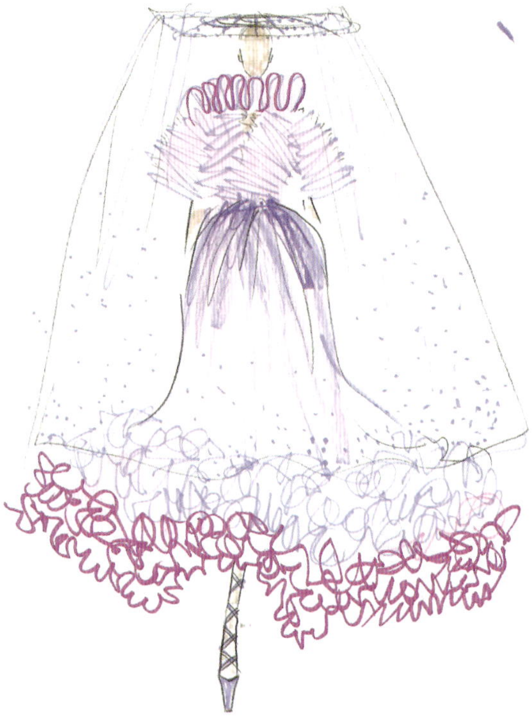
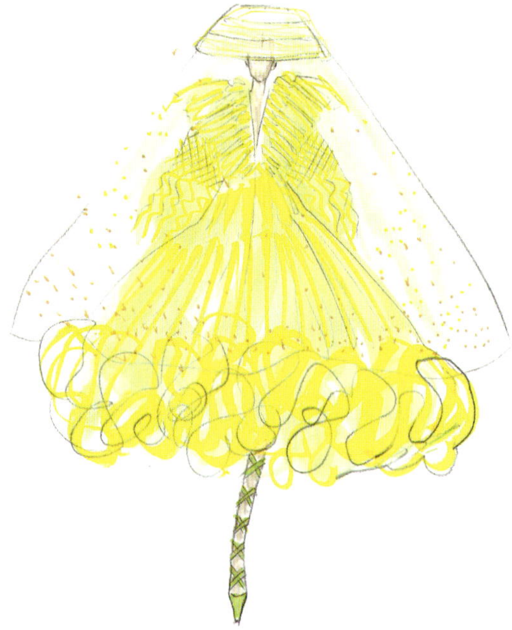
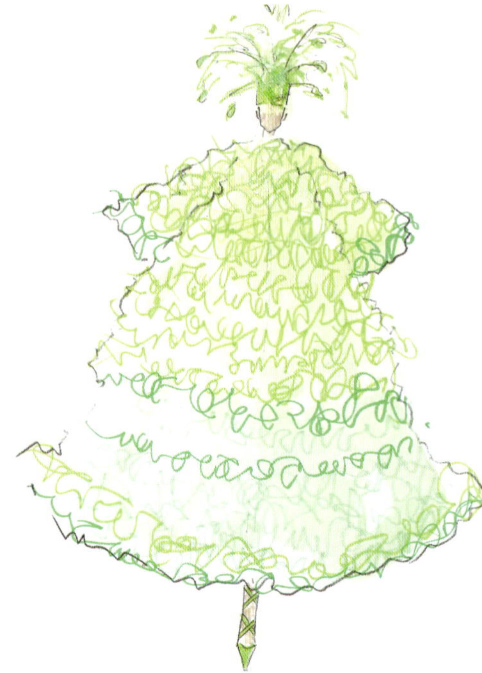
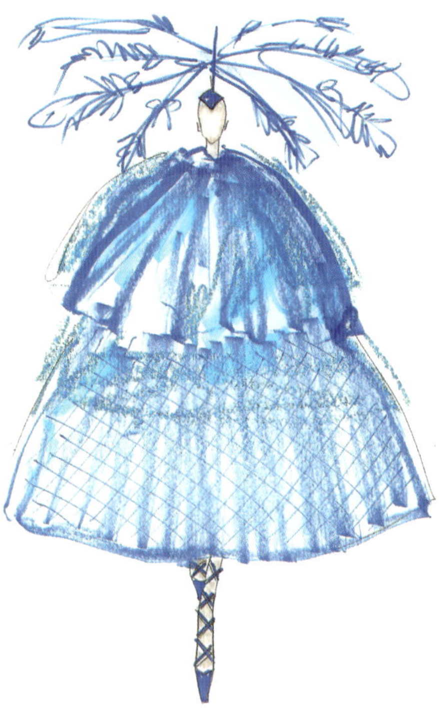
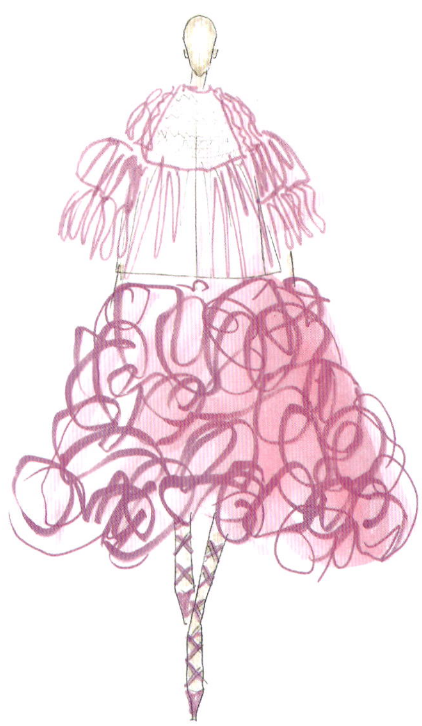
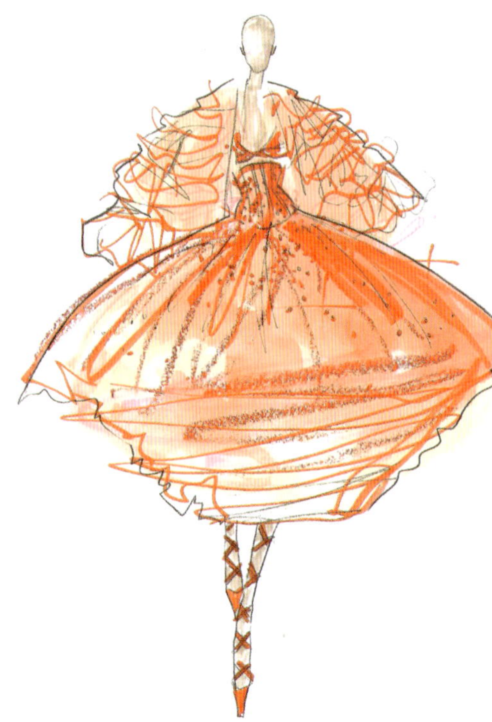
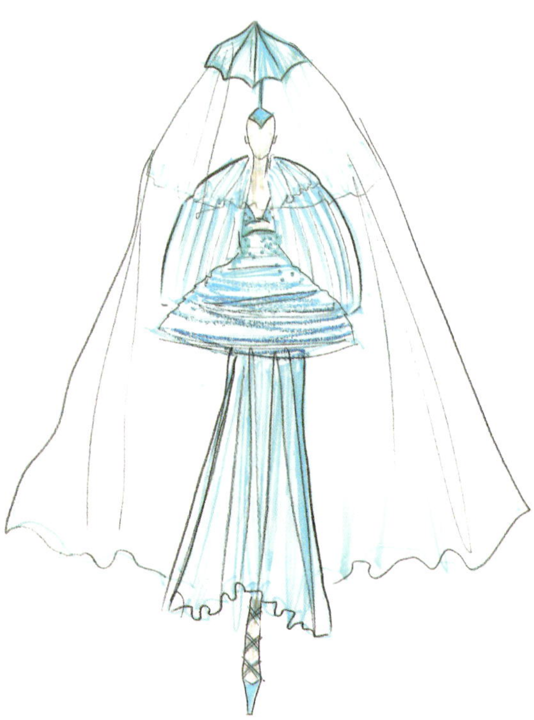
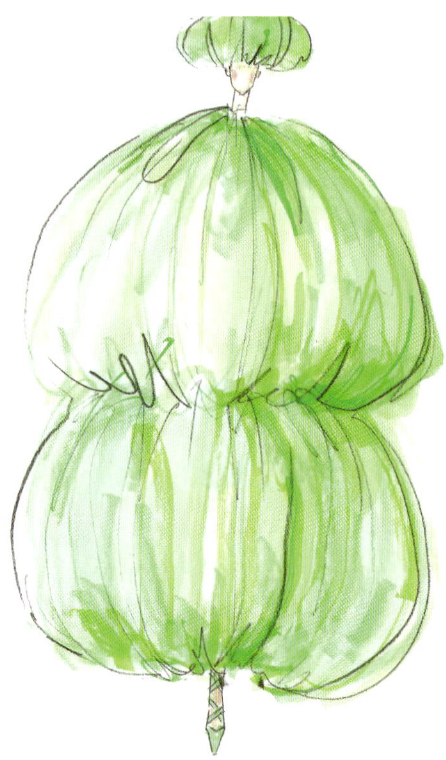
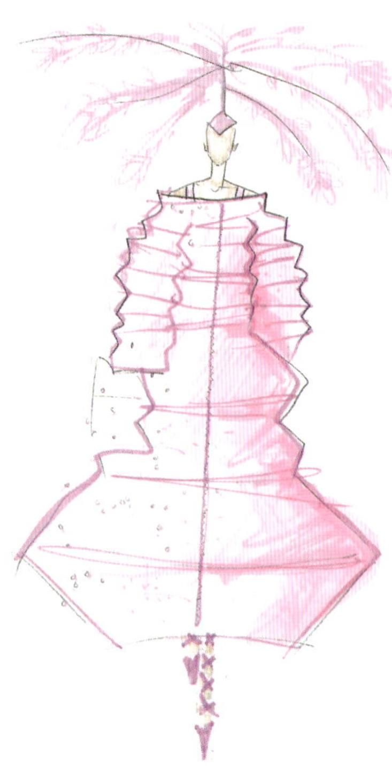

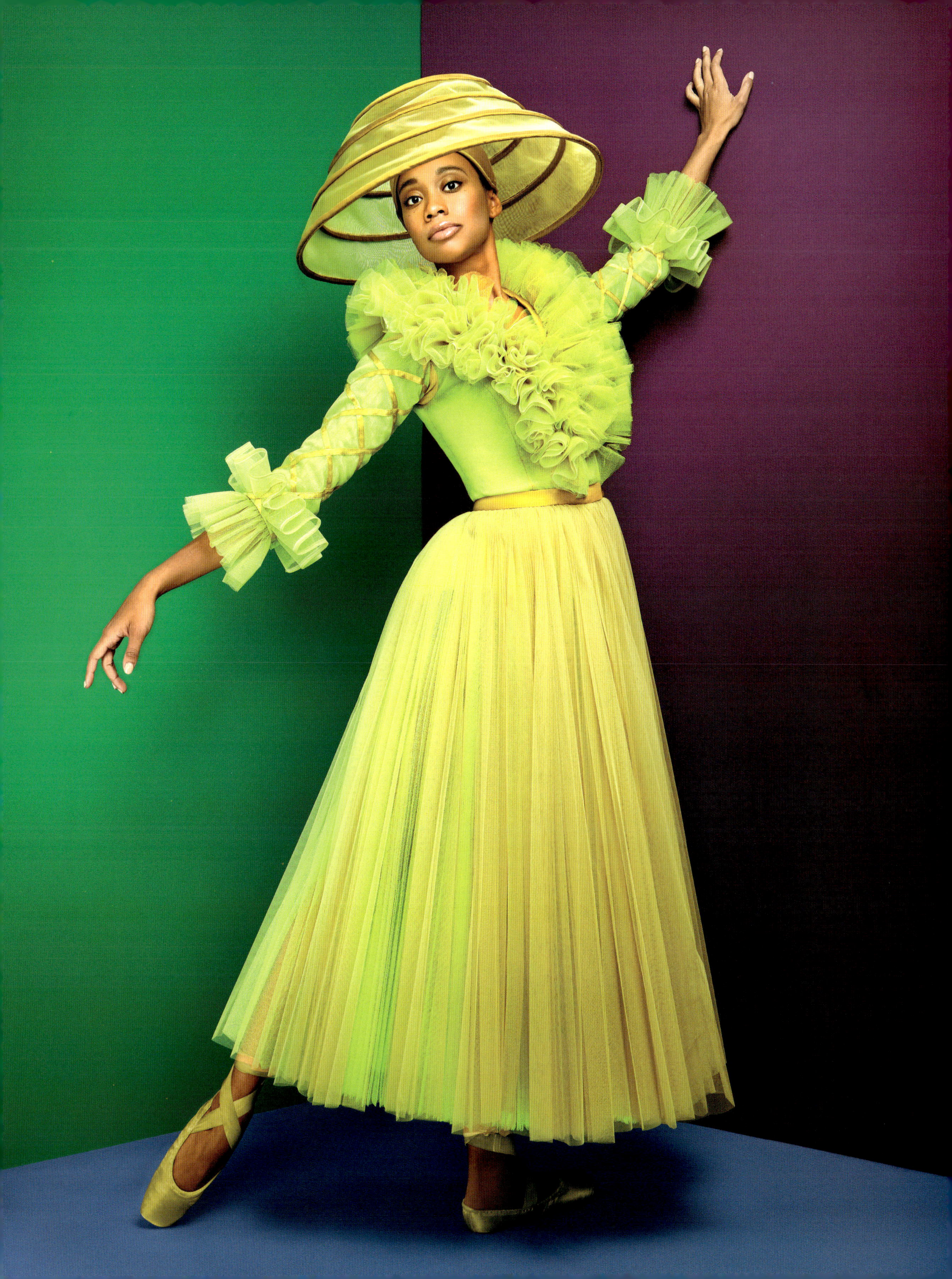

2021

ESTEBAN CORTÁZAR *SKY TO HOLD*

Witnessing the rehearsals and seeing the dancers and teams working tirelessly to achieve such perfection is an inspiration I will hold onto forever. I was inspired by the concept of "finding the light," which was talked about spontaneously in one of the first creative sessions with our amazing choreographer Andrea Miller and Colombian star singer and songwriter Lido Pimienta. Right away I thought to create fluid, light, and transparent pieces that would echo the dancers' movements. I worked with Marc and his incredible team to build the shapes and silhouettes, along with their color and dye specialist to create dégradé and ombré effects, which made every piece unique. On stage it was an explosion of color, full of enthusiasm, positivity.

—ESTEBAN CORTÁZAR

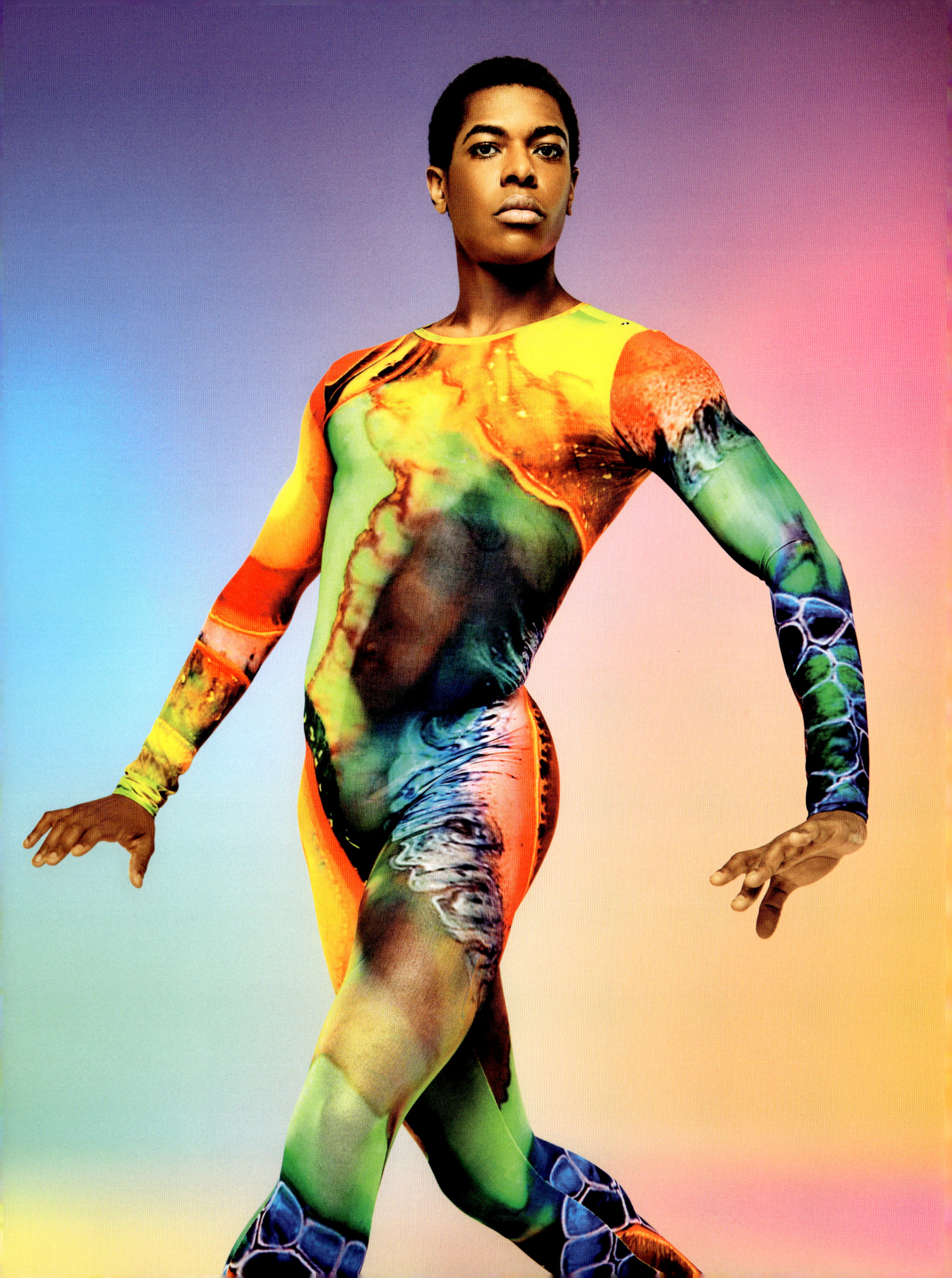

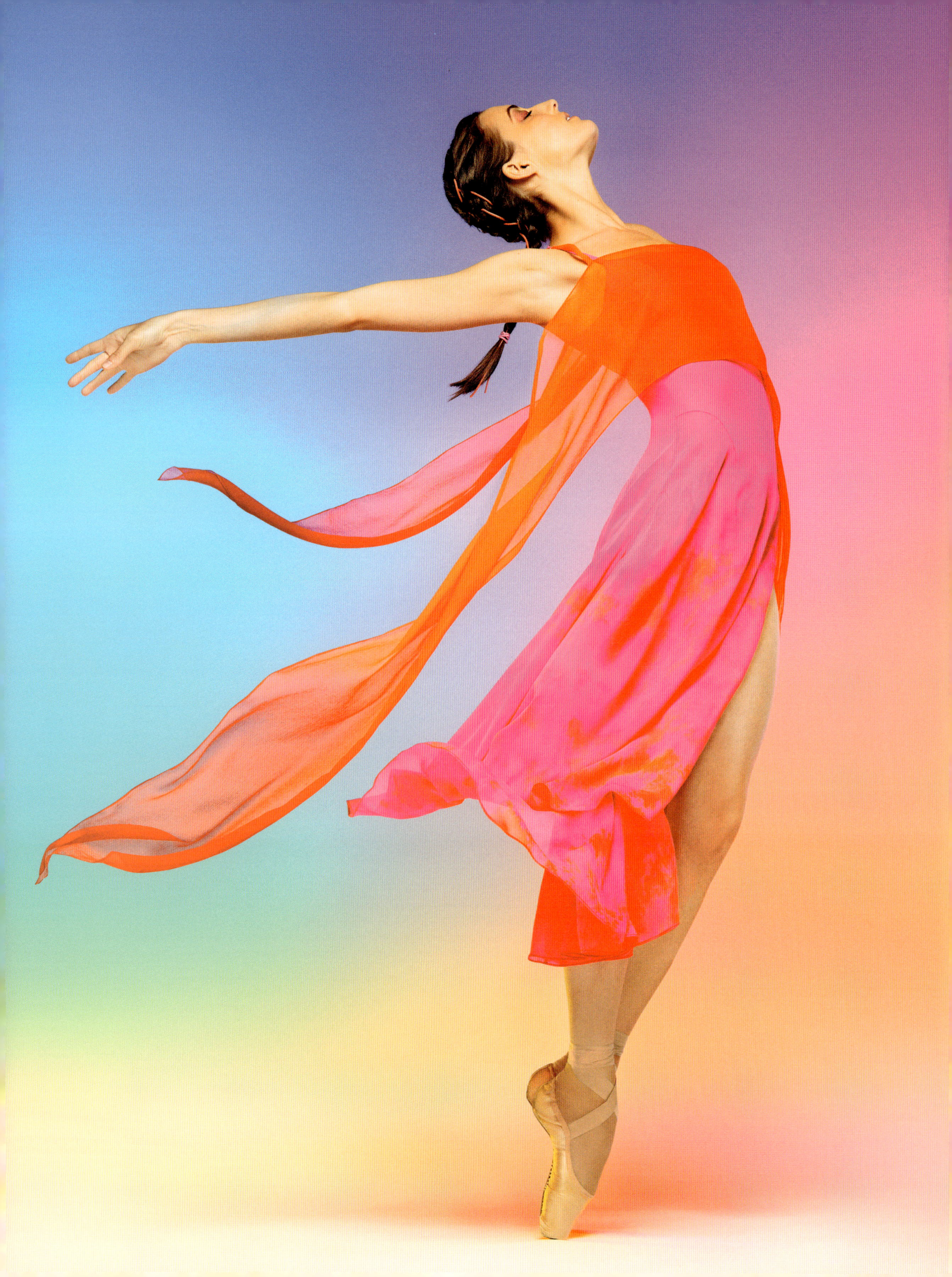

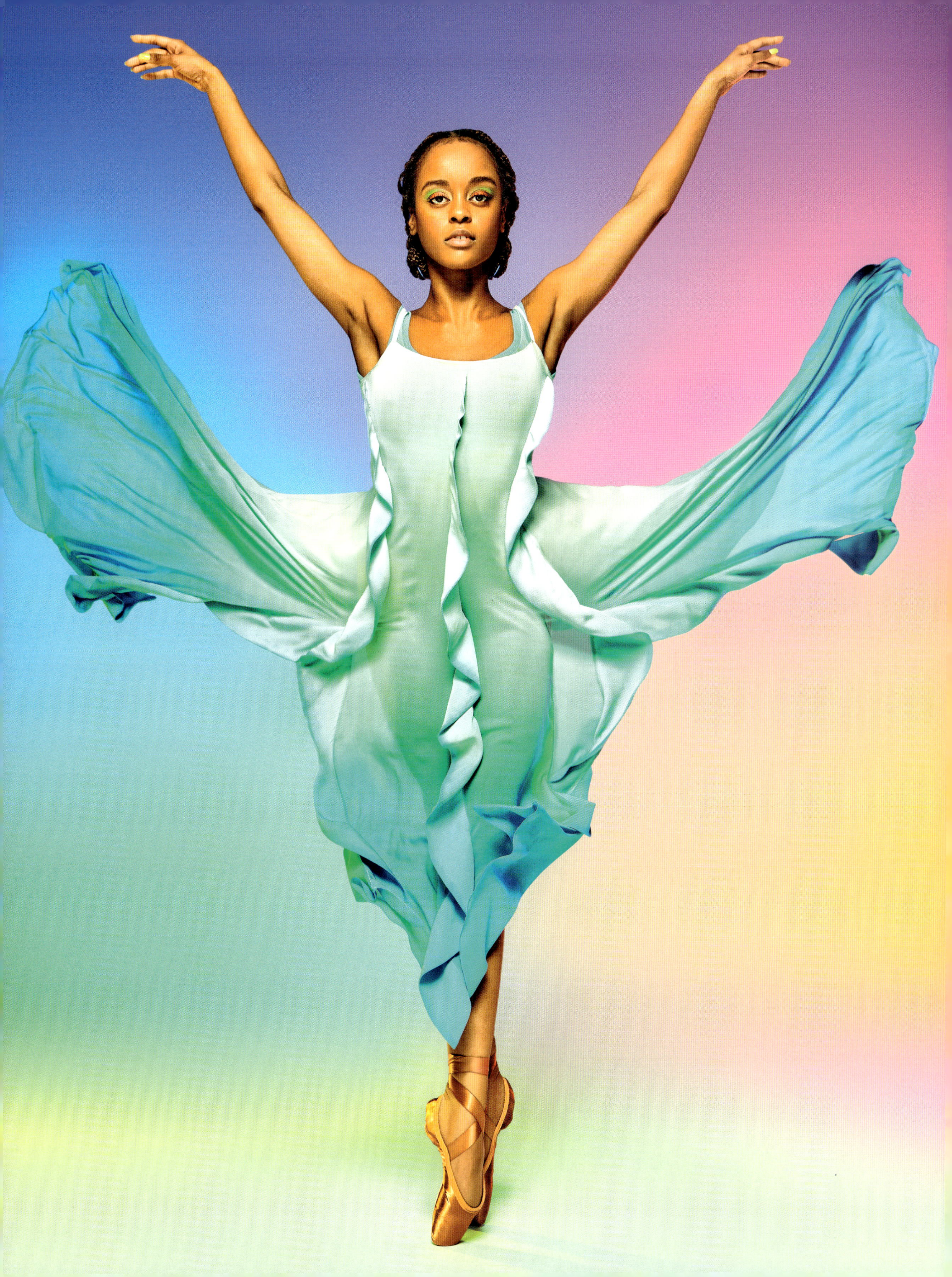

Esteban was inspired by who we were as individuals. Both he and Andrea embraced the fact that I had tattoos. It wasn't just about designing for the ballet, it was also about highlighting who we were. He brought a great energy to the collaboration, and made a real effort to make sure we felt comfortable dancing in the costumes. My favorite was the dress I wore in the first section of the piece. It was exciting to see him break gender norms in the world of ballet, and to do so with integrity. I think it is extremely powerful to embrace both the feminine and masculine qualities of a male dancer. There is strength in both, and Esteban's designs demonstrate that. —*JONATHAN FAHOURY, Dancer*

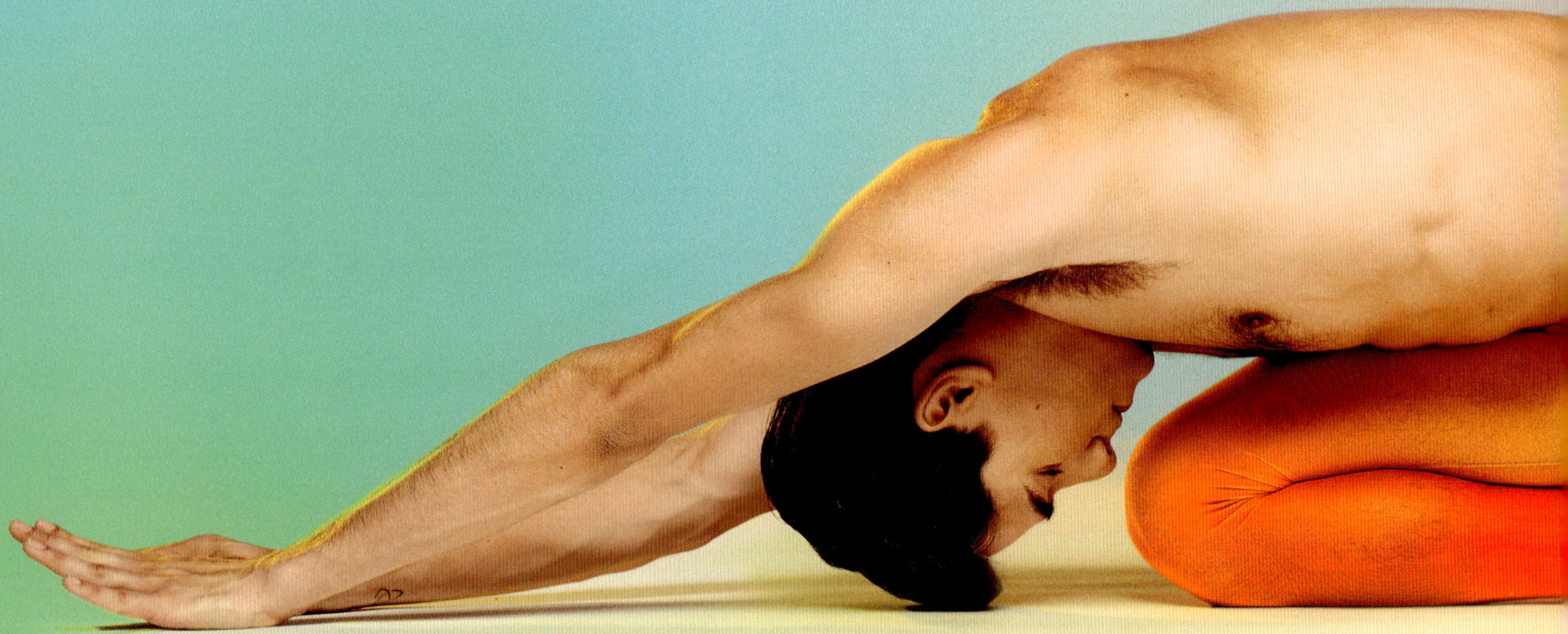

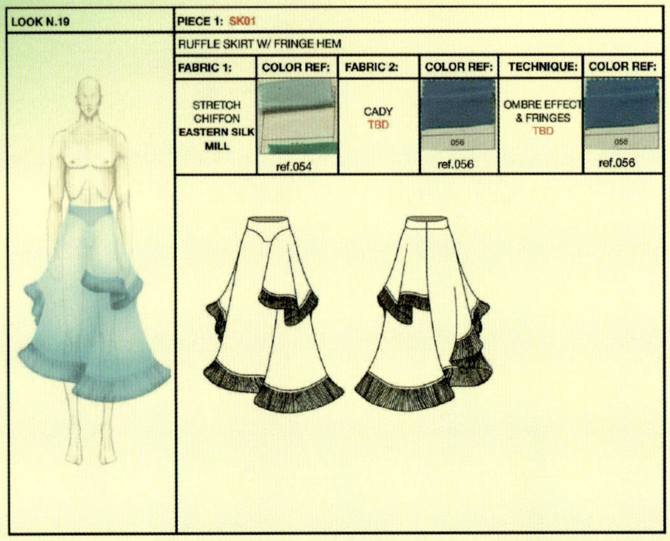

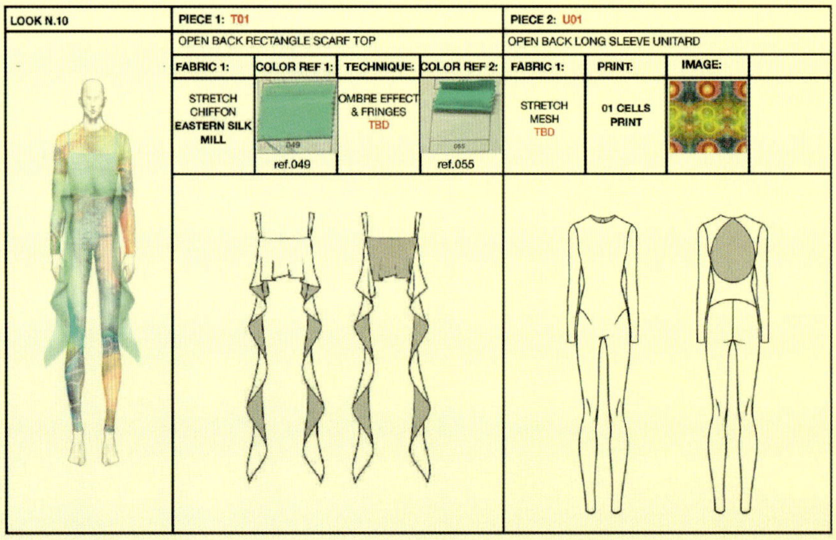

I was especially interested in the movement of heat and I asked Esteban if the color story could change over the course of the piece. Who could have imagined what Esteban would create?

He made weather.

Balancing fluidity and structure, elegance and rebelliousness, color and more color, the ballet danced from dawn to torrent, from sunset to sunrise. It was epic and sensual.

—ANDREA MILLER, Choreographer

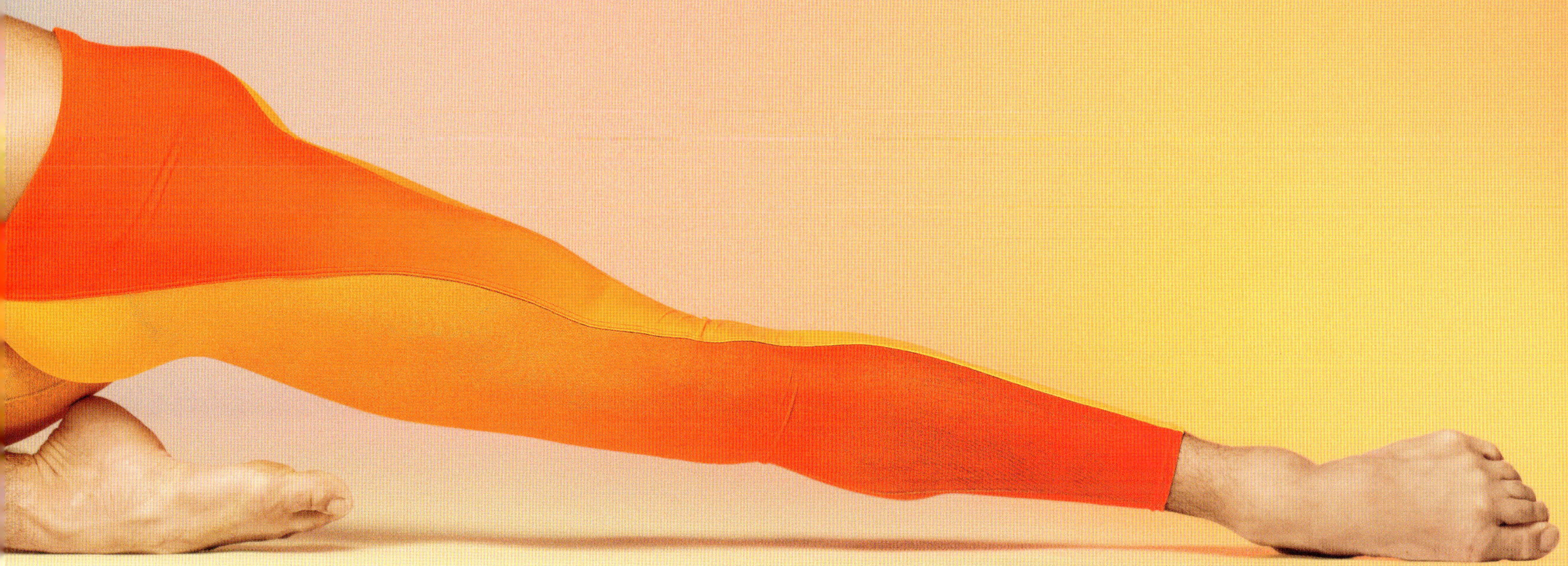

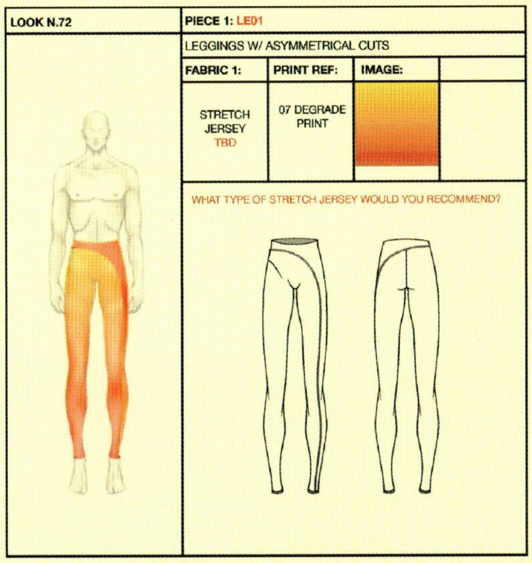

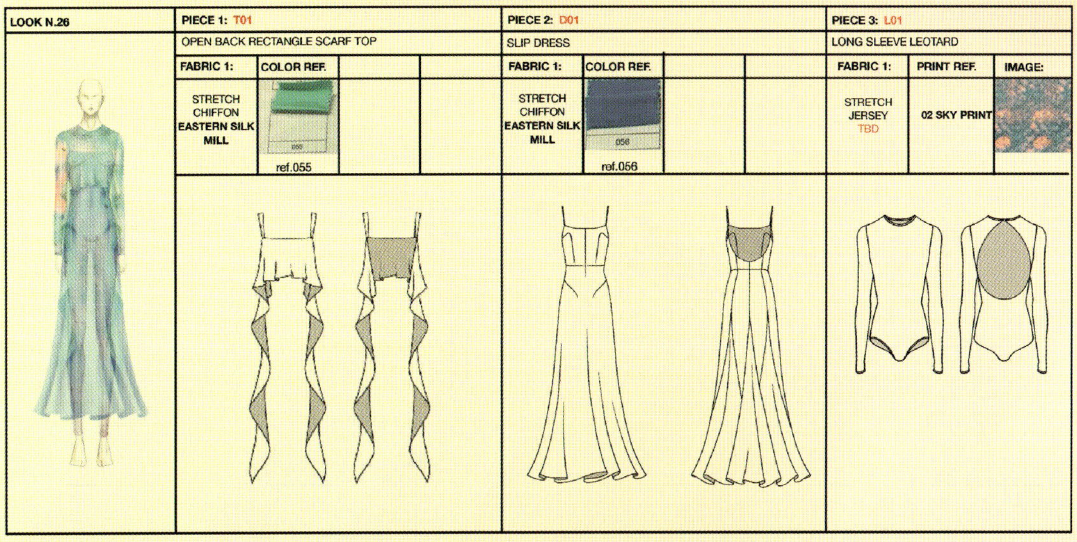

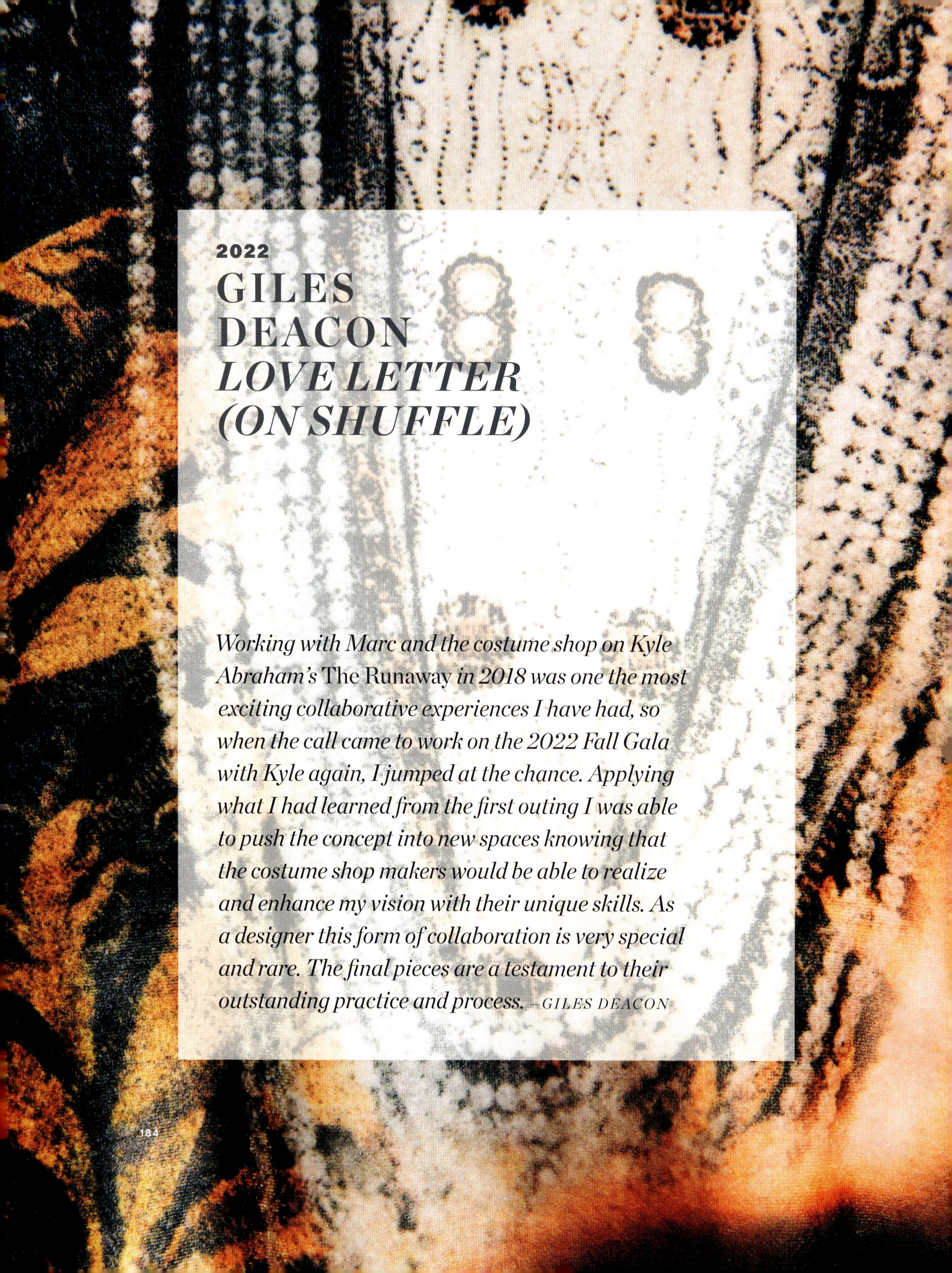

2022

GILES DEACON *LOVE LETTER (ON SHUFFLE)*

Working with Marc and the costume shop on Kyle Abraham's The Runaway *in 2018 was one the most exciting collaborative experiences I have had, so when the call came to work on the 2022 Fall Gala with Kyle again, I jumped at the chance. Applying what I had learned from the first outing I was able to push the concept into new spaces knowing that the costume shop makers would be able to realize and enhance my vision with their unique skills. As a designer this form of collaboration is very special and rare. The final pieces are a testament to their outstanding practice and process.* —GILES DEACON

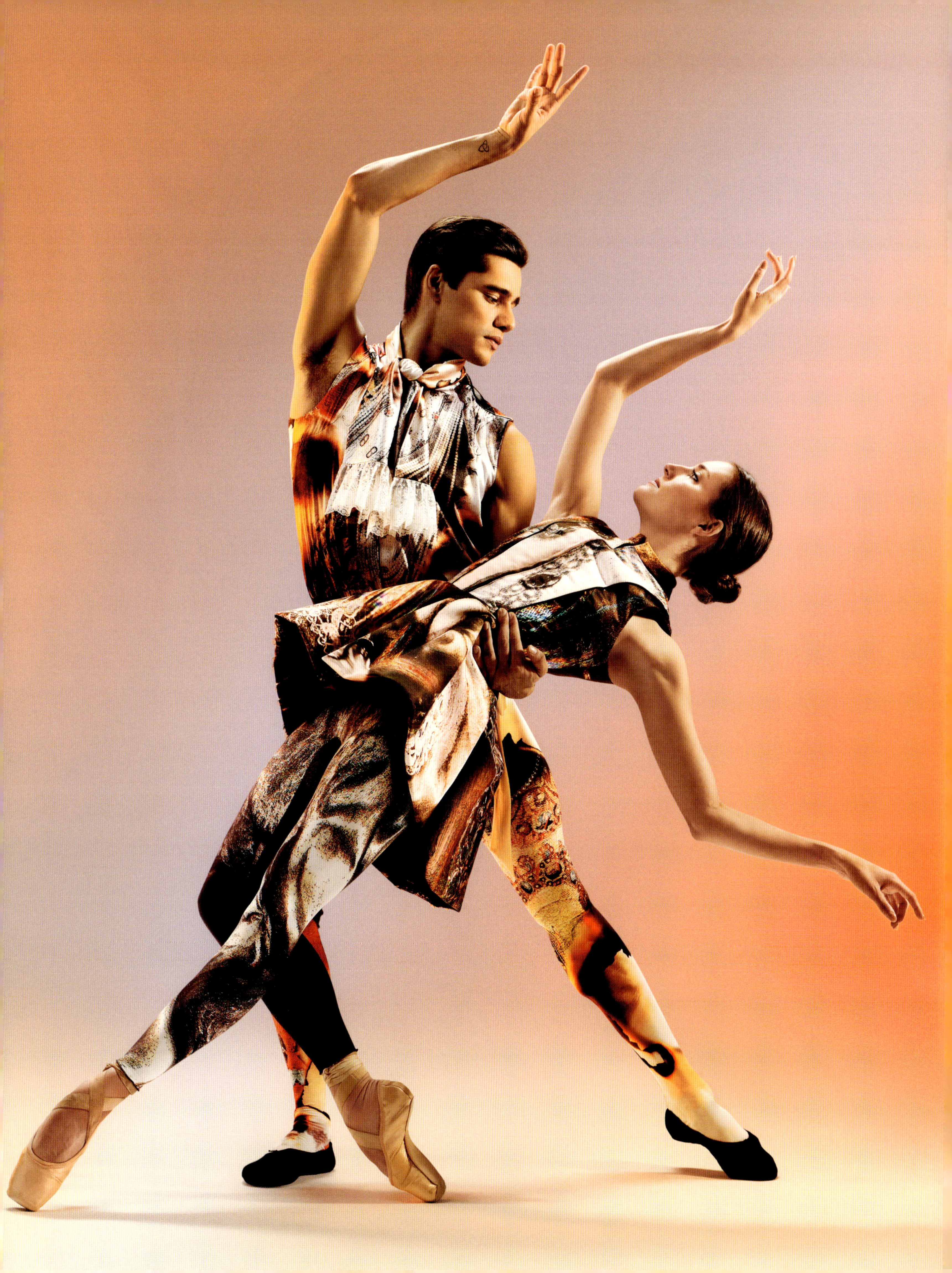

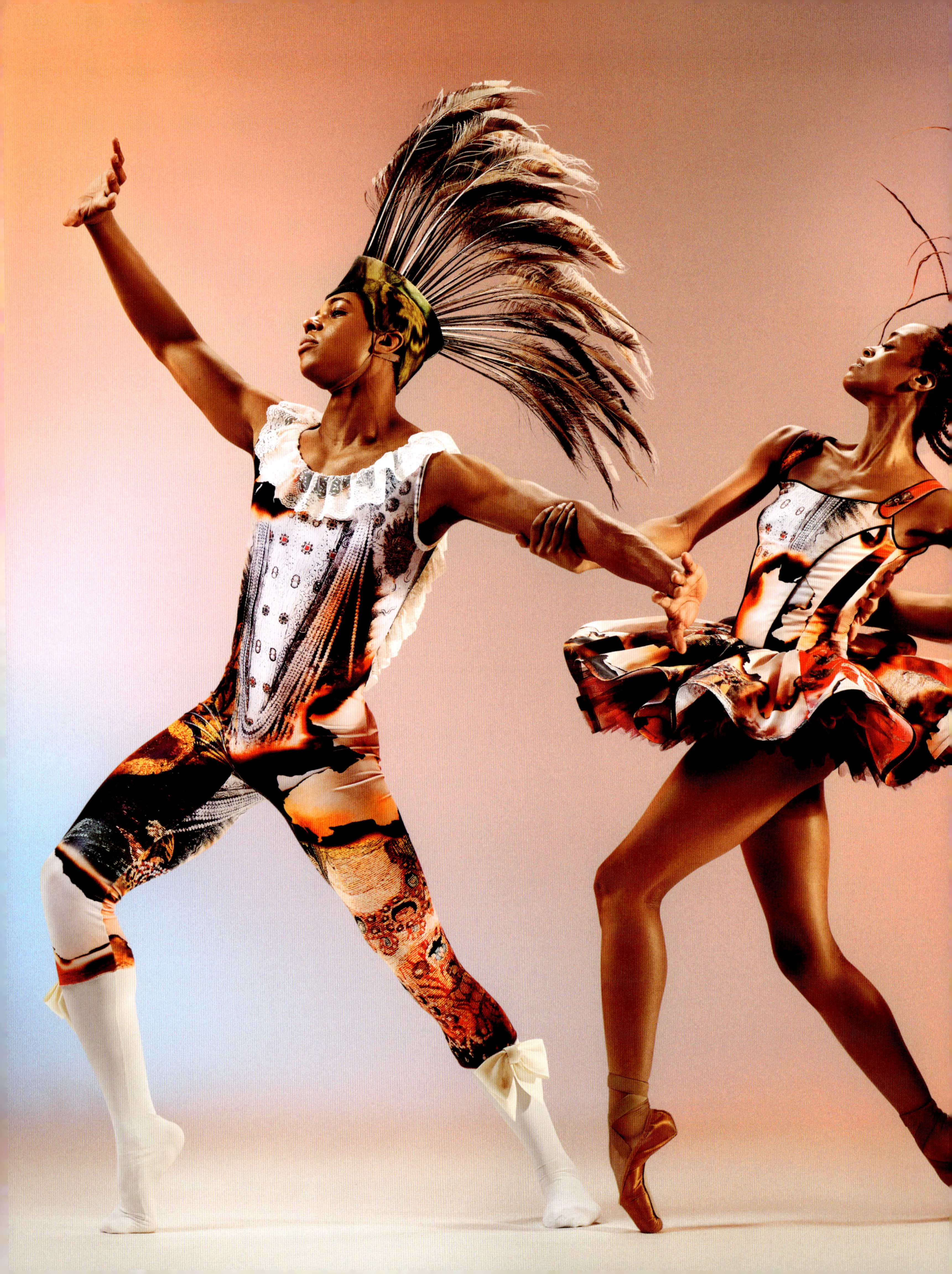

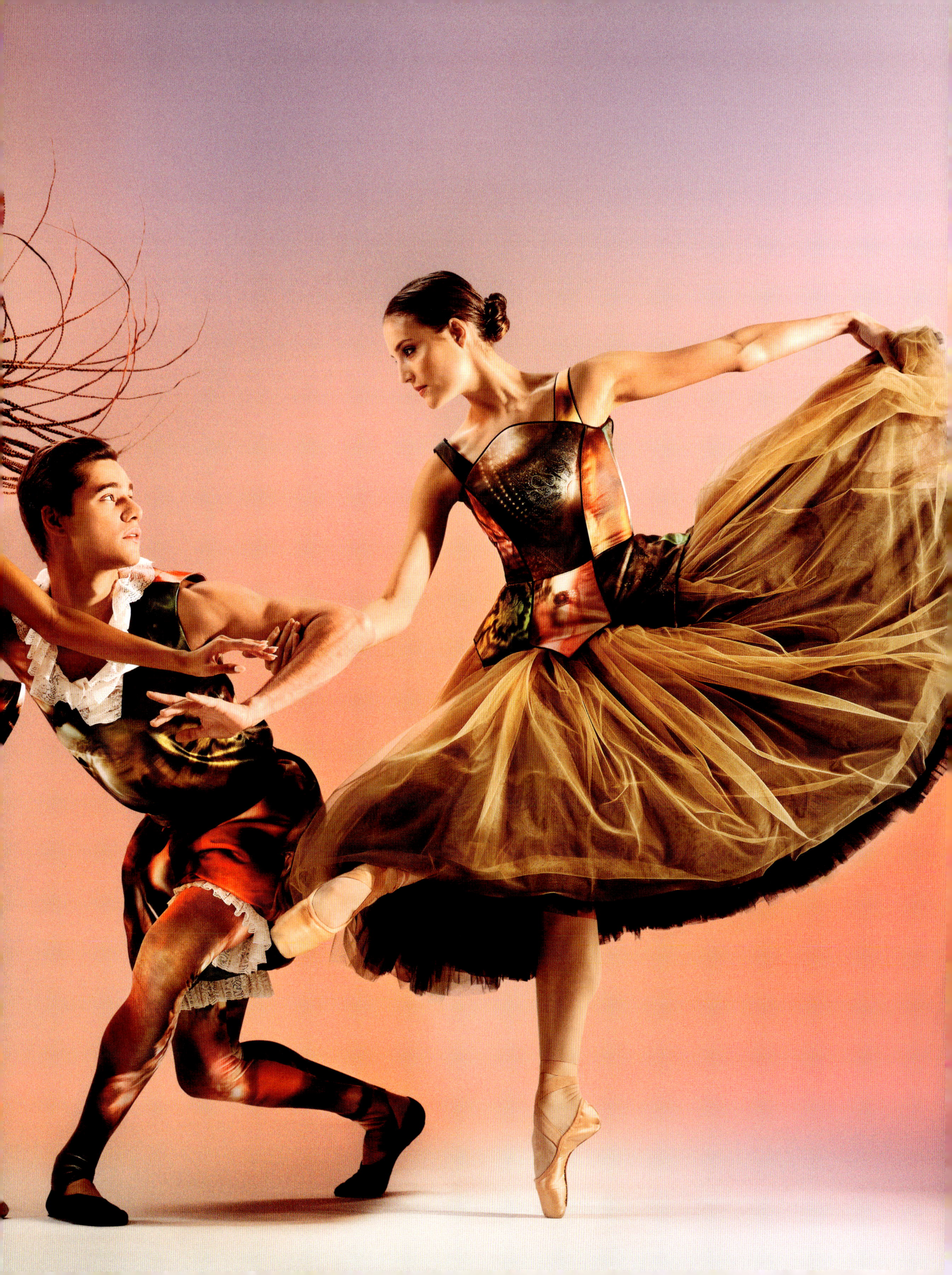

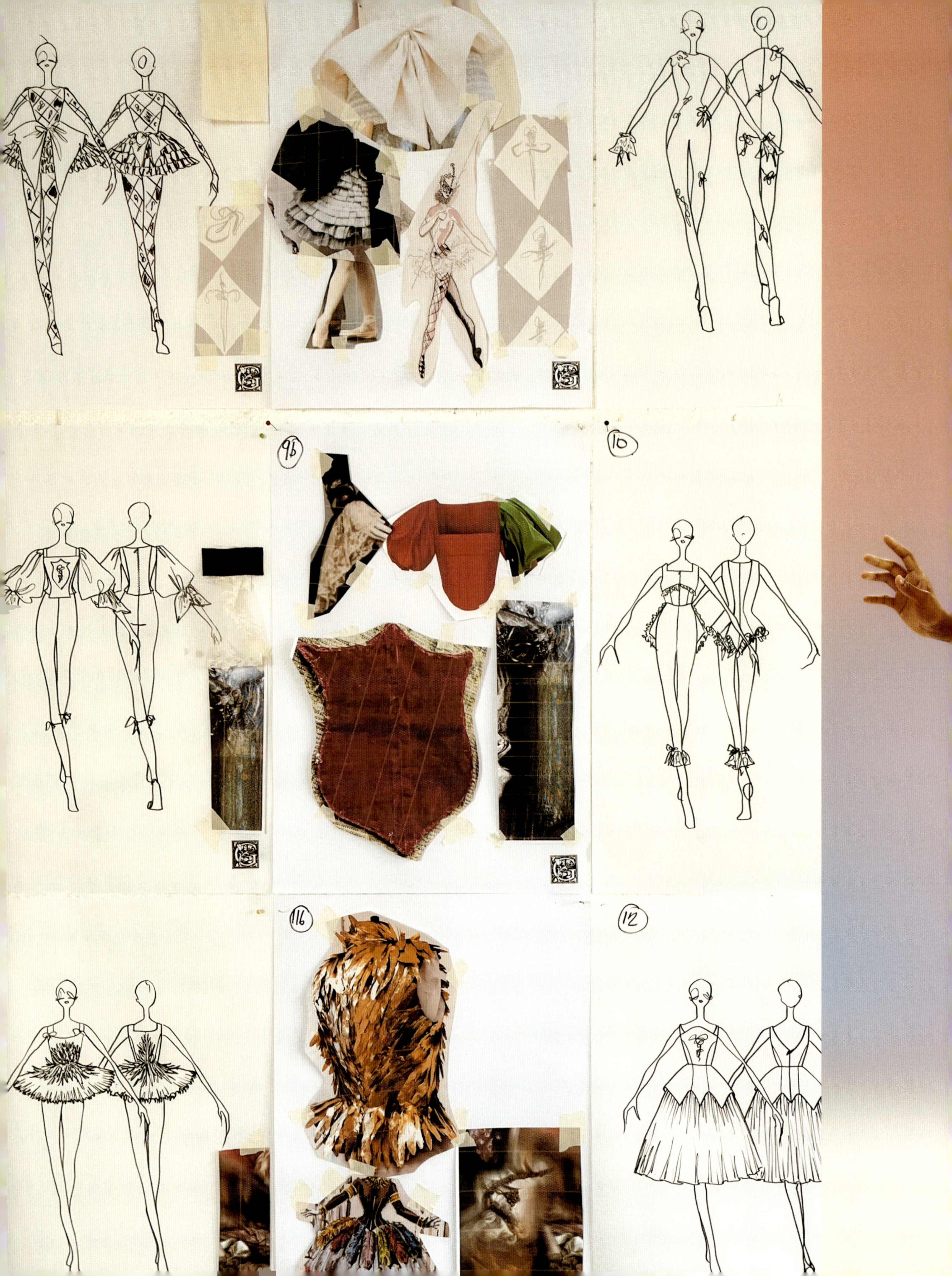
9b
10
11b
12

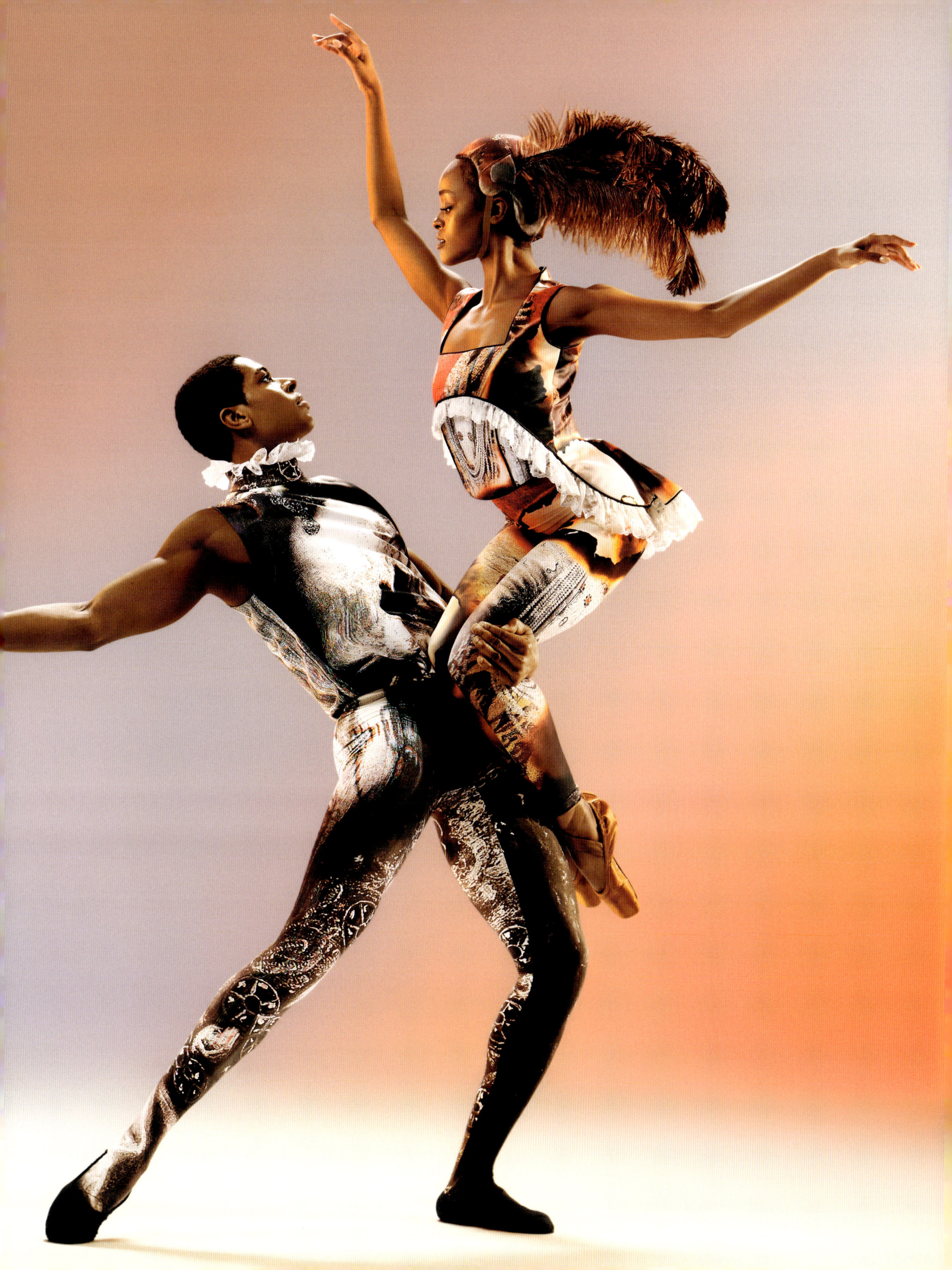

2022

RAF SIMONS *SOLO*

Collaborating with Raf Simons, we were able to approach two slightly defined looks for our two dancer interpreters: Anthony Huxley and Sara Mearns. What was so special about this process was seeing how each of these seasoned artists approached their interpretation of the same choreography. It became a wildly exhilarating experience to witness how they each found their own distinct way through the piece in performance. —JUSTIN PECK, *Choreographer*

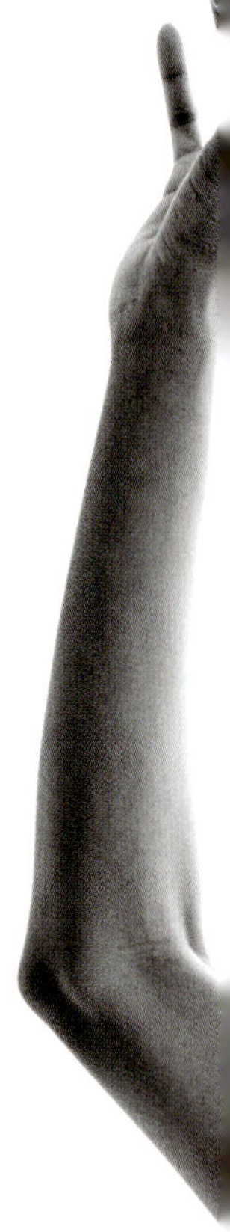

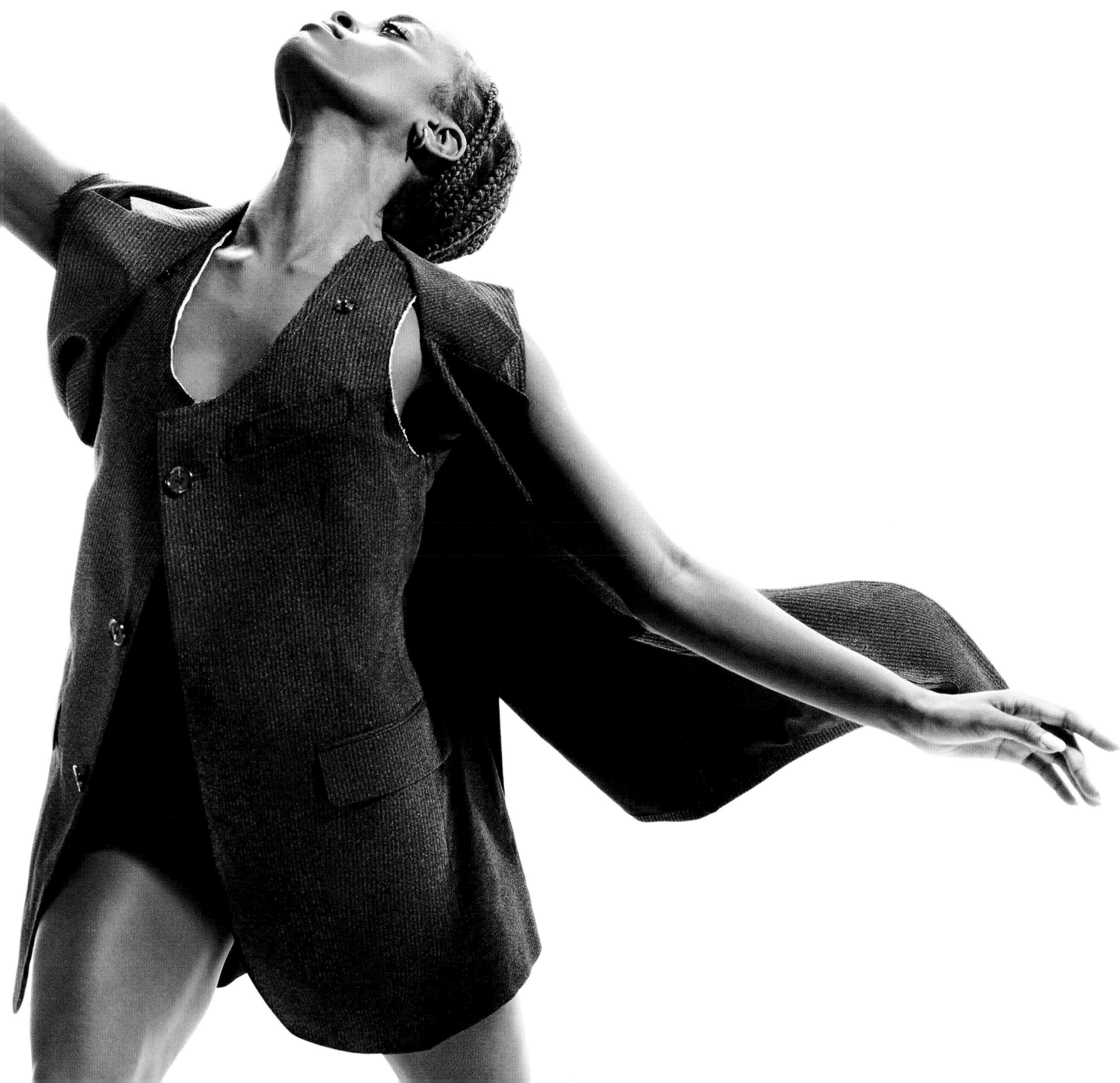

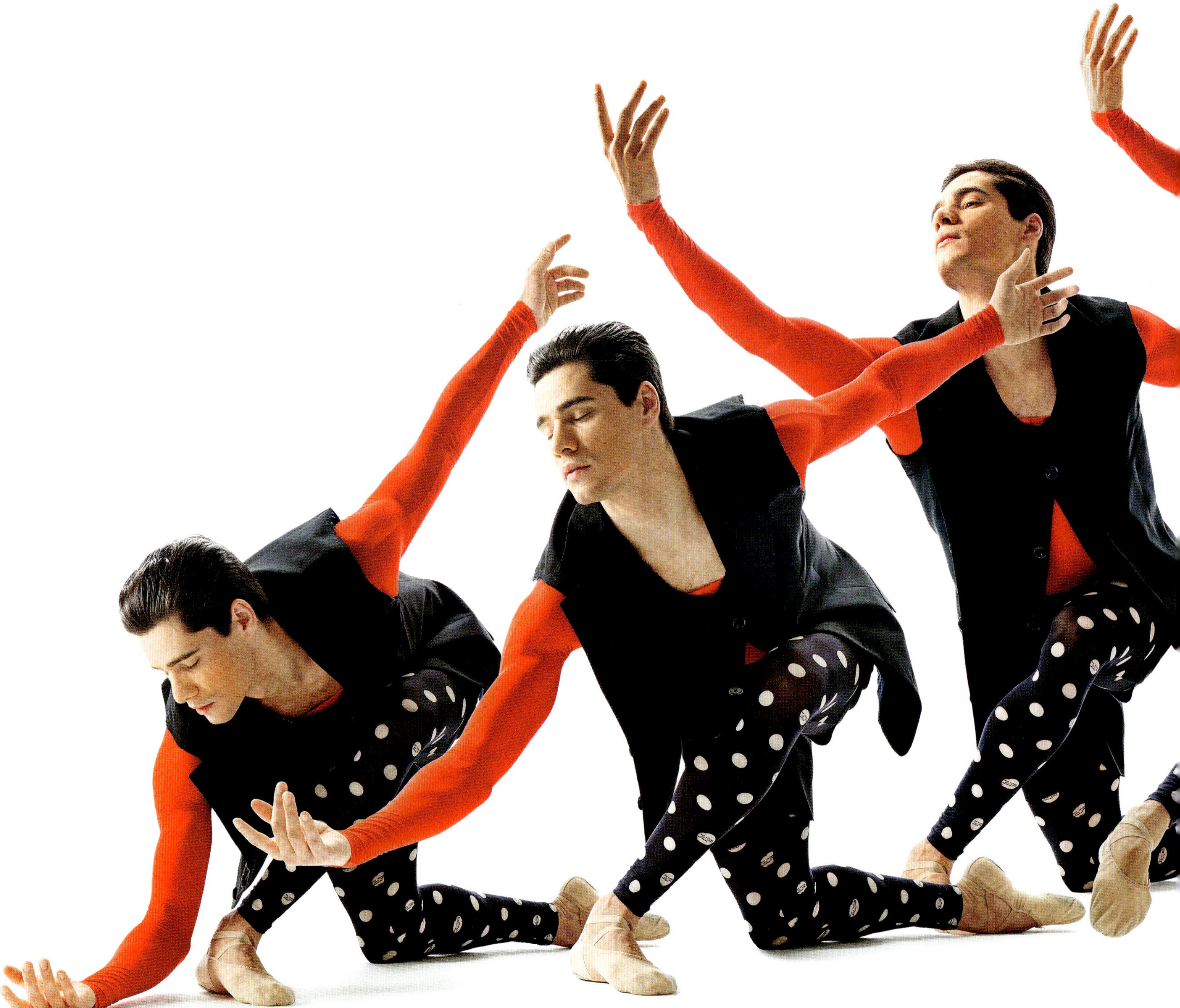

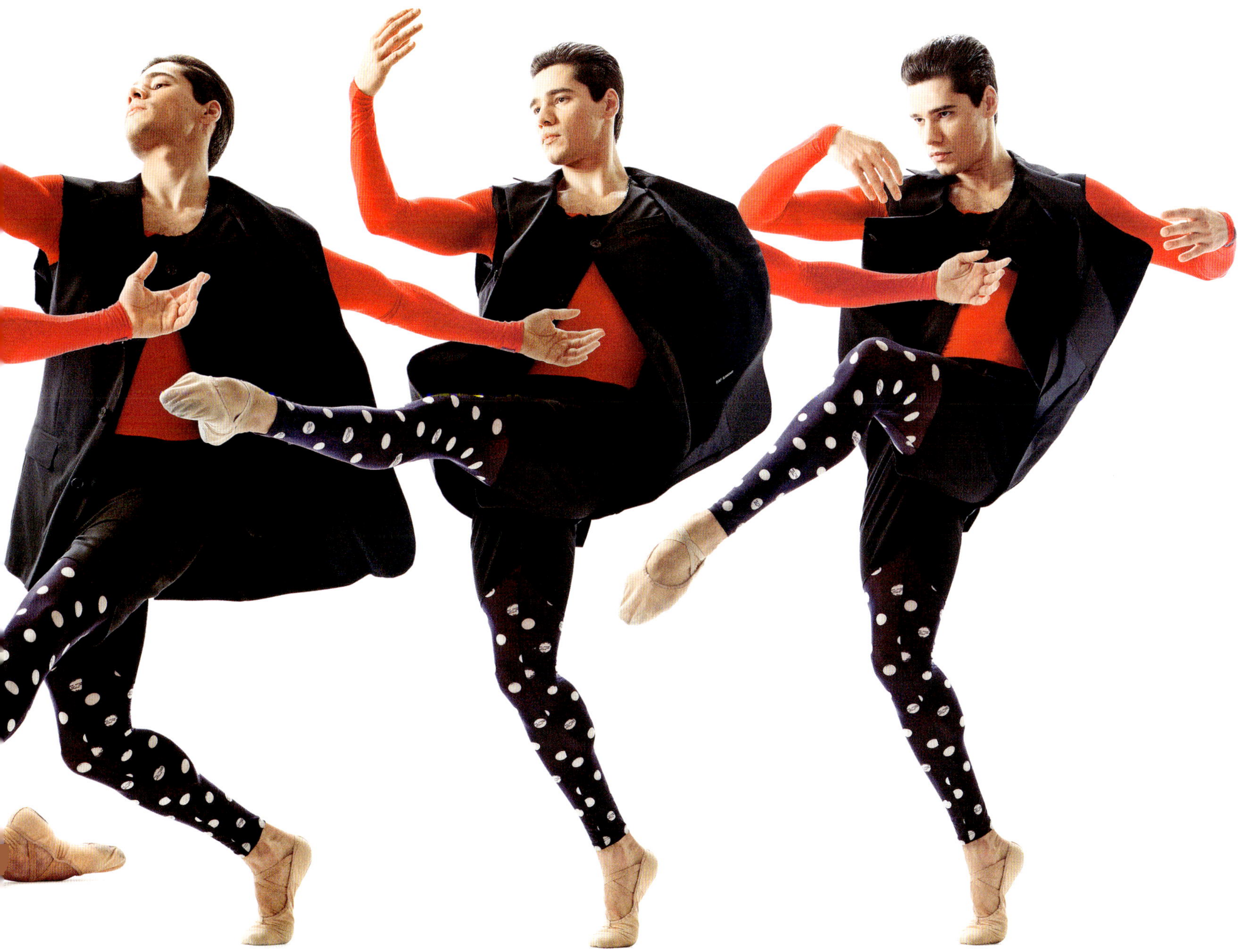

2022

ALEJANDRO GÓMEZ PALOMO FOR PALOMO SPAIN *PLAY TIME*

A work of art can be understood as a conductor from the artist's mind to the viewer's. It can be difficult to translate what one has in mind and it is only in particular moments that the artist feels his art has been perceived exactly how it was meant to be. Such was the case when the curtains of New York City Ballet were raised and the audience gasped at the view of a formation of dancers in blinding colorful designs. That one moment is one of the highlights of my life and I will cherish the experience forever. I felt so extremely honored to create such a memorable performance with the NYCB costume department, the dancers, Gianna Reisen, and Solange Knowles.

—ALEJANDRO GÓMEZ PALOMO

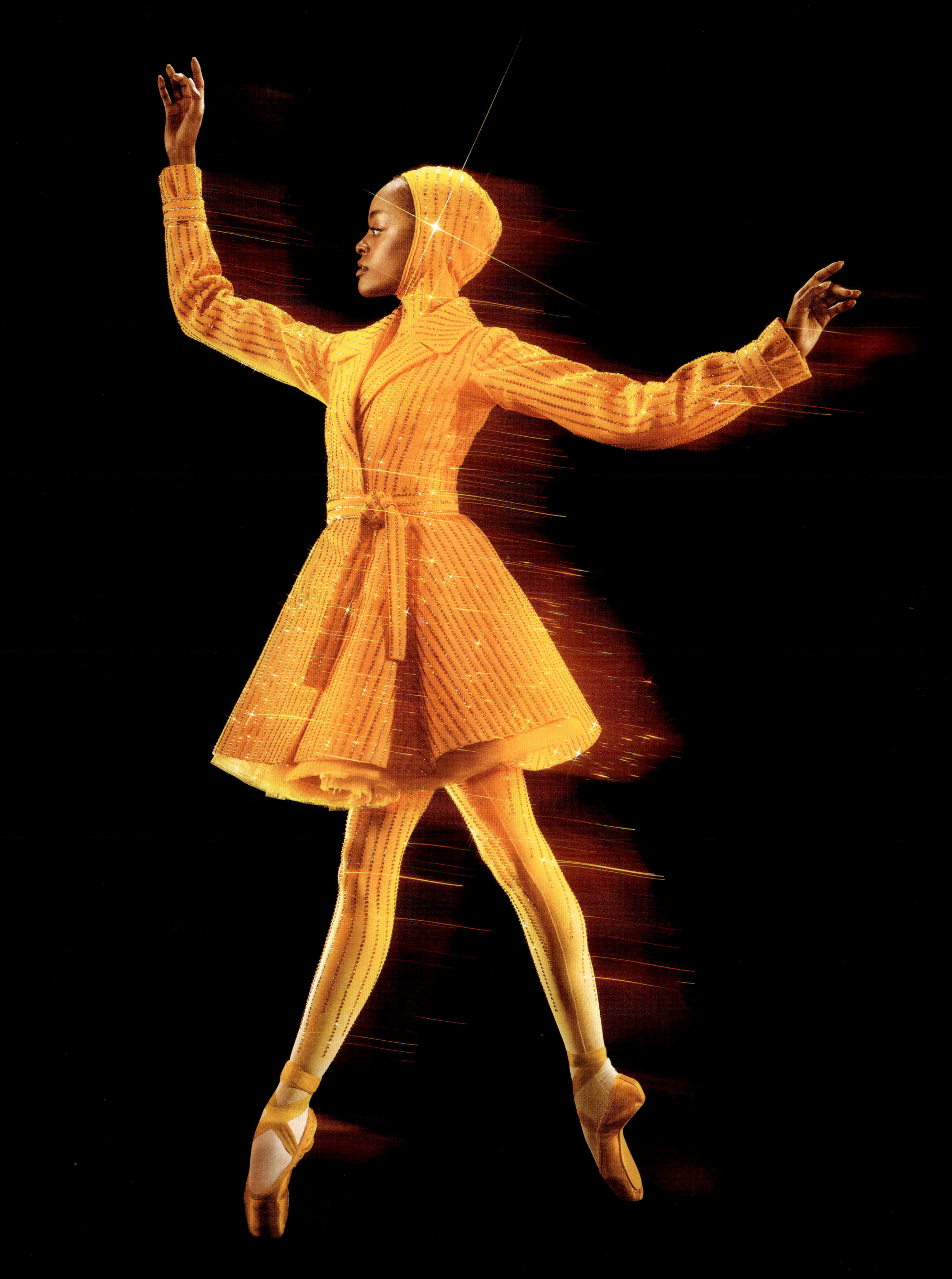

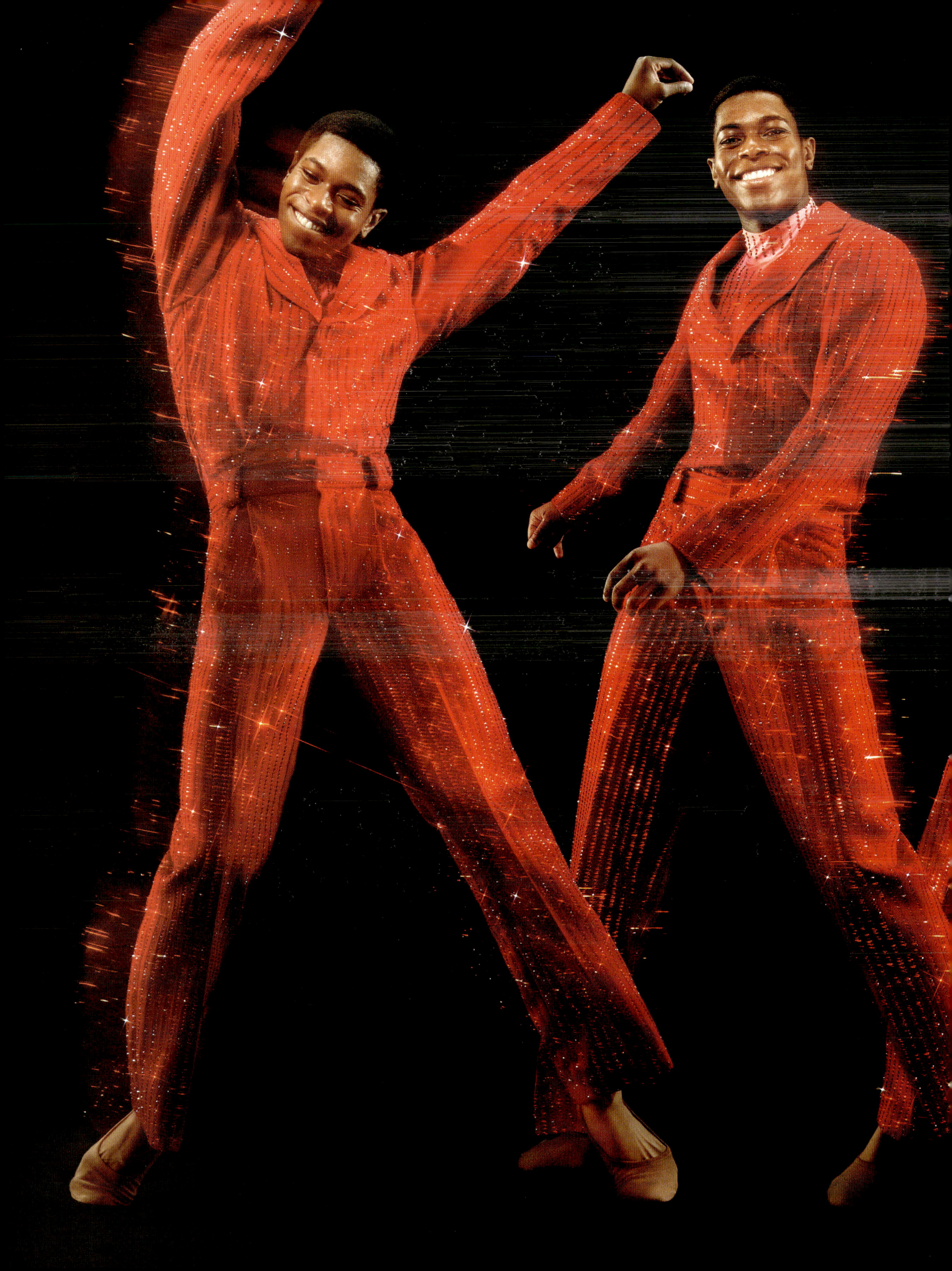

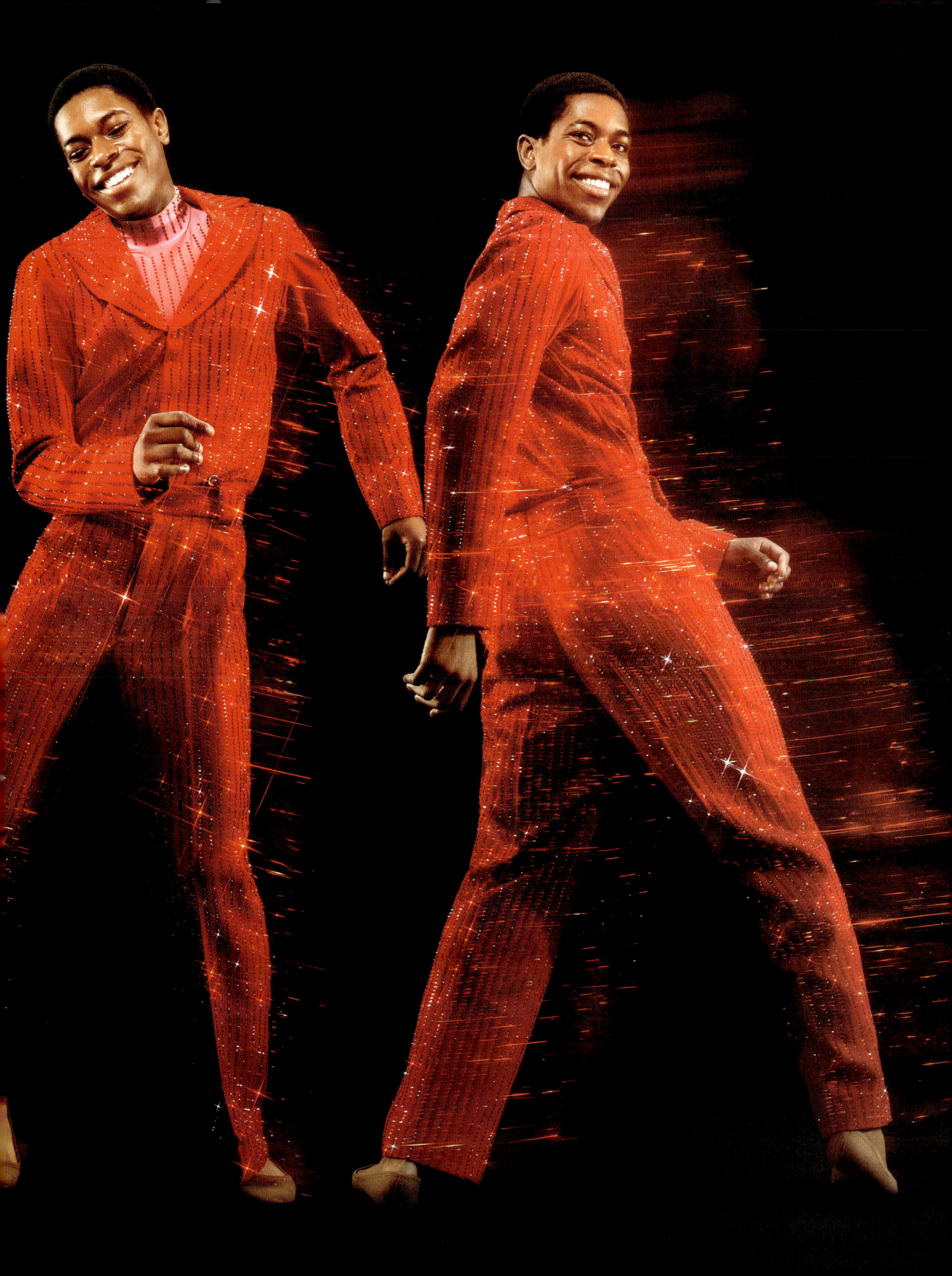

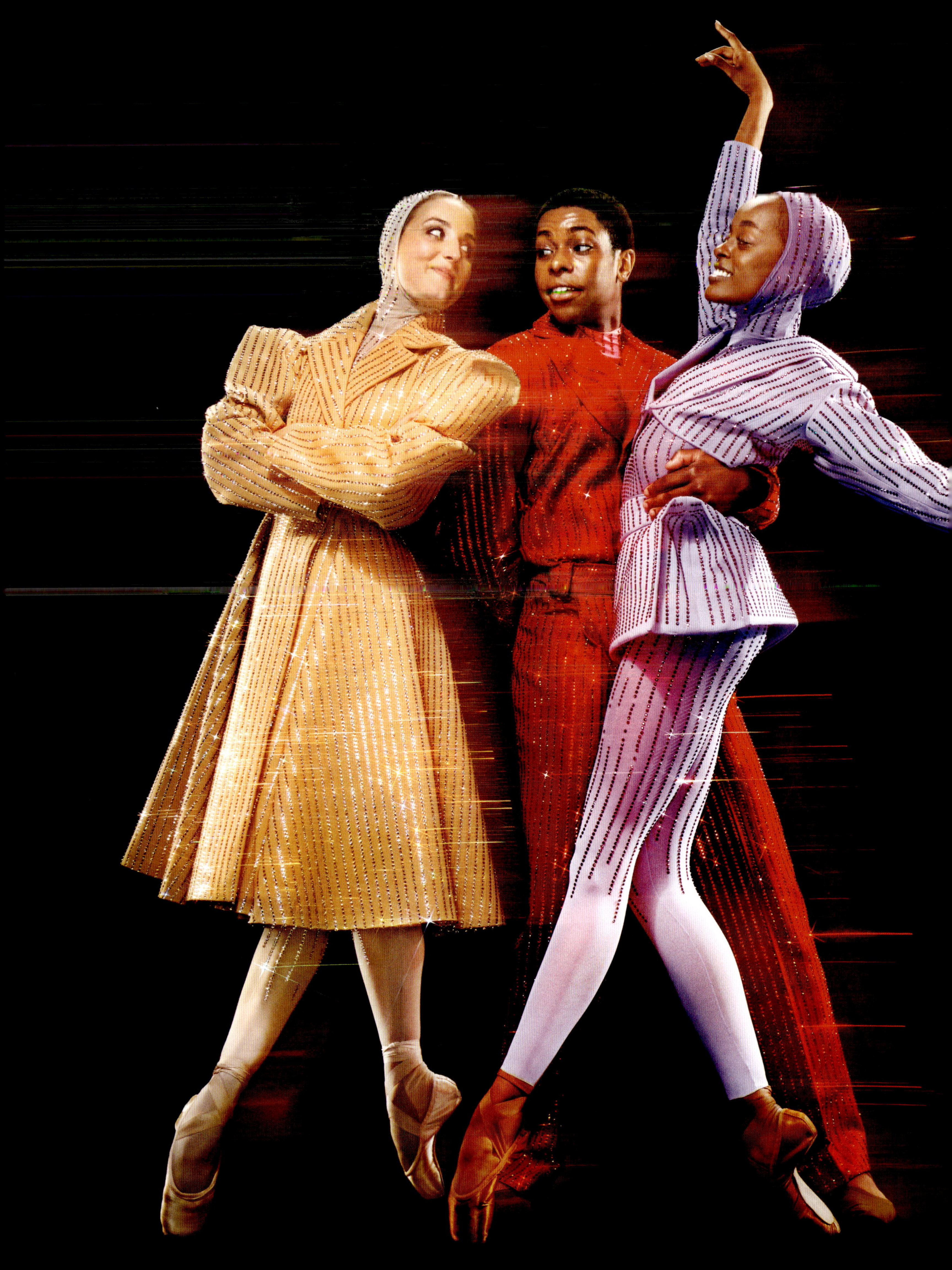

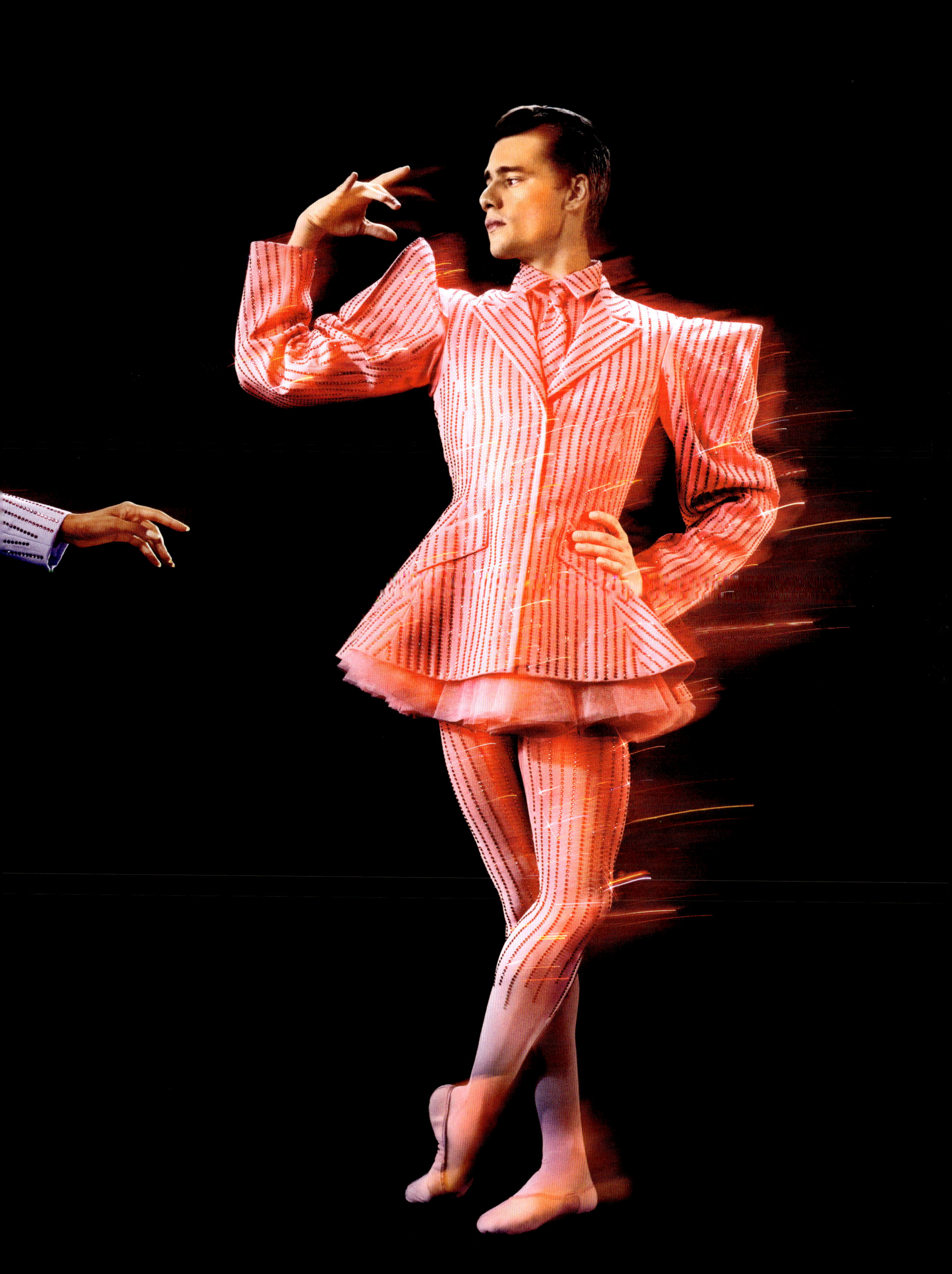

Alejandro and I were heavily inspired by '80s fashion themes, like exaggerated shoulders and block colors. I wanted a showstopper and an element of shock value within the designs, which is where the Swarovski collaboration came into play.

With an enormous effort from the costume department at NYCB, nearly 800,000 Swarovski crystals were meticulously pressed in pinstripe and chevron patterns, covering all ten men and women from head to toe.

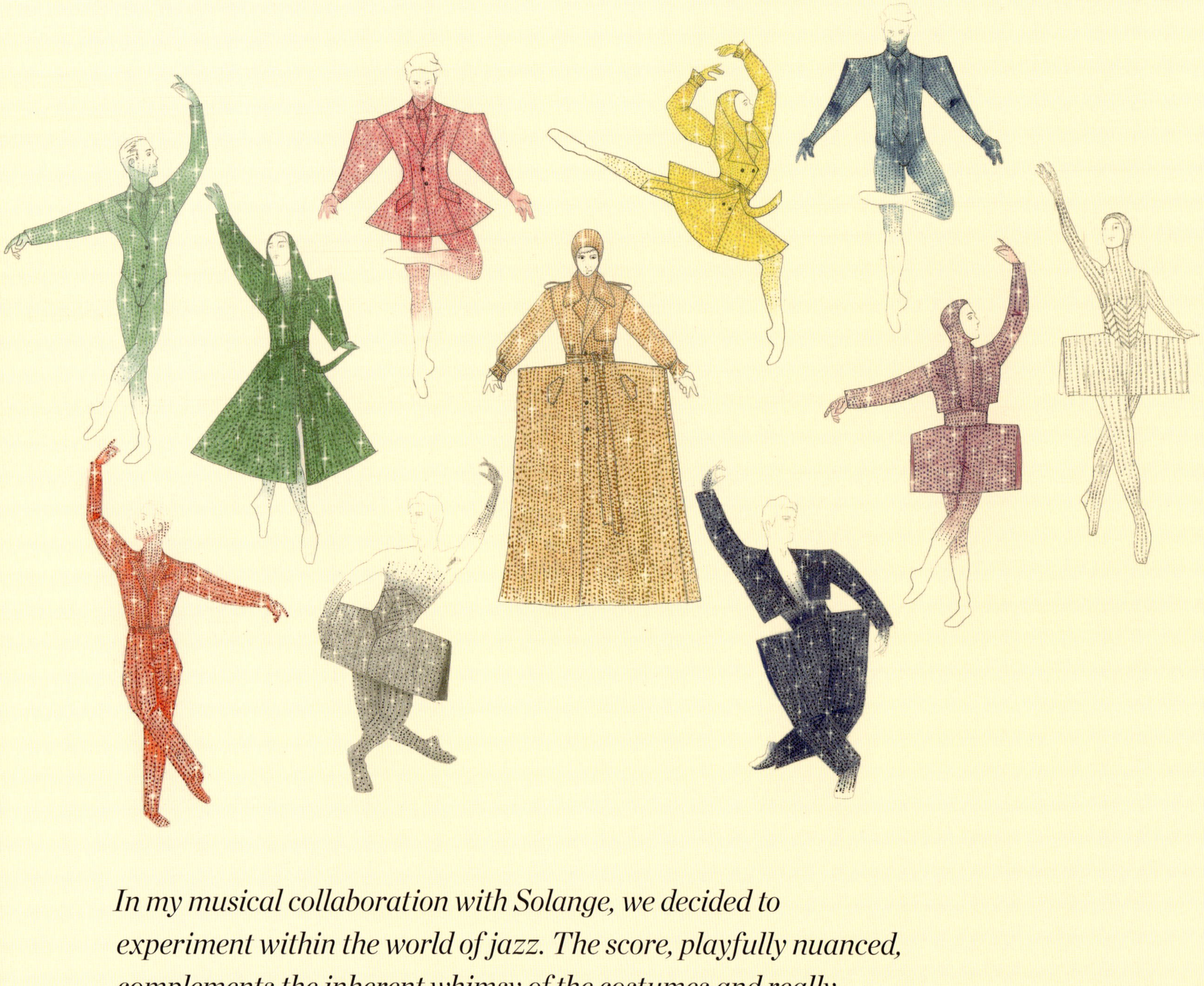

In my musical collaboration with Solange, we decided to experiment within the world of jazz. The score, playfully nuanced, complements the inherent whimsy of the costumes and really pushes the theatricality of the dance. —GIANNA REISEN, *Choreographer*

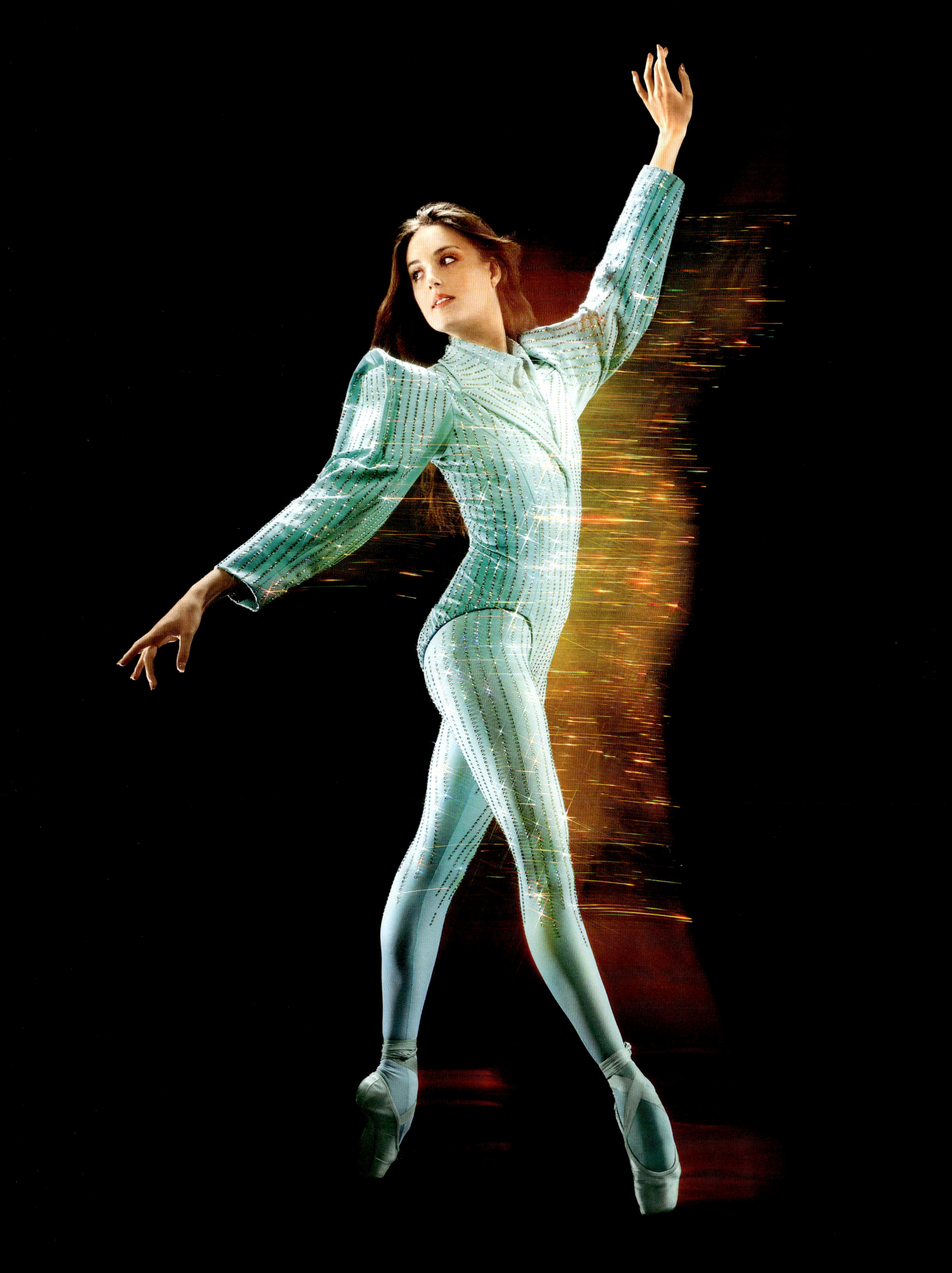

DESIGN & CHOREOGRAPHY CREDITS

2012

VALENTINO
Sophisticated Lady, Not My Girl, Bal de Couture
CHOREOGRAPHER: Peter Martins

This Bitter Earth pas de deux
CHOREOGRAPHER: Christopher Wheeldon

2013

PRABAL GURUNG
Capricious Maneuvers
CHOREOGRAPHER: Justin Peck

OLIVIER THEYSKENS
Spectral Evidence
CHOREOGRAPHER: Angelin Preljocaj

IRIS VAN HERPEN
Neverwhere
CHOREOGRAPHER: Benjamin Millepied

2014

THOM BROWNE
Clearing Dawn
CHOREOGRAPHER: Troy Schumacher

SARAH BURTON FOR ALEXANDER MCQUEEN
Funérailles
CHOREOGRAPHER: Liam Scarlett

CAROLINA HERRERA
Morgen
CHOREOGRAPHER: Peter Martins

MARY KATRANTZOU
Belles-Lettres
CHOREOGRAPHER: Justin Peck

2015

PETER COPPING OF OSCAR DE LA RENTA
Thou Swell
CHOREOGRAPHER: Peter Martins

HUMBERTO LEON OF OPENING CEREMONY AND KENZO
New Blood
CHOREOGRAPHER: Justin Peck

HANAKO MAEDA OF ADEAM
The Blue of Distance
CHOREOGRAPHER: Robert Binet

MARTA MARQUES AND PAULO ALMEIDA OF MARQUES'ALMEIDA
Common Ground
CHOREOGRAPHER: Troy Schumacher

ZUHAIR MURAD
Polaris
CHOREOGRAPHER: Myles Thatcher

2016

JASON WU
ten in seven
CHOREOGRAPHER: Peter Walker

ROSIE ASSOULIN
Unframed
CHOREOGRAPHER: Annabelle Lopez Ochoa

NARCISO RODRIGUEZ
For Clara
CHOREOGRAPHER: Lauren Lovette

DRIES VAN NOTEN
The Dreamers
CHOREOGRAPHER: Justin Peck

2017

JONATHAN SAUNDERS
The Wind Still Brings
CHOREOGRAPHER: Troy Schumacher

VIRGIL ABLOH OF OFF-WHITE™
Composer's Holiday
CHOREOGRAPHER: Gianna Reisen

FERNANDO GARCIA AND LAURA KIM OF MONSE AND OSCAR DE LA RENTA
Not Our Fate
CHOREOGRAPHER: Lauren Lovette

TSUMORI CHISATO
Pulcinella Variations
CHOREOGRAPHER: Justin Peck

2018

GILES DEACON
The Runaway
CHOREOGRAPHER: Kyle Abraham

GARETH PUGH
The Exchange
CHOREOGRAPHER: Matthew Neenan

ALBERTA FERRETTI
Judah
CHOREOGRAPHER: Gianna Reisen

2019

ANNA SUI
Lineage
CHOREOGRAPHER: Edwaard Liang

ZAC POSEN
The Shaded Line
CHOREOGRAPHER: Lauren Lovette

2021

CHRISTOPHER JOHN ROGERS
SUSPENDED ANIMATION
CHOREOGRAPHER: Sidra Bell

ESTEBAN CORTÁZAR
sky to hold
CHOREOGRAPHER: Andrea Miller

2022

GILES DEACON
Love Letter (on shuffle)
CHOREOGRAPHER: Kyle Abraham

RAF SIMONS
Solo
CHOREOGRAPHER: Justin Peck

ALEJANDRO GÓMEZ PALOMO FOR PALOMO SPAIN
Play Time
CHOREOGRAPHER: Gianna Reisen

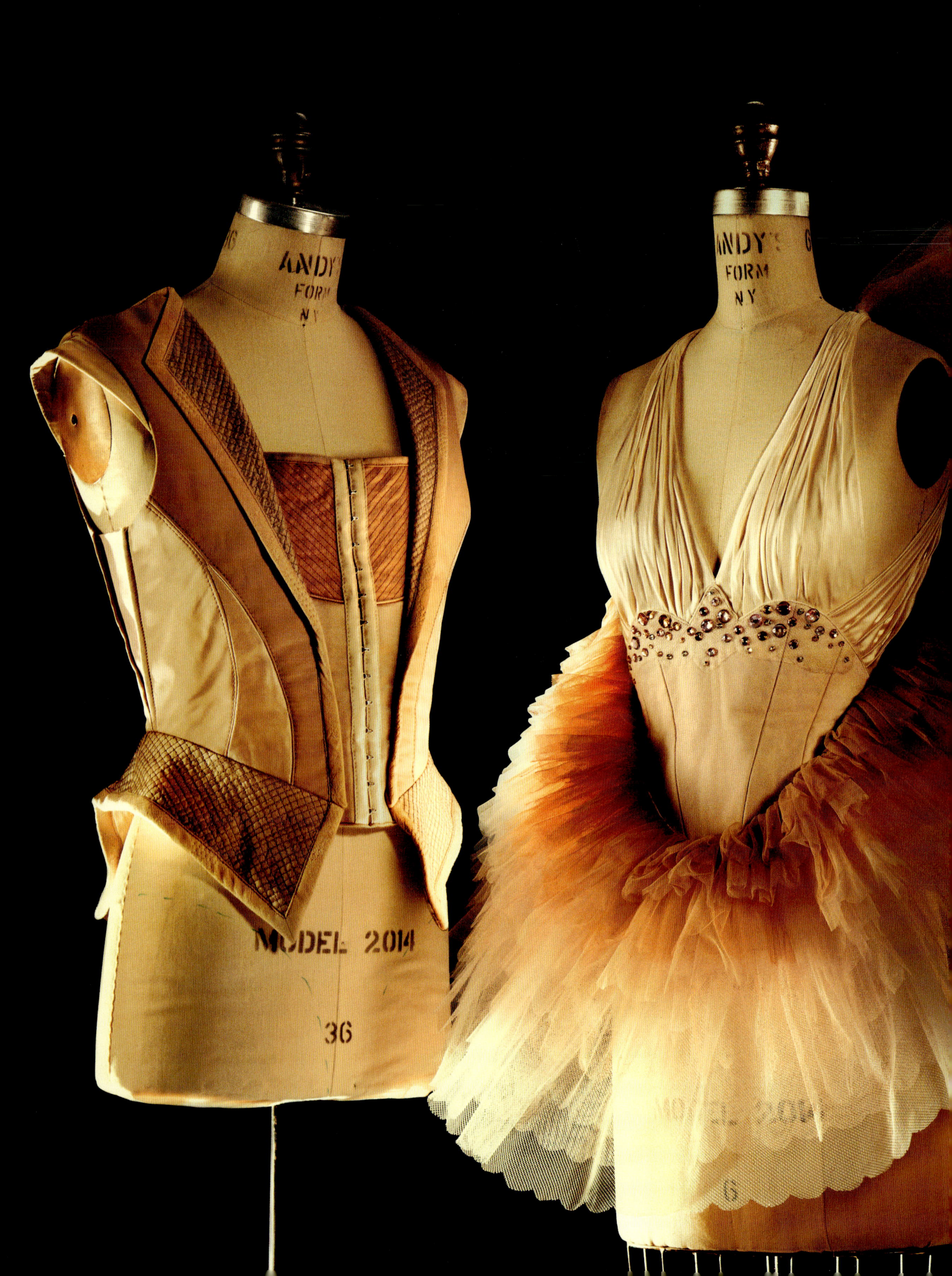
FORM
NY
MODEL 2014
36
FORM
NY
6

ACKNOWLEDGMENTS

MANY INDIVIDUALS offered support and encouragement during the production of this publication, especially:

Noriko Maeda for her inspiring generosity

All of the designers and choreographers who participated in the Fall Fashion Galas and generously offered their thoughts and inspirations in the pages of this book

New York City Ballet's leadership team—Kathy Brown, Jonathan Stafford, and Wendy Whelan

Pari Dukovic and his amazing crew: Clay, Christian, Chad, Grant, Muhammet and Vita

Gonzalo Garcia, movement director for the photo shoots, and the dancers who participated in the photo shoots with commitment and joy

Sammy Garcia, Jr., Kevin Damoah, and the Rose Building staff who helped to make the photo shoots happen

The entire staff of New York City Ballet especially Rob Daniels, Brooks Parsons, and Christine van Kipnis

Sarah Gifford

Susan Harmms

Ellen Nidy and Caitlin Leffel at Rizzoli for their guidance

Judy Zankel

In addition, it's important to recognize all former and present members of New York City Ballet's Costume Shop who helped in the creation of the costumes seen on these pages and continually make magic: Regina Abayev, Tatiyana Bakalyna, Tracee Bear, Monika Bellucci, Juan Camacho, Leonard Choo, Marie Deserto, Irina Fedosseeva, Mariah Fidago, Luba Flek, Mathew Gnagy, Richard Gregg, Kelli Haase, Jason Hadley, Ludmila Ildemenova, Lindsey Kethan, Miwako Kimura, Layton Kuchinski, Caroline La Porta, Sarah Lenigan, Jarod Lewis, Kathryn Lewis, Anna Light, Sam Meredith, Siobhan Nestor, Maria Nieto, Riona O'Malley, Makoto Osada, Mirka Owczarek, Kendell Owings, Allie Pawlukojc, Natallia Rakhmanenka, Erin Rodgers, Hannah Ross, Olga Saprikina, Tracey Shababo, Kellie Sheehan, Tyler Sherrier, Joseph Shrope, Kaitlin Smith, Marie Stair, Natalie Turturro, Sherry Wu

As well as the dancers who patiently sat through fittings and diplomatically gave feedback through the Fall Fashion Galas, some of whom also provided insights about their experiences in these pages

And, Sarah Jessica Parker, Peter Martins, and Valentino who started it all

Marc Happel would like to personally thank Maria Grady for her constant dedication and encouragement throughout the creation of this book, as well as his husband, Harvey Weiss, for his love, support, and input.

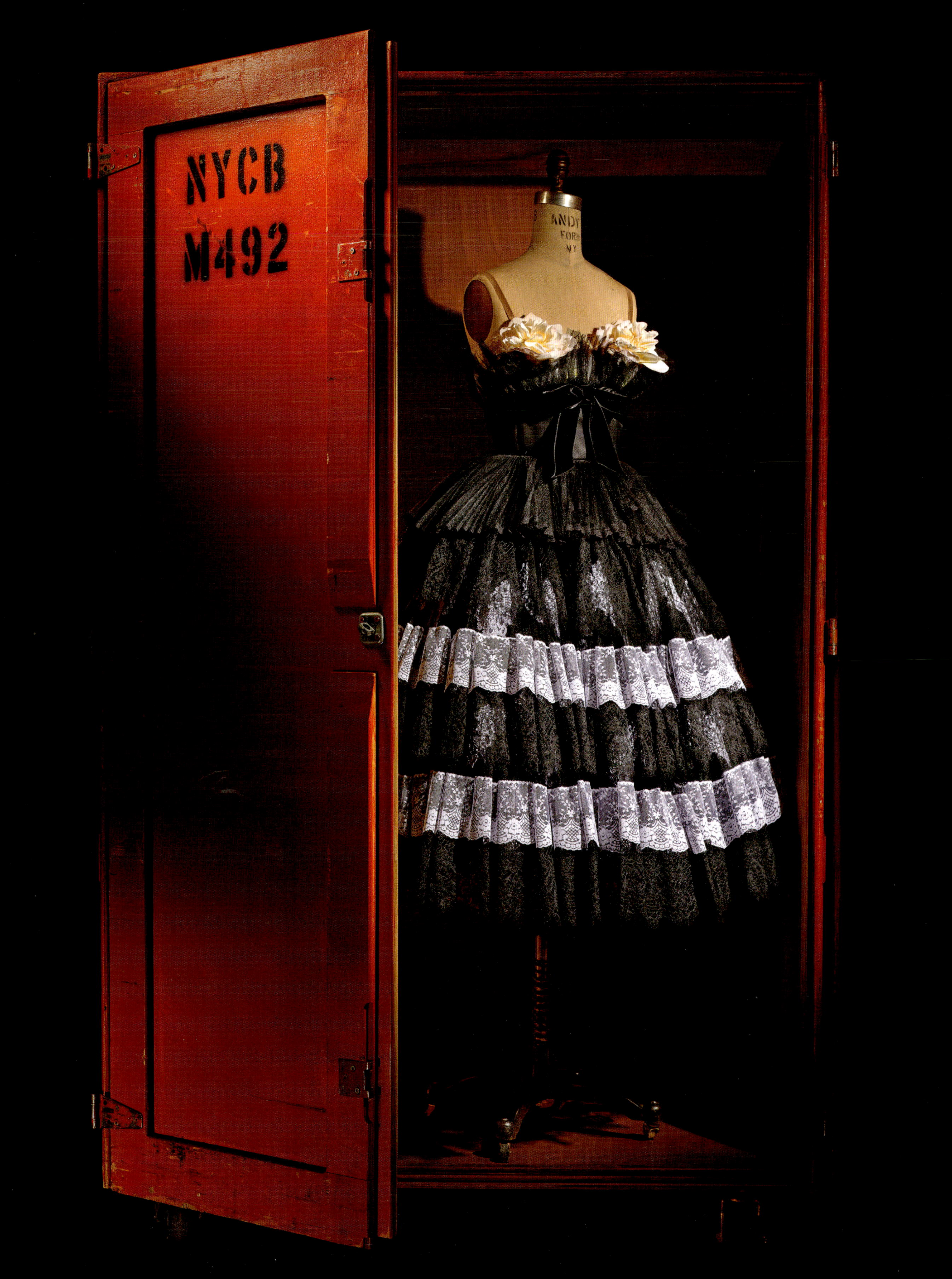
NYCB
M492